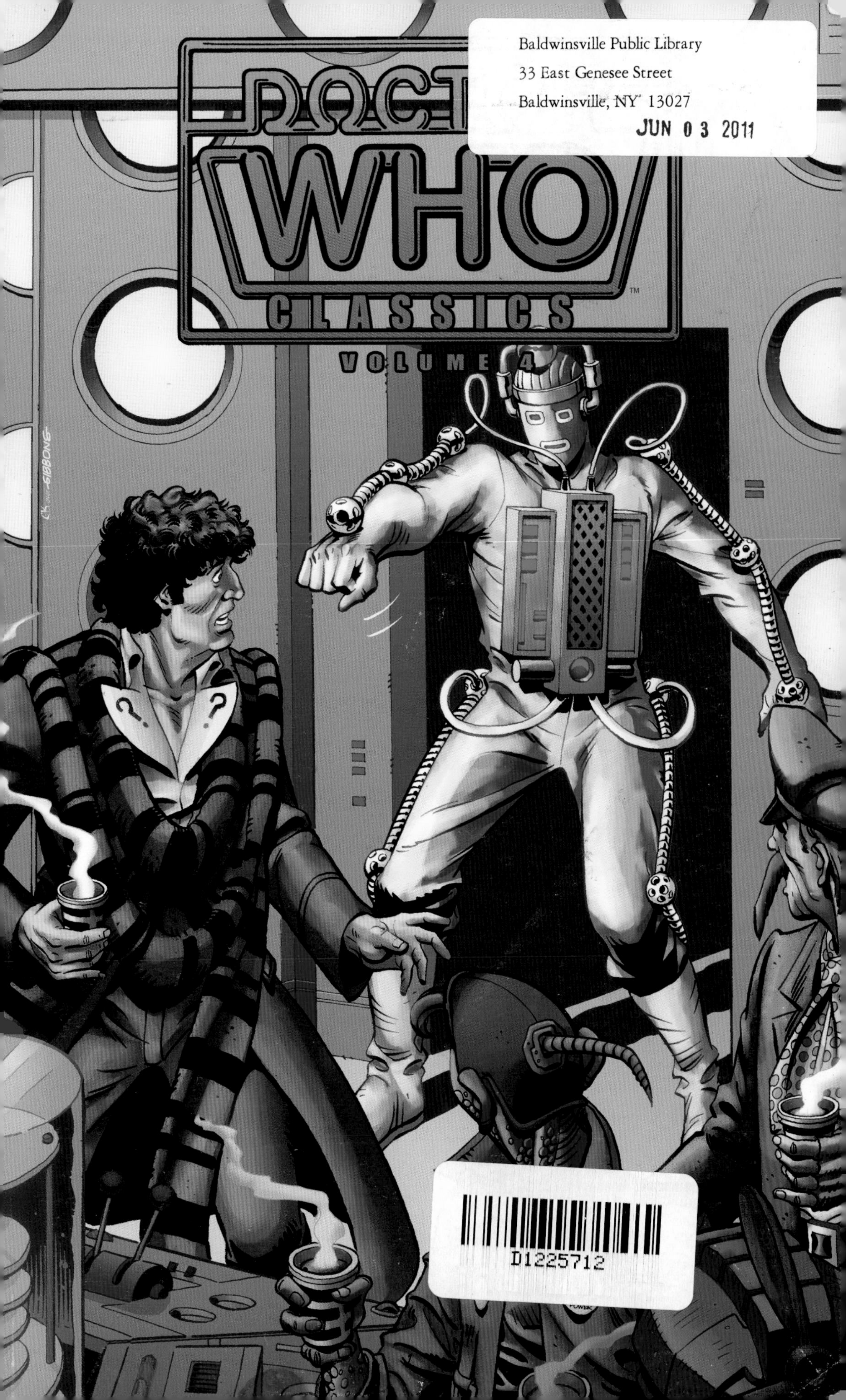
DOCTOR WHO
CLASSICS
VOLUME 4

Cover by Charlie Kirchoff over Dave Gibbons

Original Edits: Alan McKenzie • Series Edits: Denton J. Tipton
Collection Edits: Justin Eisinger • Collection Design: Amauri Osorio

IDW Publishing
Operations:
Ted Adams, Chief Executive Officer
Greg Goldstein, Chief Operating Officer
Matthew Ruzicka, CPA, Chief Financial Officer
Alan Payne, VP of Sales
Lorelei Bunjes, Dir. of Digital Services
AnnaMaria White, Marketing & PR Manager
Marci Hubbard, Executive Assistant
Alonzo Simon, Shipping Manager
Angela Loggins, Staff Accountant

Editorial:
Chris Ryall, Publisher/Editor-in-Chief
Scott Dunbier, Editor, Special Projects
Andy Schmidt, Senior Editor
Justin Eisinger, Editor
Kris Oprisko, Editor/Foreign Lic.
Denton J. Tipton, Editor
Tom Waltz, Editor
Mariah Huehner, Associate Editor
Carlos Guzman, Editorial Assistant

Design:
Robbie Robbins, EVP/Sr. Graphic Artist
Neil Uyetake, Art Director
Chris Mowry, Graphic Artist
Amauri Osorio, Graphic Artist
Gilberto Lazcano, Production Assistant

® ISBN: 978-1-60010-534-0

12 11 10 9   1 2 3 4

Special thanks to David Turbitt and Gary Russell at BBC Worldwide,
Dave Gibbons, Marc Mostman, and Mike Riddell and Tom Spilsbury at
Panini Publishing, Ltd., for their invaluable assistance.

WWW.IDWPUBLISHING.COM

DR. WHO CLASSICS VOLUME 4 TPB. NOVEMBER 2009. FIRST PRINTING. © 2009 BBC Worldwide. Doctor Who logo TM and © BBC 1973. Licensed
by BBC Worldwide Limited. All Rights Reserved. © 2009 Idea and Design Works, LLC. IDW Publishing, a division of Idea and Design Works, LLC.
Editorial offices: 5080 Santa Fe St., San Diego, CA 92109. The IDW logo is registered in the U.S. Patent and Trademark Office. All Rights Reserved.
Any similarities to persons living or dead are purely coincidental. With the exception of artwork used for review purposes, none of the contents
of this publication may be reprinted without the permission of Idea and Design Works, LLC. Printed in Korea.

IDW Publishing does not read or accept unsolicited submissions of ideas, stories, or artwork.

Originally published as DR. WHO CLASSICS SERIES TWO Issues #4–9.

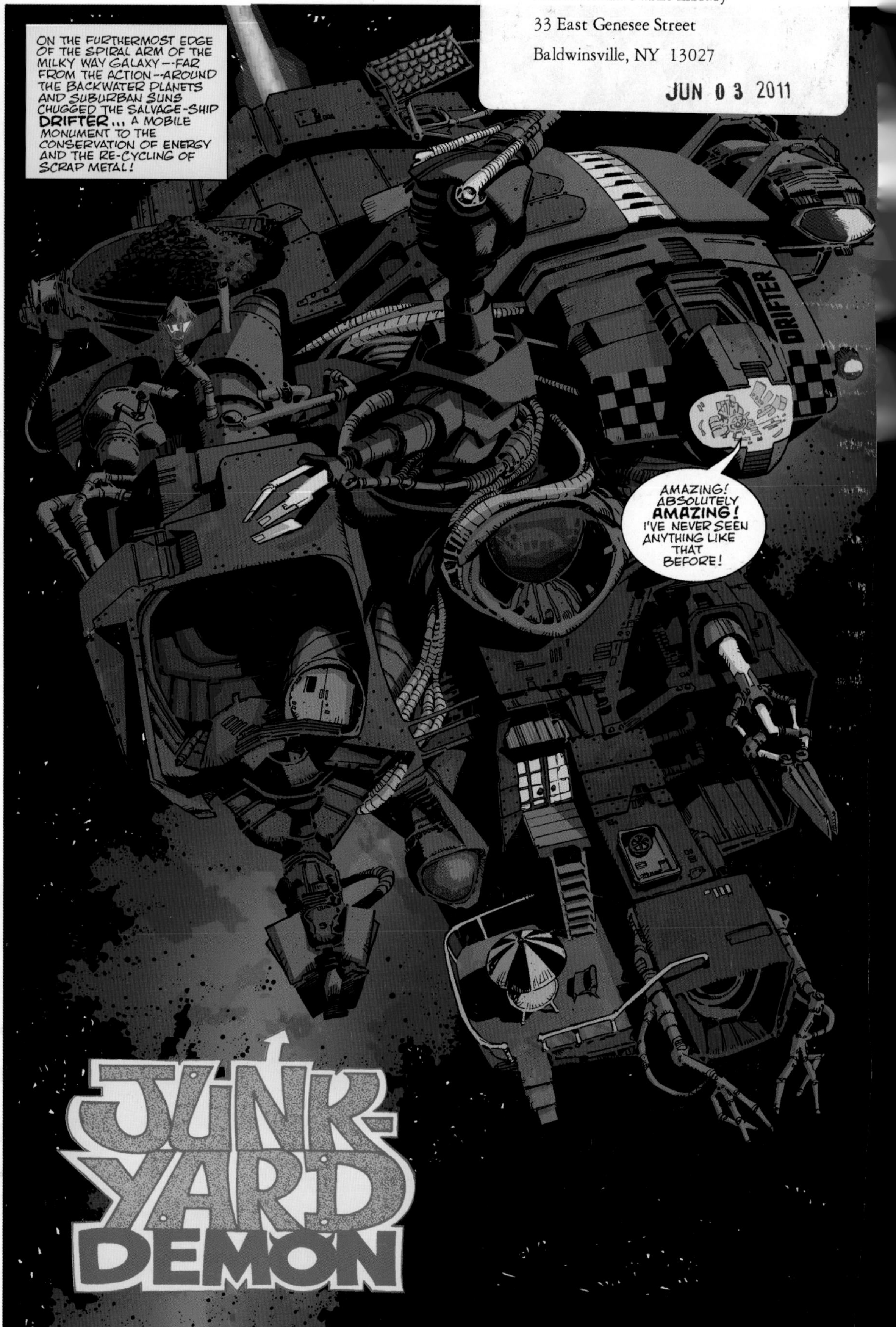
ON THE FURTHERMOST EDGE OF THE SPIRAL ARM OF THE MILKY WAY GALAXY--FAR FROM THE ACTION--AROUND THE BACKWATER PLANETS AND SUBURBAN SUNS CHUGGED THE SALVAGE-SHIP DRIFTER... A MOBILE MONUMENT TO THE CONSERVATION OF ENERGY AND THE RE-CYCLING OF SCRAP METAL!
DRIFTER
AMAZING! ABSOLUTELY AMAZING! I'VE NEVER SEEN ANYTHING LIKE THAT BEFORE!
JUNK-YARD DEMON

WRITER | STEVE PARKHOUSE | ARTISTS | MIKE McMAHON AND ADOLFO BUYLLA | EDITOR | ALAN McKENZIE

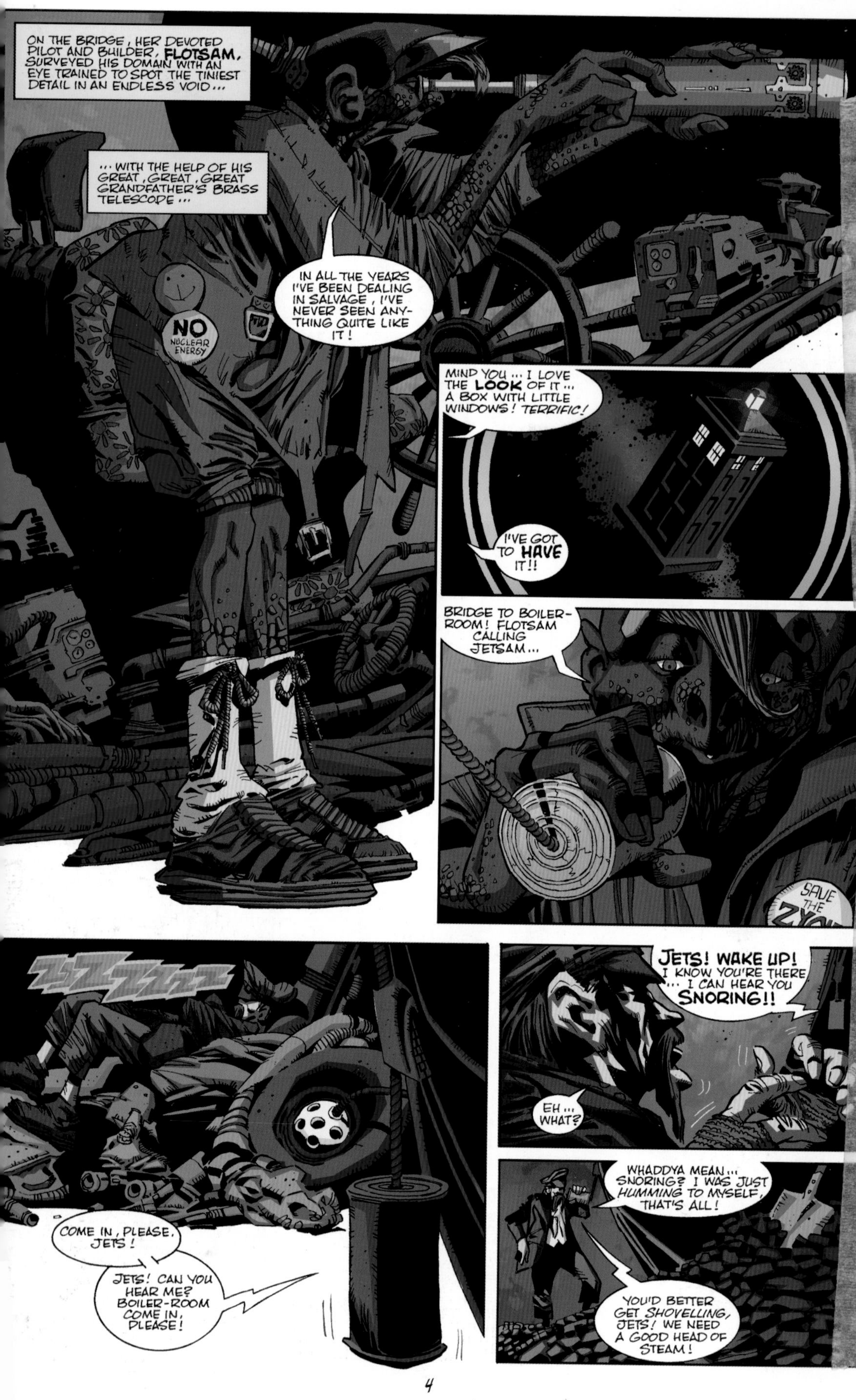

ON THE BRIDGE, HER DEVOTED PILOT AND BUILDER, FLOTSAM, SURVEYED HIS DOMAIN WITH AN EYE TRAINED TO SPOT THE TINIEST DETAIL IN AN ENDLESS VOID...
...WITH THE HELP OF HIS GREAT, GREAT, GREAT GRANDFATHER'S BRASS TELESCOPE...
IN ALL THE YEARS I'VE BEEN DEALING IN SALVAGE, I'VE NEVER SEEN ANYTHING QUITE LIKE IT!
NO NUCLEAR ENERGY
MIND YOU... I LOVE THE LOOK OF IT... A BOX WITH LITTLE WINDOWS! TERRIFIC!
I'VE GOT TO HAVE IT!!
BRIDGE TO BOILER-ROOM! FLOTSAM CALLING JETSAM...
ZZZZZZZ
COME IN, PLEASE, JETS!
JETS! CAN YOU HEAR ME? BOILER-ROOM COME IN, PLEASE!
JETS! WAKE UP! I KNOW YOU'RE THERE... I CAN HEAR YOU SNORING!!
EH... WHAT?
WHADDYA MEAN... SNORING? I WAS JUST HUMMING TO MYSELF, THAT'S ALL!
YOU'D BETTER GET SHOVELLING, JETS! WE NEED A GOOD HEAD OF STEAM!

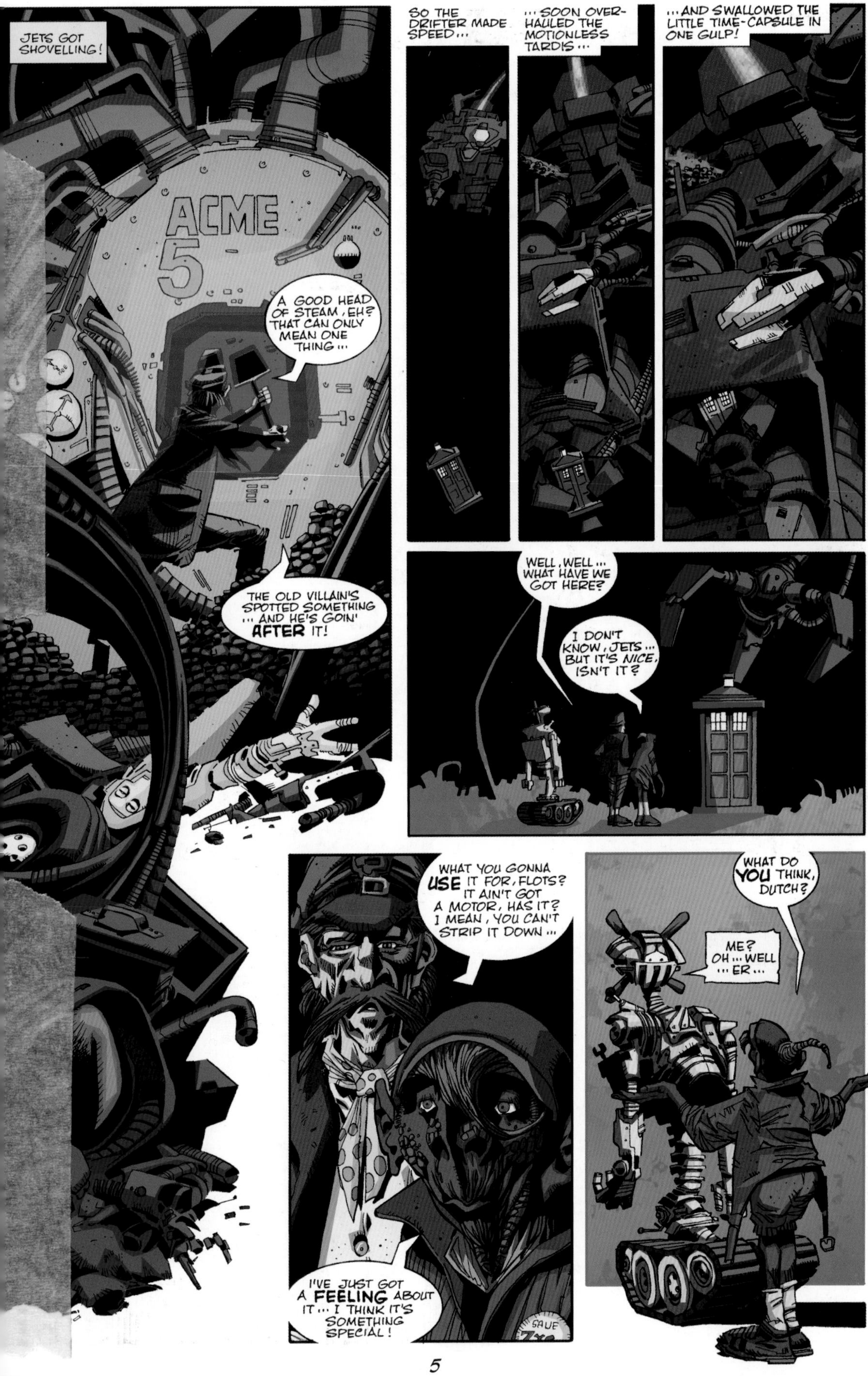
JETS GOT SHOVELLING!
A GOOD HEAD OF STEAM, EH? THAT CAN ONLY MEAN ONE THING...
THE OLD VILLAIN'S SPOTTED SOMETHING ... AND HE'S GOIN' AFTER IT!
ACME 5
SO THE DRIFTER MADE SPEED...
...SOON OVER-HAULED THE MOTIONLESS TARDIS...
...AND SWALLOWED THE LITTLE TIME-CAPSULE IN ONE GULP!
WELL, WELL... WHAT HAVE WE GOT HERE?
I DON'T KNOW, JETS... BUT IT'S NICE, ISN'T IT?
WHAT YOU GONNA USE IT FOR, FLOTS? IT AIN'T GOT A MOTOR, HAS IT? I MEAN, YOU CAN'T STRIP IT DOWN...
I'VE JUST GOT A FEELING ABOUT IT... I THINK IT'S SOMETHING SPECIAL!
WHAT DO YOU THINK, DUTCH?
ME? OH... WELL ...ER...

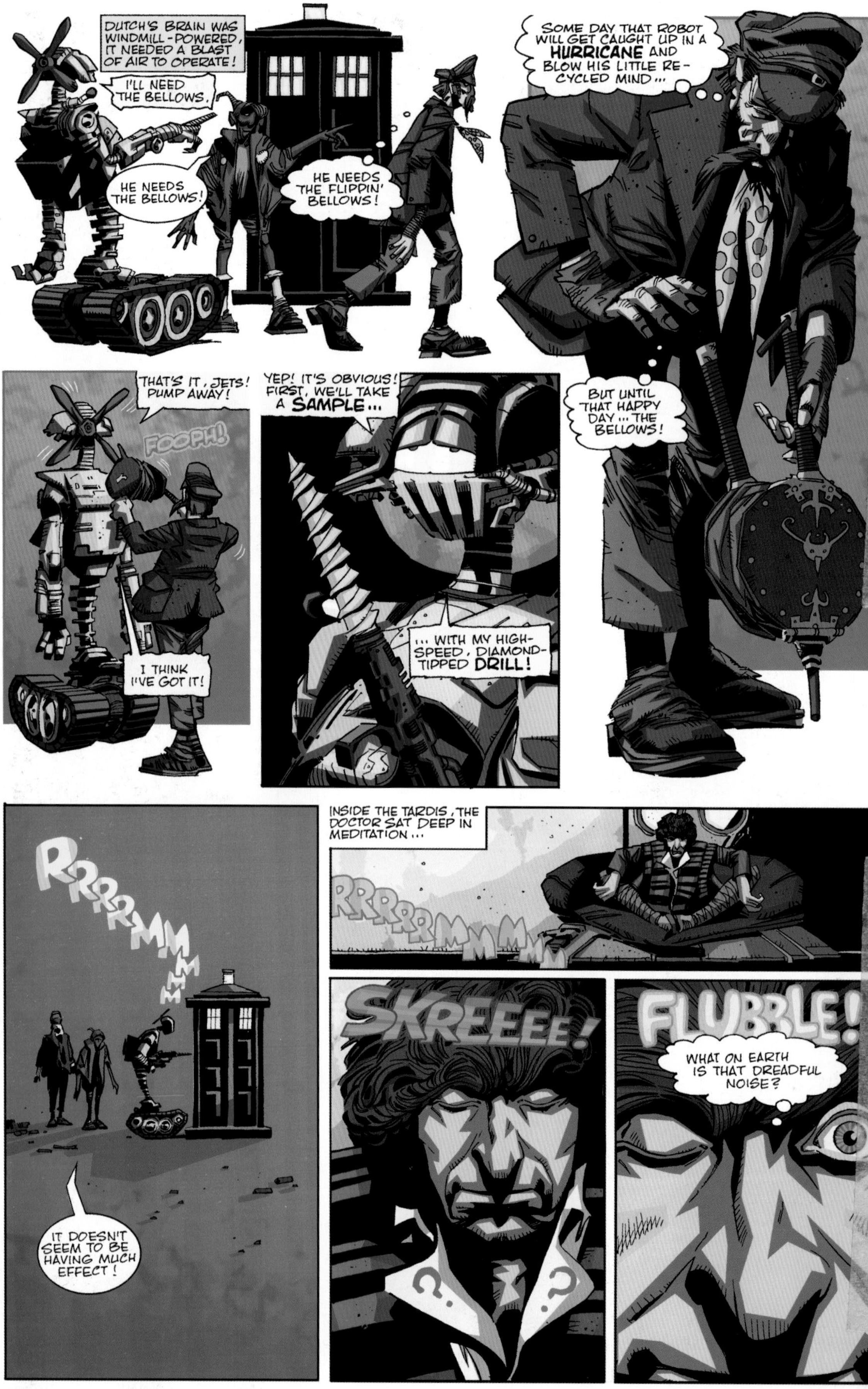
DUTCH'S BRAIN WAS WINDMILL-POWERED, IT NEEDED A BLAST OF AIR TO OPERATE!
I'LL NEED THE BELLOWS.
HE NEEDS THE BELLOWS!
HE NEEDS THE FLIPPIN' BELLOWS!
SOME DAY THAT ROBOT WILL GET CAUGHT UP IN A HURRICANE AND BLOW HIS LITTLE RE-CYCLED MIND...
BUT UNTIL THAT HAPPY DAY... THE BELLOWS!
THAT'S IT, JETS! PUMP AWAY!
FOOPH!
I THINK I'VE GOT IT!
YEP! IT'S OBVIOUS! FIRST, WE'LL TAKE A SAMPLE...
... WITH MY HIGH-SPEED, DIAMOND-TIPPED DRILL!
RRRRMMMMMM
IT DOESN'T SEEM TO BE HAVING MUCH EFFECT!
INSIDE THE TARDIS, THE DOCTOR SAT DEEP IN MEDITATION...
RRRRRMMMMM
SKREEEEE!
FLUBBLE!
WHAT ON EARTH IS THAT DREADFUL NOISE?

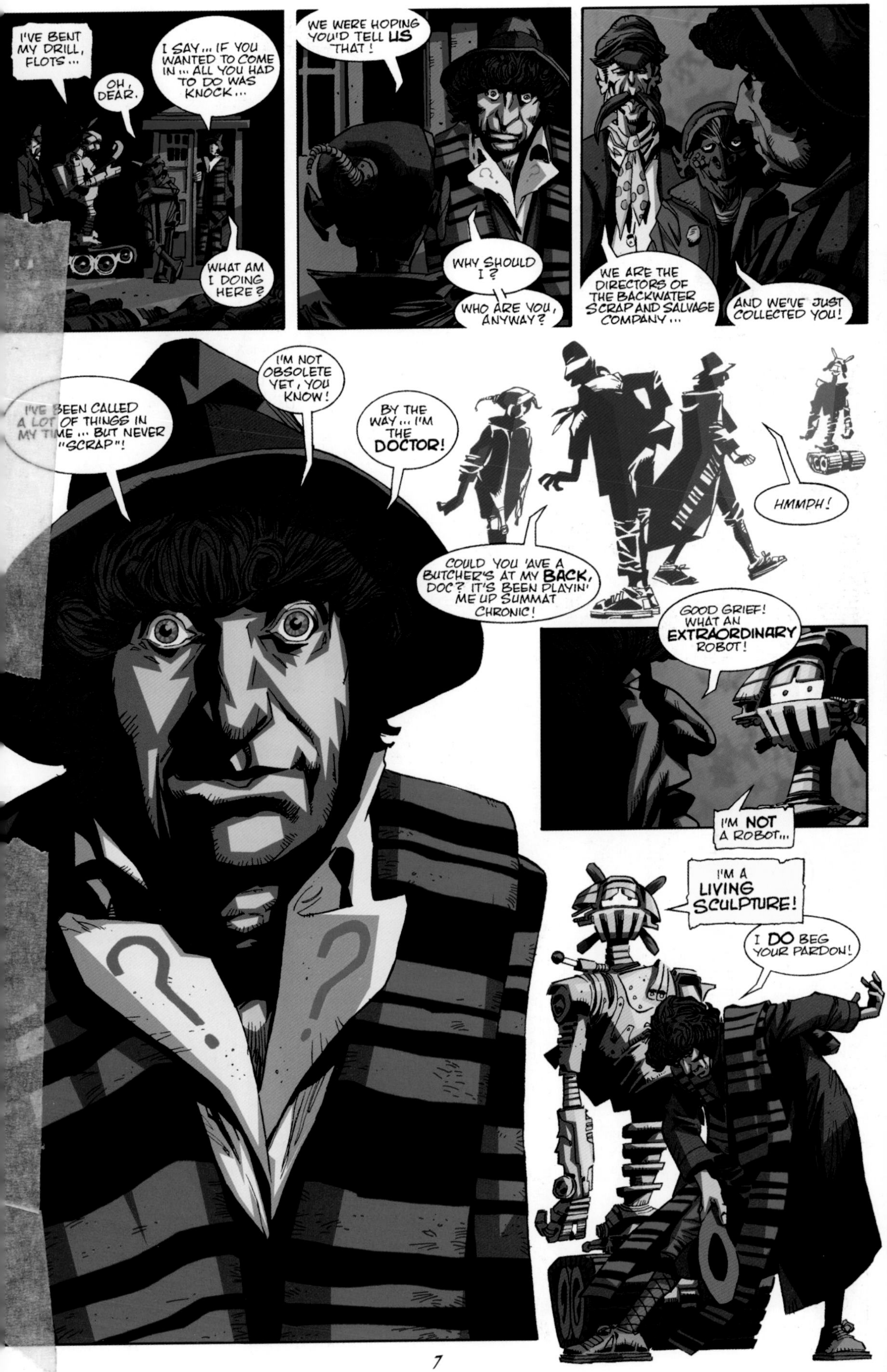
I'VE BENT MY DRILL, FLOTS...
OH, DEAR.
I SAY... IF YOU WANTED TO COME IN... ALL YOU HAD TO DO WAS KNOCK...
WHAT AM I DOING HERE?
WE WERE HOPING YOU'D TELL **US** THAT!
WHY SHOULD I?
WHO ARE YOU, ANYWAY?
WE ARE THE DIRECTORS OF THE BACKWATER SCRAP AND SALVAGE COMPANY...
AND WE'VE JUST COLLECTED YOU!
I'VE BEEN CALLED A LOT OF THINGS IN MY TIME... BUT NEVER "SCRAP"!
I'M NOT OBSOLETE YET, YOU KNOW!
BY THE WAY... I'M THE **DOCTOR!**
COULD YOU 'AVE A BUTCHER'S AT MY **BACK,** DOC? IT'S BEEN PLAYIN' ME UP SUMMAT CHRONIC!
HMMPH!
GOOD GRIEF! WHAT AN **EXTRAORDINARY** ROBOT!
I'M **NOT** A ROBOT...
I'M A **LIVING SCULPTURE!**
I **DO** BEG YOUR PARDON!

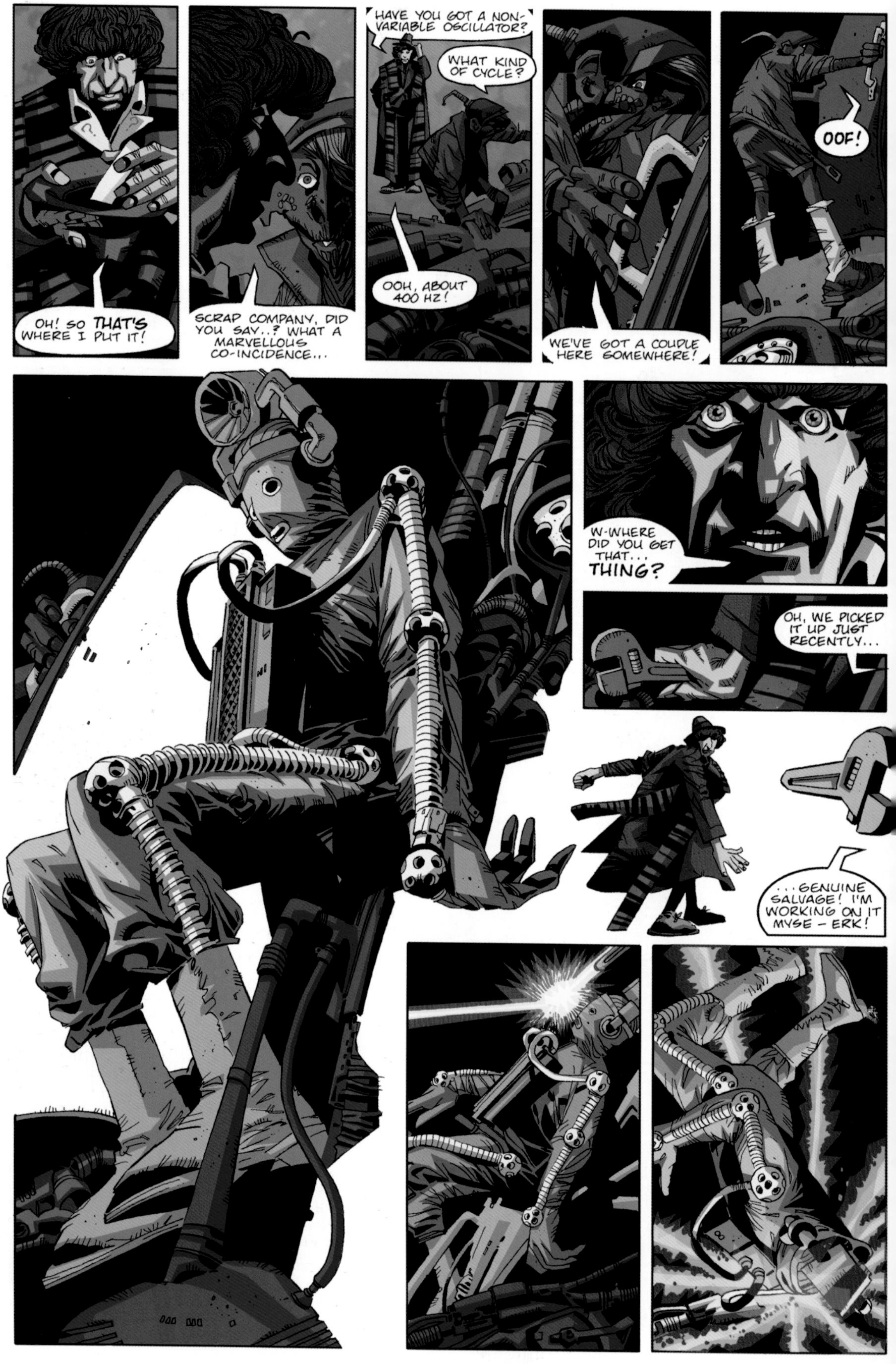
OH! SO THAT'S WHERE I PUT IT!
SCRAP COMPANY, DID YOU SAY..? WHAT A MARVELLOUS CO-INCIDENCE...
HAVE YOU GOT A NON-VARIABLE OSCILLATOR?
WHAT KIND OF CYCLE?
OOH, ABOUT 400 HZ!
WE'VE GOT A COUPLE HERE SOMEWHERE!
OOF!
W-WHERE DID YOU GET THAT... THING?
OH, WE PICKED IT UP JUST RECENTLY...
...GENUINE SALVAGE! I'M WORKING ON IT MYSE – ERK!

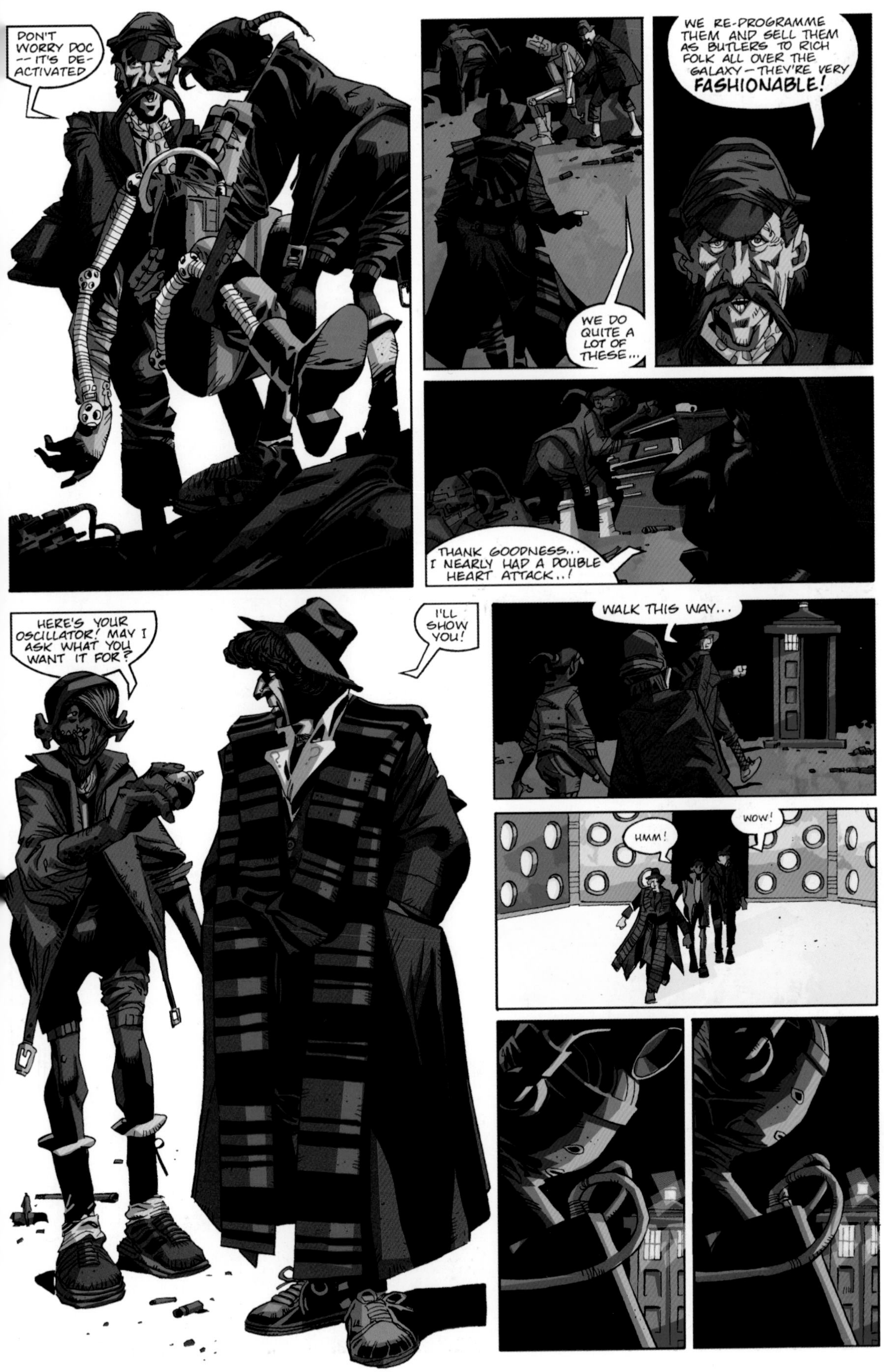

DON'T WORRY DOC -- IT'S DE-ACTIVATED
WE DO QUITE A LOT OF THESE...
WE RE-PROGRAMME THEM AND SELL THEM AS BUTLERS TO RICH FOLK ALL OVER THE GALAXY — THEY'RE VERY FASHIONABLE!
THANK GOODNESS... I NEARLY HAD A DOUBLE HEART ATTACK..!
HERE'S YOUR OSCILLATOR! MAY I ASK WHAT YOU WANT IT FOR?
I'LL SHOW YOU!
WALK THIS WAY...
HMM!
WOW!

PERFECT! WON'T BE A JIF, NOW!

BEEP! BEEP! MEEP!

MMMMM!

IT'S HOT CHOCOLATE... DRINK UP!

GANGWAY!

YEOWW!

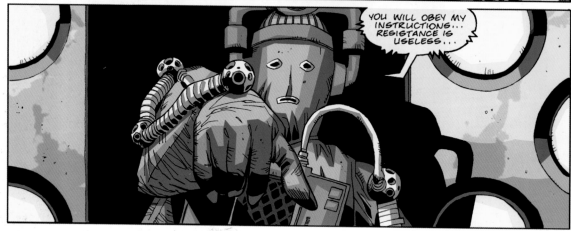

YOU WILL OBEY MY INSTRUCTIONS... RESISTANCE IS USELESS...

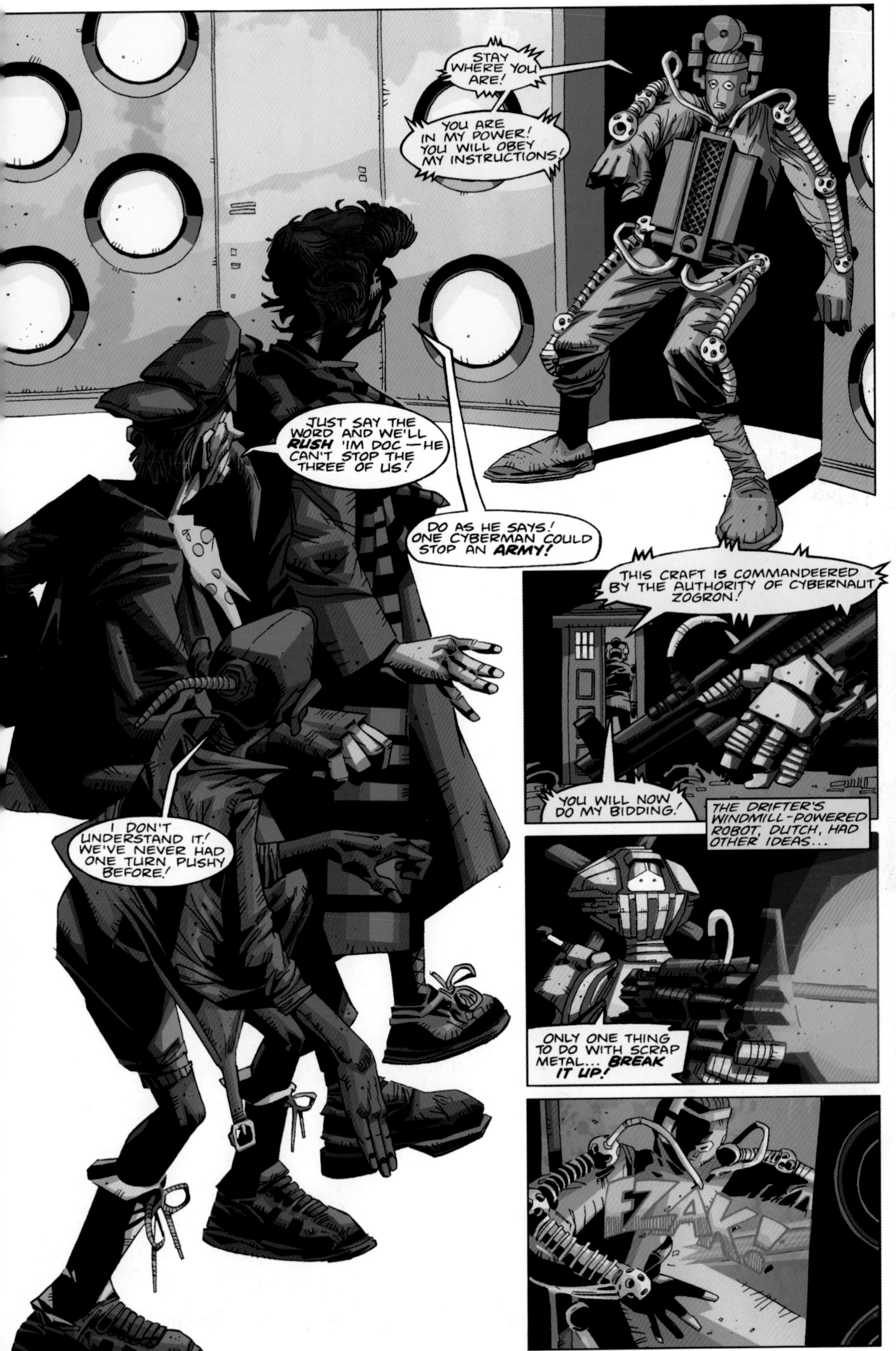
STAY WHERE YOU ARE!
YOU ARE IN MY POWER! YOU WILL OBEY MY INSTRUCTIONS!
JUST SAY THE WORD AND WE'LL RUSH 'IM DOC — HE CAN'T STOP THE THREE OF US!
DO AS HE SAYS! ONE CYBERMAN COULD STOP AN ARMY!
I DON'T UNDERSTAND IT! WE'VE NEVER HAD ONE TURN PUSHY BEFORE!
THIS CRAFT IS COMMANDEERED BY THE AUTHORITY OF CYBERNAUT ZOGRON!
YOU WILL NOW DO MY BIDDING!
THE DRIFTER'S WINDMILL-POWERED ROBOT, DUTCH, HAD OTHER IDEAS...
ONLY ONE THING TO DO WITH SCRAP METAL... BREAK IT UP!
FZAK!

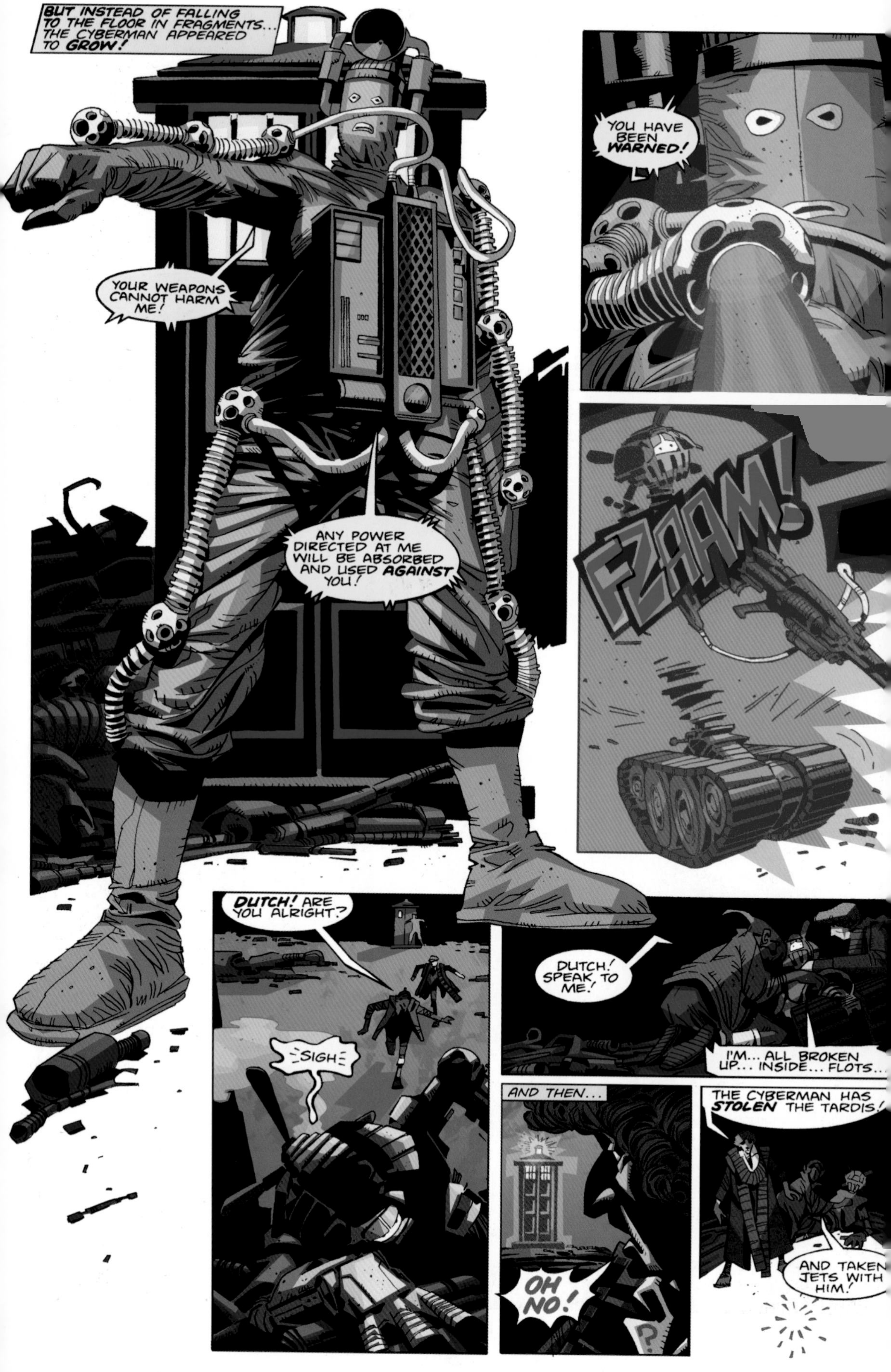
BUT INSTEAD OF FALLING TO THE FLOOR IN FRAGMENTS... THE CYBERMAN APPEARED TO GROW!
YOUR WEAPONS CANNOT HARM ME!
ANY POWER DIRECTED AT ME WILL BE ABSORBED AND USED AGAINST YOU!
YOU HAVE BEEN WARNED!
FZAAM!
DUTCH! ARE YOU ALRIGHT?
SIGH
DUTCH! SPEAK, TO ME!
I'M... ALL BROKEN UP... INSIDE... FLOTS...
AND THEN...
OH NO!
?
THE CYBERMAN HAS STOLEN THE TARDIS!
AND TAKEN JETS WITH HIM!

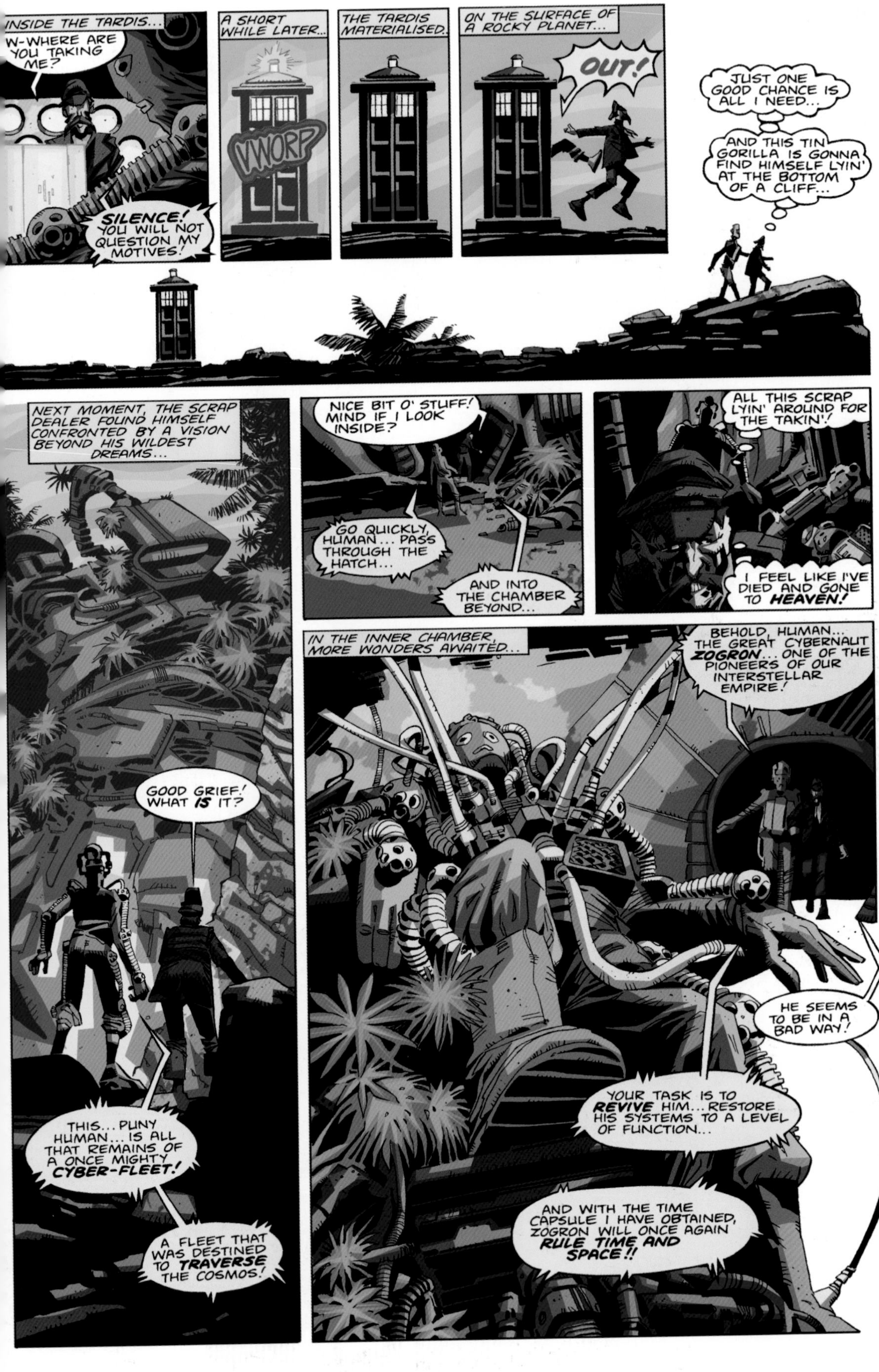
INSIDE THE TARDIS...
W-WHERE ARE YOU TAKING ME?
SILENCE! YOU WILL NOT QUESTION MY MOTIVES!
A SHORT WHILE LATER...
VWORP
THE TARDIS MATERIALISED...
ON THE SURFACE OF A ROCKY PLANET...
OUT!
JUST ONE GOOD CHANCE IS ALL I NEED...
AND THIS TIN GORILLA IS GONNA FIND HIMSELF LYIN' AT THE BOTTOM OF A CLIFF...
NEXT MOMENT, THE SCRAP DEALER FOUND HIMSELF CONFRONTED BY A VISION BEYOND HIS WILDEST DREAMS...
GOOD GRIEF! WHAT IS IT?
THIS... PUNY HUMAN... IS ALL THAT REMAINS OF A ONCE MIGHTY CYBER-FLEET!
A FLEET THAT WAS DESTINED TO TRAVERSE THE COSMOS!
NICE BIT O' STUFF! MIND IF I LOOK INSIDE?
GO QUICKLY, HUMAN... PASS THROUGH THE HATCH...
AND INTO THE CHAMBER BEYOND...
ALL THIS SCRAP LYIN' AROUND FOR THE TAKIN'!
I FEEL LIKE I'VE DIED AND GONE TO HEAVEN!
IN THE INNER CHAMBER, MORE WONDERS AWAITED...
BEHOLD, HUMAN... THE GREAT CYBERNAUT ZOGRON... ONE OF THE PIONEERS OF OUR INTERSTELLAR EMPIRE!
HE SEEMS TO BE IN A BAD WAY!
YOUR TASK IS TO REVIVE HIM... RESTORE HIS SYSTEMS TO A LEVEL OF FUNCTION...
AND WITH THE TIME CAPSULE I HAVE OBTAINED, ZOGRON WILL ONCE AGAIN RULE TIME AND SPACE!!

MEANWHILE... BACK ON THE DRIFTER...

THAT CYBERMAN HAS TAKEN THE TARDIS FOR A *REASON*, FLOTS! I'VE GOT TO FIND OUT WHAT AND WHERE!

I'M SORRY ABOUT ALL THIS, DOCTOR—LIKE WE SAID... WE'VE JUST RE-PROGRAMMED THE ODD ONE OR TWO FOR USE AS *BUTLERS*!

THEY GO FOR A *FORTUNE*!

WE DIDN'T KNOW IT WOULD CAUSE ALL THIS TROUBLE!

JUST A MINUTE...WHERE DID YOU PICK UP YOUR FIRST CYBERMAN?

ALL THE DETAILS ARE LOGGED IN THE SHIP'S COMPUTER...

LEMME SEE...

HE WAS ADRIFT IN QUADRANT 747...ARCTURIAN SYSTEM...

AND THE ONE AFTER THAT?

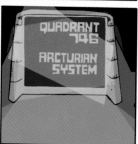

QUADRANT 746

ARCTURIAN SYSTEM

WHAT'S THE NEAREST PLANET TO THOSE TWO POINTS?

A SMALL PLANET CALLED AS4...

IT'S AN IMPOSSIBLY LONG SHOT... BUT IT'S OUR ONLY CHANCE...

CAN WE GET THERE?

WE CAN SWITCH TO SOLAR POWER— TOGETHER WITH THE ION-DRIVE MOTORS WE CAN MAKE GOOD SPEED...

BUT YOU'LL HAVE TO NAVIGATE WHILE I ATTEND TO THE MECHANICS!

THEN LET'S GO!

ENGINES BLAZING, THE DRIFTER POWERED OFF INTO THE VOID...

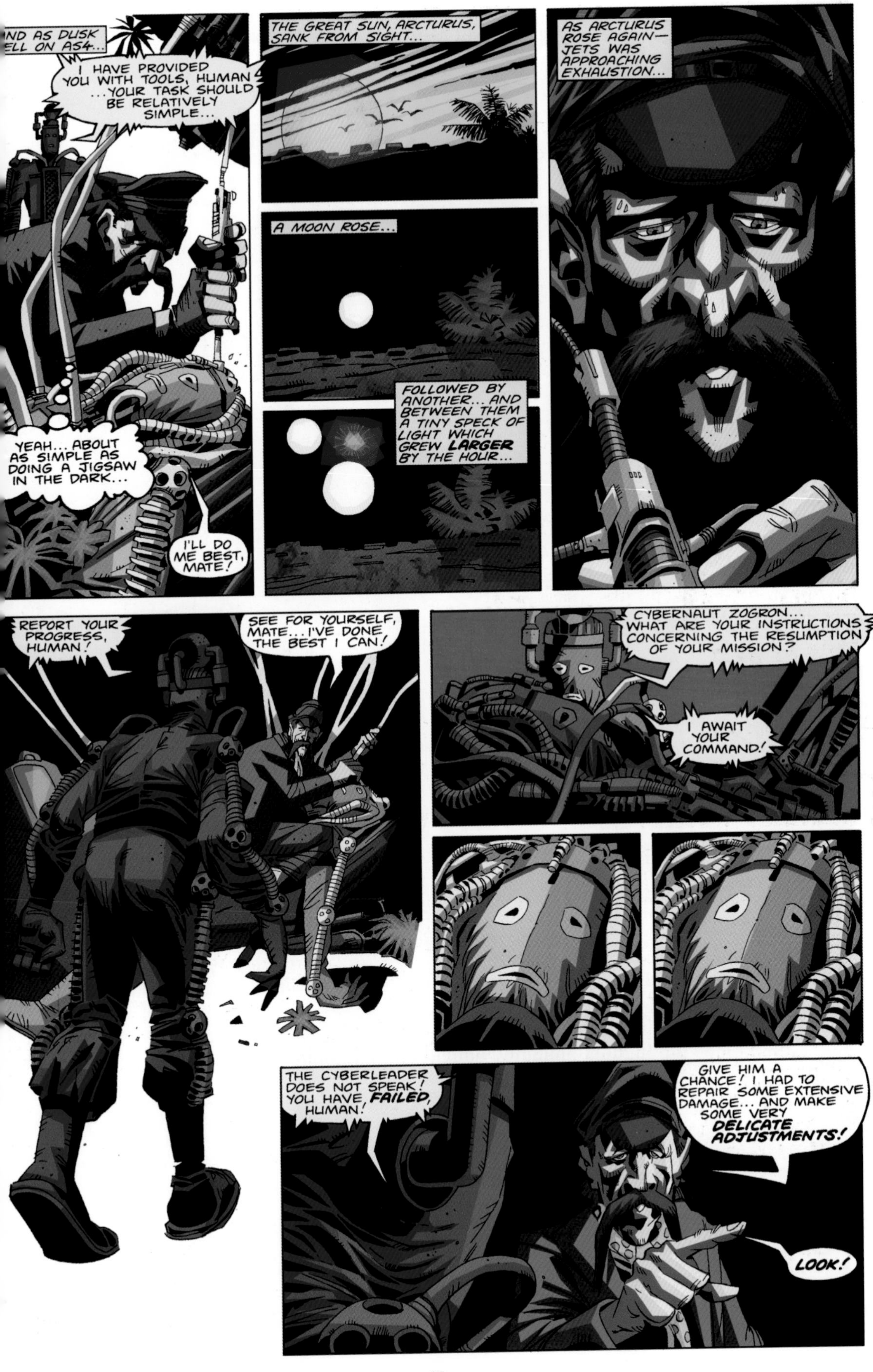

ND AS DUSK
ELL ON AS4...
I HAVE PROVIDED YOU WITH TOOLS, HUMAN ...YOUR TASK SHOULD BE RELATIVELY SIMPLE...
YEAH... ABOUT AS SIMPLE AS DOING A JIGSAW IN THE DARK...
I'LL DO ME BEST, MATE!
THE GREAT SUN, ARCTURUS, SANK FROM SIGHT...
A MOON ROSE...
FOLLOWED BY ANOTHER... AND BETWEEN THEM A TINY SPECK OF LIGHT WHICH GREW LARGER BY THE HOUR...
AS ARCTURUS ROSE AGAIN— JETS WAS APPROACHING EXHAUSTION...
REPORT YOUR PROGRESS, HUMAN!
SEE FOR YOURSELF, MATE... I'VE DONE THE BEST I CAN!
CYBERNAUT ZOGRON... WHAT ARE YOUR INSTRUCTIONS CONCERNING THE RESUMPTION OF YOUR MISSION?
I AWAIT YOUR COMMAND!
THE CYBERLEADER DOES NOT SPEAK! YOU HAVE FAILED, HUMAN!
GIVE HIM A CHANCE! I HAD TO REPAIR SOME EXTENSIVE DAMAGE... AND MAKE SOME VERY DELICATE ADJUSTMENTS!
LOOK!

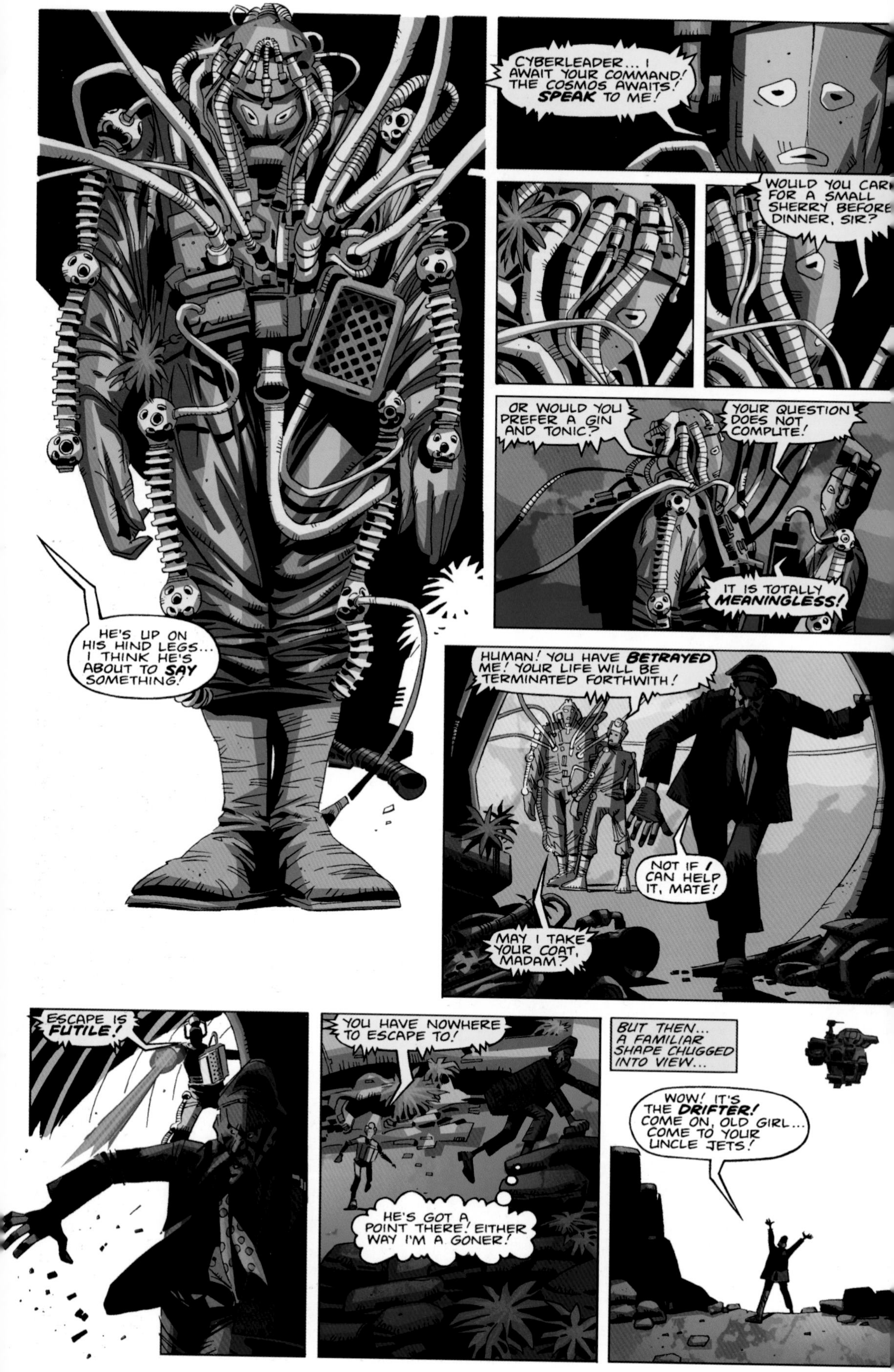

HE'S UP ON HIS HIND LEGS... I THINK HE'S ABOUT TO SAY SOMETHING!
CYBERLEADER... I AWAIT YOUR COMMAND! THE COSMOS AWAITS! SPEAK TO ME!
WOULD YOU CAR FOR A SMALL SHERRY BEFORE DINNER, SIR?
OR WOULD YOU PREFER A GIN AND TONIC?
YOUR QUESTION DOES NOT COMPUTE!
IT IS TOTALLY MEANINGLESS!
HUMAN! YOU HAVE BETRAYED ME! YOUR LIFE WILL BE TERMINATED FORTHWITH!
NOT IF I CAN HELP IT, MATE!
MAY I TAKE YOUR COAT, MADAM?
ESCAPE IS FUTILE!
YOU HAVE NOWHERE TO ESCAPE TO!
HE'S GOT A POINT THERE! EITHER WAY I'M A GONER!
BUT THEN... A FAMILIAR SHAPE CHUGGED INTO VIEW...
WOW! IT'S THE DRIFTER! COME ON, OLD GIRL... COME TO YOUR UNCLE JETS!

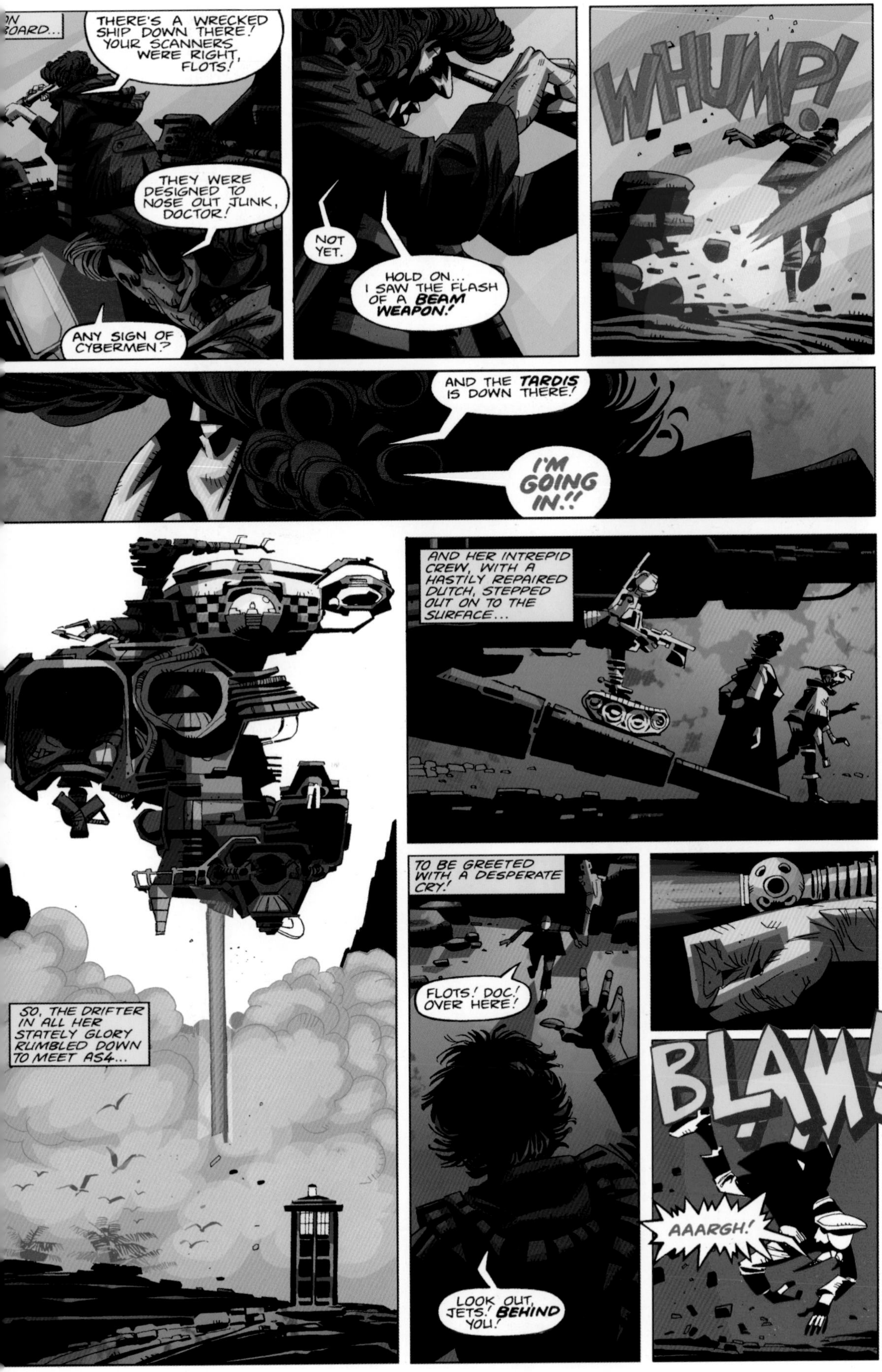
ON BOARD...
THERE'S A WRECKED SHIP DOWN THERE! YOUR SCANNERS WERE RIGHT, FLOTS!
THEY WERE DESIGNED TO NOSE OUT JUNK, DOCTOR!
ANY SIGN OF CYBERMEN?
NOT YET.
HOLD ON... I SAW THE FLASH OF A BEAM WEAPON!
WHUMP!
AND THE TARDIS IS DOWN THERE!
I'M GOING IN!!
SO, THE DRIFTER IN ALL HER STATELY GLORY RUMBLED DOWN TO MEET AS4...
AND HER INTREPID CREW, WITH A HASTILY REPAIRED DUTCH, STEPPED OUT ON TO THE SURFACE...
TO BE GREETED WITH A DESPERATE CRY!
FLOTS! DOC! OVER HERE!
LOOK OUT, JETS! BEHIND YOU!
BLAM!
AAARGH!

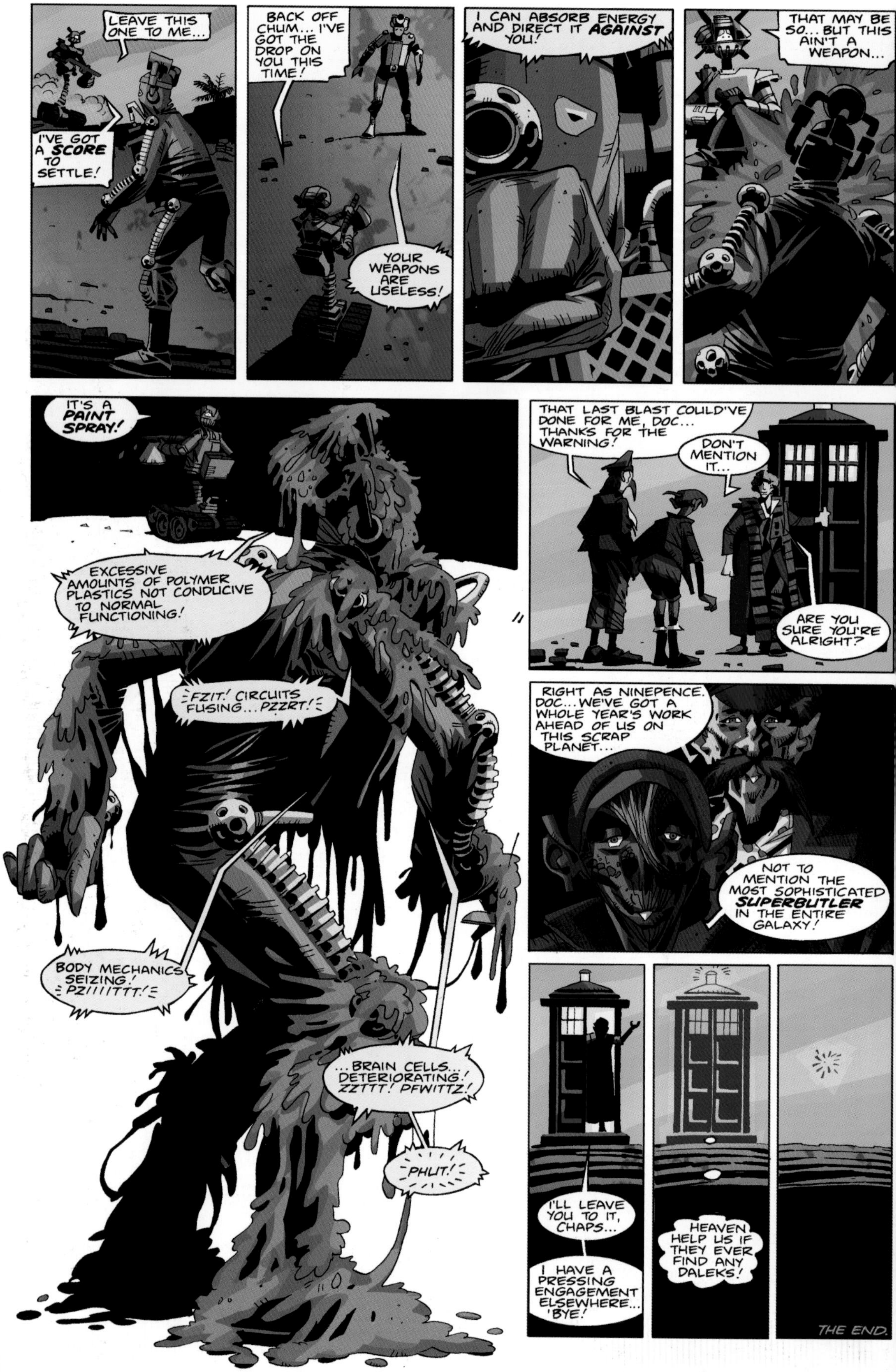
LEAVE THIS ONE TO ME...
I'VE GOT A SCORE TO SETTLE!
BACK OFF CHUM... I'VE GOT THE DROP ON YOU THIS TIME!
YOUR WEAPONS ARE USELESS!
I CAN ABSORB ENERGY AND DIRECT IT AGAINST YOU!
THAT MAY BE SO... BUT THIS AIN'T A WEAPON...
IT'S A PAINT SPRAY!
EXCESSIVE AMOUNTS OF POLYMER PLASTICS NOT CONDUCIVE TO NORMAL FUNCTIONING!
FZIT! CIRCUITS FUSING... PZZRT!
BODY MECHANICS SEIZING! PZIIIITTT!
...BRAIN CELLS... DETERIORATING! ZZTTT! PFWITTZ!
PHUT!
THAT LAST BLAST COULD'VE DONE FOR ME, DOC... THANKS FOR THE WARNING!
DON'T MENTION IT...
ARE YOU SURE YOU'RE ALRIGHT?
RIGHT AS NINEPENCE, DOC... WE'VE GOT A WHOLE YEAR'S WORK AHEAD OF US ON THIS SCRAP PLANET...
NOT TO MENTION THE MOST SOPHISTICATED SUPERBUTLER IN THE ENTIRE GALAXY!
I'LL LEAVE YOU TO IT, CHAPS...
I HAVE A PRESSING ENGAGEMENT ELSEWHERE... 'BYE!
HEAVEN HELP US IF THEY EVER FIND ANY DALEKS!
THE END.

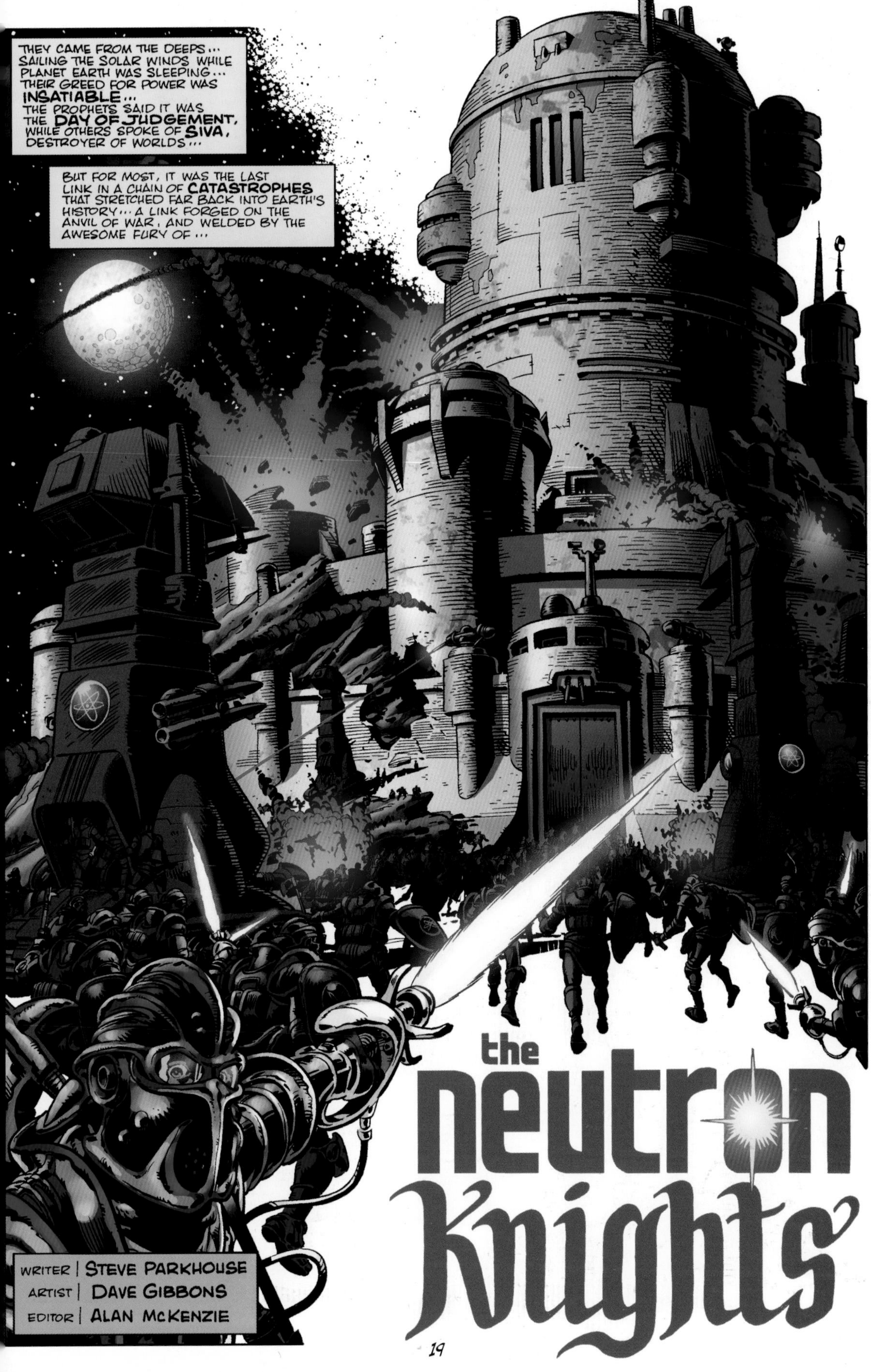
THEY CAME FROM THE DEEPS... SAILING THE SOLAR WINDS WHILE PLANET EARTH WAS SLEEPING... THEIR GREED FOR POWER WAS INSATIABLE... THE PROPHETS SAID IT WAS THE DAY OF JUDGEMENT, WHILE OTHERS SPOKE OF SIVA, DESTROYER OF WORLDS...
BUT FOR MOST, IT WAS THE LAST LINK IN A CHAIN OF CATASTROPHES THAT STRETCHED FAR BACK INTO EARTH'S HISTORY... A LINK FORGED ON THE ANVIL OF WAR, AND WELDED BY THE AWESOME FURY OF...
the neutron Knights
WRITER | STEVE PARKHOUSE
ARTIST | DAVE GIBBONS
EDITOR | ALAN McKENZIE

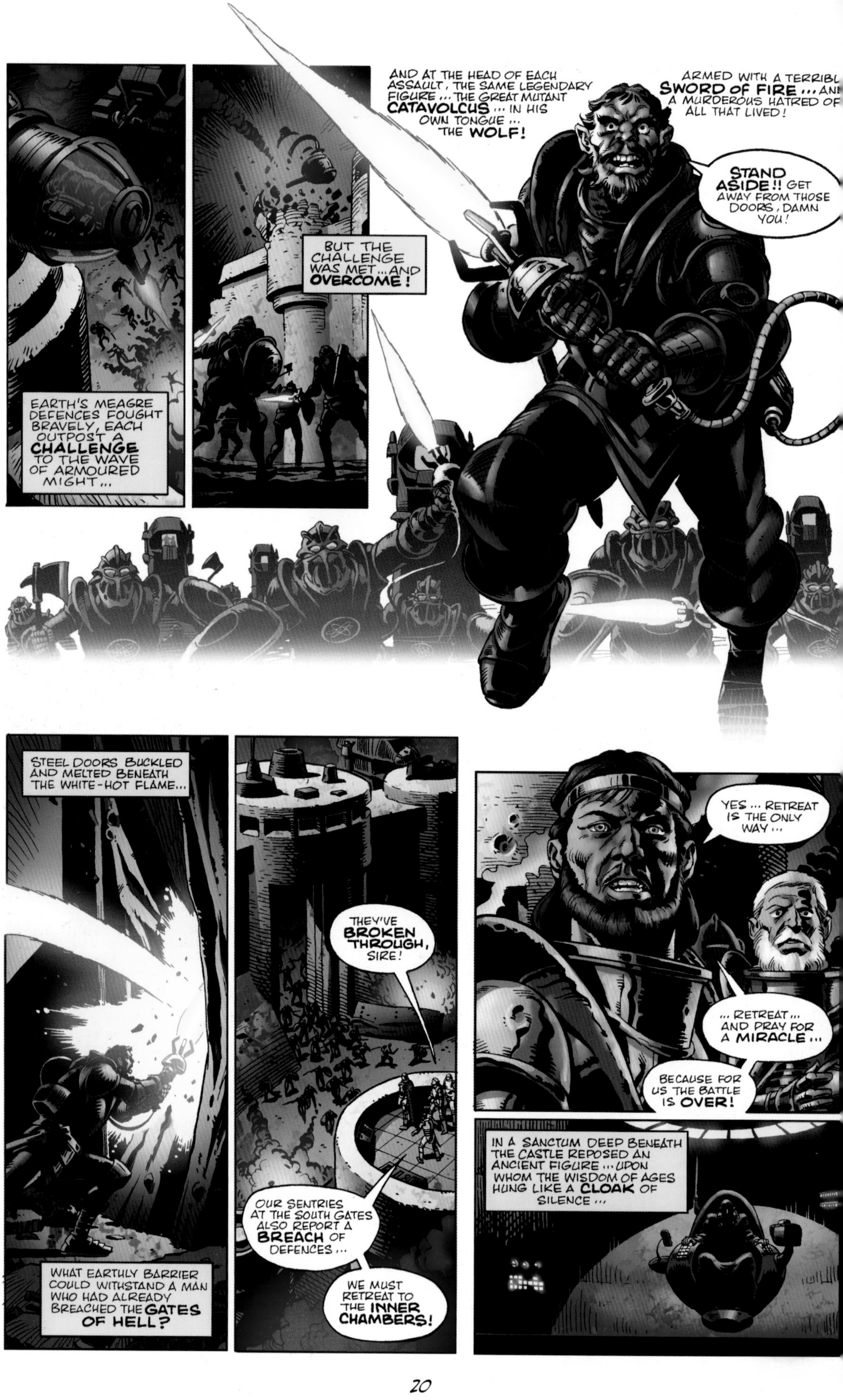
EARTH'S MEAGRE DEFENCES FOUGHT BRAVELY, EACH OUTPOST A CHALLENGE TO THE WAVE OF ARMOURED MIGHT...
BUT THE CHALLENGE WAS MET... AND OVERCOME!
AND AT THE HEAD OF EACH ASSAULT, THE SAME LEGENDARY FIGURE... THE GREAT MUTANT CATAVOLCUS... IN HIS OWN TONGUE... THE WOLF!
ARMED WITH A TERRIBL SWORD OF FIRE... AN A MURDEROUS HATRED OF ALL THAT LIVED!
STAND ASIDE!! GET AWAY FROM THOSE DOORS, DAMN YOU!
STEEL DOORS BUCKLED AND MELTED BENEATH THE WHITE-HOT FLAME...
WHAT EARTHLY BARRIER COULD WITHSTAND A MAN WHO HAD ALREADY BREACHED THE GATES OF HELL?
THEY'VE BROKEN THROUGH, SIRE!
OUR SENTRIES AT THE SOUTH GATES ALSO REPORT A BREACH OF DEFENCES...
WE MUST RETREAT TO THE INNER CHAMBERS!
YES... RETREAT IS THE ONLY WAY...
... RETREAT... AND PRAY FOR A MIRACLE...
BECAUSE FOR US THE BATTLE IS OVER!
IN A SANCTUM DEEP BENEATH THE CASTLE REPOSED AN ANCIENT FIGURE... UPON WHOM THE WISDOM OF AGES HUNG LIKE A CLOAK OF SILENCE...

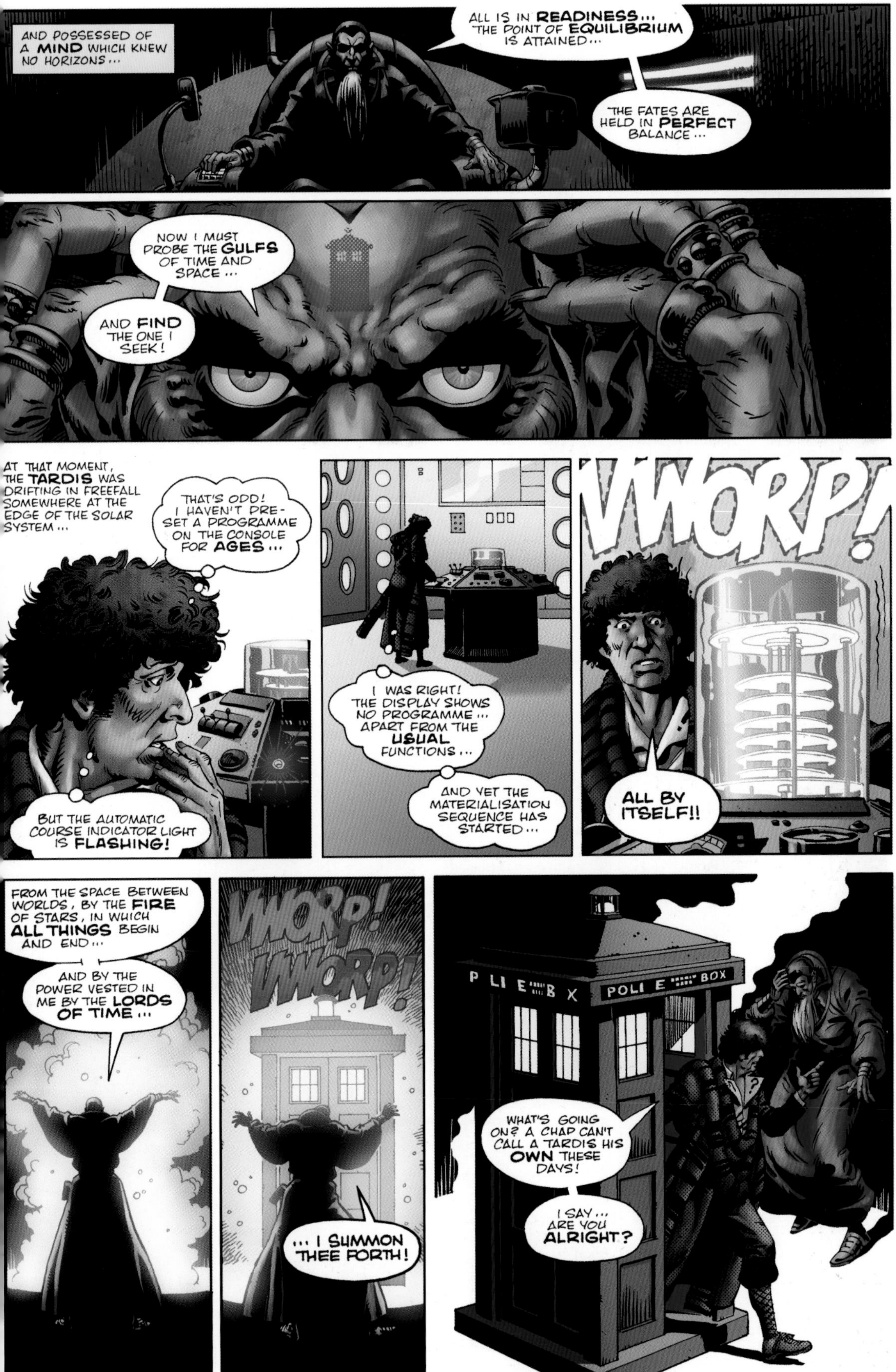
AND POSSESSED OF A MIND WHICH KNEW NO HORIZONS...
ALL IS IN READINESS... THE POINT OF EQUILIBRIUM IS ATTAINED...
THE FATES ARE HELD IN PERFECT BALANCE...
NOW I MUST PROBE THE GULFS OF TIME AND SPACE...
AND FIND THE ONE I SEEK!
AT THAT MOMENT, THE TARDIS WAS DRIFTING IN FREEFALL SOMEWHERE AT THE EDGE OF THE SOLAR SYSTEM...
THAT'S ODD! I HAVEN'T PRE-SET A PROGRAMME ON THE CONSOLE FOR AGES...
BUT THE AUTOMATIC COURSE INDICATOR LIGHT IS FLASHING!
I WAS RIGHT! THE DISPLAY SHOWS NO PROGRAMME... APART FROM THE USUAL FUNCTIONS...
AND YET THE MATERIALISATION SEQUENCE HAS STARTED...
VWORP!
ALL BY ITSELF!!
FROM THE SPACE BETWEEN WORLDS, BY THE FIRE OF STARS, IN WHICH ALL THINGS BEGIN AND END...
AND BY THE POWER VESTED IN ME BY THE LORDS OF TIME...
VWORP! VWORP!
... I SUMMON THEE FORTH!
WHAT'S GOING ON? A CHAP CAN'T CALL A TARDIS HIS OWN THESE DAYS!
I SAY... ARE YOU ALRIGHT?

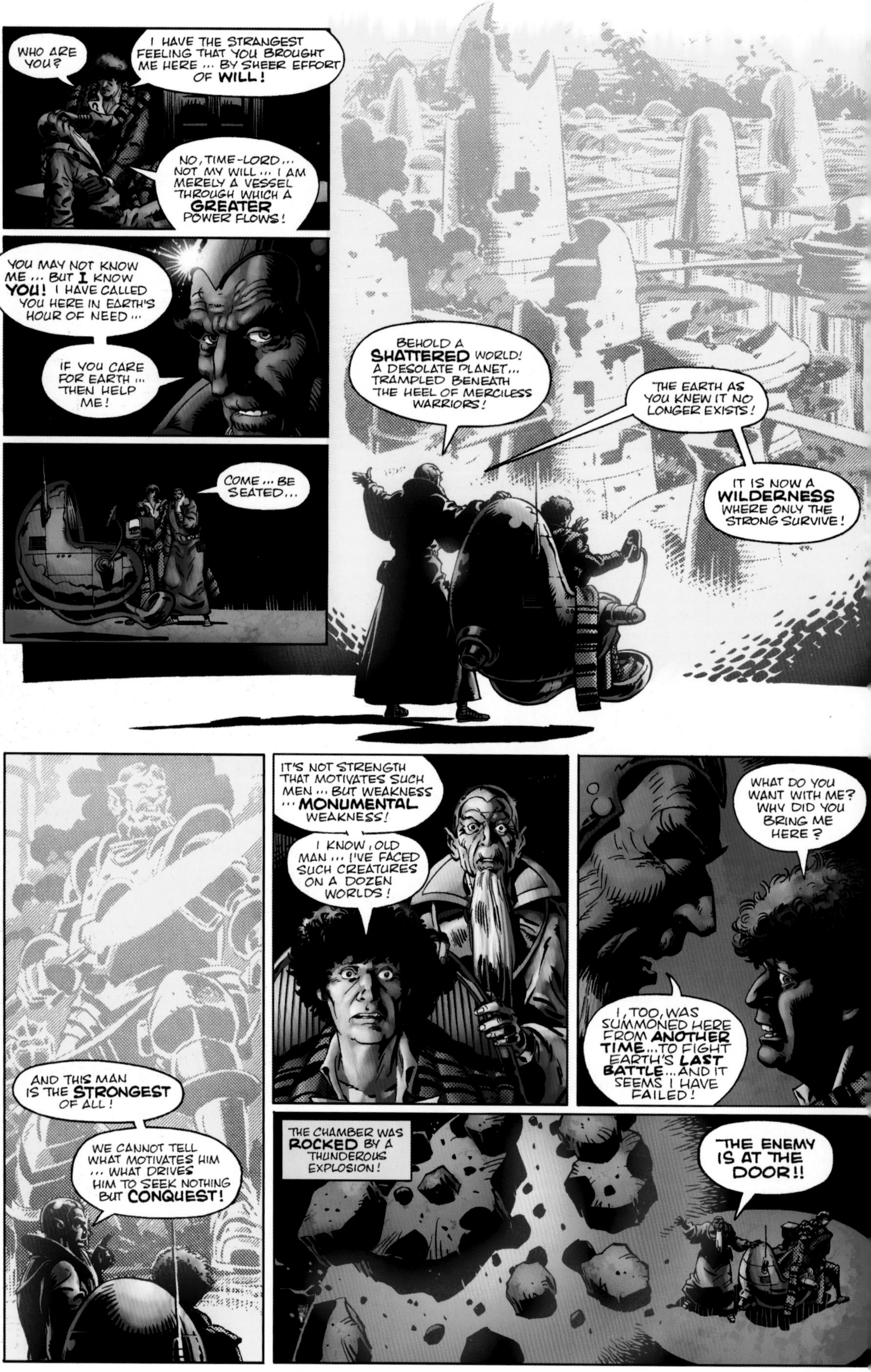
WHO ARE YOU?
I HAVE THE STRANGEST FEELING THAT YOU BROUGHT ME HERE ... BY SHEER EFFORT OF WILL!
NO, TIME-LORD... NOT MY WILL... I AM MERELY A VESSEL THROUGH WHICH A GREATER POWER FLOWS!
YOU MAY NOT KNOW ME ... BUT I KNOW YOU! I HAVE CALLED YOU HERE IN EARTH'S HOUR OF NEED...
IF YOU CARE FOR EARTH ... THEN HELP ME!
COME ... BE SEATED...
BEHOLD A SHATTERED WORLD! A DESOLATE PLANET... TRAMPLED BENEATH THE HEEL OF MERCILESS WARRIORS!
THE EARTH AS YOU KNEW IT NO LONGER EXISTS!
IT IS NOW A WILDERNESS WHERE ONLY THE STRONG SURVIVE!
IT'S NOT STRENGTH THAT MOTIVATES SUCH MEN ... BUT WEAKNESS ... MONUMENTAL WEAKNESS!
I KNOW, OLD MAN ... I'VE FACED SUCH CREATURES ON A DOZEN WORLDS!
AND THIS MAN IS THE STRONGEST OF ALL!
WE CANNOT TELL WHAT MOTIVATES HIM ... WHAT DRIVES HIM TO SEEK NOTHING BUT CONQUEST!
WHAT DO YOU WANT WITH ME? WHY DID YOU BRING ME HERE?
I, TOO, WAS SUMMONED HERE FROM ANOTHER TIME...TO FIGHT EARTH'S LAST BATTLE...AND IT SEEMS I HAVE FAILED!
THE CHAMBER WAS ROCKED BY A THUNDEROUS EXPLOSION!
THE ENEMY IS AT THE DOOR!!

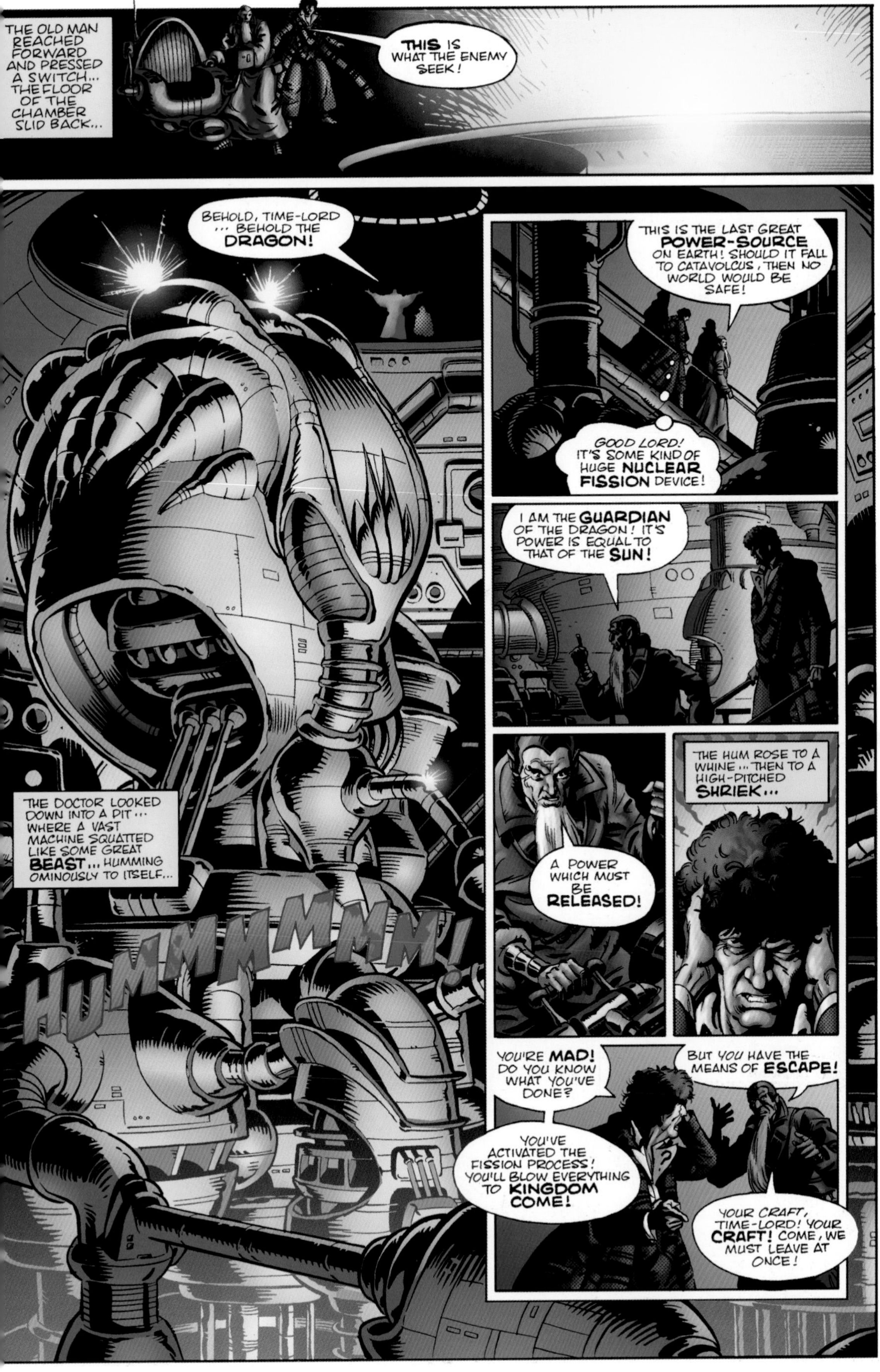
THE OLD MAN REACHED FORWARD AND PRESSED A SWITCH... THE FLOOR OF THE CHAMBER SLID BACK...
THIS IS WHAT THE ENEMY SEEK!
BEHOLD, TIME-LORD ... BEHOLD THE DRAGON!
THE DOCTOR LOOKED DOWN INTO A PIT... WHERE A VAST MACHINE SQUATTED LIKE SOME GREAT BEAST... HUMMING OMINOUSLY TO ITSELF...
HUMMMMMMM!
THIS IS THE LAST GREAT POWER-SOURCE ON EARTH! SHOULD IT FALL TO CATAVOLCUS, THEN NO WORLD WOULD BE SAFE!
GOOD LORD! IT'S SOME KIND OF HUGE NUCLEAR FISSION DEVICE!
I AM THE GUARDIAN OF THE DRAGON! IT'S POWER IS EQUAL TO THAT OF THE SUN!
A POWER WHICH MUST BE RELEASED!
THE HUM ROSE TO A WHINE... THEN TO A HIGH-PITCHED SHRIEK...
YOU'RE MAD! DO YOU KNOW WHAT YOU'VE DONE?
YOU'VE ACTIVATED THE FISSION PROCESS! YOU'LL BLOW EVERYTHING TO KINGDOM COME!
BUT YOU HAVE THE MEANS OF ESCAPE!
YOUR CRAFT, TIME-LORD! YOUR CRAFT! COME, WE MUST LEAVE AT ONCE!

BUT AT THE TOP OF THE WELL A SALVO OF SHOTS STOPPED THE FLEEING PAIR IN THEIR TRACKS!

HANG ON, OLD MAN!! I'LL TRY AND **REACH** YOU SOME-HOW!

GO! IT'S TOO LATE FOR ME NOW! GO BACK UP AND WAIT FOR THE OTHERS!

BUT THE *NEUTRON KNIGHTS* HAD INFILTRATED THE CASTLE...

GREAT GODS! THIS IS WHAT WE CAME HERE FOR!

ALL THE POWER WE'LL EVER NEED!

NO!! NOT WHILE I LIVE... YOU'LL **NEVER** TAKE IT!

THE CASTLE DEFENDERS THREW THEMSELVES INTO THE FRAY...

THEIR LEADER'S GAZE FELL TO THE LEDGE BELOW THE RIM... WHERE THE DOCTOR WAS STRUGGLING VALIANTLY...

AAAGH!!

AND A SINGLE, UNBELIEVABLE WORD BURST FROM HIS LIPS...

MERLIN!!

HOLD FAST! WE'LL SOON GET YOU OUT!

THEN HURRY, ARTHUR! AND DO NOT **HARM** THIS ONE... HE CAN SAVE US ALL!

THE DRAGON HAS DRAWN BREATH... SOO HIS FIRE WILL **SCORCH** THE WORLD...

WE MUST BE AWAY!

MERLIN? ARTHUR? AM I GOING **MAD?**

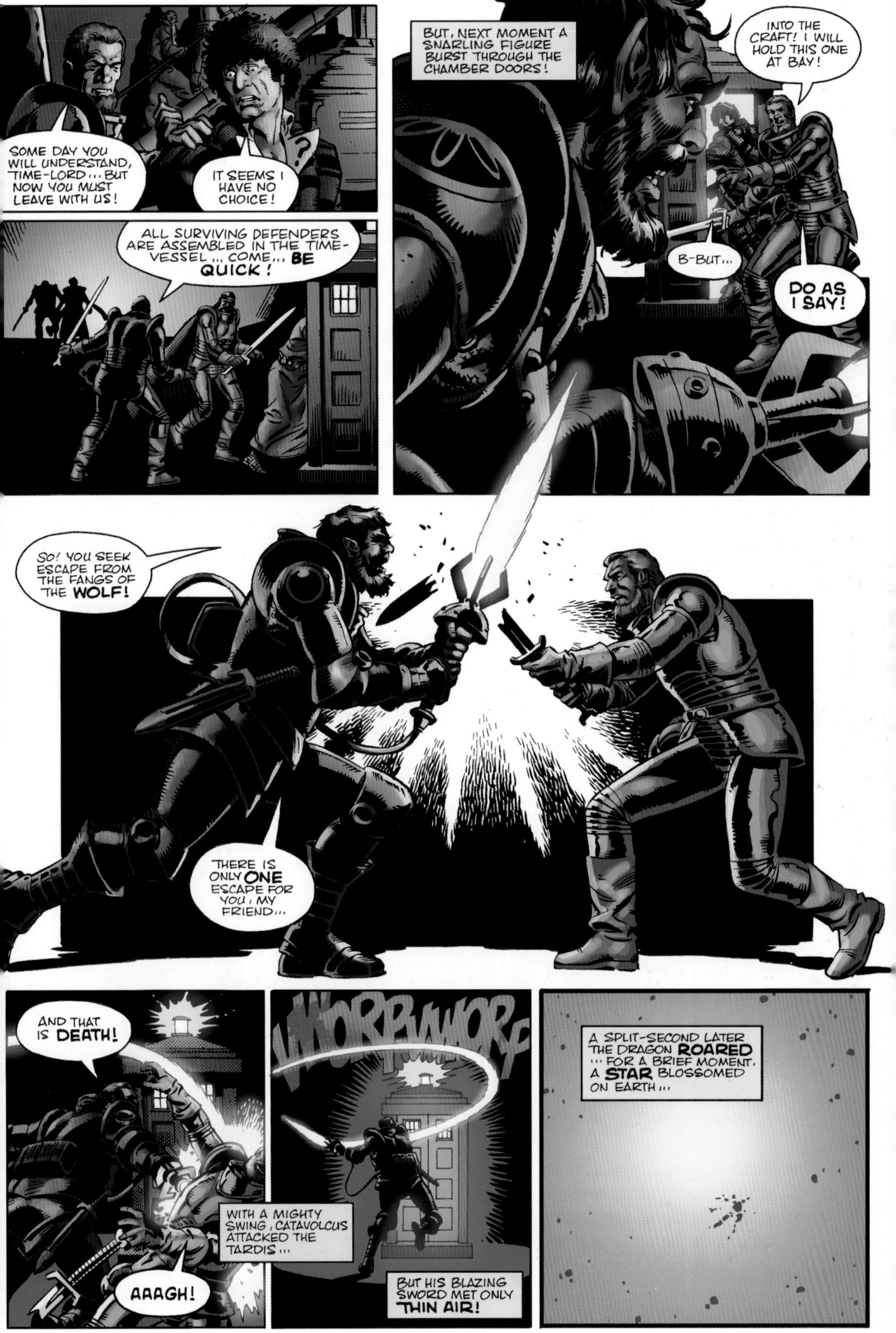
SOME DAY YOU WILL UNDERSTAND, TIME-LORD... BUT NOW YOU MUST LEAVE WITH US!
IT SEEMS I HAVE NO CHOICE!
ALL SURVIVING DEFENDERS ARE ASSEMBLED IN THE TIME-VESSEL ... COME... BE QUICK!
BUT, NEXT MOMENT A SNARLING FIGURE BURST THROUGH THE CHAMBER DOORS!
INTO THE CRAFT! I WILL HOLD THIS ONE AT BAY!
B-BUT...
DO AS I SAY!
SO! YOU SEEK ESCAPE FROM THE FANGS OF THE WOLF!
THERE IS ONLY ONE ESCAPE FOR YOU, MY FRIEND...
AND THAT IS DEATH!
WITH A MIGHTY SWING, CATAVOLCUS ATTACKED THE TARDIS...
AAAGH!
BUT HIS BLAZING SWORD MET ONLY THIN AIR!
A SPLIT-SECOND LATER THE DRAGON ROARED ... FOR A BRIEF MOMENT, A STAR BLOSSOMED ON EARTH...

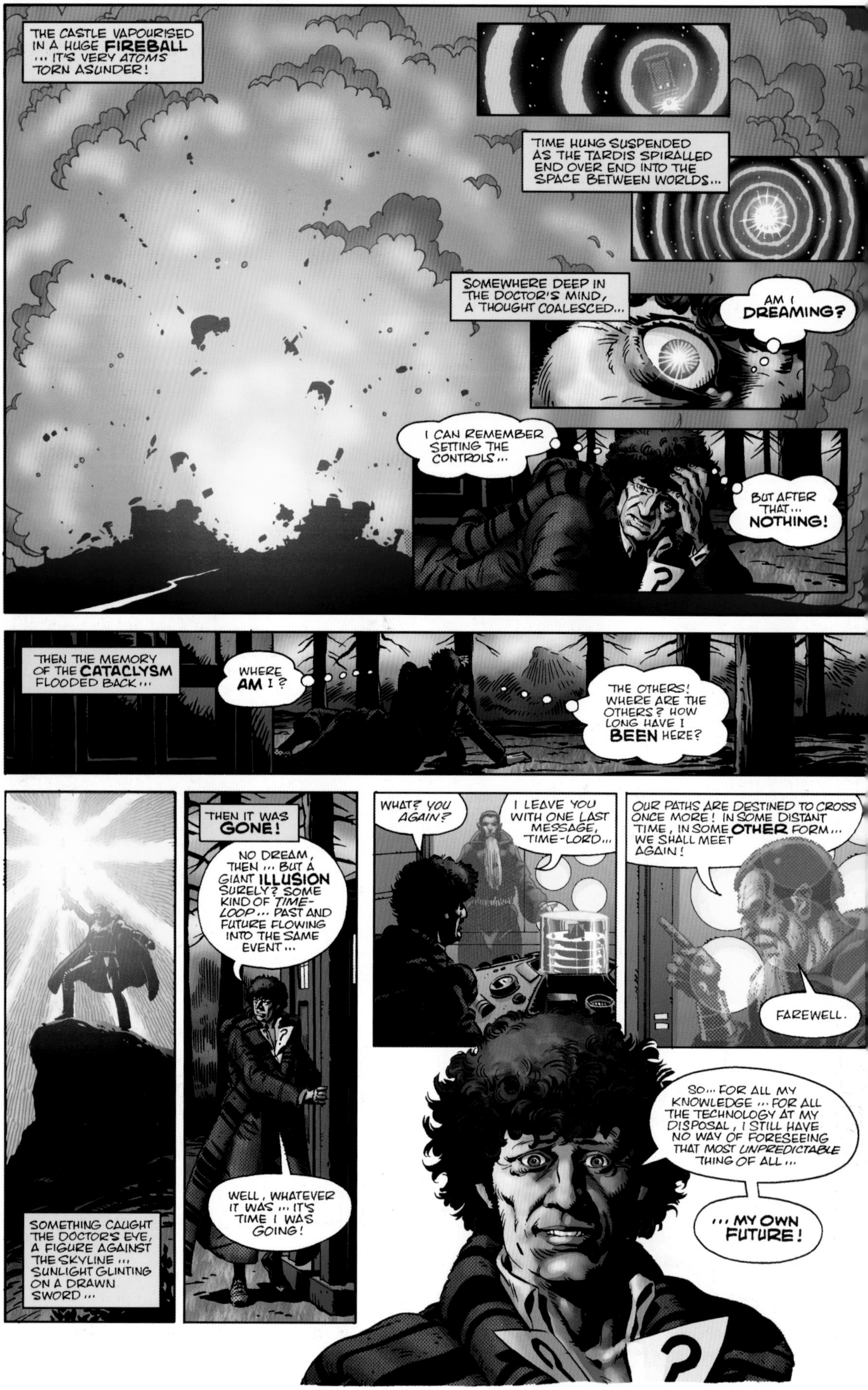
THE CASTLE VAPOURISED IN A HUGE FIREBALL ... IT'S VERY ATOMS TORN ASUNDER!
TIME HUNG SUSPENDED AS THE TARDIS SPIRALLED END OVER END INTO THE SPACE BETWEEN WORLDS...
SOMEWHERE DEEP IN THE DOCTOR'S MIND, A THOUGHT COALESCED...
AM I DREAMING?
I CAN REMEMBER SETTING THE CONTROLS...
BUT AFTER THAT... NOTHING!
THEN THE MEMORY OF THE CATACLYSM FLOODED BACK...
WHERE AM I?
THE OTHERS! WHERE ARE THE OTHERS? HOW LONG HAVE I BEEN HERE?
SOMETHING CAUGHT THE DOCTOR'S EYE, A FIGURE AGAINST THE SKYLINE ... SUNLIGHT GLINTING ON A DRAWN SWORD...
THEN IT WAS GONE!
NO DREAM, THEN ... BUT A GIANT ILLUSION SURELY? SOME KIND OF TIME-LOOP ... PAST AND FUTURE FLOWING INTO THE SAME EVENT...
WELL, WHATEVER IT WAS ... IT'S TIME I WAS GOING!
WHAT? YOU AGAIN?
I LEAVE YOU WITH ONE LAST MESSAGE, TIME-LORD...
OUR PATHS ARE DESTINED TO CROSS ONCE MORE! IN SOME DISTANT TIME, IN SOME OTHER FORM... WE SHALL MEET AGAIN!
FAREWELL.
SO... FOR ALL MY KNOWLEDGE ... FOR ALL THE TECHNOLOGY AT MY DISPOSAL, I STILL HAVE NO WAY OF FORESEEING THAT MOST UNPREDICTABLE THING OF ALL...
... MY OWN FUTURE!

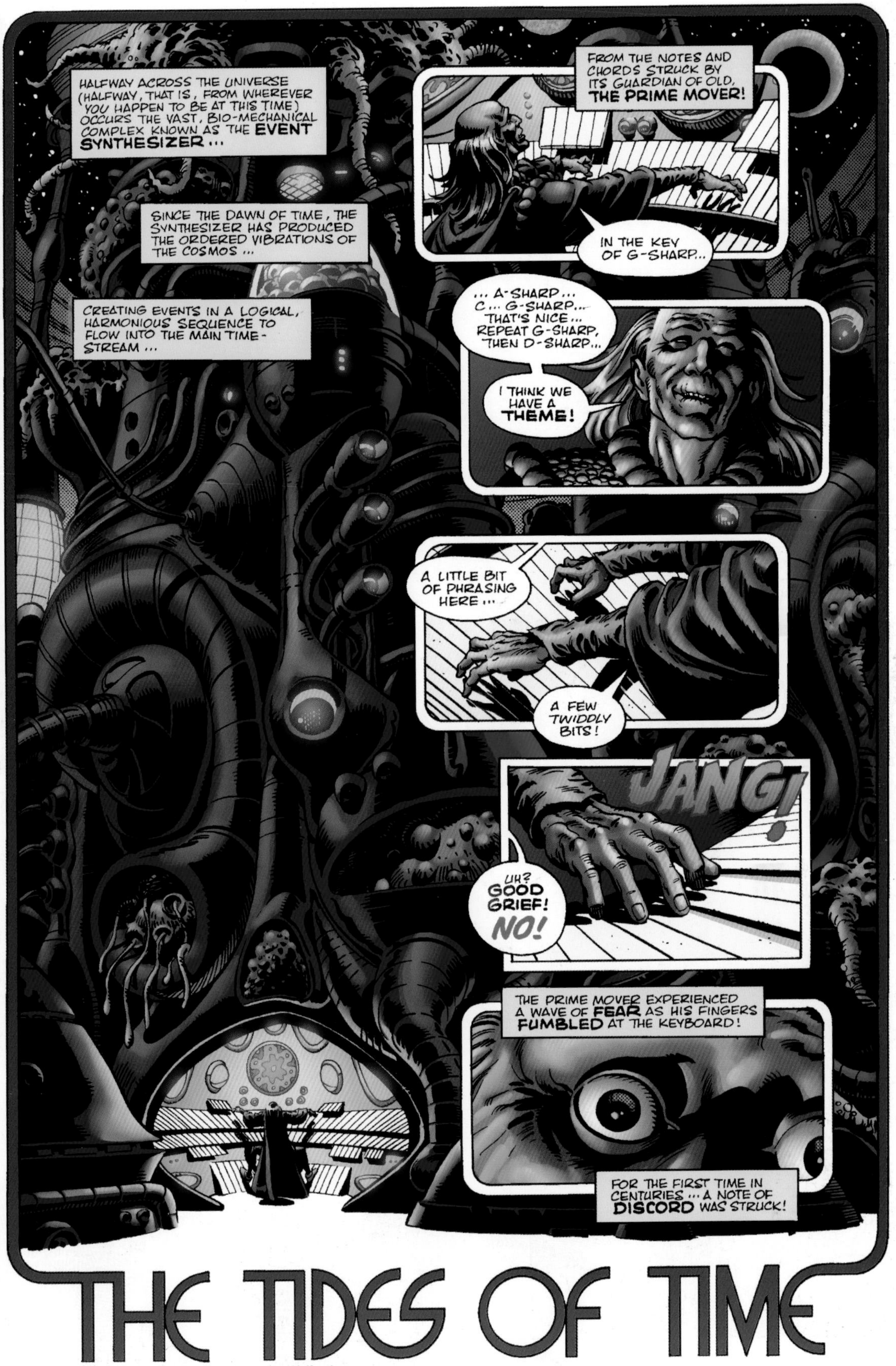
HALFWAY ACROSS THE UNIVERSE (HALFWAY, THAT IS, FROM WHEREVER YOU HAPPEN TO BE AT THIS TIME) OCCURS THE VAST, BIO-MECHANICAL COMPLEX KNOWN AS THE **EVENT SYNTHESIZER**...
SINCE THE DAWN OF TIME, THE SYNTHESIZER HAS PRODUCED THE ORDERED VIBRATIONS OF THE COSMOS...
CREATING EVENTS IN A LOGICAL, HARMONIOUS SEQUENCE TO FLOW INTO THE MAIN TIME-STREAM...
FROM THE NOTES AND CHORDS STRUCK BY ITS GUARDIAN OF OLD, **THE PRIME MOVER!**
IN THE KEY OF G-SHARP...
... A-SHARP... C... G-SHARP... THAT'S NICE... REPEAT G-SHARP, THEN D-SHARP...
I THINK WE HAVE A **THEME!**
A LITTLE BIT OF PHRASING HERE...
A FEW TWIDDLY BITS!
JANG!
UH? GOOD GRIEF! NO!
THE PRIME MOVER EXPERIENCED A WAVE OF **FEAR** AS HIS FINGERS **FUMBLED** AT THE KEYBOARD!
FOR THE FIRST TIME IN CENTURIES... A NOTE OF **DISCORD** WAS STRUCK!

THE TIDES OF TIME

Script: Steve Parkhouse Art: Dave Gibbons Editor: Alan McKenzie

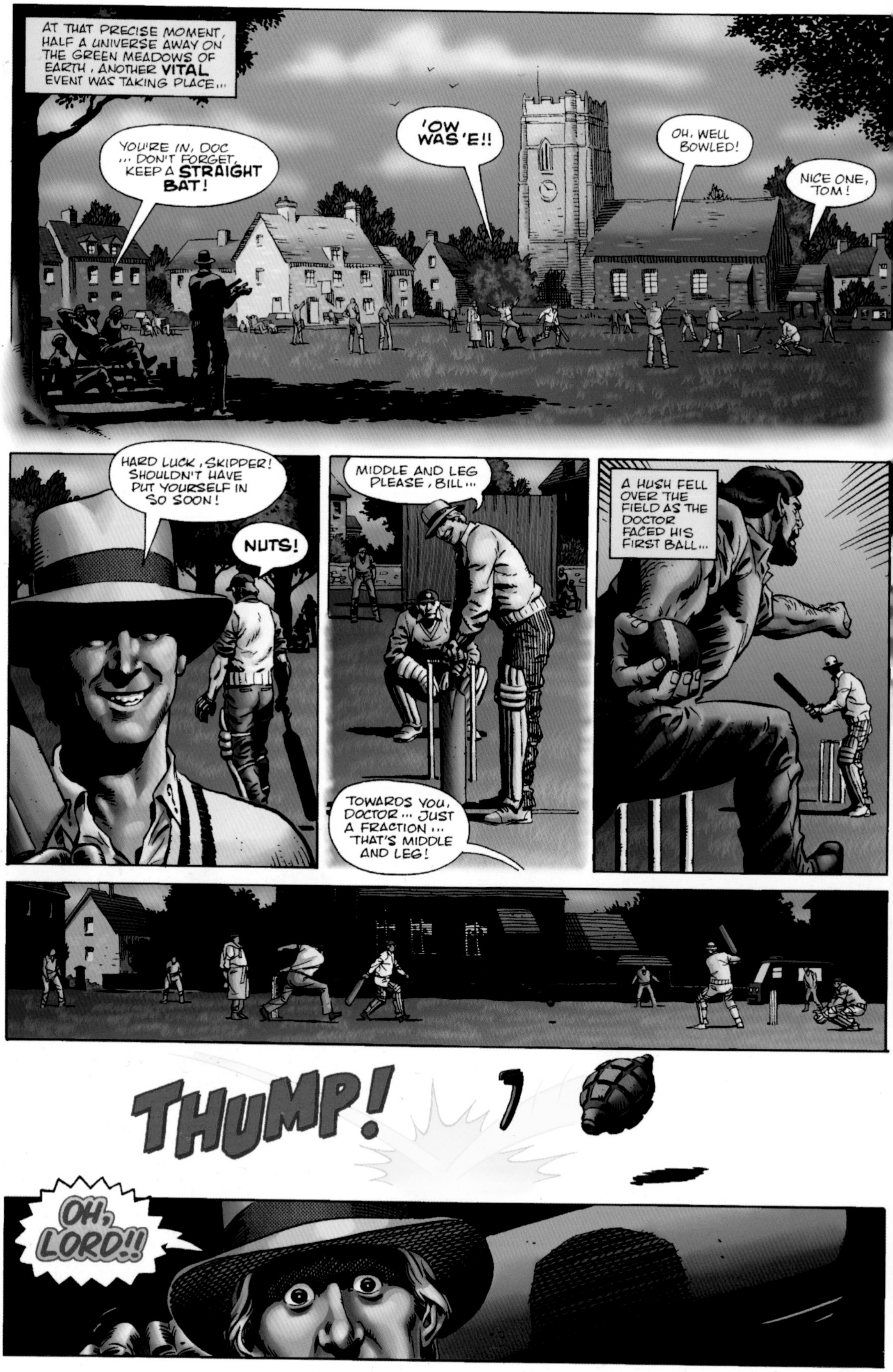

AT THAT PRECISE MOMENT, HALF A UNIVERSE AWAY ON THE GREEN MEADOWS OF EARTH, ANOTHER VITAL EVENT WAS TAKING PLACE...
YOU'RE IN, DOC ... DON'T FORGET, KEEP A STRAIGHT BAT!
'OW WAS 'E!!
OH, WELL BOWLED!
NICE ONE, TOM!
HARD LUCK, SKIPPER! SHOULDN'T HAVE PUT YOURSELF IN SO SOON!
NUTS!
MIDDLE AND LEG PLEASE, BILL...
TOWARDS YOU, DOCTOR... JUST A FRACTION... THAT'S MIDDLE AND LEG!
A HUSH FELL OVER THE FIELD AS THE DOCTOR FACED HIS FIRST BALL...
THUMP!
OH, LORD!!

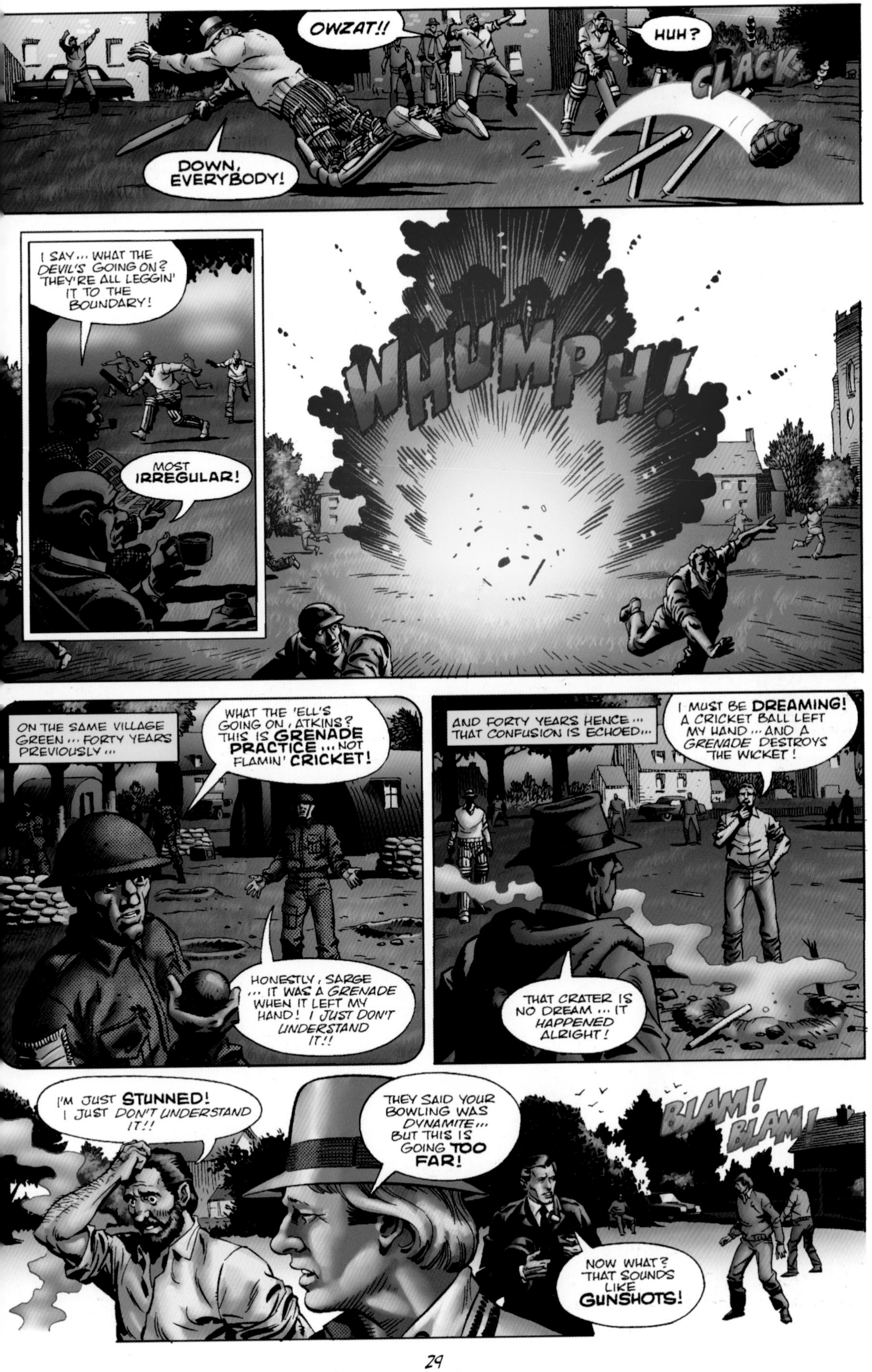
OWZAT!!
HUH?
CLACK
DOWN, EVERYBODY!
I SAY... WHAT THE DEVIL'S GOING ON? THEY'RE ALL LEGGIN' IT TO THE BOUNDARY!
MOST IRREGULAR!
WHUMPH!
ON THE SAME VILLAGE GREEN... FORTY YEARS PREVIOUSLY...
WHAT THE 'ELL'S GOING ON, ATKINS? THIS IS GRENADE PRACTICE... NOT FLAMIN' CRICKET!
HONESTLY, SARGE... IT WAS A GRENADE WHEN IT LEFT MY HAND! I JUST DON'T UNDERSTAND IT!!
AND FORTY YEARS HENCE... THAT CONFUSION IS ECHOED...
I MUST BE DREAMING! A CRICKET BALL LEFT MY HAND... AND A GRENADE DESTROYS THE WICKET!
THAT CRATER IS NO DREAM... IT HAPPENED ALRIGHT!
I'M JUST STUNNED! I JUST DON'T UNDERSTAND IT!!
THEY SAID YOUR BOWLING WAS DYNAMITE... BUT THIS IS GOING TOO FAR!
BLAM! BLAM!
NOW WHAT? THAT SOUNDS LIKE GUNSHOTS!

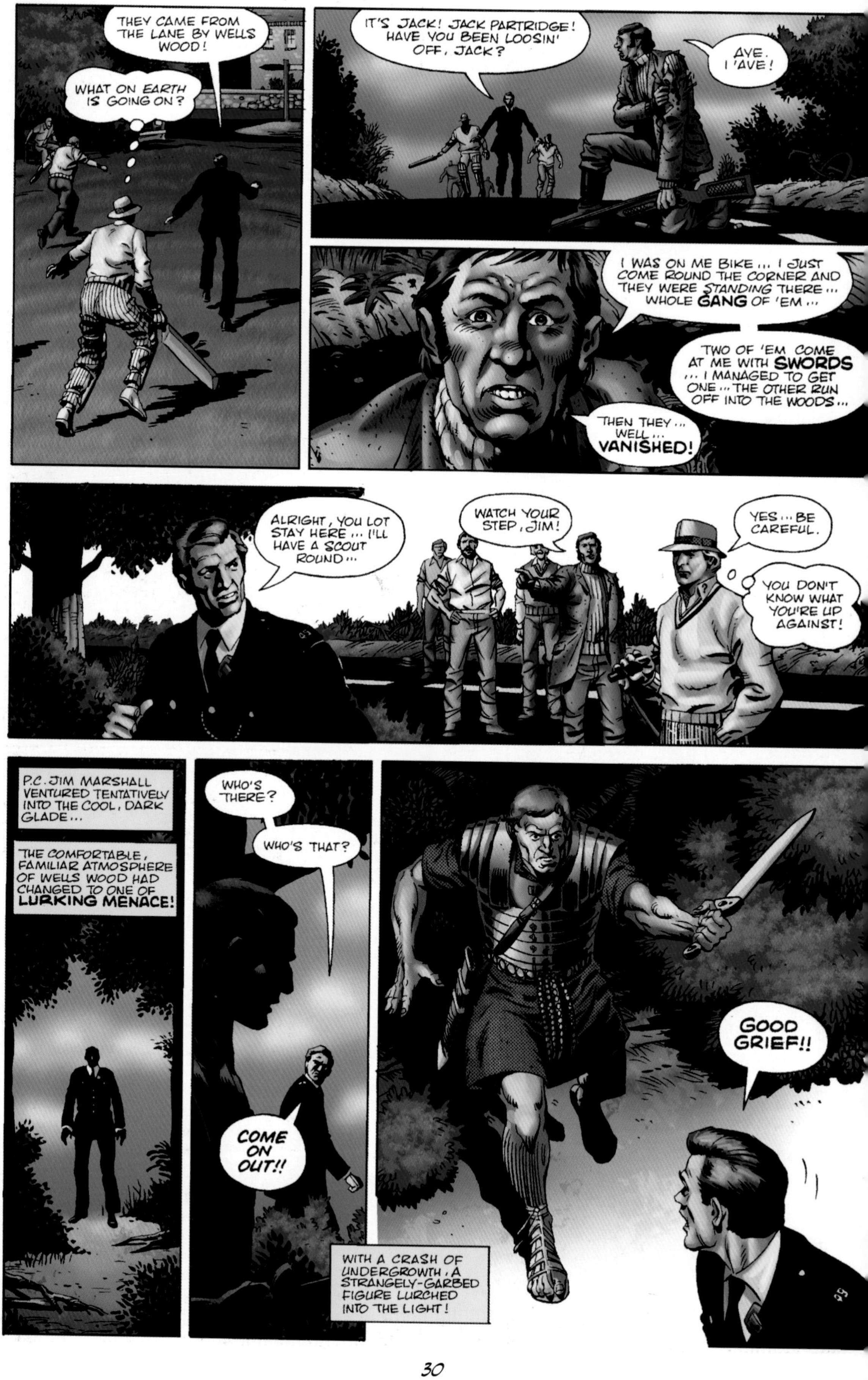
THEY CAME FROM THE LANE BY WELLS WOOD!
WHAT ON EARTH IS GOING ON?
IT'S JACK! JACK PARTRIDGE! HAVE YOU BEEN LOOSIN' OFF, JACK?
AYE. I 'AVE!
I WAS ON ME BIKE ... I JUST COME ROUND THE CORNER AND THEY WERE STANDING THERE ... WHOLE GANG OF 'EM ...
TWO OF 'EM COME AT ME WITH SWORDS ... I MANAGED TO GET ONE ... THE OTHER RUN OFF INTO THE WOODS ...
THEN THEY ... WELL ... VANISHED!
ALRIGHT, YOU LOT STAY HERE ... I'LL HAVE A SCOUT ROUND ...
WATCH YOUR STEP, JIM!
YES ... BE CAREFUL.
YOU DON'T KNOW WHAT YOU'RE UP AGAINST!
P.C. JIM MARSHALL VENTURED TENTATIVELY INTO THE COOL, DARK GLADE ...
THE COMFORTABLE, FAMILIAR ATMOSPHERE OF WELLS WOOD HAD CHANGED TO ONE OF LURKING MENACE!
WHO'S THERE?
WHO'S THAT?
COME ON OUT!!
WITH A CRASH OF UNDERGROWTH, A STRANGELY-GARBED FIGURE LURCHED INTO THE LIGHT!
GOOD GRIEF!!

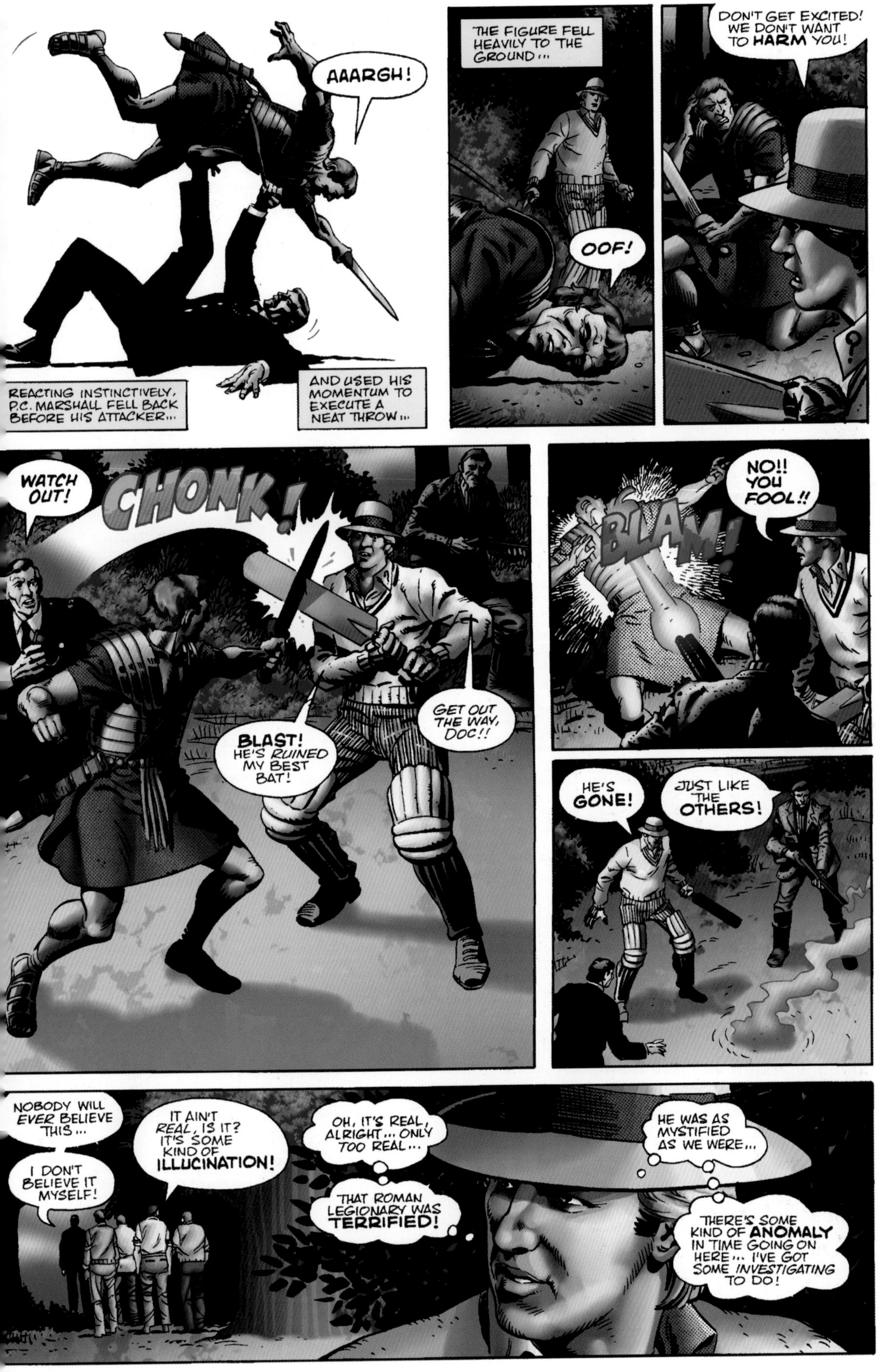
AAARGH!
REACTING INSTINCTIVELY, P.C. MARSHALL FELL BACK BEFORE HIS ATTACKER...
AND USED HIS MOMENTUM TO EXECUTE A NEAT THROW...
THE FIGURE FELL HEAVILY TO THE GROUND...
OOF!
DON'T GET EXCITED! WE DON'T WANT TO HARM YOU!
WATCH OUT!
CHONK!
BLAST! HE'S RUINED MY BEST BAT!
GET OUT THE WAY, DOC!!
BLAM!
NO!! YOU FOOL!!
HE'S GONE!
JUST LIKE THE OTHERS!
NOBODY WILL EVER BELIEVE THIS...
I DON'T BELIEVE IT MYSELF!
IT AIN'T REAL, IS IT? IT'S SOME KIND OF ILLUCINATION!
OH, IT'S REAL, ALRIGHT... ONLY TOO REAL...
THAT ROMAN LEGIONARY WAS TERRIFIED!
HE WAS AS MYSTIFIED AS WE WERE...
THERE'S SOME KIND OF ANOMALY IN TIME GOING ON HERE... I'VE GOT SOME INVESTIGATING TO DO!

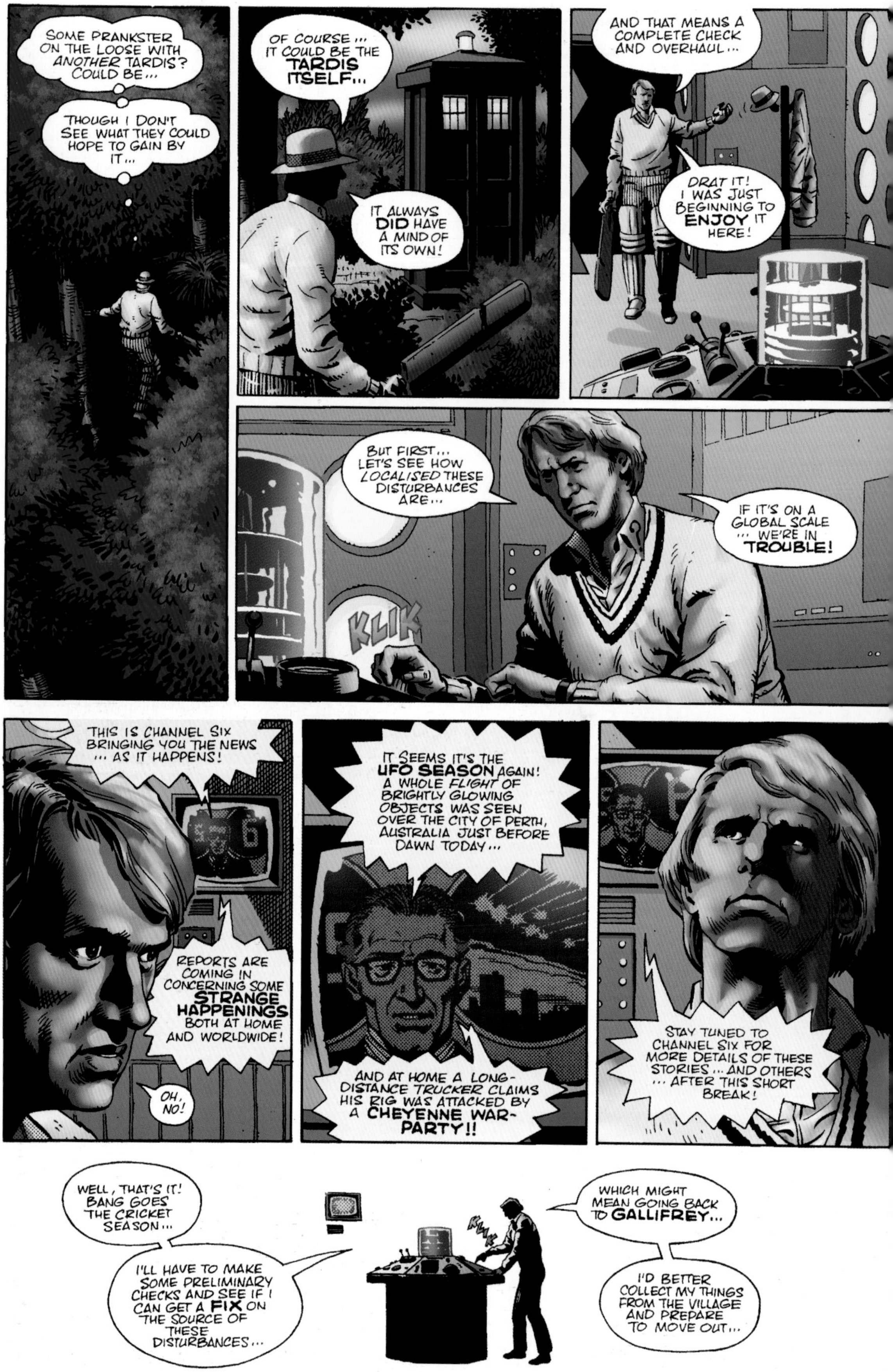
SOME PRANKSTER ON THE LOOSE WITH ANOTHER TARDIS? COULD BE...
THOUGH I DON'T SEE WHAT THEY COULD HOPE TO GAIN BY IT...
OF COURSE... IT COULD BE THE TARDIS ITSELF...
IT ALWAYS DID HAVE A MIND OF ITS OWN!
AND THAT MEANS A COMPLETE CHECK AND OVERHAUL...
DRAT IT! I WAS JUST BEGINNING TO ENJOY IT HERE!
BUT FIRST... LET'S SEE HOW LOCALISED THESE DISTURBANCES ARE...
IF IT'S ON A GLOBAL SCALE ... WE'RE IN TROUBLE!
KLIK
THIS IS CHANNEL SIX BRINGING YOU THE NEWS ... AS IT HAPPENS!
REPORTS ARE COMING IN CONCERNING SOME STRANGE HAPPENINGS BOTH AT HOME AND WORLDWIDE!
OH, NO!
IT SEEMS IT'S THE UFO SEASON AGAIN! A WHOLE FLIGHT OF BRIGHTLY GLOWING OBJECTS WAS SEEN OVER THE CITY OF PERTH, AUSTRALIA JUST BEFORE DAWN TODAY...
AND AT HOME A LONG-DISTANCE TRUCKER CLAIMS HIS RIG WAS ATTACKED BY A CHEYENNE WAR-PARTY!!
STAY TUNED TO CHANNEL SIX FOR MORE DETAILS OF THESE STORIES... AND OTHERS ... AFTER THIS SHORT BREAK!
WELL, THAT'S IT! BANG GOES THE CRICKET SEASON...
I'LL HAVE TO MAKE SOME PRELIMINARY CHECKS AND SEE IF I CAN GET A FIX ON THE SOURCE OF THESE DISTURBANCES...
WHICH MIGHT MEAN GOING BACK TO GALLIFREY...
I'D BETTER COLLECT MY THINGS FROM THE VILLAGE AND PREPARE TO MOVE OUT...

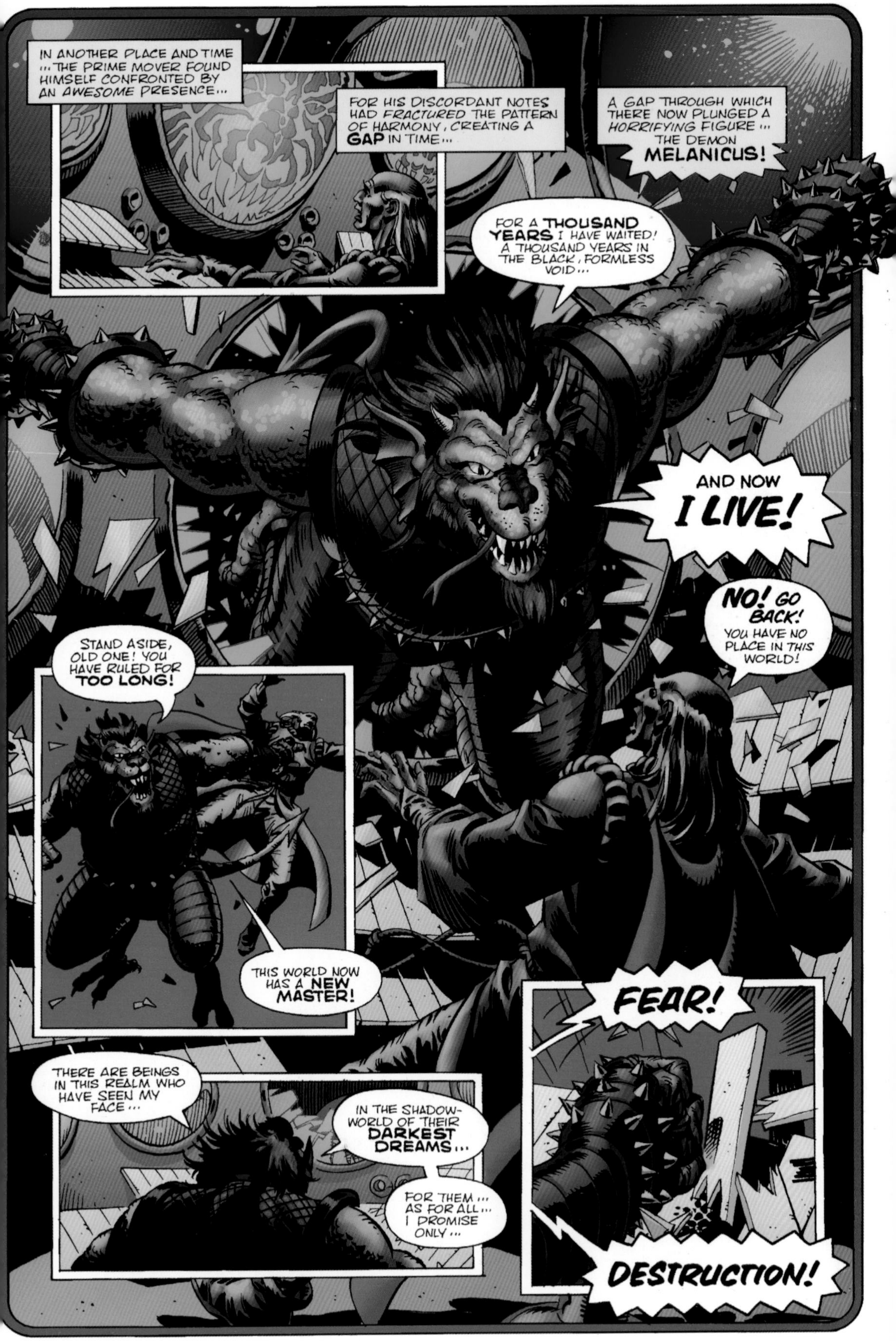
IN ANOTHER PLACE AND TIME ...THE PRIME MOVER FOUND HIMSELF CONFRONTED BY AN AWESOME PRESENCE...
FOR HIS DISCORDANT NOTES HAD FRACTURED THE PATTERN OF HARMONY, CREATING A GAP IN TIME...
A GAP THROUGH WHICH THERE NOW PLUNGED A HORRIFYING FIGURE... THE DEMON MELANICUS!
FOR A THOUSAND YEARS I HAVE WAITED! A THOUSAND YEARS IN THE BLACK, FORMLESS VOID...
AND NOW I LIVE!
NO! GO BACK! YOU HAVE NO PLACE IN THIS WORLD!
STAND ASIDE, OLD ONE! YOU HAVE RULED FOR TOO LONG!
THIS WORLD NOW HAS A NEW MASTER!
THERE ARE BEINGS IN THIS REALM WHO HAVE SEEN MY FACE...
IN THE SHADOW-WORLD OF THEIR DARKEST DREAMS...
FOR THEM... AS FOR ALL... I PROMISE ONLY...
FEAR!
DESTRUCTION!

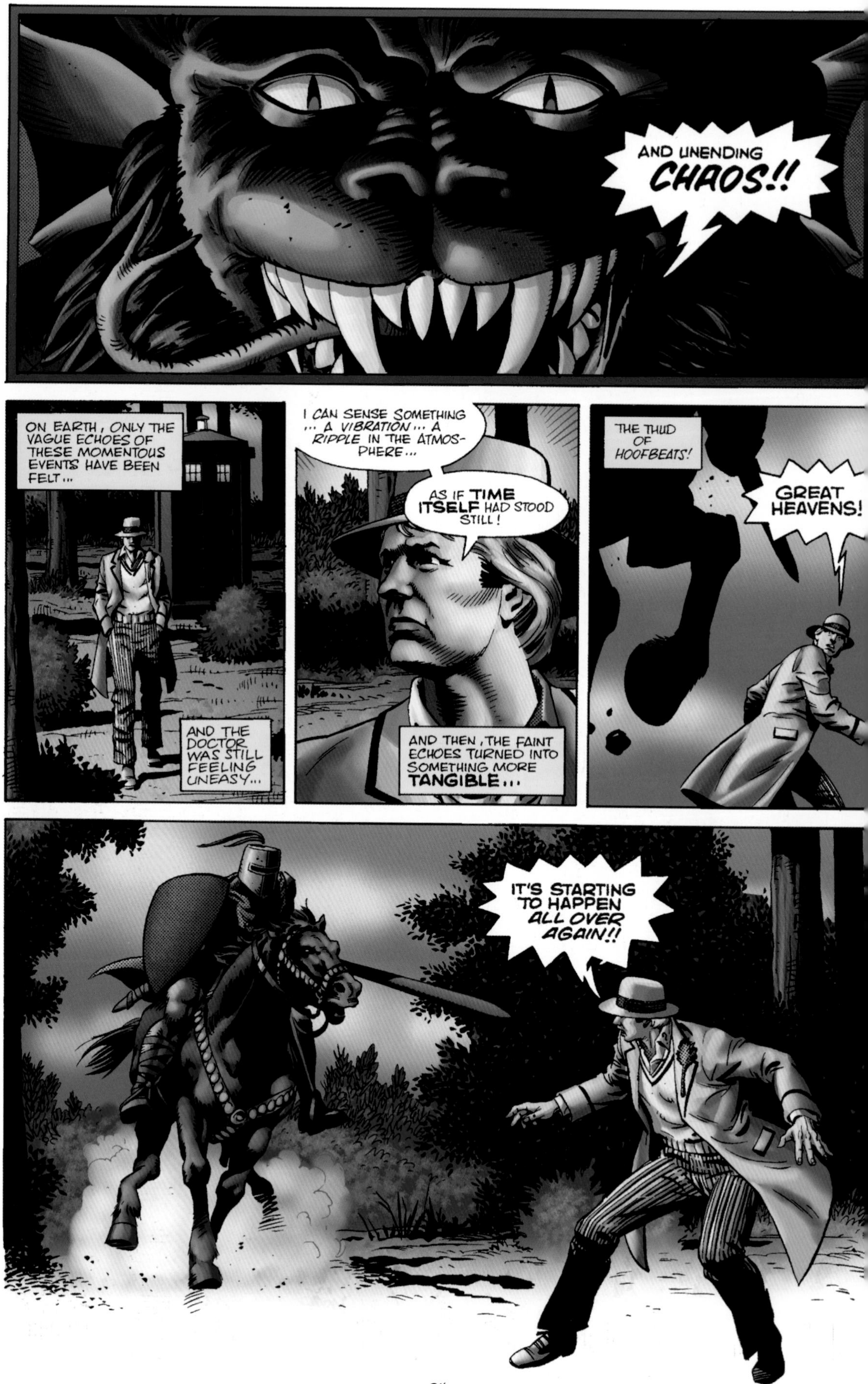
AND UNENDING CHAOS!!
ON EARTH, ONLY THE VAGUE ECHOES OF THESE MOMENTOUS EVENTS HAVE BEEN FELT...
AND THE DOCTOR WAS STILL FEELING UNEASY...
I CAN SENSE SOMETHING ... A VIBRATION ... A RIPPLE IN THE ATMOSPHERE...
AS IF TIME ITSELF HAD STOOD STILL!
AND THEN, THE FAINT ECHOES TURNED INTO SOMETHING MORE TANGIBLE...
THE THUD OF HOOFBEATS!
GREAT HEAVENS!
IT'S STARTING TO HAPPEN ALL OVER AGAIN!!

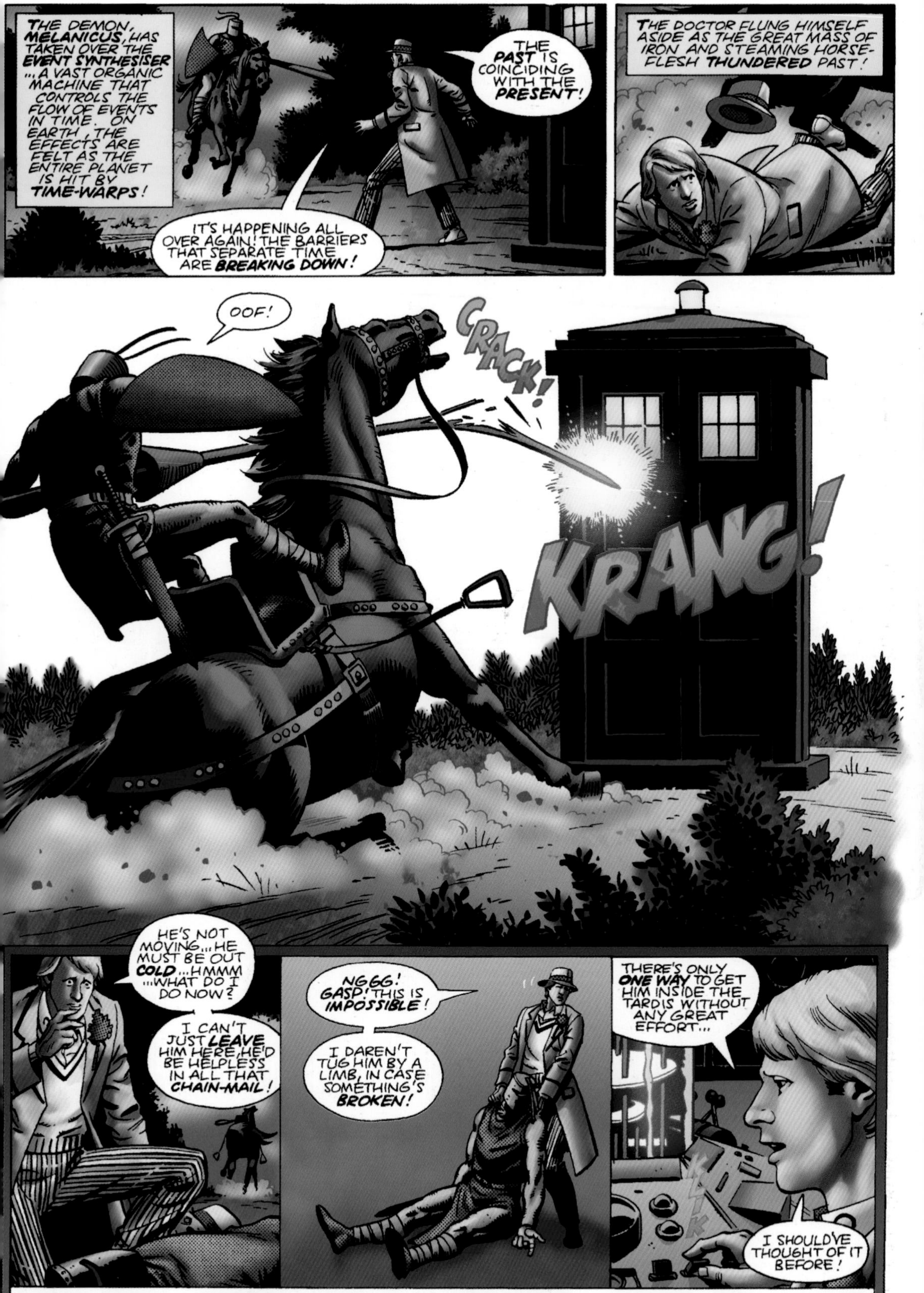
THE DEMON, MELANICUS, HAS TAKEN OVER THE EVENT SYNTHESISER ...A VAST ORGANIC MACHINE THAT CONTROLS THE FLOW OF EVENTS IN TIME. ON EARTH, THE EFFECTS ARE FELT AS THE ENTIRE PLANET IS HIT BY TIME-WARPS!
THE PAST IS COINCIDING WITH THE PRESENT!
IT'S HAPPENING ALL OVER AGAIN! THE BARRIERS THAT SEPARATE TIME ARE BREAKING DOWN!
THE DOCTOR FLUNG HIMSELF ASIDE AS THE GREAT MASS OF IRON AND STEAMING HORSE-FLESH THUNDERED PAST!
OOF!
CRACK!
KRANG!
HE'S NOT MOVING... HE MUST BE OUT COLD... HMMM ...WHAT DO I DO NOW?
I CAN'T JUST LEAVE HIM HERE, HE'D BE HELPLESS IN ALL THAT CHAIN-MAIL!
NGGG! GASP! THIS IS IMPOSSIBLE!
I DAREN'T TUG HIM BY A LIMB, IN CASE SOMETHING'S BROKEN!
THERE'S ONLY ONE WAY TO GET HIM INSIDE THE TARDIS WITHOUT ANY GREAT EFFORT...
I SHOULD'VE THOUGHT OF IT BEFORE!

THE TIDES OF TIME PART TWO

SCRIPT – STEVE PARKHOUSE ART – DAVE GIBBONS EDITOR – ALAN McKENZIE

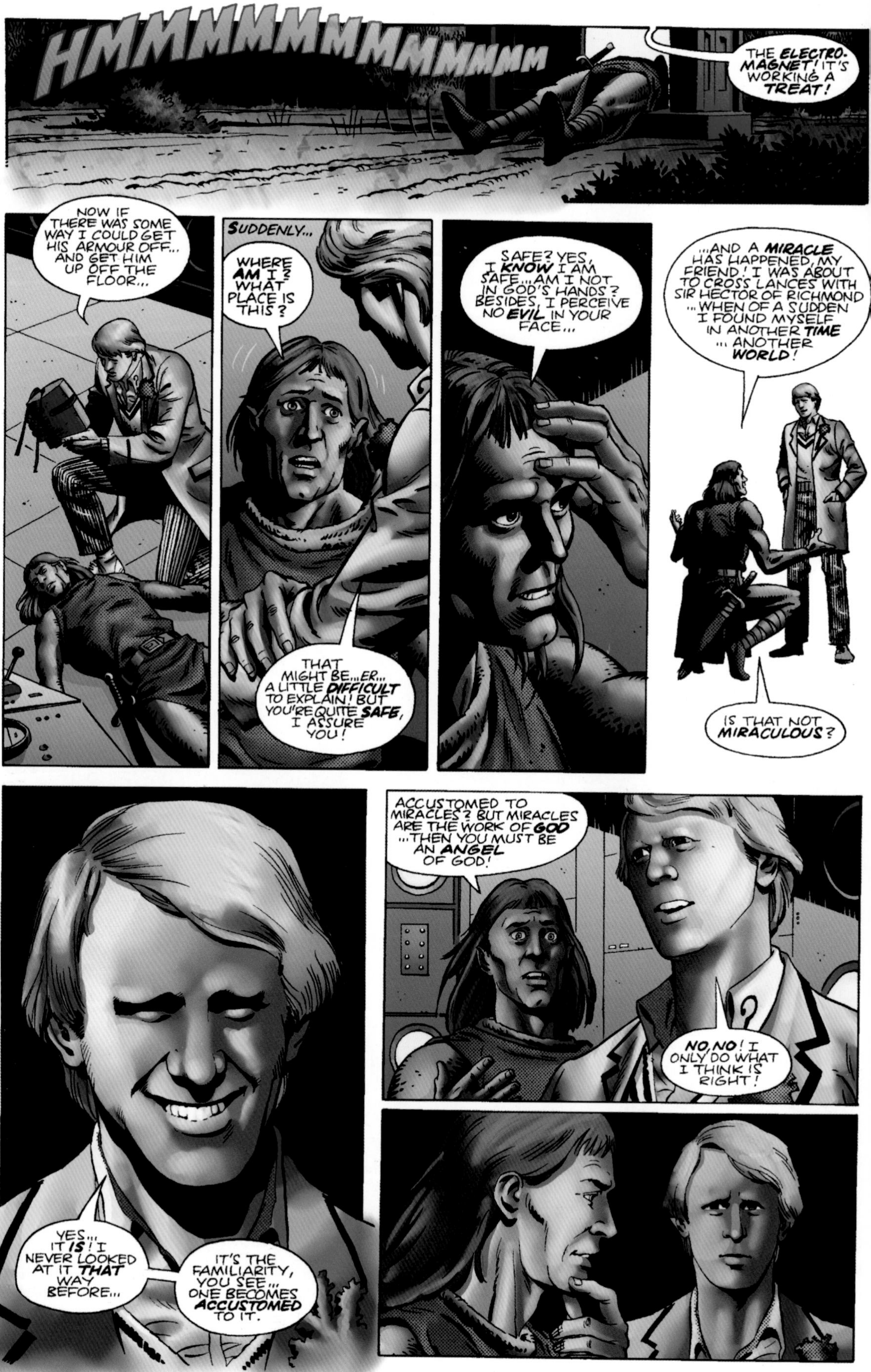
HMMMMMMMMMMMMMM
THE ELECTRO-MAGNET! IT'S WORKING A TREAT!
NOW IF THERE WAS SOME WAY I COULD GET HIS ARMOUR OFF... AND GET HIM UP OFF THE FLOOR...
SUDDENLY...
WHERE AM I? WHAT PLACE IS THIS?
THAT MIGHT BE...ER... A LITTLE DIFFICULT TO EXPLAIN! BUT YOU'RE QUITE SAFE, I ASSURE YOU!
SAFE? YES, I KNOW I AM SAFE...AM I NOT IN GOD'S HANDS? BESIDES, I PERCEIVE NO EVIL IN YOUR FACE...
...AND A MIRACLE HAS HAPPENED, MY FRIEND! I WAS ABOUT TO CROSS LANCES WITH SIR HECTOR OF RICHMOND ...WHEN OF A SUDDEN I FOUND MYSELF IN ANOTHER TIME ...ANOTHER WORLD!
IS THAT NOT MIRACULOUS?
YES... IT IS! I NEVER LOOKED AT IT THAT WAY BEFORE...
IT'S THE FAMILIARITY, YOU SEE... ONE BECOMES ACCUSTOMED TO IT.
ACCUSTOMED TO MIRACLES? BUT MIRACLES ARE THE WORK OF GOD ...THEN YOU MUST BE AN ANGEL OF GOD!
NO, NO! I ONLY DO WHAT I THINK IS RIGHT!

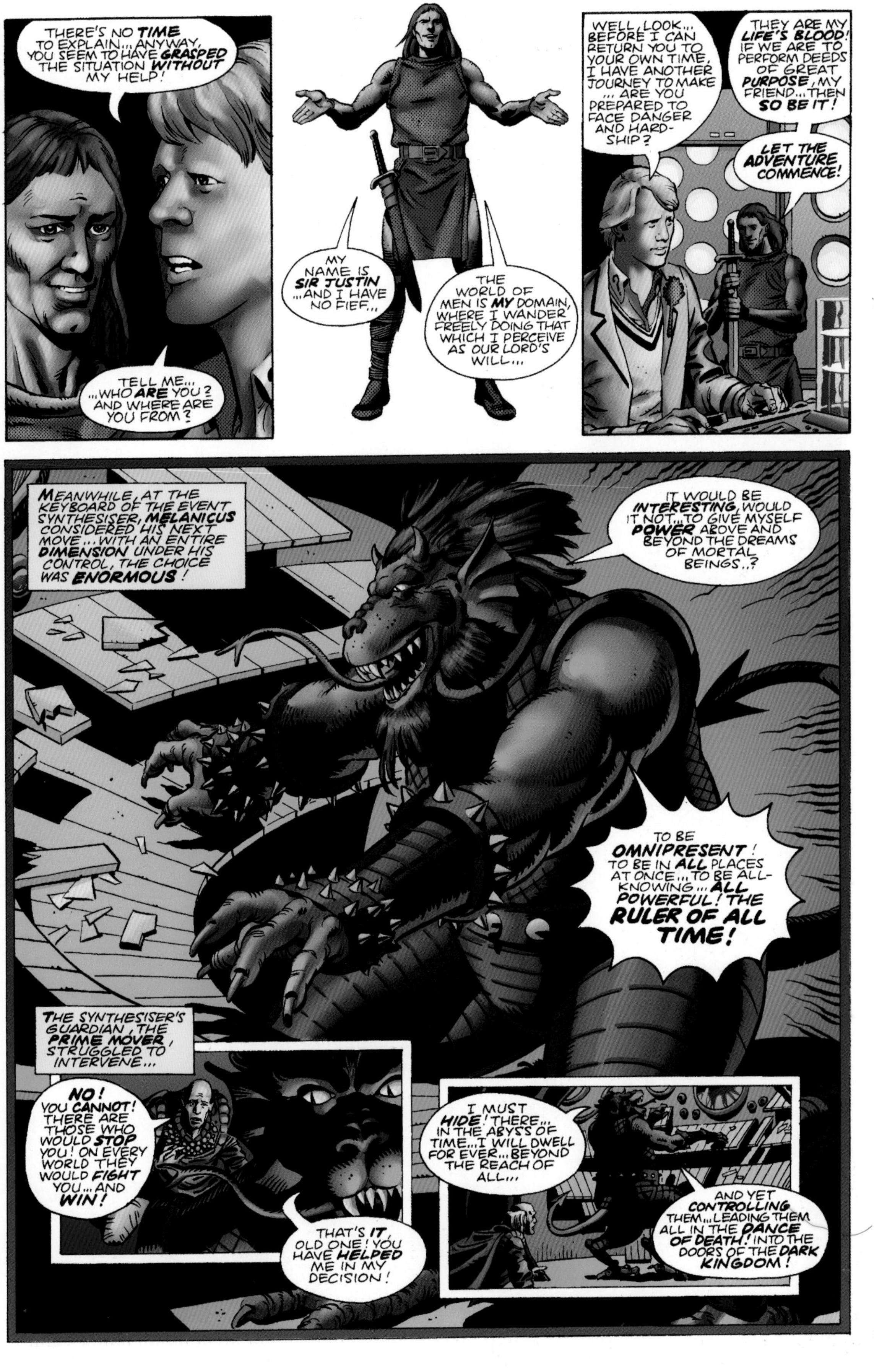

THERE'S NO TIME TO EXPLAIN... ANYWAY, YOU SEEM TO HAVE GRASPED THE SITUATION WITHOUT MY HELP!
TELL ME... ...WHO ARE YOU? AND WHERE ARE YOU FROM?
MY NAME IS SIR JUSTIN ...AND I HAVE NO FIEF...
THE WORLD OF MEN IS MY DOMAIN, WHERE I WANDER FREELY DOING THAT WHICH I PERCEIVE AS OUR LORD'S WILL...
WELL, LOOK... BEFORE I CAN RETURN YOU TO YOUR OWN TIME, I HAVE ANOTHER JOURNEY TO MAKE ... ARE YOU PREPARED TO FACE DANGER AND HARDSHIP?
THEY ARE MY LIFE'S BLOOD! IF WE ARE TO PERFORM DEEDS OF GREAT PURPOSE, MY FRIEND... THEN SO BE IT!
LET THE ADVENTURE COMMENCE!
MEANWHILE, AT THE KEYBOARD OF THE EVENT SYNTHESISER, MELANICUS CONSIDERED HIS NEXT MOVE... WITH AN ENTIRE DIMENSION UNDER HIS CONTROL, THE CHOICE WAS ENORMOUS!
IT WOULD BE INTERESTING, WOULD IT NOT... TO GIVE MYSELF POWER ABOVE AND BEYOND THE DREAMS OF MORTAL BEINGS..?
TO BE OMNIPRESENT! TO BE IN ALL PLACES AT ONCE... TO BE ALL-KNOWING... ALL POWERFUL! THE RULER OF ALL TIME!
THE SYNTHESISER'S GUARDIAN, THE PRIME MOVER, STRUGGLED TO INTERVENE...
NO! YOU CANNOT! THERE ARE THOSE WHO WOULD STOP YOU! ON EVERY WORLD THEY WOULD FIGHT YOU... AND WIN!
THAT'S IT, OLD ONE! YOU HAVE HELPED ME IN MY DECISION!
I MUST HIDE! THERE... IN THE ABYSS OF TIME... I WILL DWELL FOR EVER... BEYOND THE REACH OF ALL...
AND YET CONTROLLING THEM... LEADING THEM ALL IN THE DANCE OF DEATH! INTO THE DOORS OF THE DARK KINGDOM!

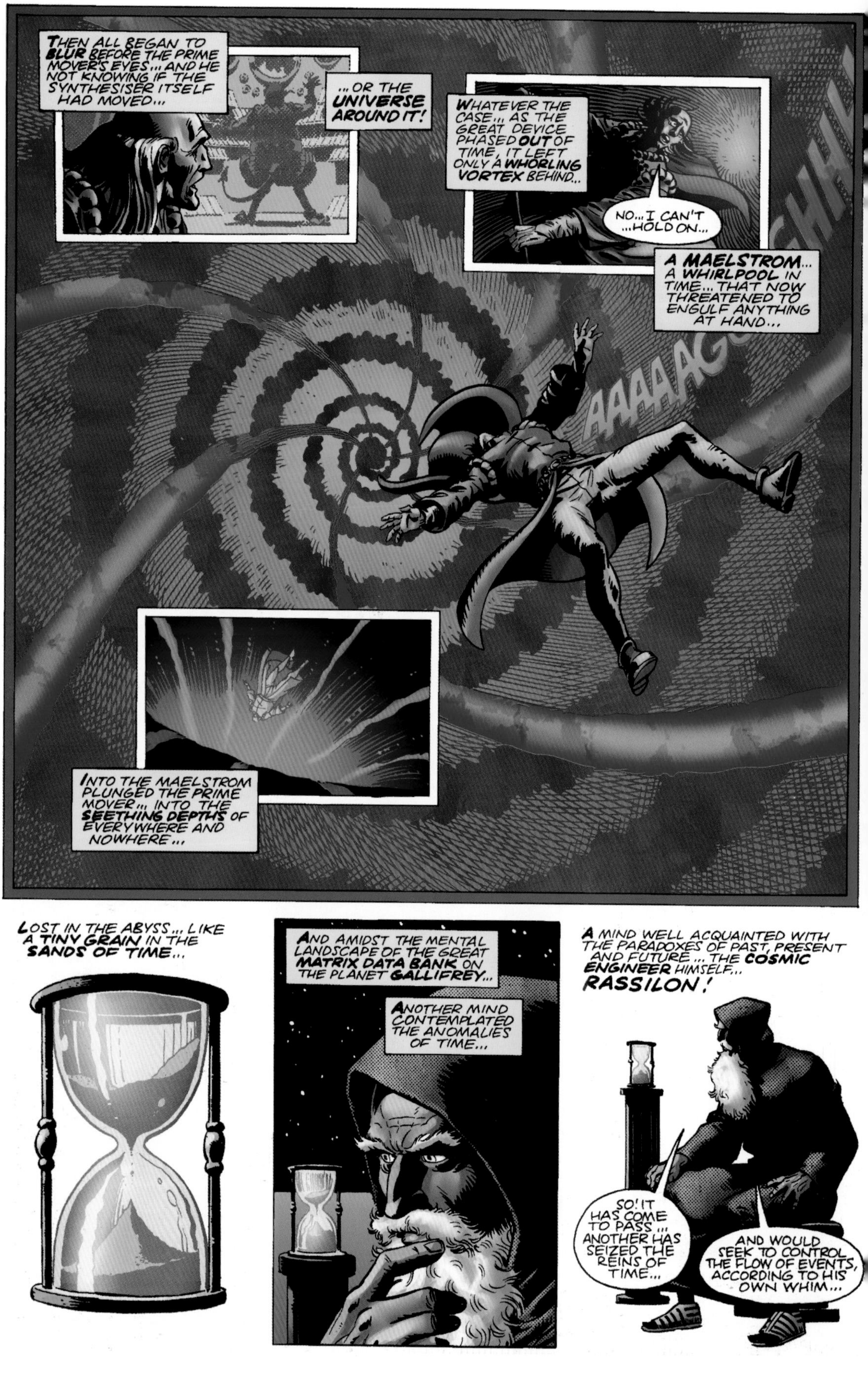

THEN ALL BEGAN TO BLUR BEFORE THE PRIME MOVER'S EYES... AND HE NOT KNOWING IF THE SYNTHESISER ITSELF HAD MOVED...
...OR THE UNIVERSE AROUND IT!
WHATEVER THE CASE... AS THE GREAT DEVICE PHASED OUT OF TIME, IT LEFT ONLY A WHORLING VORTEX BEHIND...
NO... I CAN'T ...HOLD ON...
A MAELSTROM... A WHIRLPOOL IN TIME... THAT NOW THREATENED TO ENGULF ANYTHING AT HAND...
AAAAAG
INTO THE MAELSTROM PLUNGED THE PRIME MOVER... INTO THE SEETHING DEPTHS OF EVERYWHERE AND NOWHERE...
LOST IN THE ABYSS... LIKE A TINY GRAIN IN THE SANDS OF TIME...
AND AMIDST THE MENTAL LANDSCAPE OF THE GREAT MATRIX DATA BANK ON THE PLANET GALLIFREY...
ANOTHER MIND CONTEMPLATED THE ANOMALIES OF TIME...
A MIND WELL ACQUAINTED WITH THE PARADOXES OF PAST, PRESENT AND FUTURE... THE COSMIC ENGINEER HIMSELF... RASSILON!
SO! IT HAS COME TO PASS... ANOTHER HAS SEIZED THE REINS OF TIME...
AND WOULD SEEK TO CONTROL THE FLOW OF EVENTS, ACCORDING TO HIS OWN WHIM...

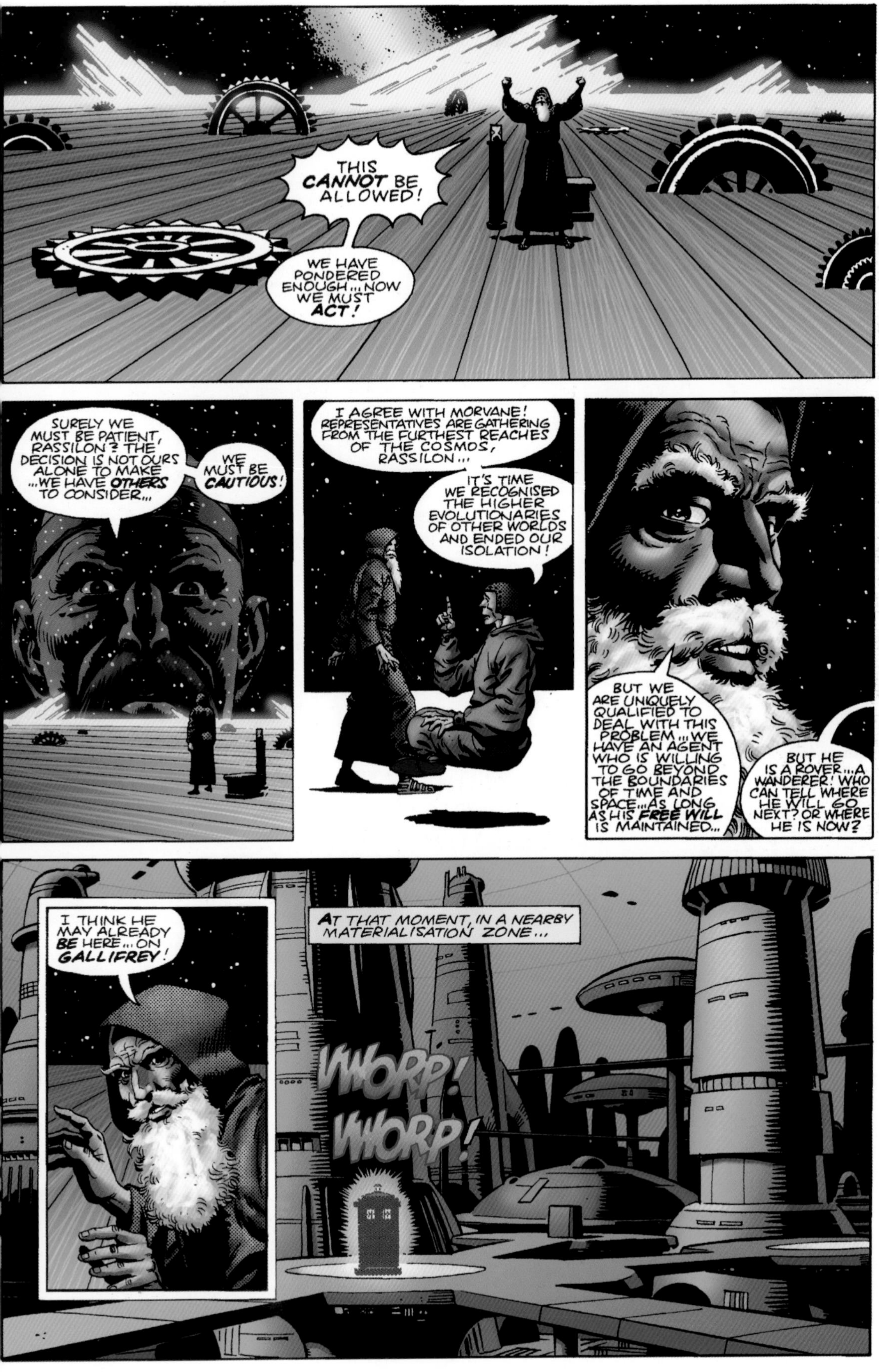
THIS CANNOT BE ALLOWED!
WE HAVE PONDERED ENOUGH... NOW WE MUST ACT!
SURELY WE MUST BE PATIENT, RASSILON? THE DECISION IS NOT OURS ALONE TO MAKE ...WE HAVE OTHERS TO CONSIDER...
WE MUST BE CAUTIOUS!
I AGREE WITH MORVANE! REPRESENTATIVES ARE GATHERING FROM THE FURTHEST REACHES OF THE COSMOS, RASSILON...
IT'S TIME WE RECOGNISED THE HIGHER EVOLUTIONARIES OF OTHER WORLDS AND ENDED OUR ISOLATION!
BUT WE ARE UNIQUELY QUALIFIED TO DEAL WITH THIS PROBLEM... WE HAVE AN AGENT WHO IS WILLING TO GO BEYOND THE BOUNDARIES OF TIME AND SPACE... AS LONG AS HIS FREE WILL IS MAINTAINED...
BUT HE IS A ROVER... A WANDERER! WHO CAN TELL WHERE HE WILL GO NEXT? OR WHERE HE IS NOW?
I THINK HE MAY ALREADY BE HERE... ON GALLIFREY!
AT THAT MOMENT, IN A NEARBY MATERIALISATION ZONE...
VWORP! VWORP!

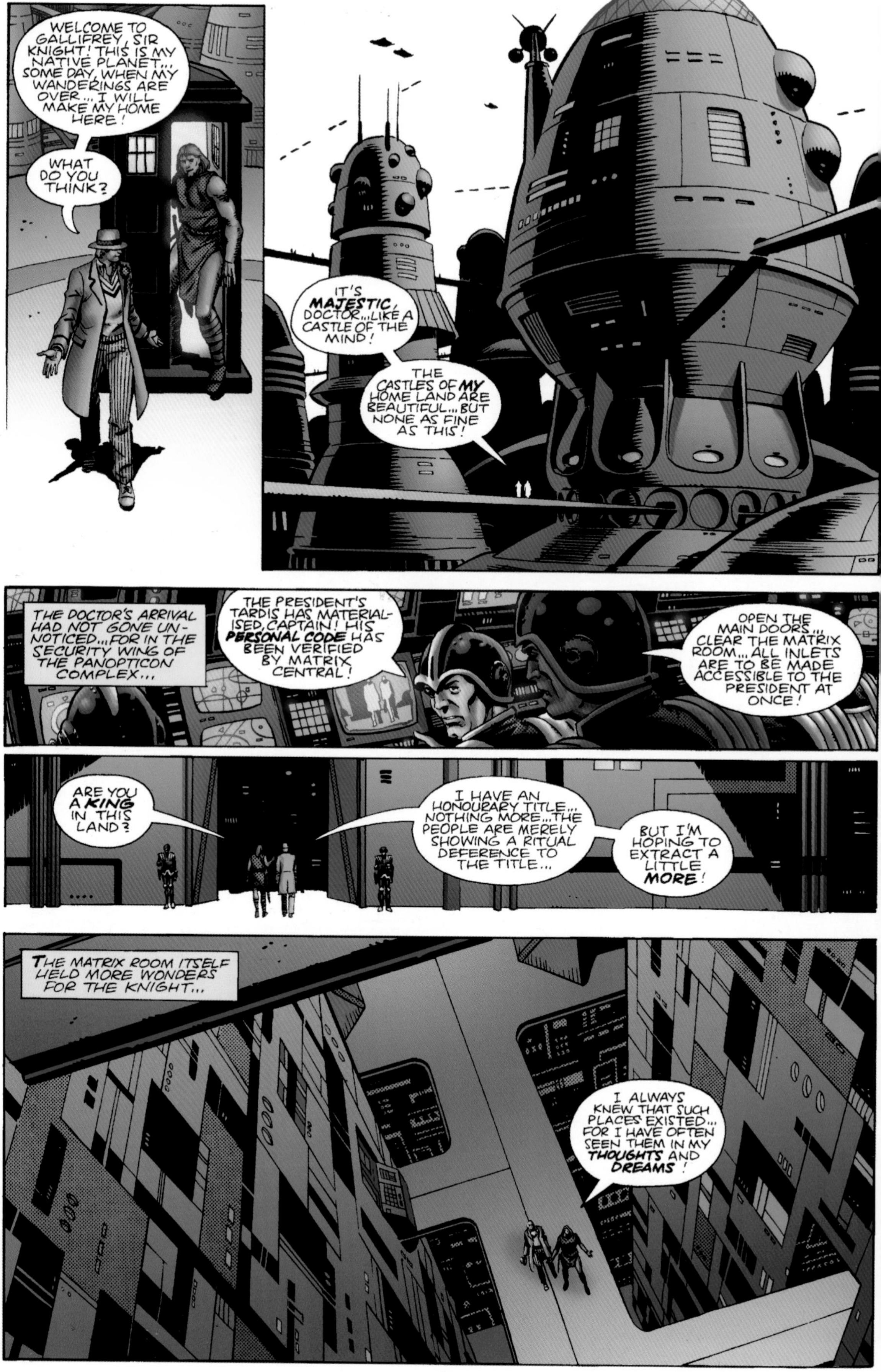
WELCOME TO GALLIFREY, SIR KNIGHT! THIS IS MY NATIVE PLANET... SOME DAY, WHEN MY WANDERINGS ARE OVER... I WILL MAKE MY HOME HERE!
WHAT DO YOU THINK?
IT'S MAJESTIC, DOCTOR... LIKE A CASTLE OF THE MIND!
THE CASTLES OF MY HOME LAND ARE BEAUTIFUL... BUT NONE AS FINE AS THIS!
THE DOCTOR'S ARRIVAL HAD NOT GONE UN-NOTICED... FOR IN THE SECURITY WING OF THE PANOPTICON COMPLEX...
THE PRESIDENT'S TARDIS HAS MATERIAL-ISED, CAPTAIN! HIS PERSONAL CODE HAS BEEN VERIFIED BY MATRIX CENTRAL!
OPEN THE MAIN DOORS... CLEAR THE MATRIX ROOM... ALL INLETS ARE TO BE MADE ACCESSIBLE TO THE PRESIDENT AT ONCE!
ARE YOU A KING IN THIS LAND?
I HAVE AN HONOURARY TITLE... NOTHING MORE... THE PEOPLE ARE MERELY SHOWING A RITUAL DEFERENCE TO THE TITLE...
BUT I'M HOPING TO EXTRACT A LITTLE MORE!
THE MATRIX ROOM ITSELF HELD MORE WONDERS FOR THE KNIGHT...
I ALWAYS KNEW THAT SUCH PLACES EXISTED... FOR I HAVE OFTEN SEEN THEM IN MY THOUGHTS AND DREAMS!

JUSTIN...YOU'RE AN **AMAZING MAN**! THERE ARE MEN FROM HIGHLY ADVANCED CIVILISATIONS', MEN FROM YOUR **OWN FUTURE** WHO WOULD BE PHASED BY THE MATRIX ROOM...

BUT YOU JUST TAKE IT IN YOUR **STRIDE**!

WELL, WHAT IS THE PASSAGE OF TIME? IT IS ALL **ONE GREAT MOMENT**, IS IT NOT?

ONLY THE NARROW PATH OF MEN'S MINDS CREATES CONFUSION...

WHAT A MARVELLOUS TIME-LORD YOU'D MAKE!

BUT FOR NOW, I ASK YOU TO EXCUSE ME... I MUST COMMUNICATE WITH MY MASTERS...

AH... IT IS AN ACT OF COMMUNION? I UNDERSTAND ...I WILL WAIT **ELSEWHERE**!

WITH ALL SECURITY FOCUSSED ON THE DOCTOR ... NOBODY NOTICED THE ARRIVAL OF A **SINGLE FIGURE** BY THE TARDIS ...

NOR **COULD** ANYBODY HAVE NOTICED ... BECAUSE, IN ESSENCE, THE FIGURE **DID NOT EXIST** ... AT LEAST NOT TO THE SECURITY WING'S OPTICAL SYSTEMS ... NOR TO THE MECHANISMS BY WHICH THE MANY FUNCTIONAL TARDISES ANNOUNCED THEIR ARRIVALS AND DEPARTURES ...

...FOR THIS MAN, VERY FEW BARRIERS EXISTED ...HE HAD BOOKED A **PERSONAL PASSAGE** IN TIME...

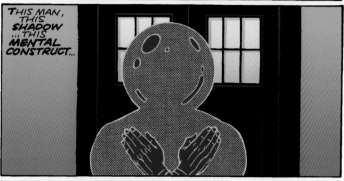

THIS MAN, THIS **SHADOW** ...THIS **MENTAL CONSTRUCT**...

...WAS NOT ONLY **IMMORTAL, TIMELESS** ...AND **VERY, VERY DANGEROUS**...

...HE WAS ALSO **WAITING FOR THE DOCTOR**!

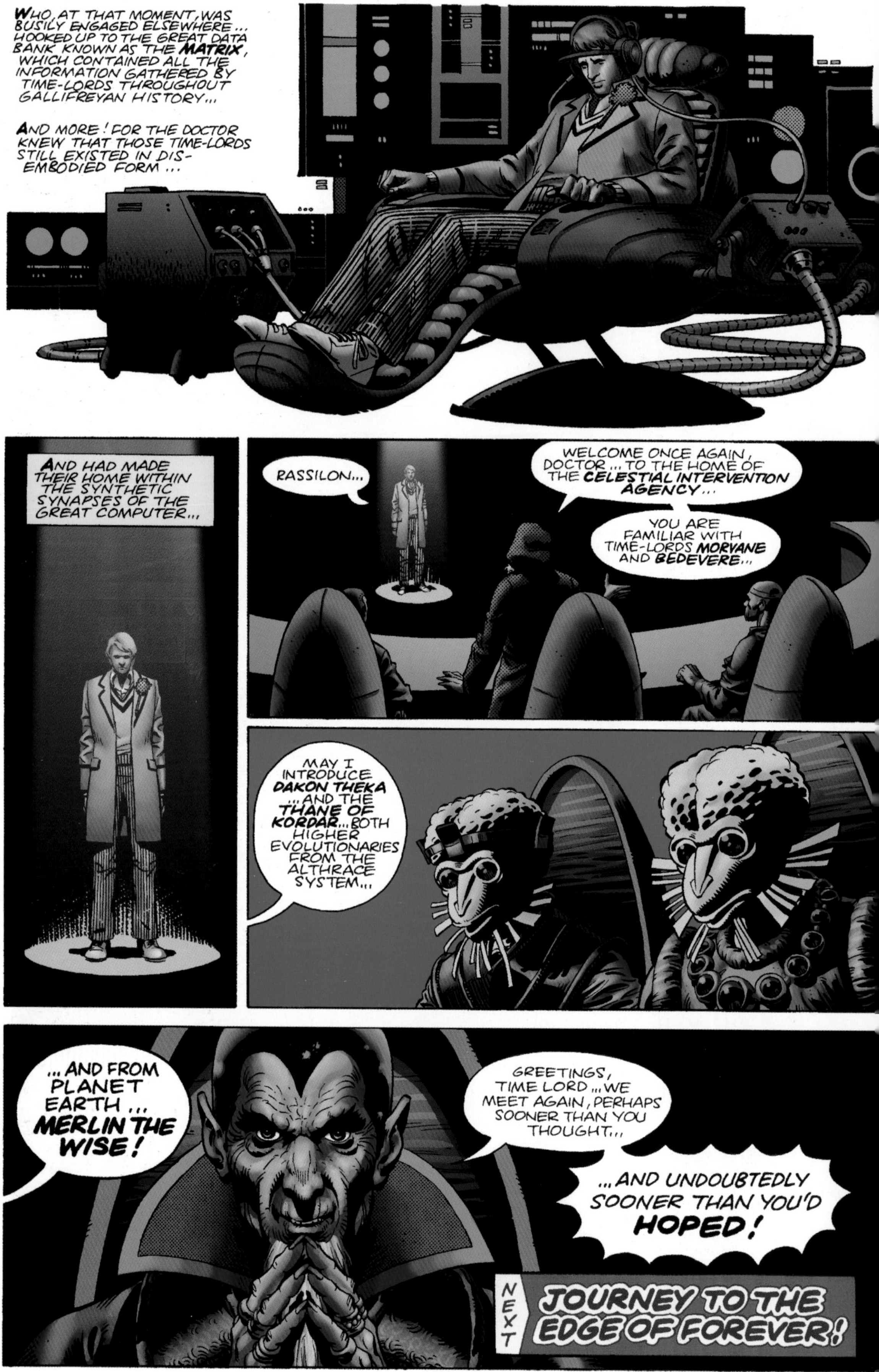
WHO, AT THAT MOMENT, WAS BUSILY ENGAGED ELSEWHERE... HOOKED UP TO THE GREAT DATA BANK KNOWN AS THE MATRIX, WHICH CONTAINED ALL THE INFORMATION GATHERED BY TIME-LORDS THROUGHOUT GALLIFREYAN HISTORY...
AND MORE! FOR THE DOCTOR KNEW THAT THOSE TIME-LORDS STILL EXISTED IN DIS-EMBODIED FORM...
AND HAD MADE THEIR HOME WITHIN THE SYNTHETIC SYNAPSES OF THE GREAT COMPUTER...
RASSILON...
WELCOME ONCE AGAIN, DOCTOR... TO THE HOME OF THE CELESTIAL INTERVENTION AGENCY...
YOU ARE FAMILIAR WITH TIME-LORDS MORVANE AND BEDEVERE...
MAY I INTRODUCE DAKON THEKA ...AND THE THANE OF KORDAR... BOTH HIGHER EVOLUTIONARIES FROM THE ALTHRACE SYSTEM...
...AND FROM PLANET EARTH... MERLIN THE WISE!
GREETINGS, TIME LORD... WE MEET AGAIN, PERHAPS SOONER THAN YOU THOUGHT...
...AND UNDOUBTEDLY SOONER THAN YOU'D HOPED!
NEXT
JOURNEY TO THE EDGE OF FOREVER!

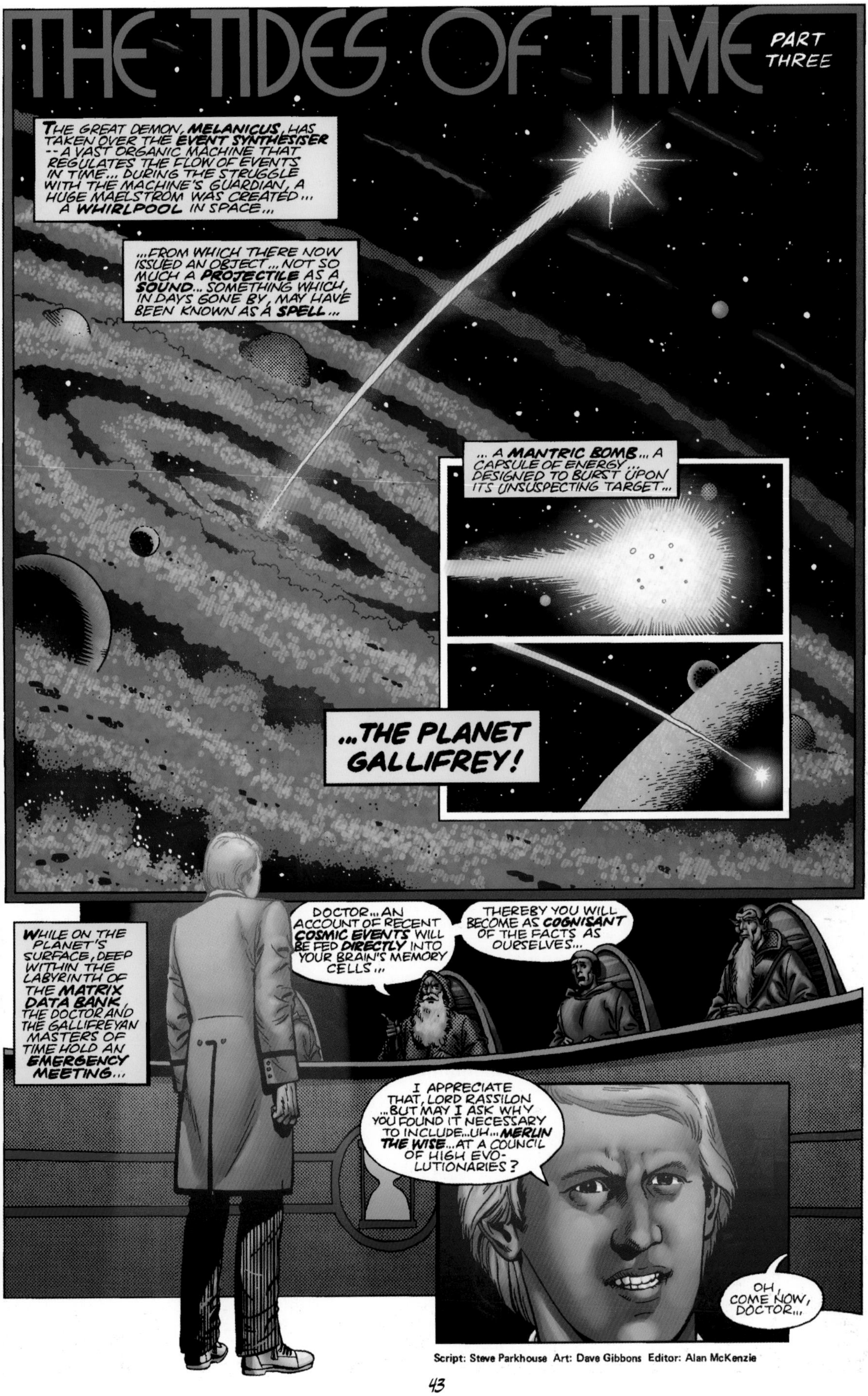
THE TIDES OF TIME
PART THREE
THE GREAT DEMON, MELANICUS, HAS TAKEN OVER THE EVENT SYNTHESISER -- A VAST ORGANIC MACHINE THAT REGULATES THE FLOW OF EVENTS IN TIME... DURING THE STRUGGLE WITH THE MACHINE'S GUARDIAN, A HUGE MAELSTROM WAS CREATED... A WHIRLPOOL IN SPACE...
...FROM WHICH THERE NOW ISSUED AN OBJECT... NOT SO MUCH A PROJECTILE AS A SOUND... SOMETHING WHICH, IN DAYS GONE BY, MAY HAVE BEEN KNOWN AS A SPELL...
... A MANTRIC BOMB... A CAPSULE OF ENERGY... DESIGNED TO BURST UPON ITS UNSUSPECTING TARGET...
...THE PLANET GALLIFREY!
WHILE ON THE PLANET'S SURFACE, DEEP WITHIN THE LABYRINTH OF THE MATRIX DATA BANK, THE DOCTOR AND THE GALLIFREYAN MASTERS OF TIME HOLD AN EMERGENCY MEETING...
DOCTOR... AN ACCOUNT OF RECENT COSMIC EVENTS WILL BE FED DIRECTLY INTO YOUR BRAIN'S MEMORY CELLS...
THEREBY YOU WILL BECOME AS COGNISANT OF THE FACTS AS OURSELVES...
I APPRECIATE THAT, LORD RASSILON ...BUT MAY I ASK WHY YOU FOUND IT NECESSARY TO INCLUDE...UH... MERLIN THE WISE...AT A COUNCIL OF HIGH EVO-LUTIONARIES?
OH, COME NOW, DOCTOR...

Script: Steve Parkhouse Art: Dave Gibbons Editor: Alan McKenzie

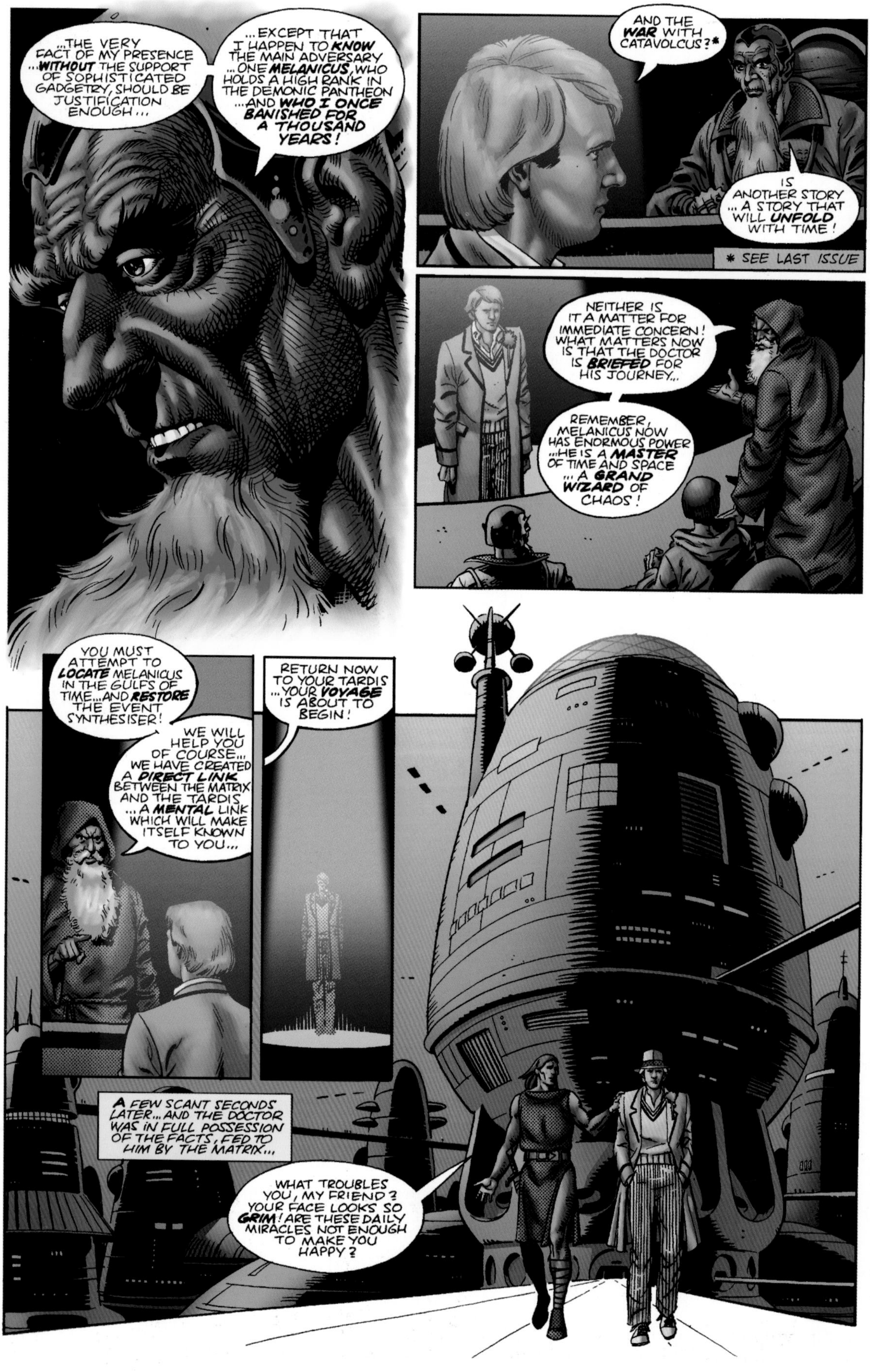
...THE VERY FACT OF MY PRESENCE ...WITHOUT THE SUPPORT OF SOPHISTICATED GADGETRY, SHOULD BE JUSTIFICATION ENOUGH...
...EXCEPT THAT I HAPPEN TO KNOW THE MAIN ADVERSARY ...ONE MELANICUS, WHO HOLDS A HIGH RANK IN THE DEMONIC PANTHEON ...AND WHO I ONCE BANISHED FOR A THOUSAND YEARS!
AND THE WAR WITH CATAVOLCUS?*
IS ANOTHER STORY ...A STORY THAT WILL UNFOLD WITH TIME!
* SEE LAST ISSUE
NEITHER IS IT A MATTER FOR IMMEDIATE CONCERN! WHAT MATTERS NOW IS THAT THE DOCTOR IS BRIEFED FOR HIS JOURNEY...
REMEMBER, MELANICUS NOW HAS ENORMOUS POWER ...HE IS A MASTER OF TIME AND SPACE ...A GRAND WIZARD OF CHAOS!
YOU MUST ATTEMPT TO LOCATE MELANICUS IN THE GULFS OF TIME...AND RESTORE THE EVENT SYNTHESISER!
WE WILL HELP YOU OF COURSE... WE HAVE CREATED A DIRECT LINK BETWEEN THE MATRIX AND THE TARDIS ...A MENTAL LINK WHICH WILL MAKE ITSELF KNOWN TO YOU...
RETURN NOW TO YOUR TARDIS ...YOUR VOYAGE IS ABOUT TO BEGIN!
A FEW SCANT SECONDS LATER... AND THE DOCTOR WAS IN FULL POSSESSION OF THE FACTS, FED TO HIM BY THE MATRIX...
WHAT TROUBLES YOU, MY FRIEND? YOUR FACE LOOKS SO GRIM! ARE THESE DAILY MIRACLES NOT ENOUGH TO MAKE YOU HAPPY?

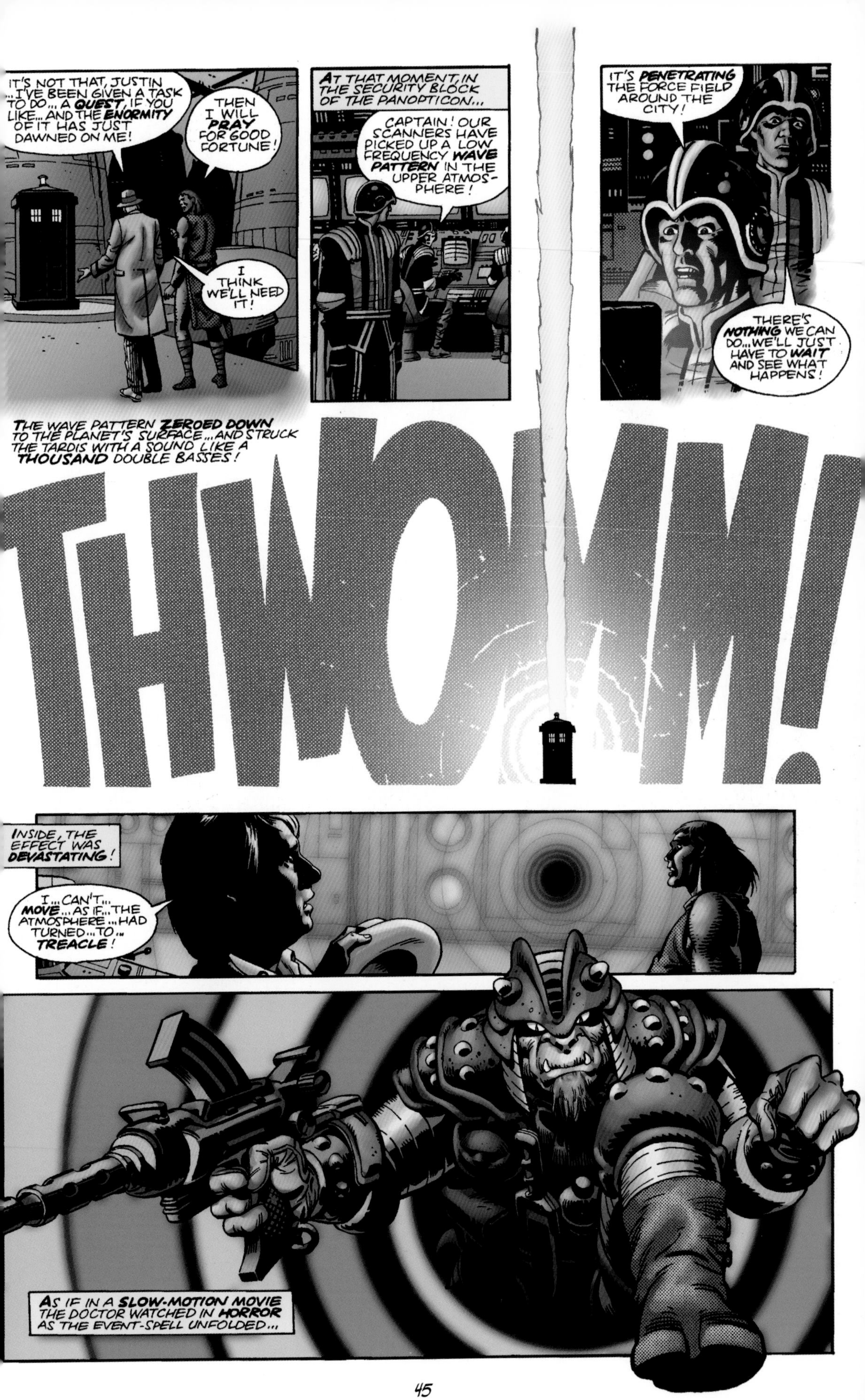
IT'S NOT THAT, JUSTIN ...I'VE BEEN GIVEN A TASK TO DO... A QUEST, IF YOU LIKE... AND THE ENORMITY OF IT HAS JUST DAWNED ON ME!
THEN I WILL PRAY FOR GOOD FORTUNE!
I THINK WE'LL NEED IT!
AT THAT MOMENT, IN THE SECURITY BLOCK OF THE PANOPTICON...
CAPTAIN! OUR SCANNERS HAVE PICKED UP A LOW FREQUENCY WAVE PATTERN IN THE UPPER ATMOS-PHERE!
IT'S PENETRATING THE FORCE FIELD AROUND THE CITY!
THERE'S NOTHING WE CAN DO... WE'LL JUST HAVE TO WAIT AND SEE WHAT HAPPENS!
THE WAVE PATTERN ZEROED DOWN TO THE PLANET'S SURFACE... AND STRUCK THE TARDIS WITH A SOUND LIKE A THOUSAND DOUBLE BASSES!
THWOMM!
INSIDE, THE EFFECT WAS DEVASTATING!
I... CAN'T... MOVE... AS IF... THE ATMOSPHERE... HAD TURNED... TO... TREACLE!
AS IF IN A SLOW-MOTION MOVIE THE DOCTOR WATCHED IN HORROR AS THE EVENT-SPELL UNFOLDED...

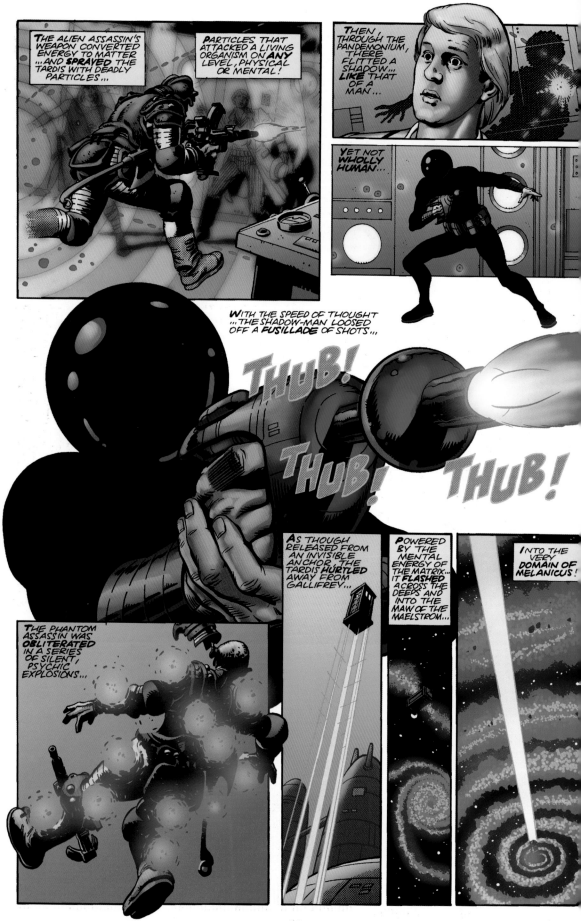

THE ALIEN ASSASSIN'S WEAPON CONVERTED ENERGY TO MATTER ...AND **SPRAYED** THE TARDIS WITH DEADLY PARTICLES...

PARTICLES THAT ATTACKED A LIVING ORGANISM ON **ANY** LEVEL, PHYSICAL OR MENTAL!

THEN, THROUGH THE PANDEMONIUM, THERE FLITTED A SHADOW... **LIKE** THAT OF A MAN...

YET NOT WHOLLY HUMAN...

WITH THE SPEED OF THOUGHT ...THE SHADOW-MAN LOOSED OFF A **FUSILLADE** OF SHOTS...

THUB!

THUB!

THUB!

AS THOUGH RELEASED FROM AN INVISIBLE ANCHOR, THE TARDIS **HURTLED** AWAY FROM GALLIFREY...

POWERED BY THE MENTAL ENERGY OF THE MATRIX... IT **FLASHED** ACROSS THE DEEPS AND INTO THE MAW OF THE MAELSTROM...

INTO THE VERY DOMAIN OF MELANICUS!

THE PHANTOM ASSASSIN WAS **OBLITERATED** IN A SERIES OF SILENT, PSYCHIC EXPLOSIONS...

46

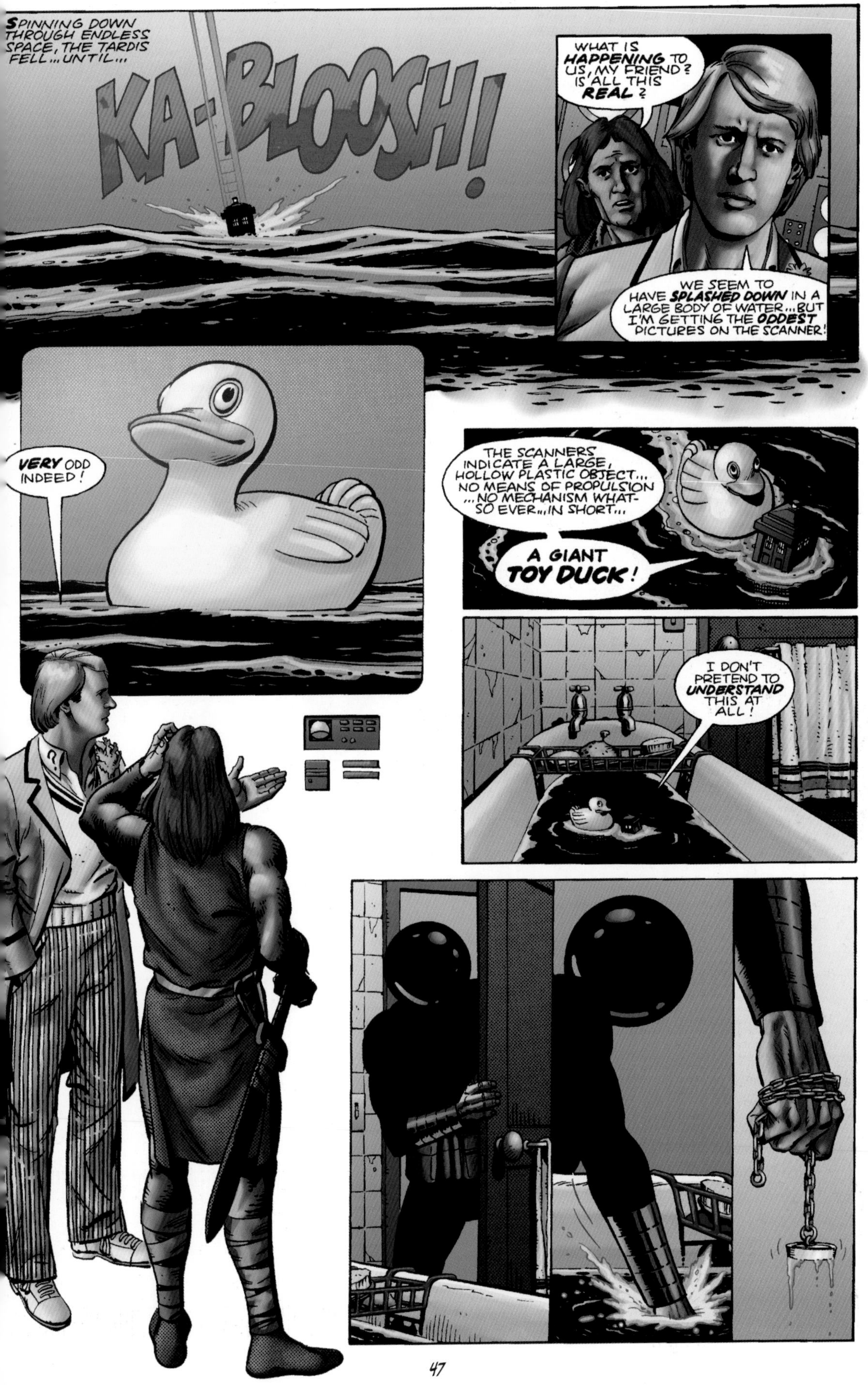

SPINNING DOWN THROUGH ENDLESS SPACE, THE TARDIS FELL... UNTIL...
KA-BLOOSH!
WHAT IS HAPPENING TO US, MY FRIEND? IS ALL THIS REAL?
WE SEEM TO HAVE SPLASHED DOWN IN A LARGE BODY OF WATER... BUT I'M GETTING THE ODDEST PICTURES ON THE SCANNER!
VERY ODD INDEED!
THE SCANNERS INDICATE A LARGE, HOLLOW PLASTIC OBJECT... NO MEANS OF PROPULSION ... NO MECHANISM WHAT-SO EVER... IN SHORT...
A GIANT TOY DUCK!
I DON'T PRETEND TO UNDERSTAND THIS AT ALL!

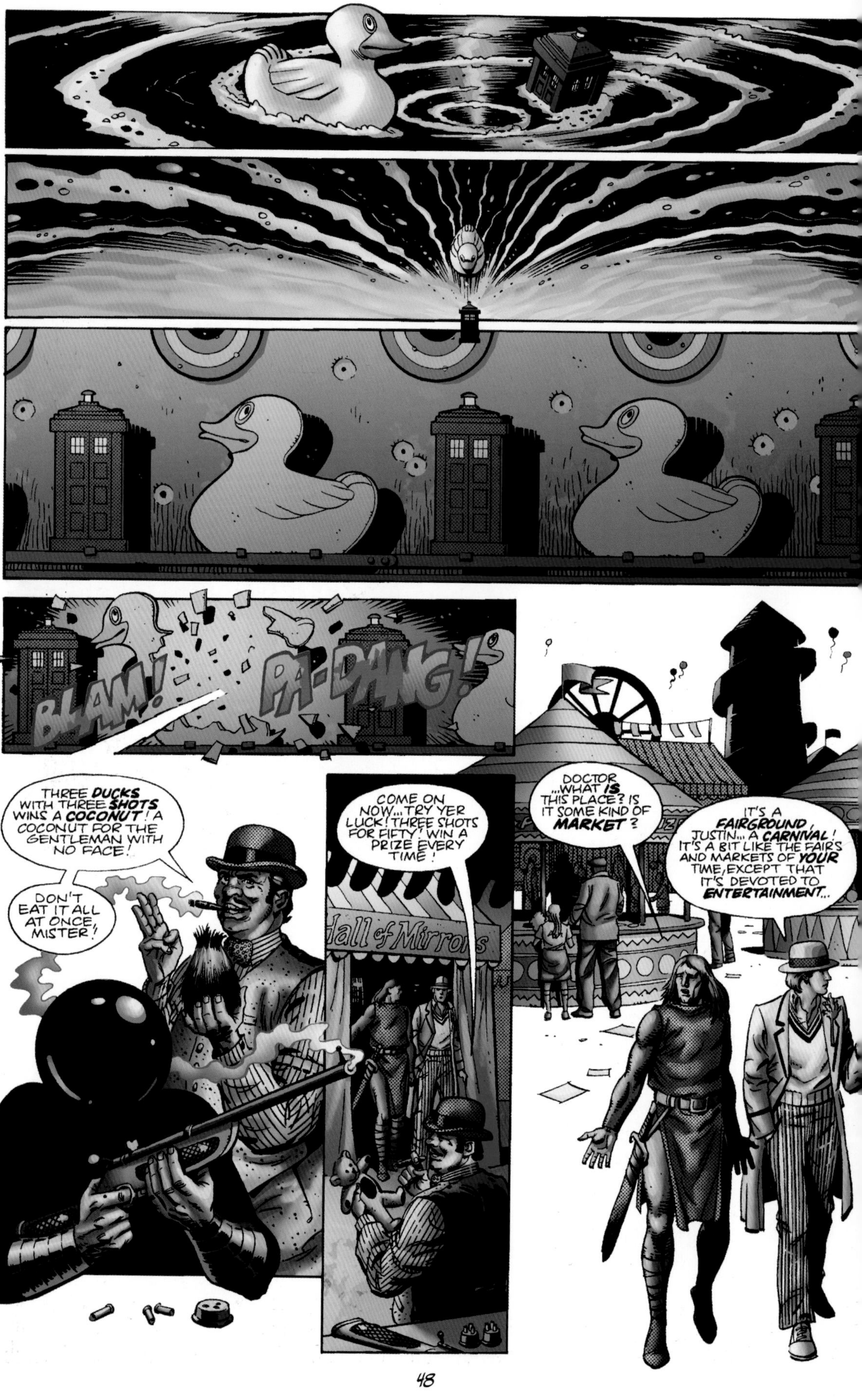
BLAM!
PA-DANG!
THREE DUCKS WITH THREE SHOTS WINS A COCONUT! A COCONUT FOR THE GENTLEMAN WITH NO FACE!
DON'T EAT IT ALL AT ONCE, MISTER!
COME ON NOW... TRY YER LUCK! THREE SHOTS FOR FIFTY! WIN A PRIZE EVERY TIME!
Hall of Mirrors
DOCTOR ...WHAT IS THIS PLACE? IS IT SOME KIND OF MARKET?
IT'S A FAIRGROUND, JUSTIN... A CARNIVAL! IT'S A BIT LIKE THE FAIRS AND MARKETS OF YOUR TIME, EXCEPT THAT IT'S DEVOTED TO ENTERTAINMENT...

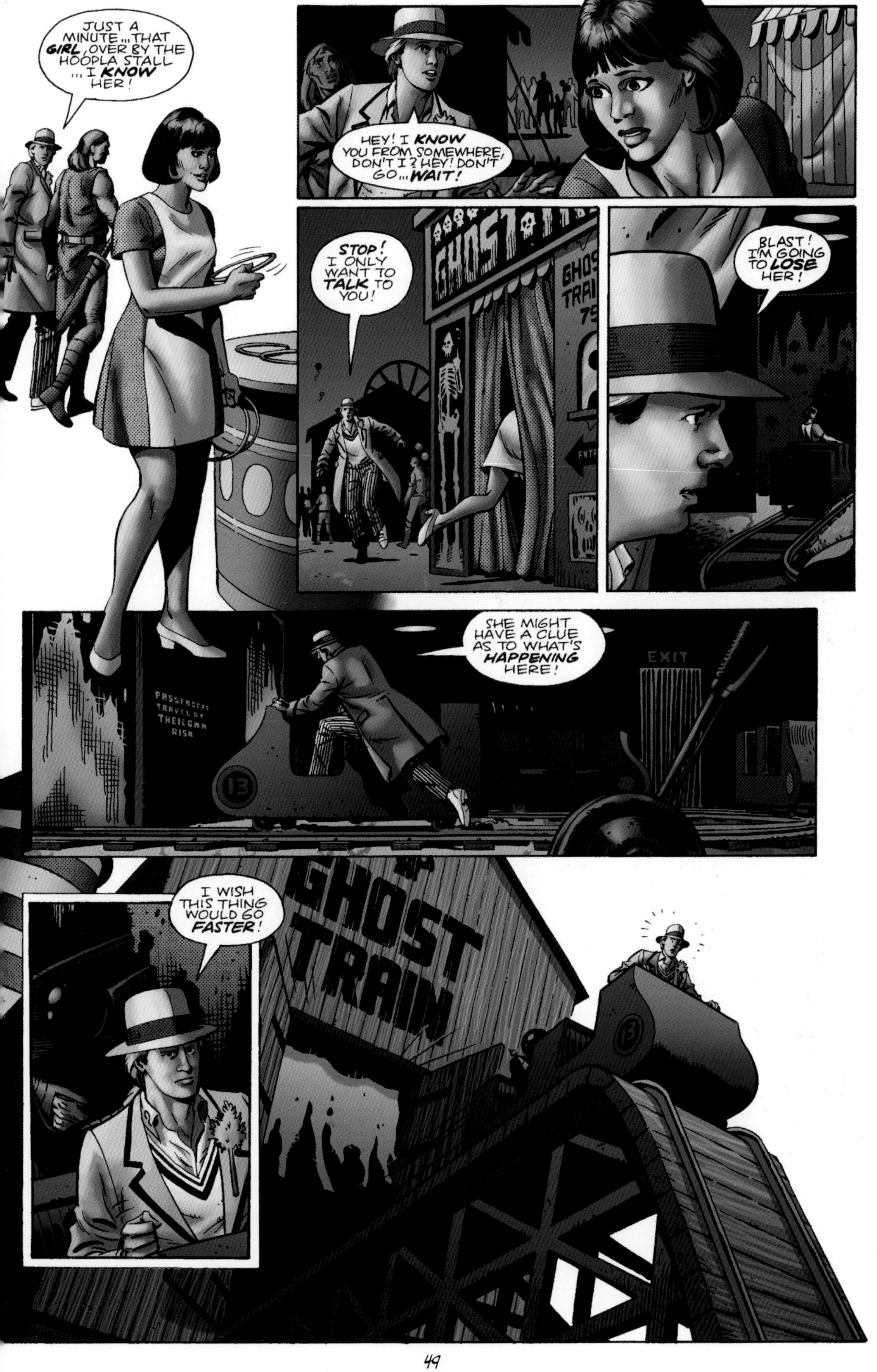

JUST A MINUTE... THAT GIRL, OVER BY THE HOOPLA STALL ... I KNOW HER!
HEY! I KNOW YOU FROM SOMEWHERE, DON'T I? HEY! DON'T GO... WAIT!
STOP! I ONLY WANT TO TALK TO YOU!
BLAST! I'M GOING TO LOSE HER!
SHE MIGHT HAVE A CLUE AS TO WHAT'S HAPPENING HERE!
PASSENGERS TRAVEL AT THEIR OWN RISK
EXIT
I WISH THIS THING WOULD GO FASTER!
GHOST TRAIN

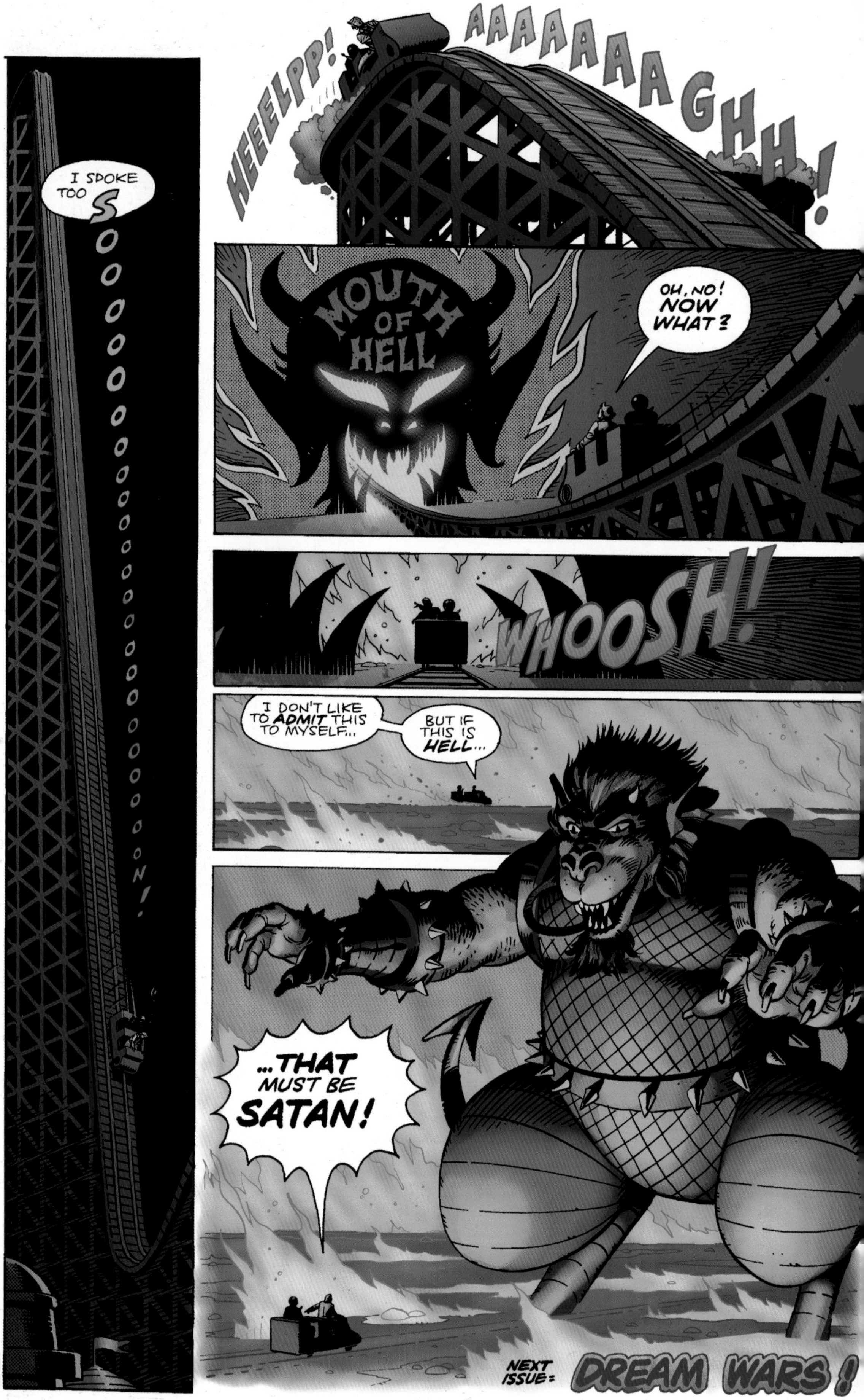
I SPOKE TOO SOOOOOOOOOOOOOOOOOOOOOOOOON!
HEEELPP! AAAAAAAAAGHH!
MOUTH OF HELL
OH, NO! NOW WHAT?
WHOOSH!
I DON'T LIKE TO ADMIT THIS TO MYSELF...
BUT IF THIS IS HELL...
...THAT MUST BE SATAN!
NEXT ISSUE: DREAM WARS!

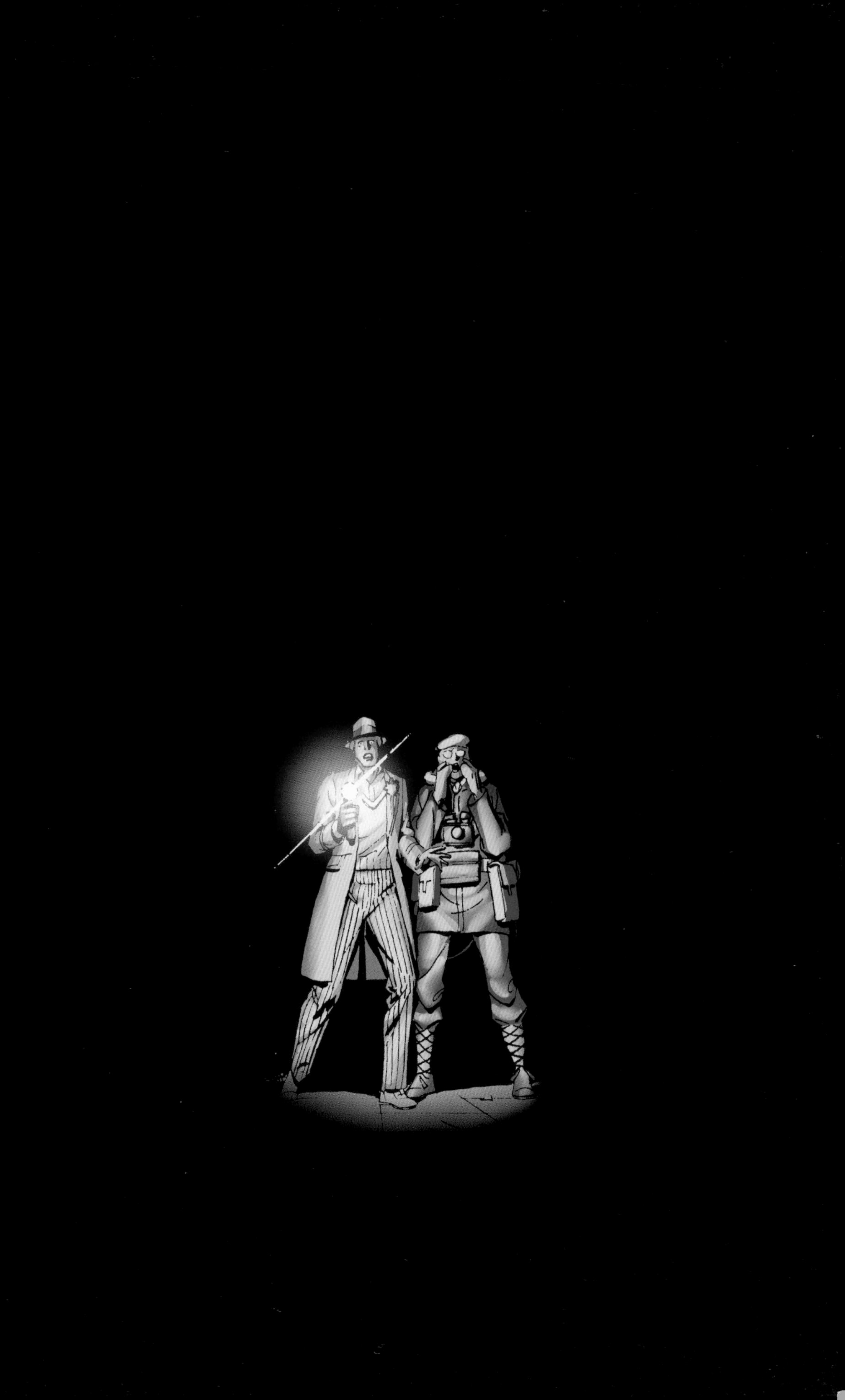

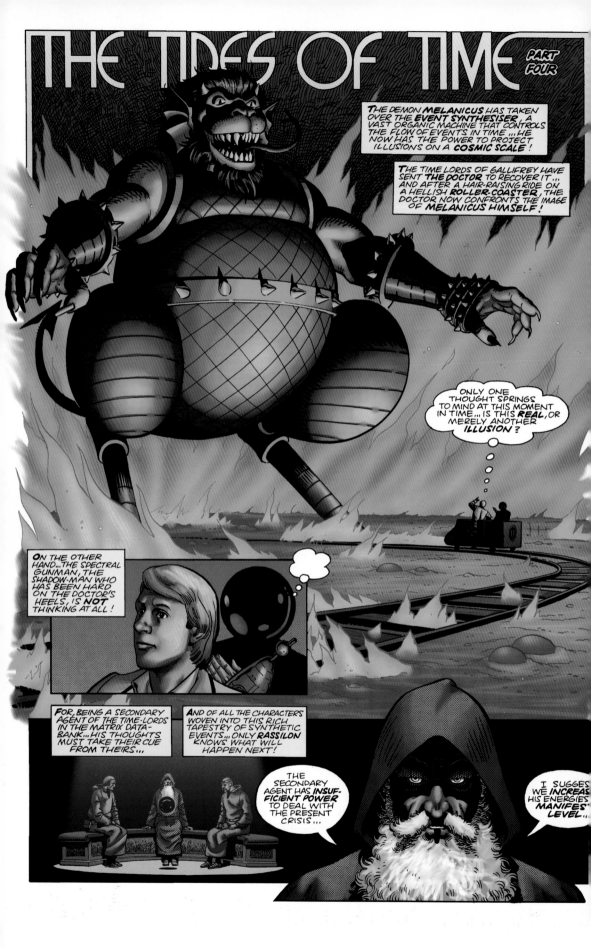

THE TIDES OF TIME PART FOUR

THE DEMON **MELANICUS** HAS TAKEN OVER THE **EVENT SYNTHESISER**, A VAST ORGANIC MACHINE THAT CONTROLS THE FLOW OF EVENTS IN TIME ... HE NOW HAS THE POWER TO PROJECT ILLUSIONS ON A **COSMIC SCALE**!

THE TIME LORDS OF GALLIFREY HAVE SENT **THE DOCTOR** TO RECOVER IT ... AND AFTER A HAIR-RAISING RIDE ON A HELLISH **ROLLER-COASTER**, THE DOCTOR NOW CONFRONTS THE IMAGE OF **MELANICUS HIMSELF**!

ONLY ONE THOUGHT SPRINGS TO MIND AT THIS MOMENT IN TIME ... IS THIS **REAL**, OR MERELY ANOTHER **ILLUSION**?

ON THE OTHER HAND ... THE SPECTRAL GUNMAN, THE SHADOW-MAN WHO HAS BEEN HARD ON THE DOCTOR'S HEELS, IS **NOT** THINKING AT ALL!

FOR, BEING A SECONDARY AGENT OF THE TIME-LORDS IN THE MATRIX DATA-BANK ... HIS THOUGHTS MUST TAKE THEIR CUE FROM THEIRS ...

AND OF ALL THE CHARACTERS WOVEN INTO THIS RICH TAPESTRY OF SYNTHETIC EVENTS ... ONLY **RASSILON** KNOWS WHAT WILL HAPPEN NEXT!

THE SECONDARY AGENT HAS **INSUF-FICIENT POWER** TO DEAL WITH THE PRESENT CRISIS ...

I SUGGES[T] WE INCREAS[E] HIS ENERGIES' MANIFES[T] LEVEL ...

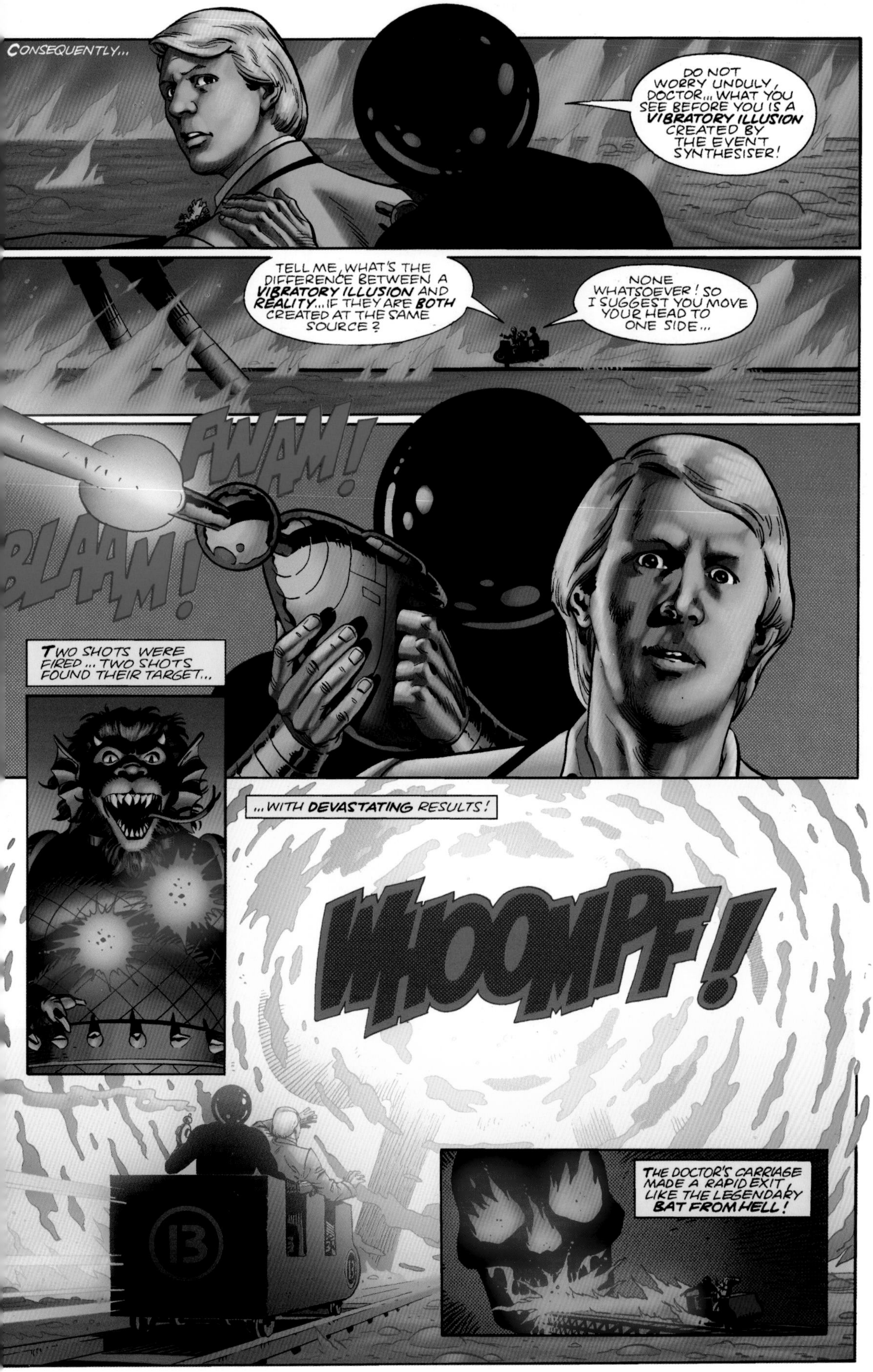
CONSEQUENTLY...
DO NOT WORRY UNDULY, DOCTOR... WHAT YOU SEE BEFORE YOU IS A VIBRATORY ILLUSION CREATED BY THE EVENT SYNTHESISER!
TELL ME, WHAT'S THE DIFFERENCE BETWEEN A VIBRATORY ILLUSION AND REALITY... IF THEY ARE BOTH CREATED AT THE SAME SOURCE?
NONE WHATSOEVER! SO I SUGGEST YOU MOVE YOUR HEAD TO ONE SIDE...
FWAM!
BLAAM!
TWO SHOTS WERE FIRED... TWO SHOTS FOUND THEIR TARGET...
...WITH DEVASTATING RESULTS!
WHOOMPF!
13
THE DOCTOR'S CARRIAGE MADE A RAPID EXIT, LIKE THE LEGENDARY BAT FROM HELL!

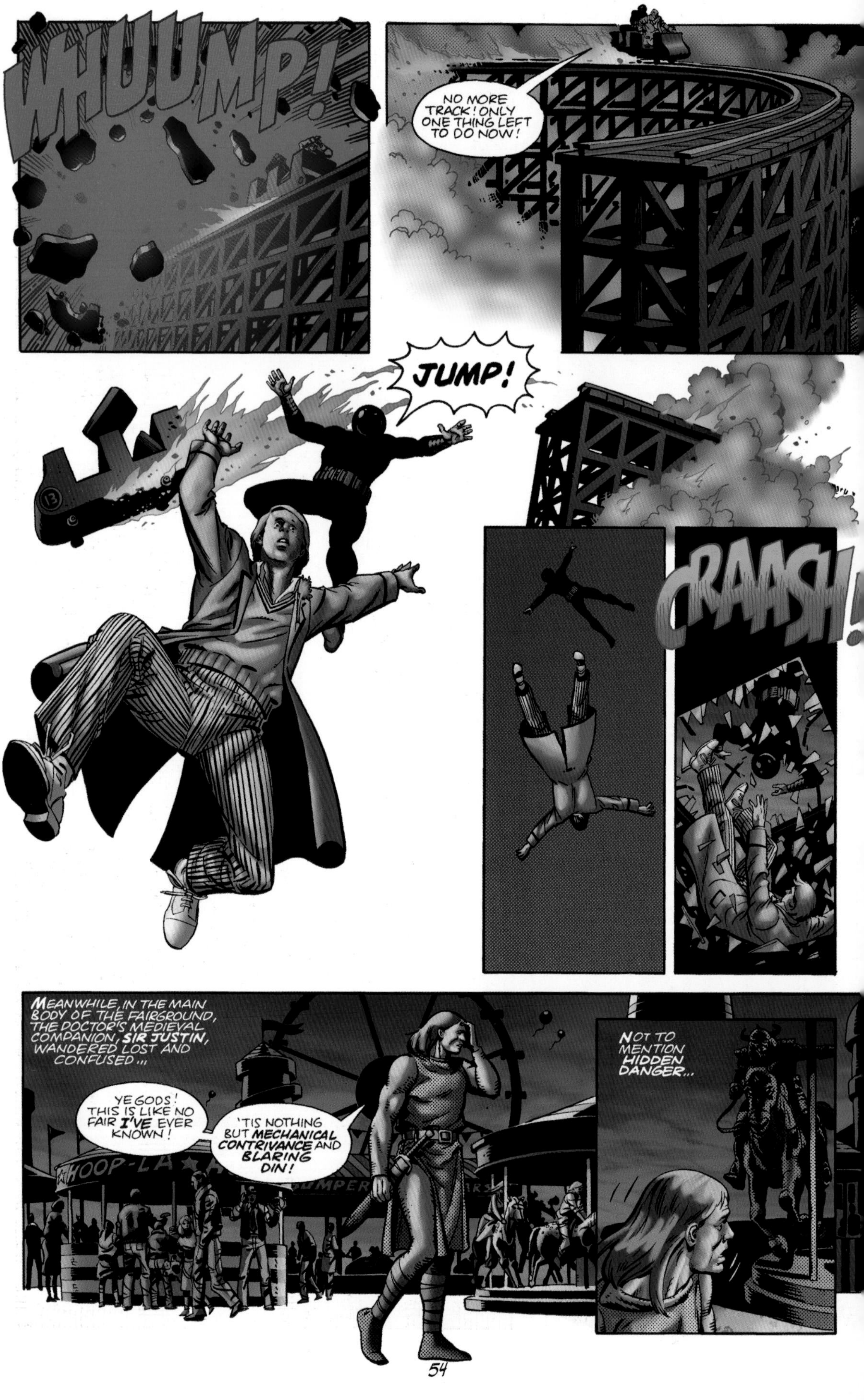
WHUUMP!
NO MORE TRACK! ONLY ONE THING LEFT TO DO NOW!
JUMP!
CRAASH!
MEANWHILE, IN THE MAIN BODY OF THE FAIRGROUND, THE DOCTOR'S MEDIEVAL COMPANION, SIR JUSTIN, WANDERED LOST AND CONFUSED...
YE GODS! THIS IS LIKE NO FAIR I'VE EVER KNOWN!
'TIS NOTHING BUT MECHANICAL CONTRIVANCE AND BLARING DIN!
NOT TO MENTION HIDDEN DANGER...

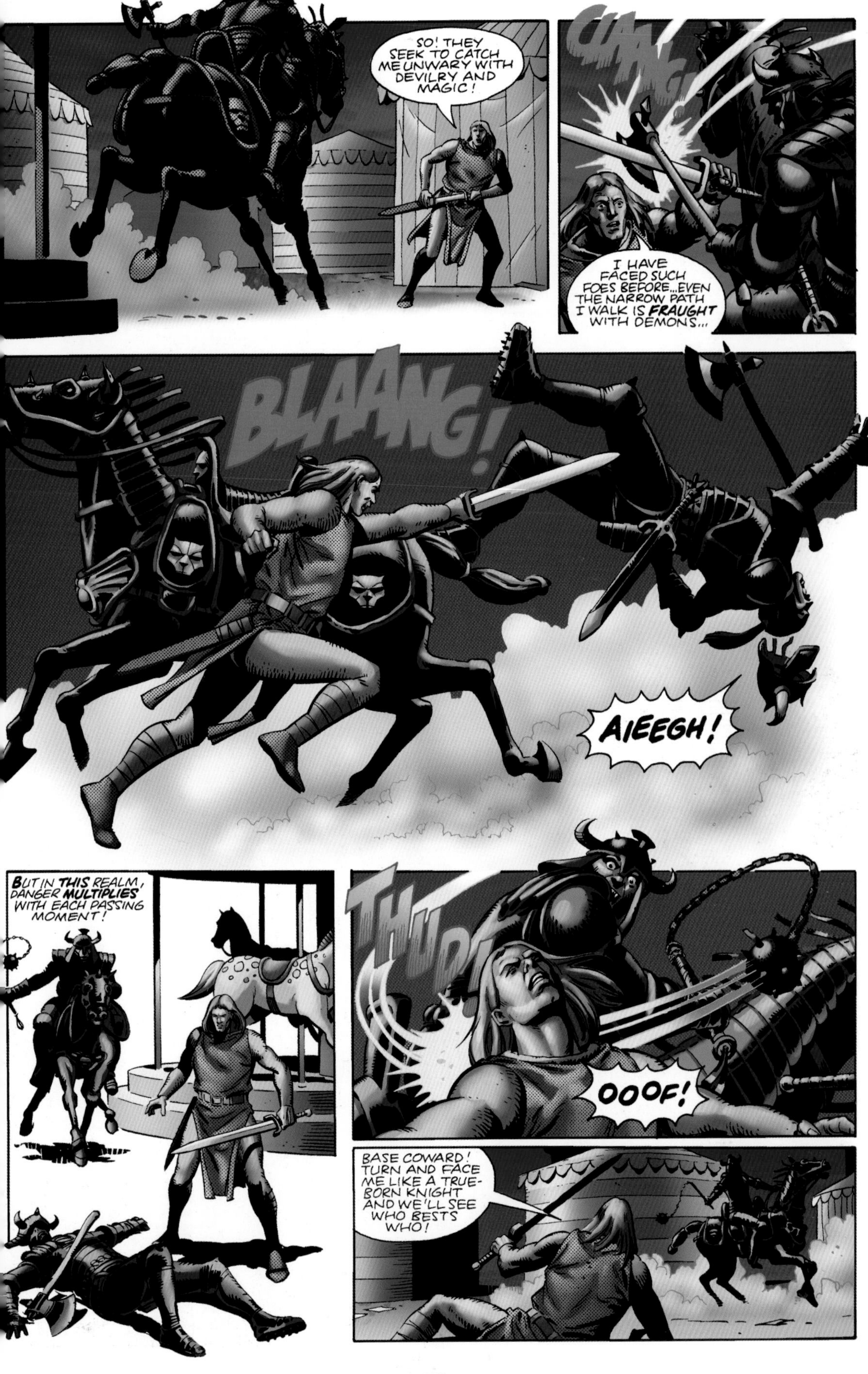
SO! THEY SEEK TO CATCH ME UNWARY WITH DEVILRY AND MAGIC!
CLAAANG!
I HAVE FACED SUCH FOES BEFORE...EVEN THE NARROW PATH I WALK IS FRAUGHT WITH DEMONS...
BLAANG!
AIEEGH!
BUT IN THIS REALM, DANGER MULTIPLIES WITH EACH PASSING MOMENT!
THUD!
OOOF!
BASE COWARD! TURN AND FACE ME LIKE A TRUE-BORN KNIGHT AND WE'LL SEE WHO BESTS WHO!

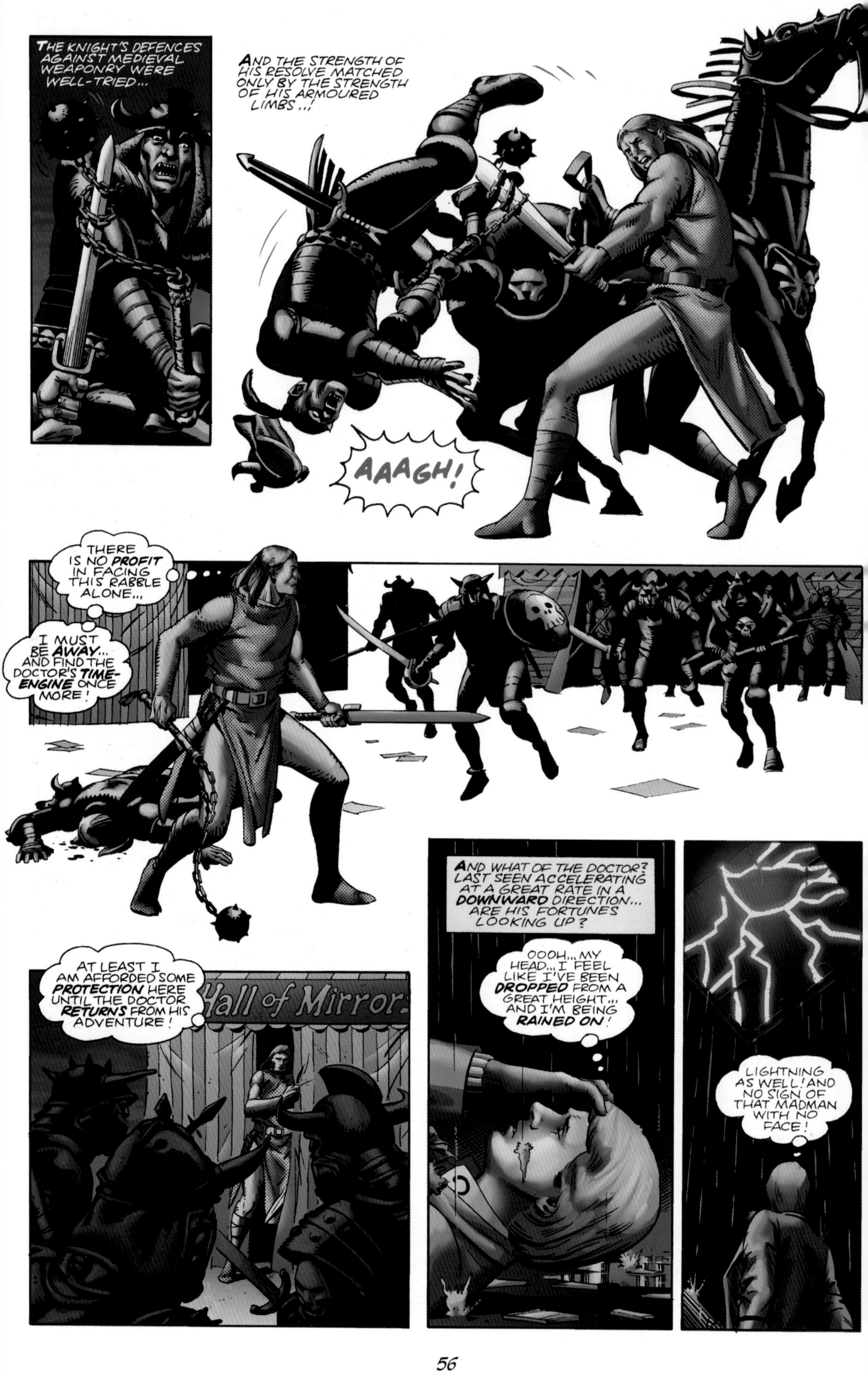
THE KNIGHT'S DEFENCES AGAINST MEDIEVAL WEAPONRY WERE WELL-TRIED...
AND THE STRENGTH OF HIS RESOLVE MATCHED ONLY BY THE STRENGTH OF HIS ARMOURED LIMBS...!
AAAGH!
THERE IS NO PROFIT IN FACING THIS RABBLE ALONE...
I MUST BE AWAY... AND FIND THE DOCTOR'S TIME-ENGINE ONCE MORE!
AT LEAST I AM AFFORDED SOME PROTECTION HERE UNTIL THE DOCTOR RETURNS FROM HIS ADVENTURE!
Hall of Mirrors
AND WHAT OF THE DOCTOR? LAST SEEN ACCELERATING AT A GREAT RATE IN A DOWNWARD DIRECTION... ARE HIS FORTUNES LOOKING UP?
OOOH... MY HEAD... I FEEL LIKE I'VE BEEN DROPPED FROM A GREAT HEIGHT... AND I'M BEING RAINED ON!
LIGHTNING AS WELL! AND NO SIGN OF THAT MADMAN WITH NO FACE!

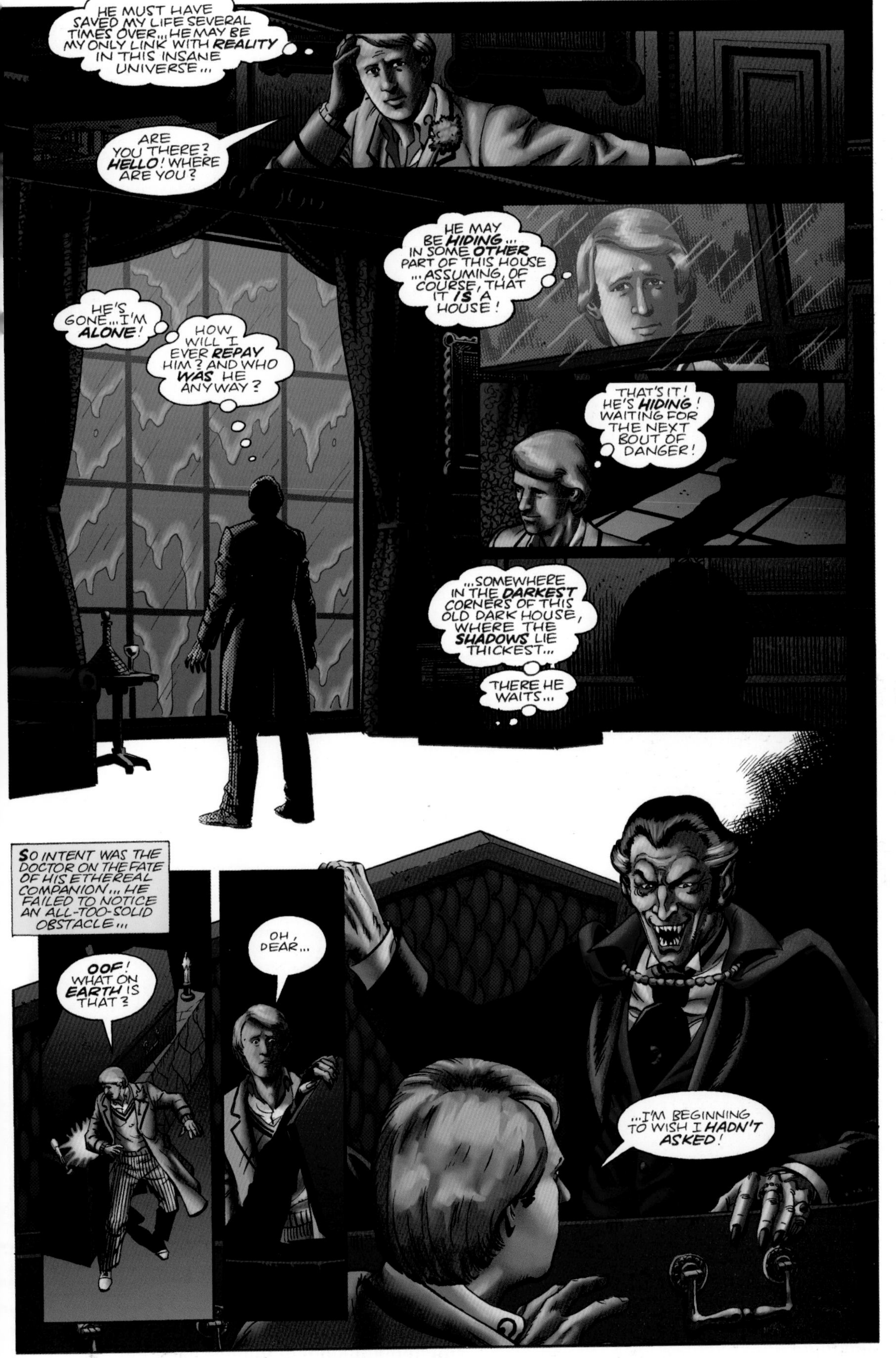
HE MUST HAVE SAVED MY LIFE SEVERAL TIMES OVER... HE MAY BE MY ONLY LINK WITH REALITY IN THIS INSANE UNIVERSE...
ARE YOU THERE? HELLO! WHERE ARE YOU?
HE'S GONE... I'M ALONE!
HOW WILL I EVER REPAY HIM? AND WHO WAS HE ANYWAY?
HE MAY BE HIDING... IN SOME OTHER PART OF THIS HOUSE ...ASSUMING, OF COURSE, THAT IT IS A HOUSE!
THAT'S IT! HE'S HIDING! WAITING FOR THE NEXT BOUT OF DANGER!
...SOMEWHERE IN THE DARKEST CORNERS OF THIS OLD DARK HOUSE, WHERE THE SHADOWS LIE THICKEST...
THERE HE WAITS...
SO INTENT WAS THE DOCTOR ON THE FATE OF HIS ETHEREAL COMPANION... HE FAILED TO NOTICE AN ALL-TOO-SOLID OBSTACLE...
OOF! WHAT ON EARTH IS THAT?
OH, DEAR...
...I'M BEGINNING TO WISH I HADN'T ASKED!

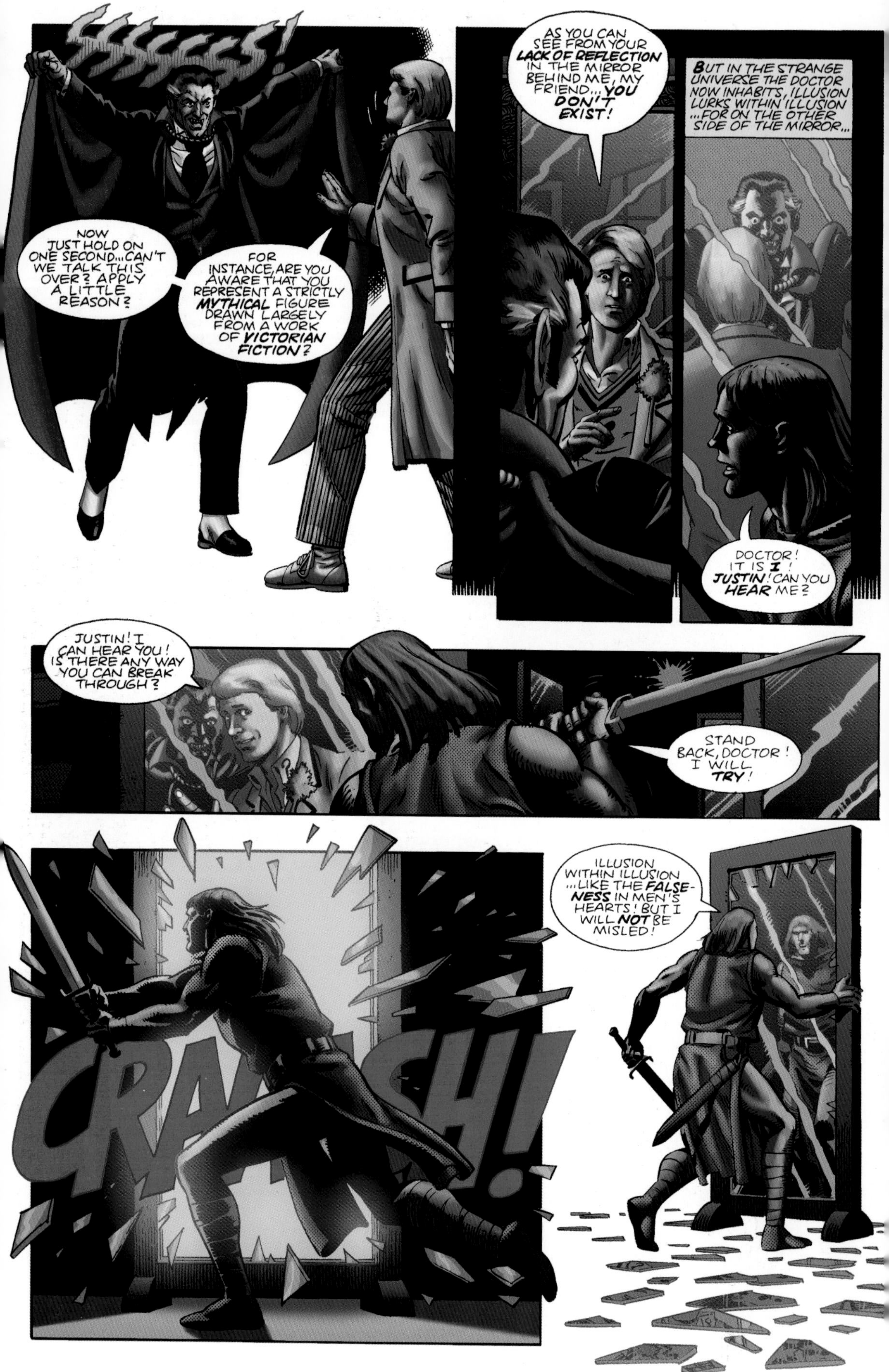
SSSSSS!
NOW JUST HOLD ON ONE SECOND...CAN'T WE TALK THIS OVER? APPLY A LITTLE REASON?
FOR INSTANCE, ARE YOU AWARE THAT YOU REPRESENT A STRICTLY MYTHICAL FIGURE DRAWN LARGELY FROM A WORK OF VICTORIAN FICTION?
AS YOU CAN SEE FROM YOUR LACK OF REFLECTION IN THE MIRROR BEHIND ME, MY FRIEND... YOU DON'T EXIST!
BUT IN THE STRANGE UNIVERSE THE DOCTOR NOW INHABITS, ILLUSION LURKS WITHIN ILLUSION ...FOR ON THE OTHER SIDE OF THE MIRROR...
DOCTOR! IT IS I! JUSTIN! CAN YOU HEAR ME?
JUSTIN! I CAN HEAR YOU! IS THERE ANY WAY YOU CAN BREAK THROUGH?
STAND BACK, DOCTOR! I WILL TRY!
CRAAASH!
ILLUSION WITHIN ILLUSION ...LIKE THE FALSENESS IN MEN'S HEARTS! BUT I WILL NOT BE MISLED!

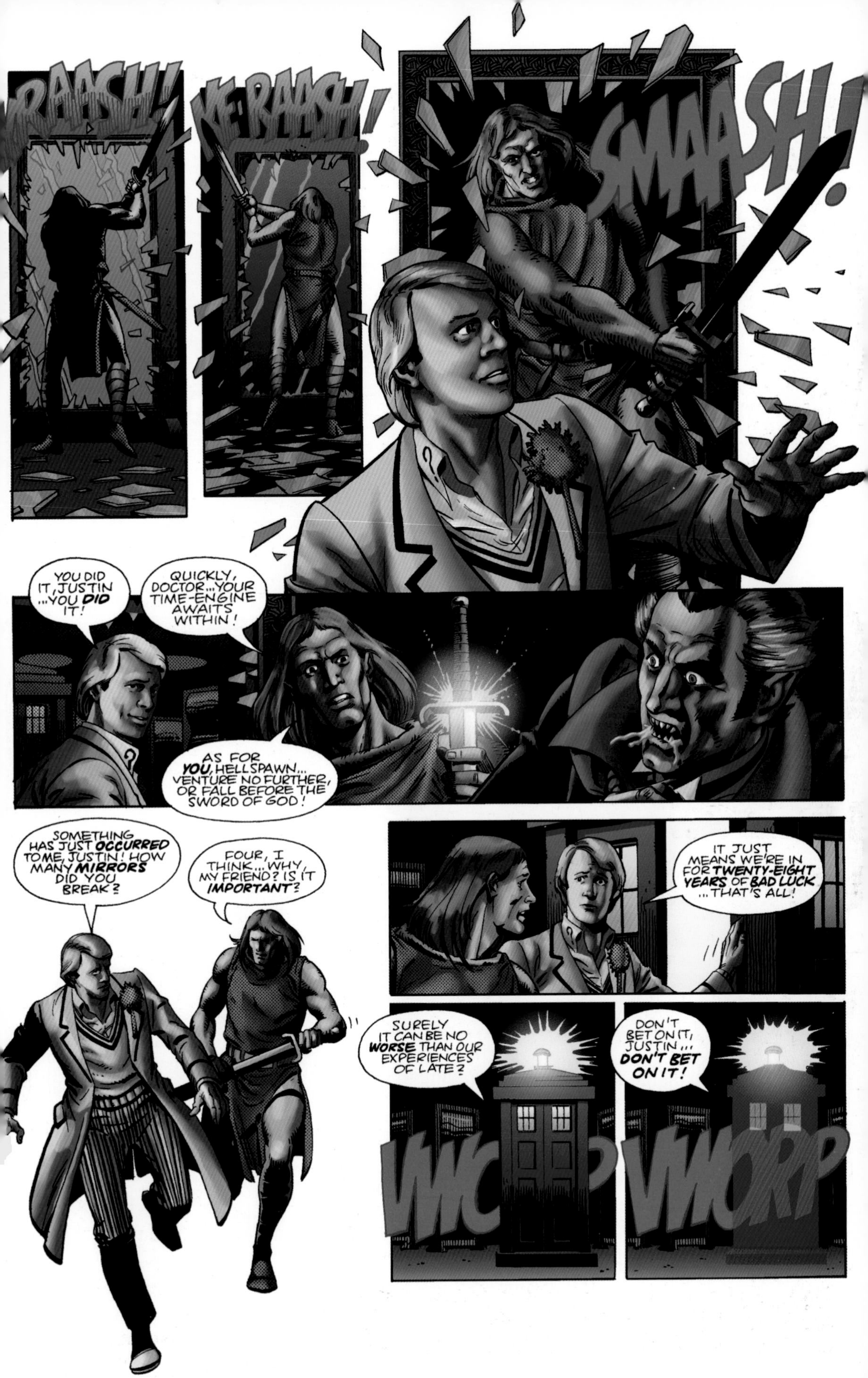
KRAASH!
KE-RAASH!
SMAASH!
YOU DID IT, JUSTIN ...YOU DID IT!
QUICKLY, DOCTOR... YOUR TIME-ENGINE AWAITS WITHIN!
AS FOR YOU, HELLSPAWN... VENTURE NO FURTHER, OR FALL BEFORE THE SWORD OF GOD!
SOMETHING HAS JUST OCCURRED TO ME, JUSTIN! HOW MANY MIRRORS DID YOU BREAK?
FOUR, I THINK... WHY, MY FRIEND? IS IT IMPORTANT?
IT JUST MEANS WE'RE IN FOR TWENTY-EIGHT YEARS OF BAD LUCK ...THAT'S ALL!
SURELY IT CAN BE NO WORSE THAN OUR EXPERIENCES OF LATE?
DON'T BET ON IT, JUSTIN... DON'T BET ON IT!
VWORP
VWORP

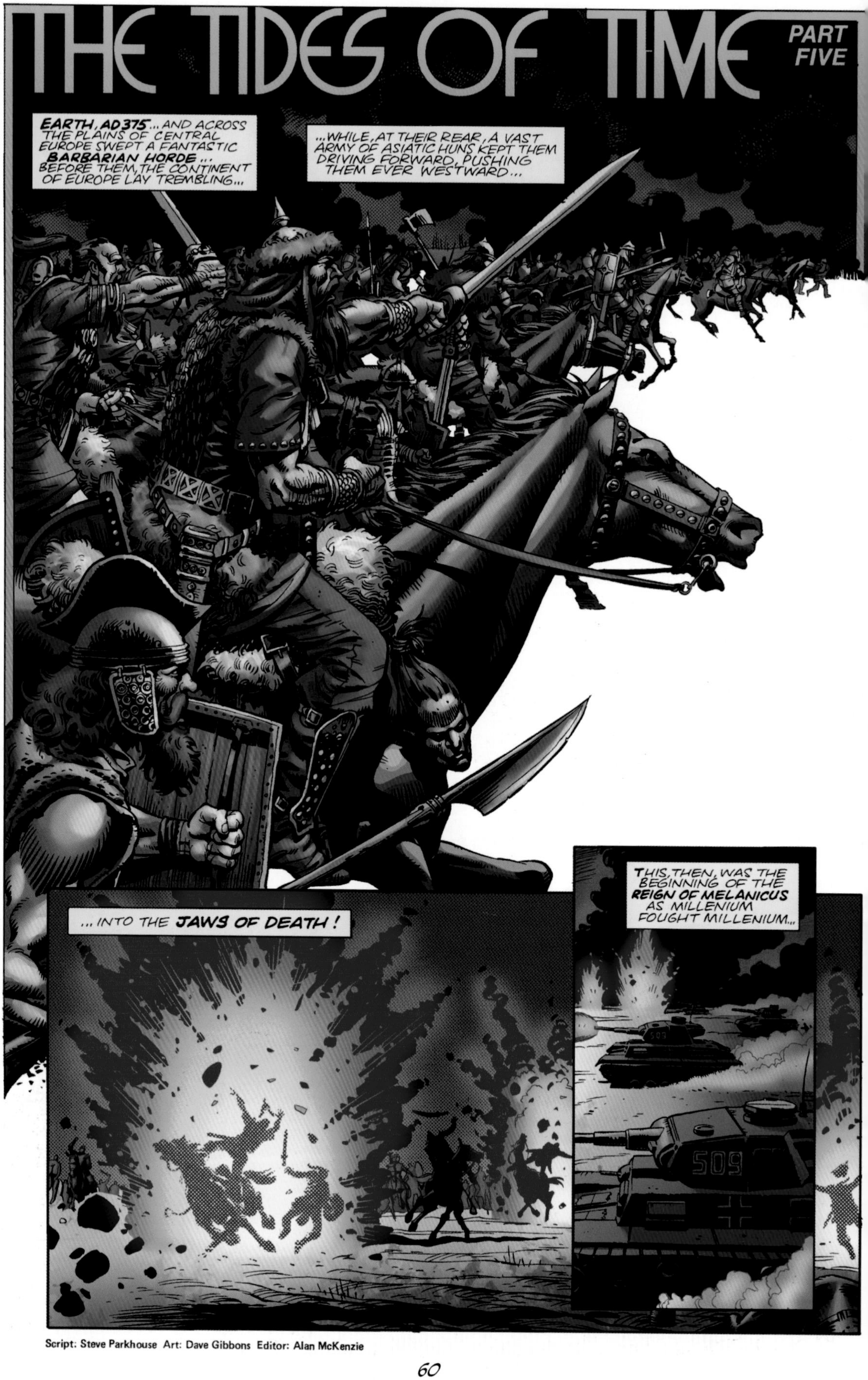
THE TIDES OF TIME
PART FIVE
EARTH, AD 375... AND ACROSS THE PLAINS OF CENTRAL EUROPE SWEPT A FANTASTIC BARBARIAN HORDE... BEFORE THEM, THE CONTINENT OF EUROPE LAY TREMBLING...
...WHILE, AT THEIR REAR, A VAST ARMY OF ASIATIC HUNS KEPT THEM DRIVING FORWARD, PUSHING THEM EVER WESTWARD...
... INTO THE JAWS OF DEATH!
THIS, THEN, WAS THE BEGINNING OF THE REIGN OF MELANICUS AS MILLENIUM FOUGHT MILLENIUM...
509

Script: Steve Parkhouse Art: Dave Gibbons Editor: Alan McKenzie

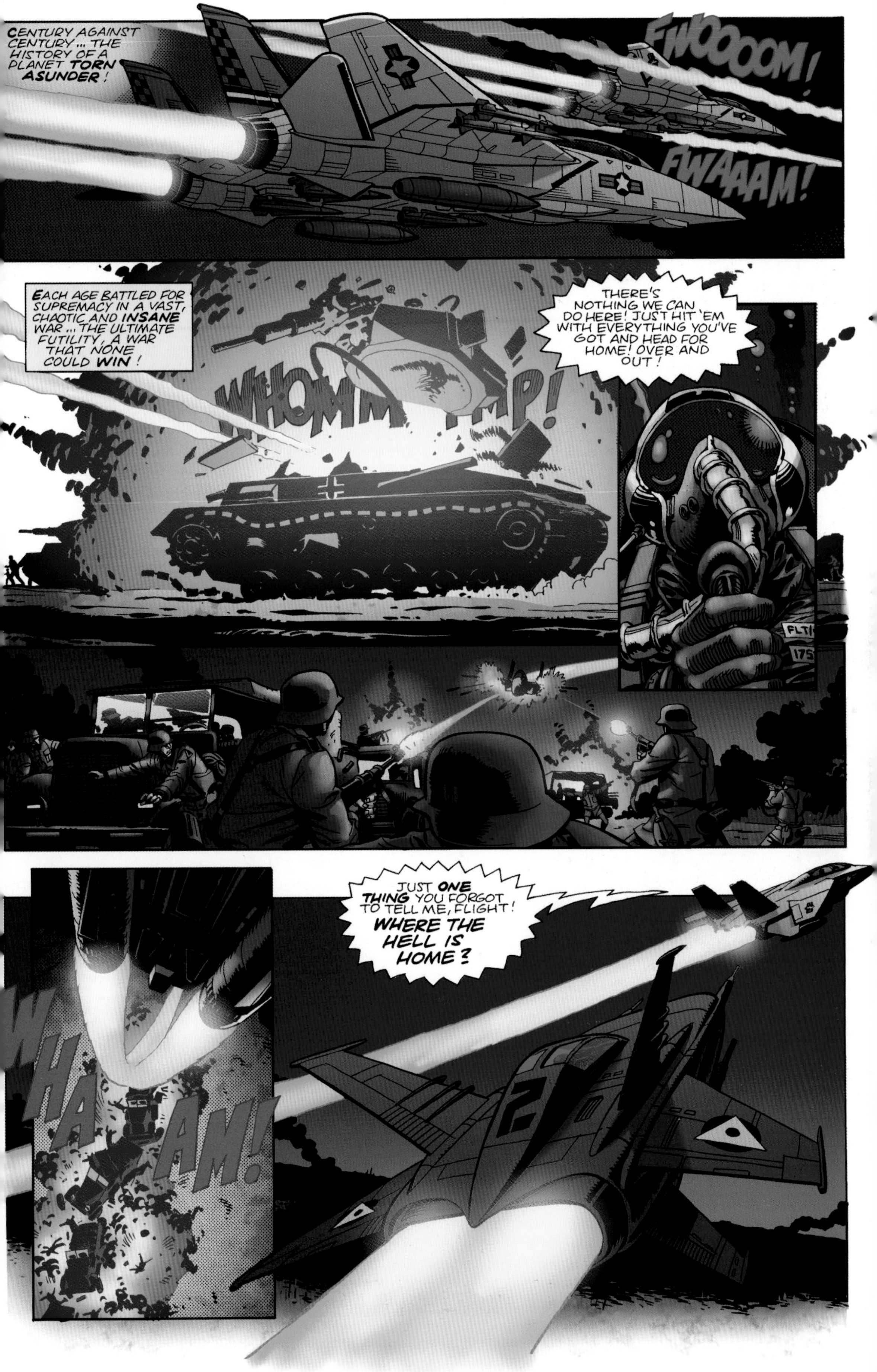
CENTURY AGAINST CENTURY... THE HISTORY OF A PLANET TORN ASUNDER!
FWOOOOM!
FWAAAM!
EACH AGE BATTLED FOR SUPREMACY IN A VAST, CHAOTIC AND INSANE WAR... THE ULTIMATE FUTILITY, A WAR THAT NONE COULD WIN!
WHOMM MP!
THERE'S NOTHING WE CAN DO HERE! JUST HIT 'EM WITH EVERYTHING YOU'VE GOT AND HEAD FOR HOME! OVER AND OUT!
JUST ONE THING YOU FORGOT TO TELL ME, FLIGHT! WHERE THE HELL IS HOME?
WHA AM!

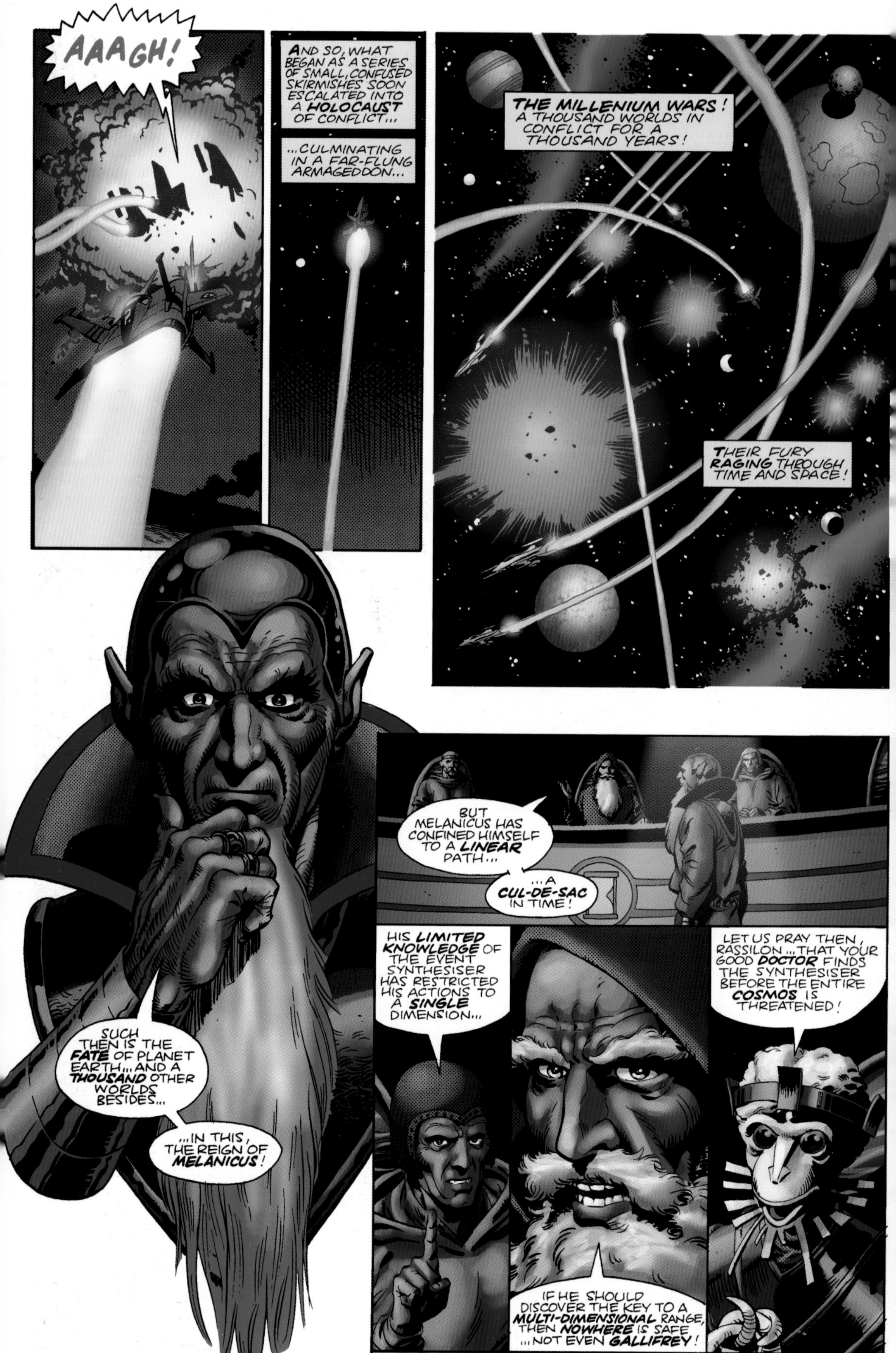
AAAGH!
AND SO, WHAT BEGAN AS A SERIES OF SMALL, CONFUSED SKIRMISHES SOON ESCALATED INTO A HOLOCAUST OF CONFLICT...
...CULMINATING IN A FAR-FLUNG ARMAGEDDON...
THE MILLENIUM WARS! A THOUSAND WORLDS IN CONFLICT FOR A THOUSAND YEARS!
THEIR FURY RAGING THROUGH TIME AND SPACE!
SUCH THEN IS THE FATE OF PLANET EARTH... AND A THOUSAND OTHER WORLDS BESIDES...
...IN THIS, THE REIGN OF MELANICUS!
BUT MELANICUS HAS CONFINED HIMSELF TO A LINEAR PATH...
...A CUL-DE-SAC IN TIME!
HIS LIMITED KNOWLEDGE OF THE EVENT SYNTHESISER HAS RESTRICTED HIS ACTIONS TO A SINGLE DIMENSION...
IF HE SHOULD DISCOVER THE KEY TO A MULTI-DIMENSIONAL RANGE, THEN NOWHERE IS SAFE ...NOT EVEN GALLIFREY!
LET US PRAY THEN, RASSILON... THAT YOUR GOOD DOCTOR FINDS THE SYNTHESISER BEFORE THE ENTIRE COSMOS IS THREATENED!

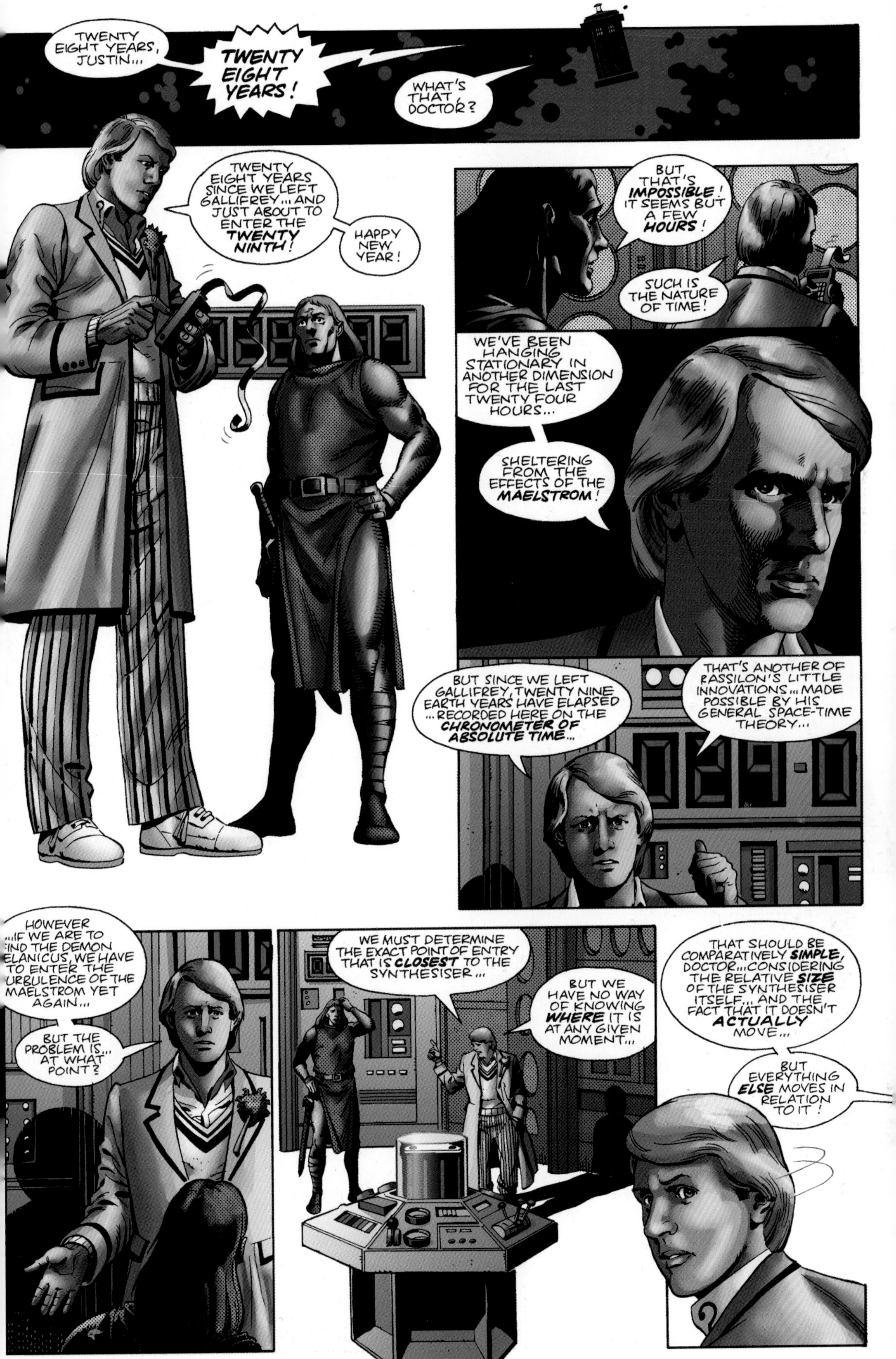

TWENTY EIGHT YEARS, JUSTIN...
TWENTY EIGHT YEARS!
WHAT'S THAT, DOCTOR?
TWENTY EIGHT YEARS SINCE WE LEFT GALLIFREY... AND JUST ABOUT TO ENTER THE TWENTY NINTH!
HAPPY NEW YEAR!
BUT THAT'S IMPOSSIBLE! IT SEEMS BUT A FEW HOURS!
SUCH IS THE NATURE OF TIME!
WE'VE BEEN HANGING STATIONARY IN ANOTHER DIMENSION FOR THE LAST TWENTY FOUR HOURS...
SHELTERING FROM THE EFFECTS OF THE MAELSTROM!
BUT SINCE WE LEFT GALLIFREY, TWENTY NINE EARTH YEARS HAVE ELAPSED ...RECORDED HERE ON THE CHRONOMETER OF ABSOLUTE TIME...
THAT'S ANOTHER OF RASSILON'S LITTLE INNOVATIONS... MADE POSSIBLE BY HIS GENERAL SPACE-TIME THEORY...
HOWEVER ...IF WE ARE TO FIND THE DEMON ELANICUS, WE HAVE TO ENTER THE TURBULENCE OF THE MAELSTROM YET AGAIN...
BUT THE PROBLEM IS... AT WHAT POINT?
WE MUST DETERMINE THE EXACT POINT OF ENTRY THAT IS CLOSEST TO THE SYNTHESISER...
BUT WE HAVE NO WAY OF KNOWING WHERE IT IS AT ANY GIVEN MOMENT...
THAT SHOULD BE COMPARATIVELY SIMPLE, DOCTOR... CONSIDERING THE RELATIVE SIZE OF THE SYNTHESISER ITSELF... AND THE FACT THAT IT DOESN'T ACTUALLY MOVE...
BUT EVERYTHING ELSE MOVES IN RELATION TO IT!

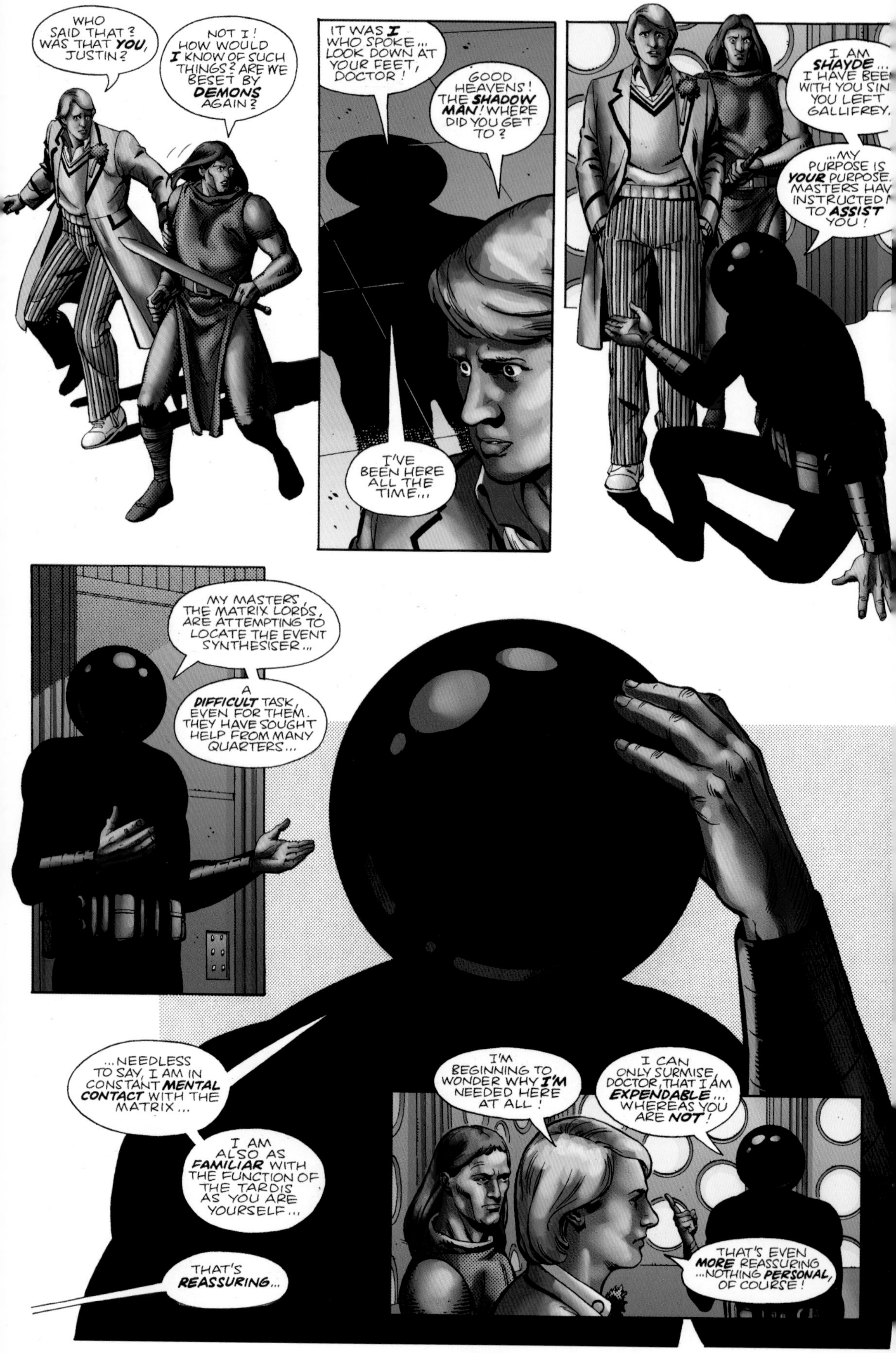
WHO SAID THAT? WAS THAT YOU, JUSTIN?
NOT I! HOW WOULD I KNOW OF SUCH THINGS? ARE WE BESET BY DEMONS AGAIN?
IT WAS I WHO SPOKE... LOOK DOWN AT YOUR FEET, DOCTOR!
GOOD HEAVENS! THE SHADOW MAN! WHERE DID YOU GET TO?
I'VE BEEN HERE ALL THE TIME...
I AM SHAYDE... I HAVE BEE WITH YOU SIN YOU LEFT GALLIFREY.
...MY PURPOSE IS YOUR PURPOSE. MASTERS HAV INSTRUCTED TO ASSIST YOU!
MY MASTERS, THE MATRIX LORDS, ARE ATTEMPTING TO LOCATE THE EVENT SYNTHESISER...
A DIFFICULT TASK, EVEN FOR THEM. THEY HAVE SOUGHT HELP FROM MANY QUARTERS...
...NEEDLESS TO SAY, I AM IN CONSTANT MENTAL CONTACT WITH THE MATRIX...
I AM ALSO AS FAMILIAR WITH THE FUNCTION OF THE TARDIS AS YOU ARE YOURSELF...
THAT'S REASSURING...
I'M BEGINNING TO WONDER WHY I'M NEEDED HERE AT ALL!
I CAN ONLY SURMISE, DOCTOR, THAT I AM EXPENDABLE... WHEREAS YOU ARE NOT!
THAT'S EVEN MORE REASSURING ...NOTHING PERSONAL, OF COURSE!

THE **MOTIVES** OF THE MATRIX LORDS ARE NOT MINE TO QUESTION... HOWEVER, I FEEL I **AM** QUALIFIED TO POINT OUT THAT THE TARDIS CONSOLE IS REGISTERING A **READING!**

YOU'RE RIGHT! THERE'S SOMETHING **OUTSIDE!**

HMM... I HAVE A **SCANNER READING...** IT'S **EXTRAORDINARY!**

NO MOVING PARTS...NO MAGNETIC FIELD...POWER SOURCE UNKNOWN! THE OBJECT APPEARS TO BE COMPOSED OF AN **EXTREMELY REFINED** SUBSTANCE...HARDLY **MATTER** AT ALL!

...IT'S SOMETHING LIKE **CRYSTALLISED ENERGY!** WHOEVER SENT THIS OBJECT, THIS **CRAFT...** THEY'RE A VERY HIGHLY EVOLVED SPECIES!

I WONDER IF WE CAN ASSUME THEIR INTENTIONS ARE...OH! HE'S **GONE!**

BEING EXPOSED TO **VACUUM**...IN THE DEEP SPACE OF ANOTHER **DIMENSION,** SEEMED HARDLY TO AFFECT SHAYDE AT ALL...

IN FACT, HE MOVED WITH THE ASSURANCE AND GRACE OF A FISH IN WATER...

NO ALARMS, NO RUNNING GUARDS...NO PANIC OR AGRESSION GREETED THE SHADOW MAN FROM GALLIFREY UPON HIS SUDDEN AND DRAMATIC INTRUSION...

...BUT A FEW SIMPLE WORDS OF **WELCOME...**

GREETINGS SHAYDE...OUR FELICITATIONS TO YOU AND YOUR MASTERS!

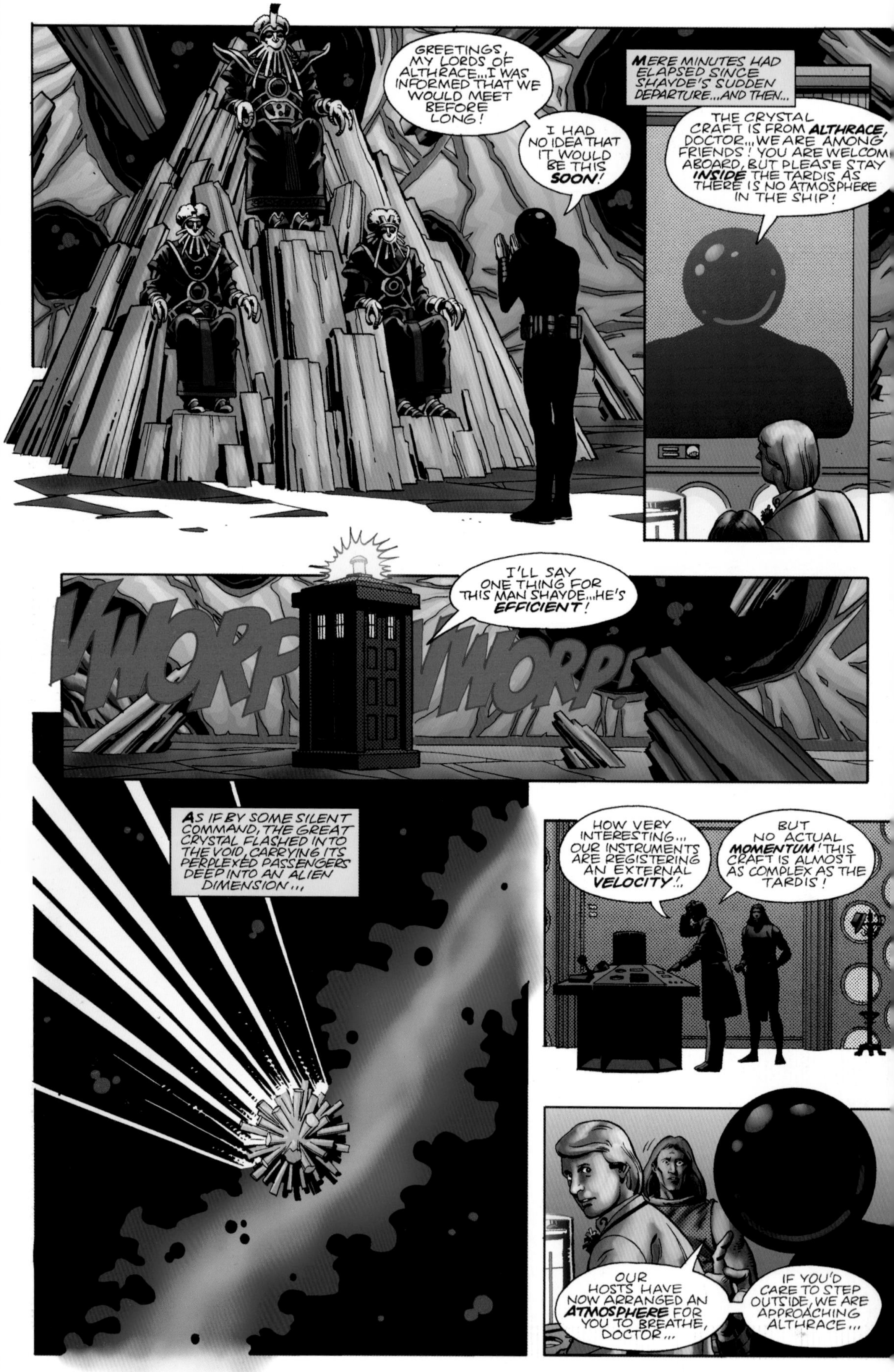
GREETINGS, MY LORDS OF ALTHRACE... I WAS INFORMED THAT WE WOULD MEET BEFORE LONG!
I HAD NO IDEA THAT IT WOULD BE THIS SOON!
MERE MINUTES HAD ELAPSED SINCE SHAYDE'S SUDDEN DEPARTURE... AND THEN...
THE CRYSTAL CRAFT IS FROM ALTHRACE, DOCTOR... WE ARE AMONG FRIENDS! YOU ARE WELCOM ABOARD, BUT PLEASE STAY INSIDE THE TARDIS AS THERE IS NO ATMOSPHERE IN THE SHIP!
VWORP VWORP!
I'LL SAY ONE THING FOR THIS MAN SHAYDE... HE'S EFFICIENT!
AS IF BY SOME SILENT COMMAND, THE GREAT CRYSTAL FLASHED INTO THE VOID, CARRYING ITS PERPLEXED PASSENGERS DEEP INTO AN ALIEN DIMENSION...
HOW VERY INTERESTING... OUR INSTRUMENTS ARE REGISTERING AN EXTERNAL VELOCITY!..
BUT NO ACTUAL MOMENTUM! THIS CRAFT IS ALMOST AS COMPLEX AS THE TARDIS!
OUR HOSTS HAVE NOW ARRANGED AN ATMOSPHERE FOR YOU TO BREATHE, DOCTOR...
IF YOU'D CARE TO STEP OUTSIDE, WE ARE APPROACHING ALTHRACE...

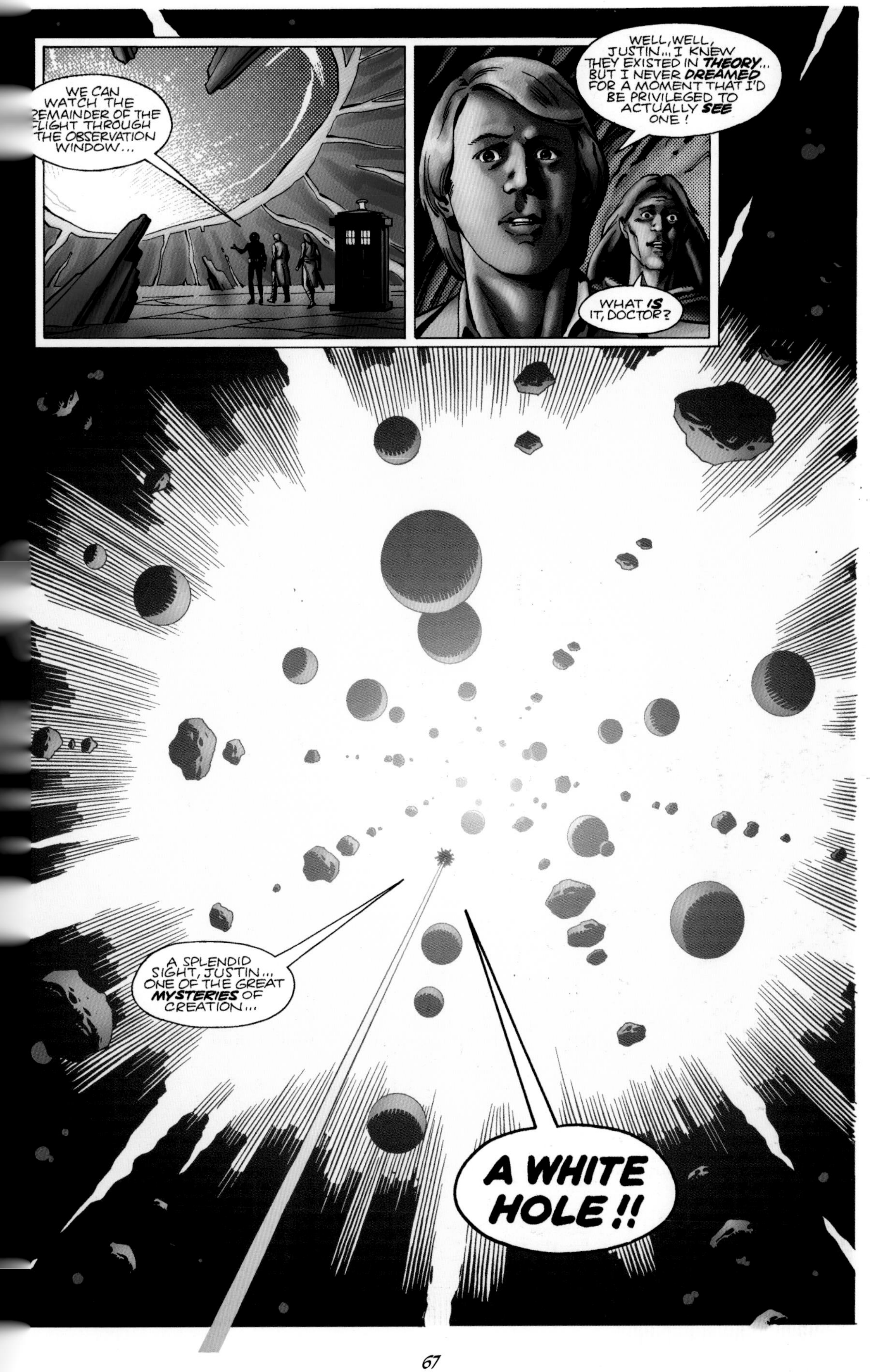
WE CAN WATCH THE REMAINDER OF THE FLIGHT THROUGH THE OBSERVATION WINDOW...
WELL, WELL, JUSTIN... I KNEW THEY EXISTED IN THEORY... BUT I NEVER DREAMED FOR A MOMENT THAT I'D BE PRIVILEGED TO ACTUALLY SEE ONE!
WHAT IS IT, DOCTOR?
A SPLENDID SIGHT, JUSTIN... ONE OF THE GREAT MYSTERIES OF CREATION...
A WHITE HOLE!!

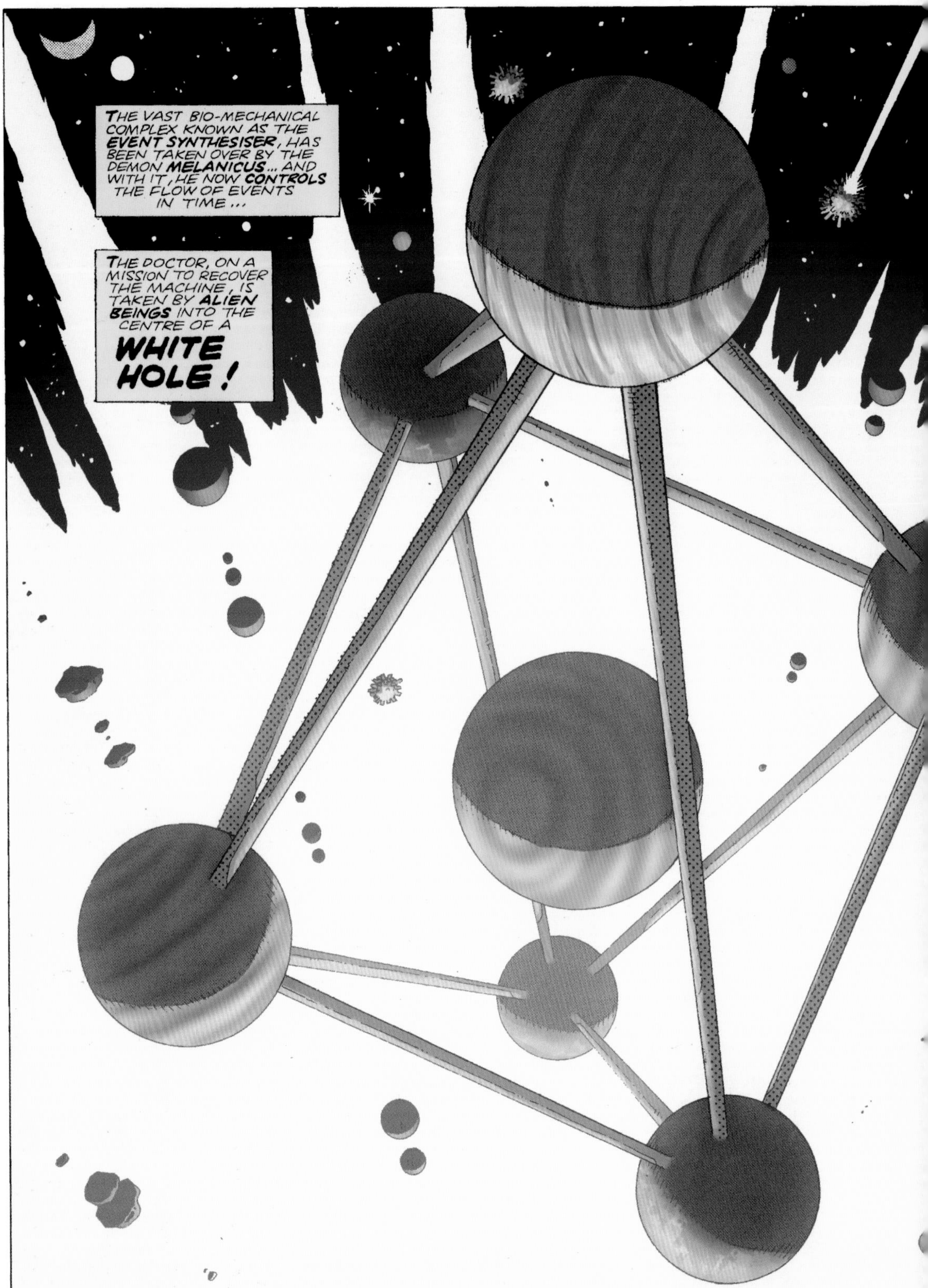
THE VAST BIO-MECHANICAL COMPLEX KNOWN AS THE EVENT SYNTHESISER, HAS BEEN TAKEN OVER BY THE DEMON MELANICUS... AND WITH IT, HE NOW CONTROLS THE FLOW OF EVENTS IN TIME...
THE DOCTOR, ON A MISSION TO RECOVER THE MACHINE, IS TAKEN BY ALIEN BEINGS INTO THE CENTRE OF A WHITE HOLE!

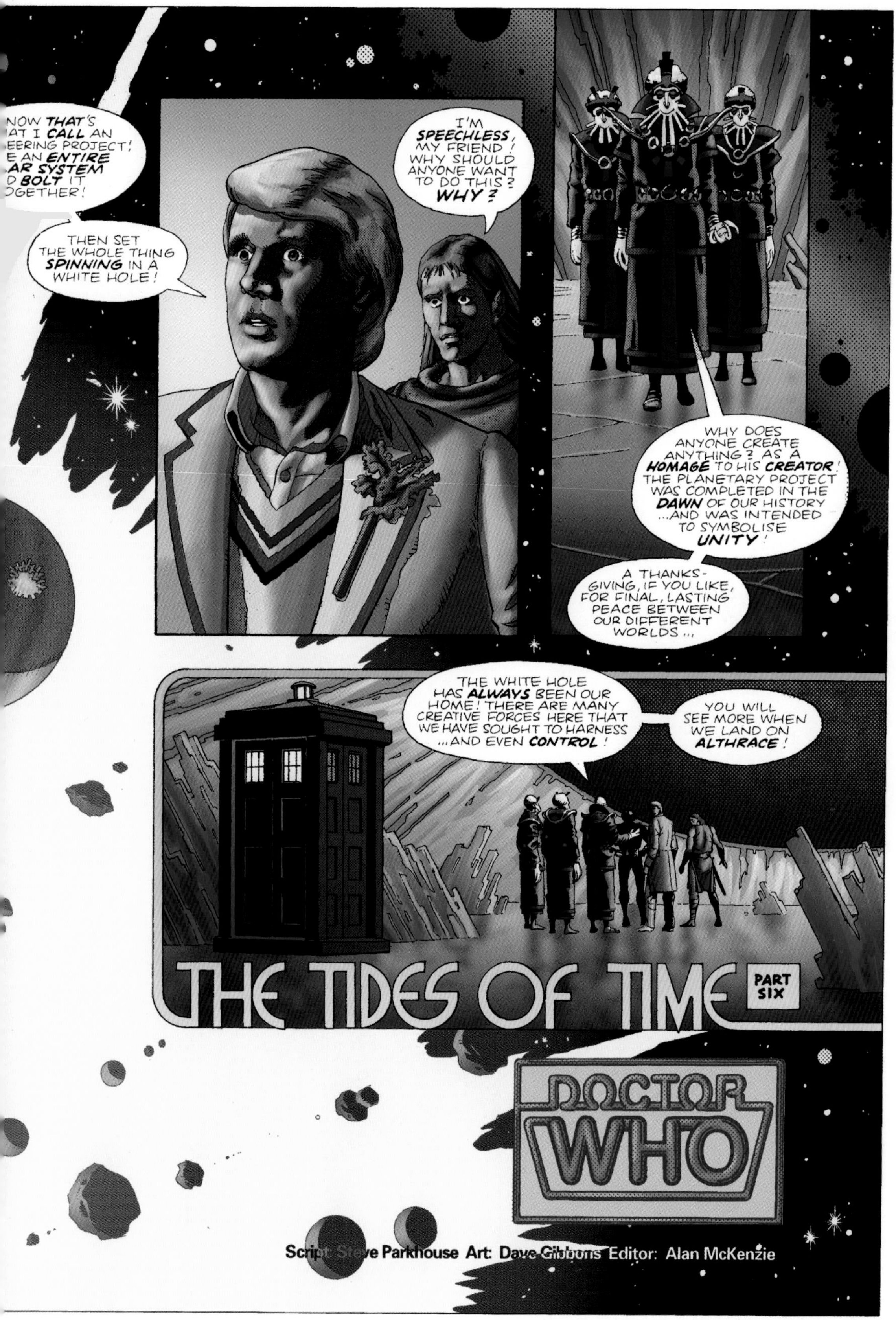
NOW THAT'S AT I CALL AN EERING PROJECT! E AN ENTIRE AR SYSTEM D BOLT IT OGETHER!
THEN SET THE WHOLE THING SPINNING IN A WHITE HOLE!
I'M SPEECHLESS, MY FRIEND! WHY SHOULD ANYONE WANT TO DO THIS? WHY?
WHY DOES ANYONE CREATE ANYTHING? AS A HOMAGE TO HIS CREATOR! THE PLANETARY PROJECT WAS COMPLETED IN THE DAWN OF OUR HISTORY ...AND WAS INTENDED TO SYMBOLISE UNITY!
A THANKS-GIVING, IF YOU LIKE, FOR FINAL, LASTING PEACE BETWEEN OUR DIFFERENT WORLDS...
THE WHITE HOLE HAS ALWAYS BEEN OUR HOME! THERE ARE MANY CREATIVE FORCES HERE THAT WE HAVE SOUGHT TO HARNESS ...AND EVEN CONTROL!
YOU WILL SEE MORE WHEN WE LAND ON ALTHRACE!
THE TIDES OF TIME
PART SIX
DOCTOR WHO
Script: Steve Parkhouse Art: Dave Gibbons Editor: Alan McKenzie

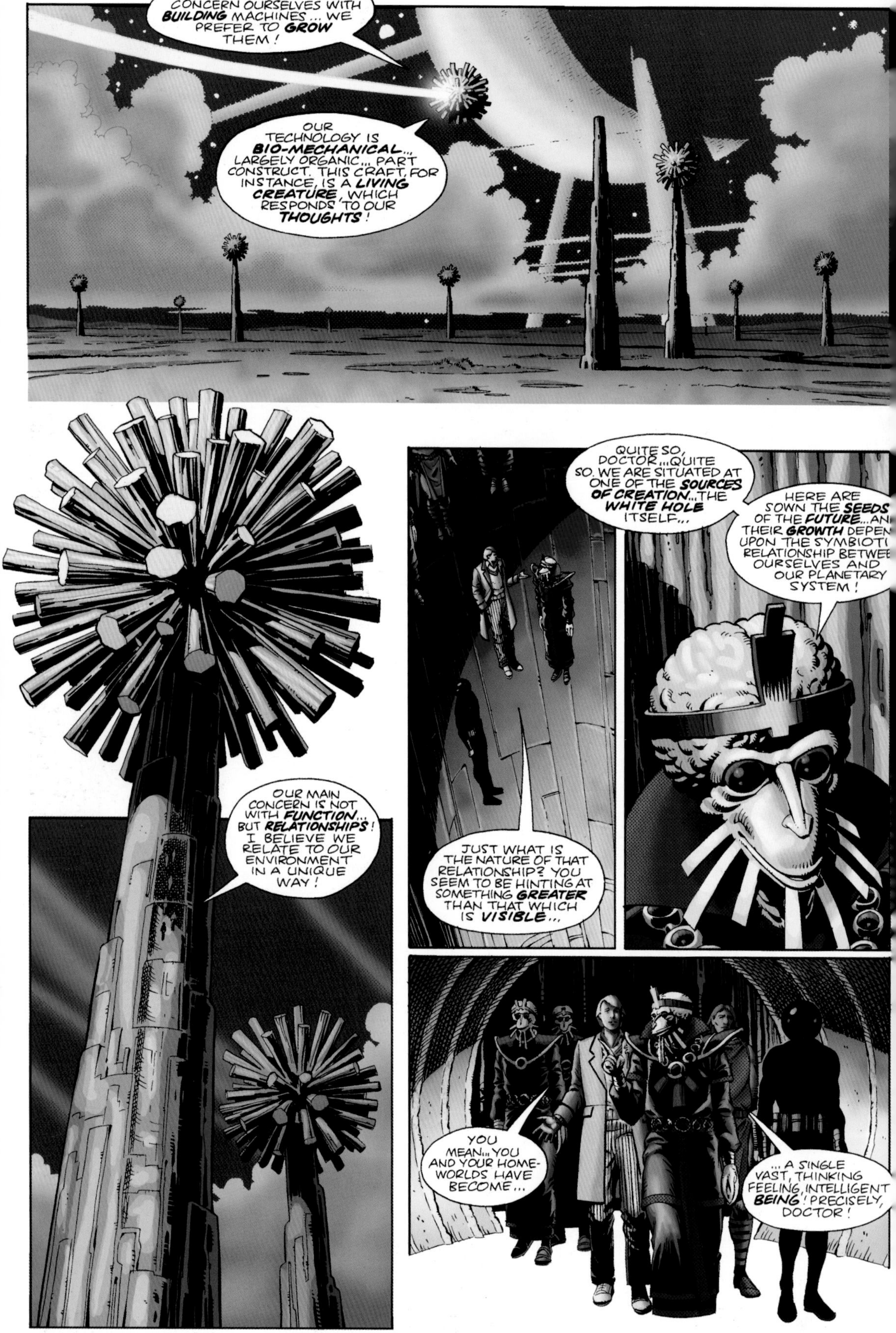
WE NO LONGER CONCERN OURSELVES WITH BUILDING MACHINES... WE PREFER TO GROW THEM!
OUR TECHNOLOGY IS BIO-MECHANICAL... LARGELY ORGANIC... PART CONSTRUCT. THIS CRAFT, FOR INSTANCE, IS A LIVING CREATURE, WHICH RESPONDS TO OUR THOUGHTS!
OUR MAIN CONCERN IS NOT WITH FUNCTION... BUT RELATIONSHIPS! I BELIEVE WE RELATE TO OUR ENVIRONMENT IN A UNIQUE WAY!
JUST WHAT IS THE NATURE OF THAT RELATIONSHIP? YOU SEEM TO BE HINTING AT SOMETHING GREATER THAN THAT WHICH IS VISIBLE...
QUITE SO, DOCTOR... QUITE SO. WE ARE SITUATED AT ONE OF THE SOURCES OF CREATION... THE WHITE HOLE ITSELF...
HERE ARE SOWN THE SEEDS OF THE FUTURE... AN THEIR GROWTH DEPEN UPON THE SYMBIOTI RELATIONSHIP BETWEE OURSELVES AND OUR PLANETARY SYSTEM!
YOU MEAN... YOU AND YOUR HOME-WORLDS HAVE BECOME...
...A SINGLE VAST, THINKING FEELING, INTELLIGENT BEING! PRECISELY, DOCTOR!

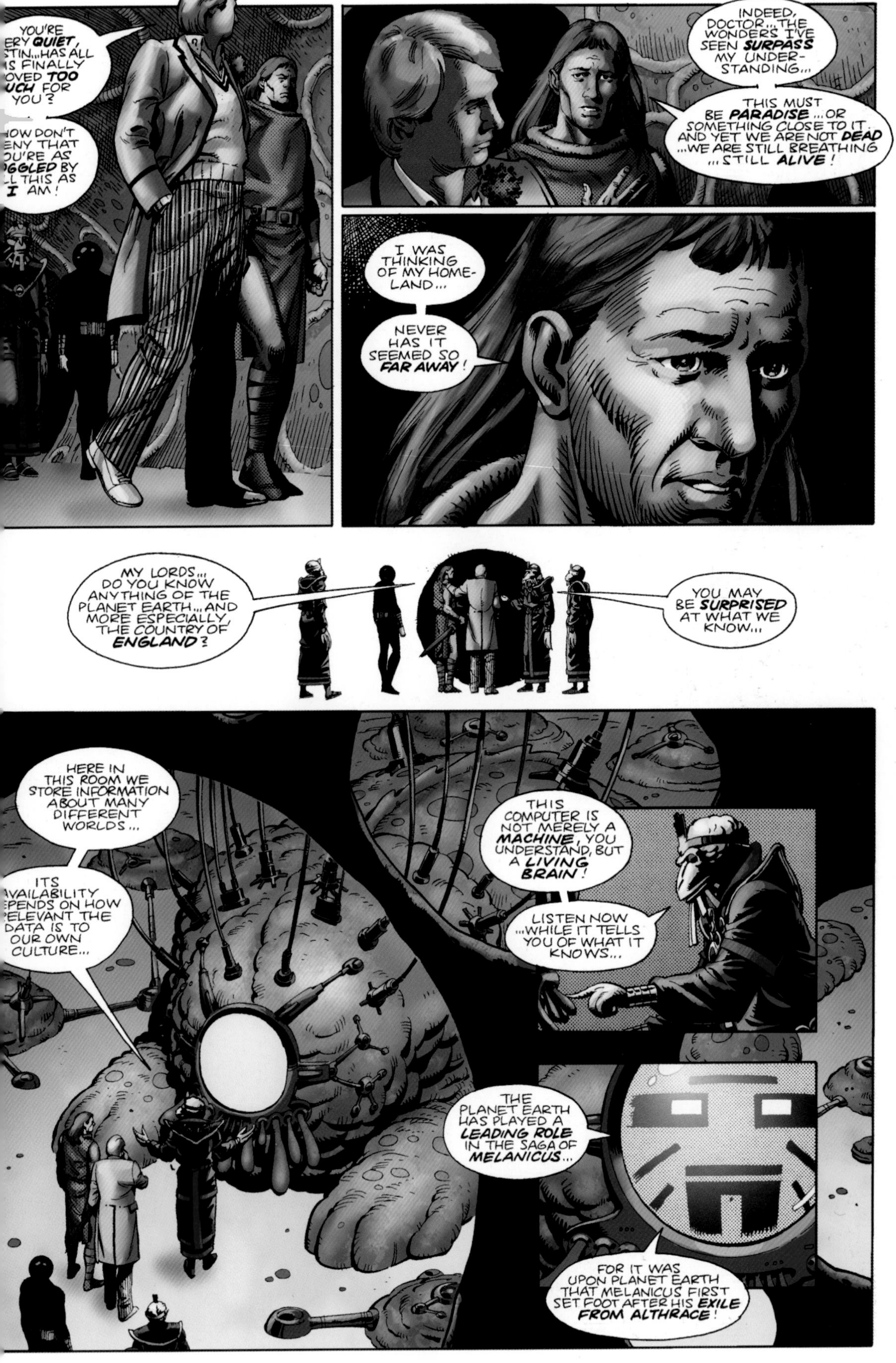
YOU'RE ERY QUIET, STIN... HAS ALL IS FINALLY OVED TOO UCH FOR YOU?
HOW DON'T ENY THAT OU'RE AS OGGLED BY LL THIS AS I AM!
INDEED, DOCTOR... THE WONDERS I'VE SEEN SURPASS MY UNDER-STANDING...
THIS MUST BE PARADISE ... OR SOMETHING CLOSE TO IT. AND YET WE ARE NOT DEAD ...WE ARE STILL BREATHING ... STILL ALIVE!
I WAS THINKING OF MY HOME-LAND...
NEVER HAS IT SEEMED SO FAR AWAY!
MY LORDS... DO YOU KNOW ANYTHING OF THE PLANET EARTH... AND MORE ESPECIALLY, THE COUNTRY OF ENGLAND?
YOU MAY BE SURPRISED AT WHAT WE KNOW...
HERE IN THIS ROOM WE STORE INFORMATION ABOUT MANY DIFFERENT WORLDS...
ITS AVAILABILITY EPENDS ON HOW ELEVANT THE DATA IS TO OUR OWN CULTURE...
THIS COMPUTER IS NOT MERELY A MACHINE, YOU UNDERSTAND, BUT A LIVING BRAIN!
LISTEN NOW ...WHILE IT TELLS YOU OF WHAT IT KNOWS...
THE PLANET EARTH HAS PLAYED A LEADING ROLE IN THE SAGA OF MELANICUS...
FOR IT WAS UPON PLANET EARTH THAT MELANICUS FIRST SET FOOT AFTER HIS EXILE FROM ALTHRACE!

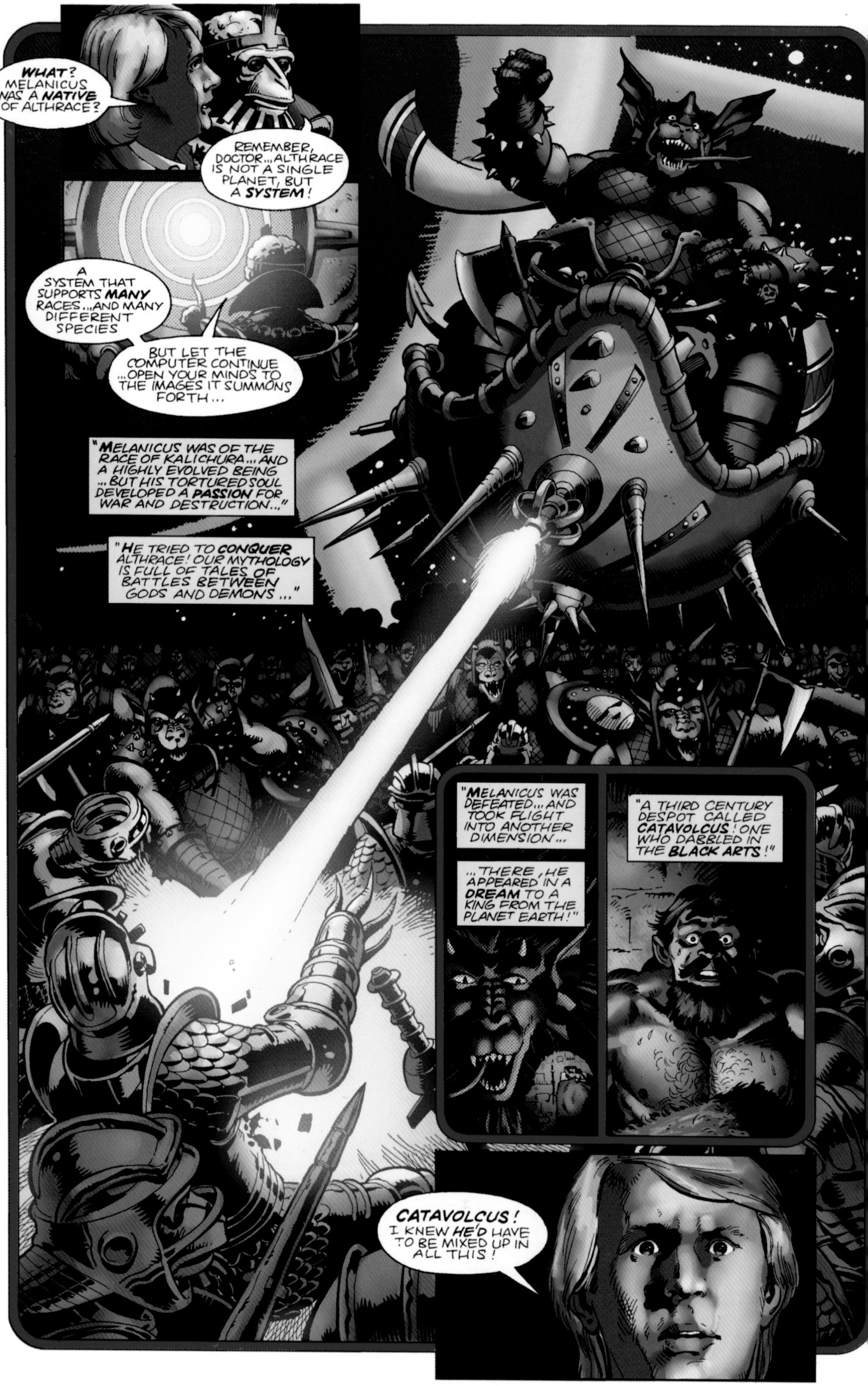
WHAT? MELANICUS WAS A NATIVE OF ALTHRACE?
REMEMBER, DOCTOR... ALTHRACE IS NOT A SINGLE PLANET, BUT A SYSTEM!
A SYSTEM THAT SUPPORTS MANY RACES... AND MANY DIFFERENT SPECIES
BUT LET THE COMPUTER CONTINUE ...OPEN YOUR MINDS TO THE IMAGES IT SUMMONS FORTH...
"MELANICUS WAS OF THE RACE OF KALICHURA... AND A HIGHLY EVOLVED BEING ...BUT HIS TORTURED SOUL DEVELOPED A PASSION FOR WAR AND DESTRUCTION..."
"HE TRIED TO CONQUER ALTHRACE! OUR MYTHOLOGY IS FULL OF TALES OF BATTLES BETWEEN GODS AND DEMONS..."
"MELANICUS WAS DEFEATED... AND TOOK FLIGHT INTO ANOTHER DIMENSION...
...THERE, HE APPEARED IN A DREAM TO A KING FROM THE PLANET EARTH!"
"A THIRD CENTURY DESPOT CALLED CATAVOLCUS! ONE WHO DABBLED IN THE BLACK ARTS!"
CATAVOLCUS! I KNEW HE'D HAVE TO BE MIXED UP IN ALL THIS!

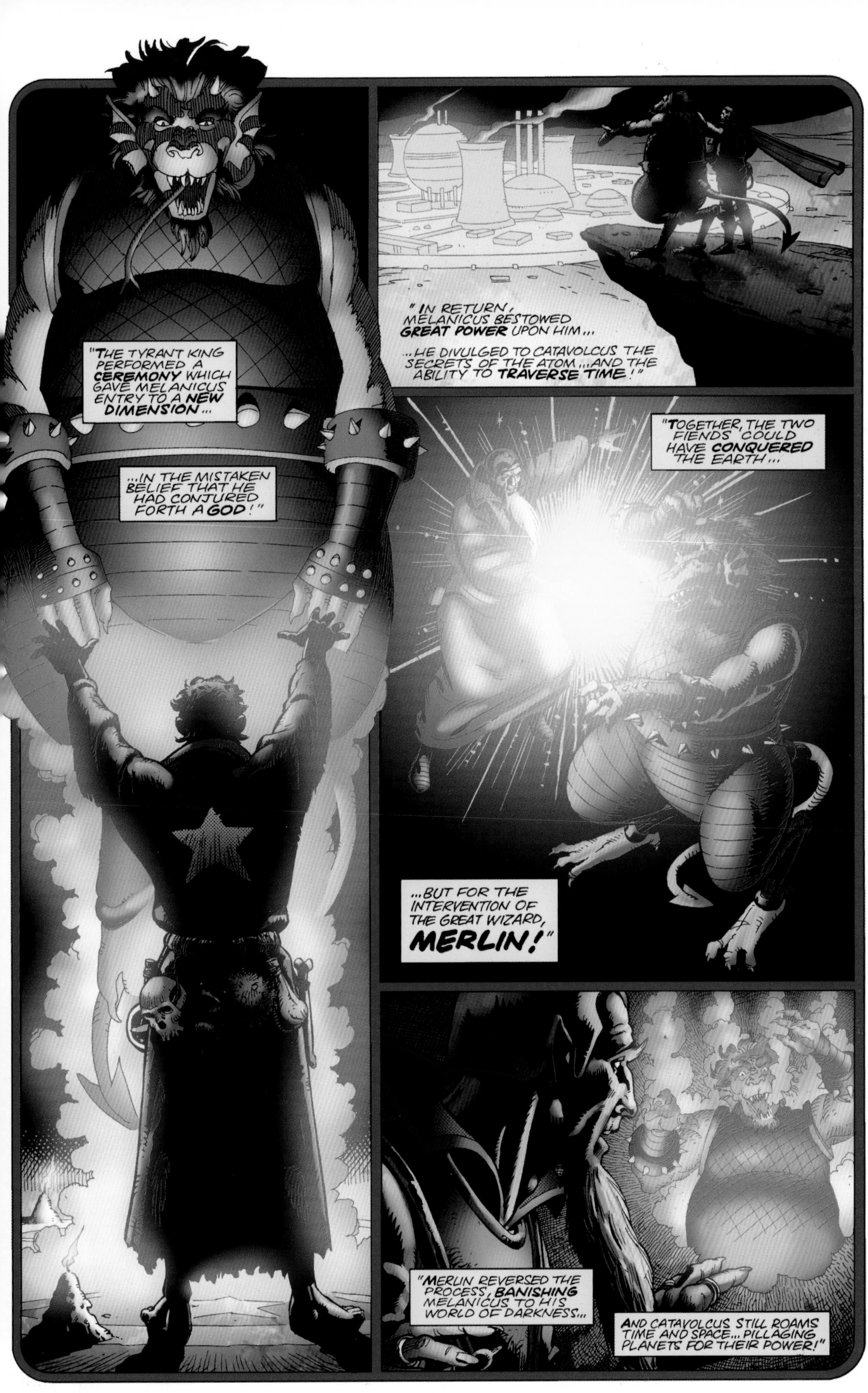
"THE TYRANT KING PERFORMED A CEREMONY WHICH GAVE MELANICUS ENTRY TO A NEW DIMENSION...
...IN THE MISTAKEN BELIEF THAT HE HAD CONJURED FORTH A GOD!"
"IN RETURN, MELANICUS BESTOWED GREAT POWER UPON HIM...
...HE DIVULGED TO CATAVOLCUS THE SECRETS OF THE ATOM...AND THE ABILITY TO TRAVERSE TIME!"
"TOGETHER, THE TWO FIENDS COULD HAVE CONQUERED THE EARTH...
...BUT FOR THE INTERVENTION OF THE GREAT WIZARD, MERLIN!"
"MERLIN REVERSED THE PROCESS, BANISHING MELANICUS TO HIS WORLD OF DARKNESS...
AND CATAVOLCUS STILL ROAMS TIME AND SPACE... PILLAGING PLANETS FOR THEIR POWER!"

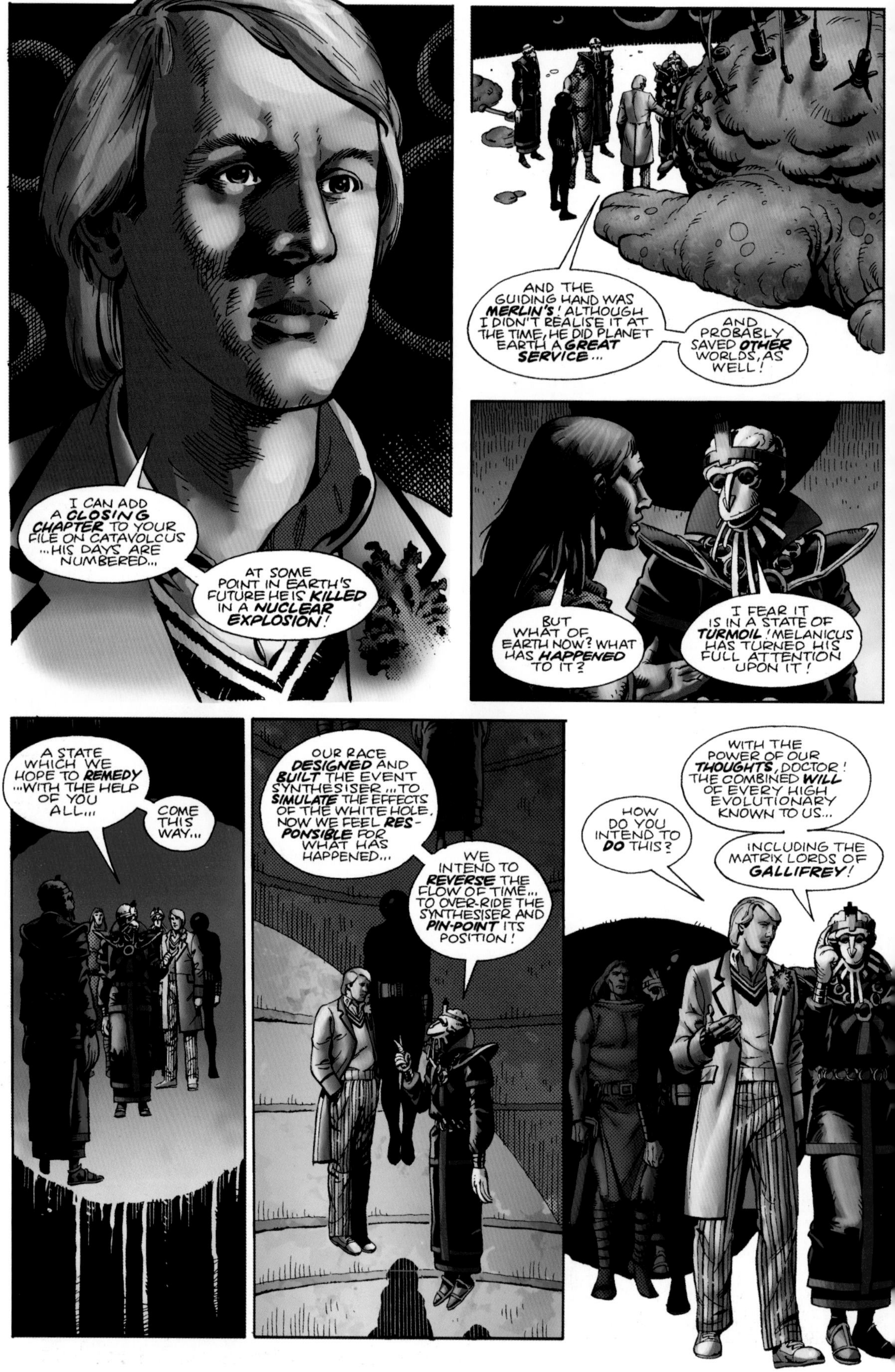
I CAN ADD A CLOSING CHAPTER TO YOUR FILE ON CATAVOLCUS ...HIS DAYS ARE NUMBERED...
AT SOME POINT IN EARTH'S FUTURE HE IS KILLED IN A NUCLEAR EXPLOSION!
AND THE GUIDING HAND WAS MERLIN'S! ALTHOUGH I DIDN'T REALISE IT AT THE TIME, HE DID PLANET EARTH A GREAT SERVICE...
AND PROBABLY SAVED OTHER WORLDS, AS WELL!
BUT WHAT OF EARTH NOW? WHAT HAS HAPPENED TO IT?
I FEAR IT IS IN A STATE OF TURMOIL! MELANICUS HAS TURNED HIS FULL ATTENTION UPON IT!
A STATE WHICH WE HOPE TO REMEDY ...WITH THE HELP OF YOU ALL...
COME THIS WAY...
OUR RACE DESIGNED AND BUILT THE EVENT SYNTHESISER ...TO SIMULATE THE EFFECTS OF THE WHITE HOLE. NOW WE FEEL RES-PONSIBLE FOR WHAT HAS HAPPENED...
WE INTEND TO REVERSE THE FLOW OF TIME... TO OVER-RIDE THE SYNTHESISER AND PIN-POINT ITS POSITION!
HOW DO YOU INTEND TO DO THIS?
WITH THE POWER OF OUR THOUGHTS, DOCTOR! THE COMBINED WILL OF EVERY HIGH EVOLUTIONARY KNOWN TO US...
INCLUDING THE MATRIX LORDS OF GALLIFREY!

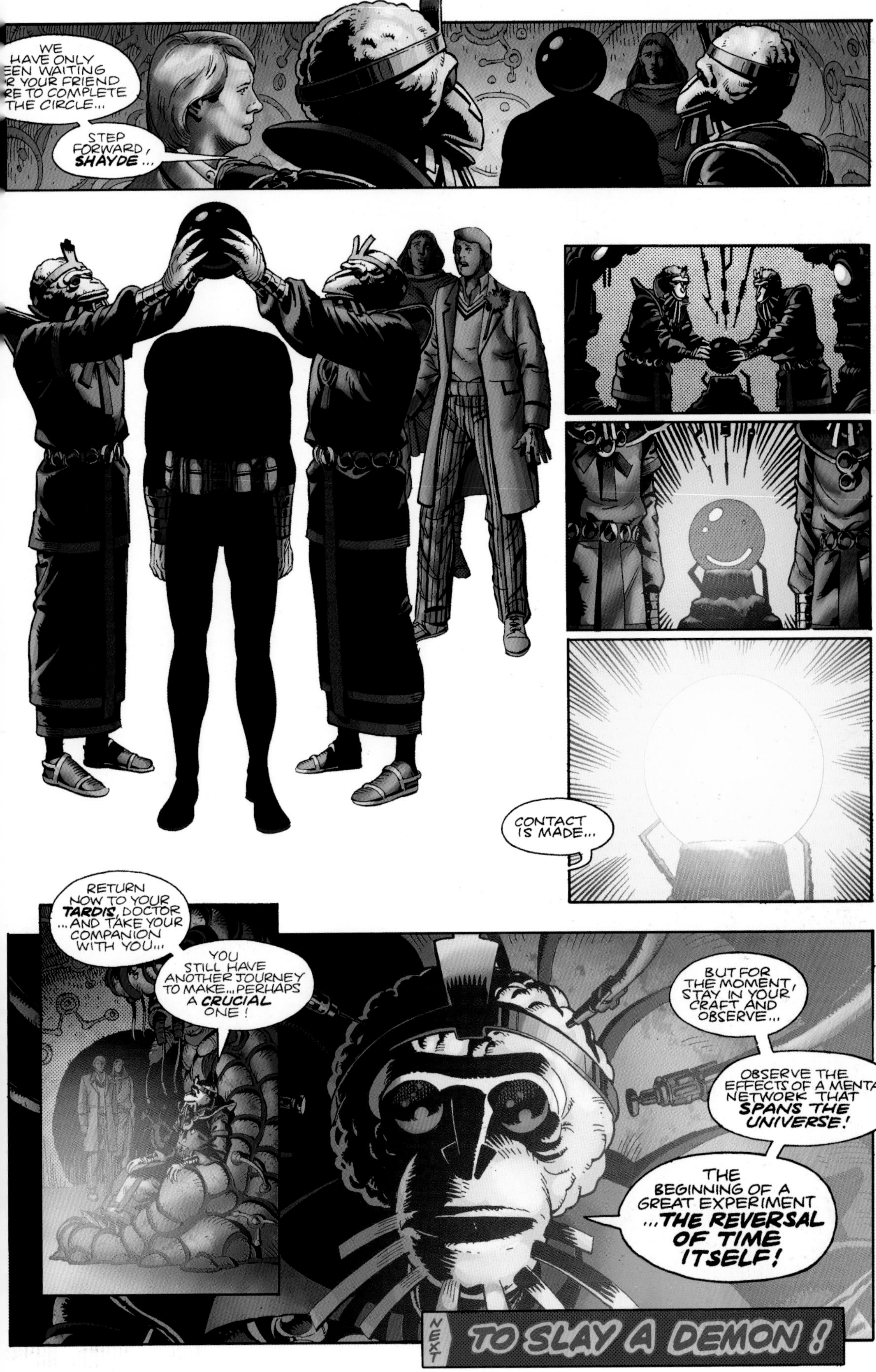

WE HAVE ONLY EEN WAITING R YOUR FRIEND RE TO COMPLETE THE CIRCLE...
STEP FORWARD, SHAYDE...
CONTACT IS MADE...
RETURN NOW TO YOUR TARDIS, DOCTOR ...AND TAKE YOUR COMPANION WITH YOU...
YOU STILL HAVE ANOTHER JOURNEY TO MAKE...PERHAPS A CRUCIAL ONE!
BUT FOR THE MOMENT, STAY IN YOUR CRAFT AND OBSERVE...
OBSERVE THE EFFECTS OF A MENTAL NETWORK THAT SPANS THE UNIVERSE!
THE BEGINNING OF A GREAT EXPERIMENT ...THE REVERSAL OF TIME ITSELF!
NEXT
TO SLAY A DEMON!

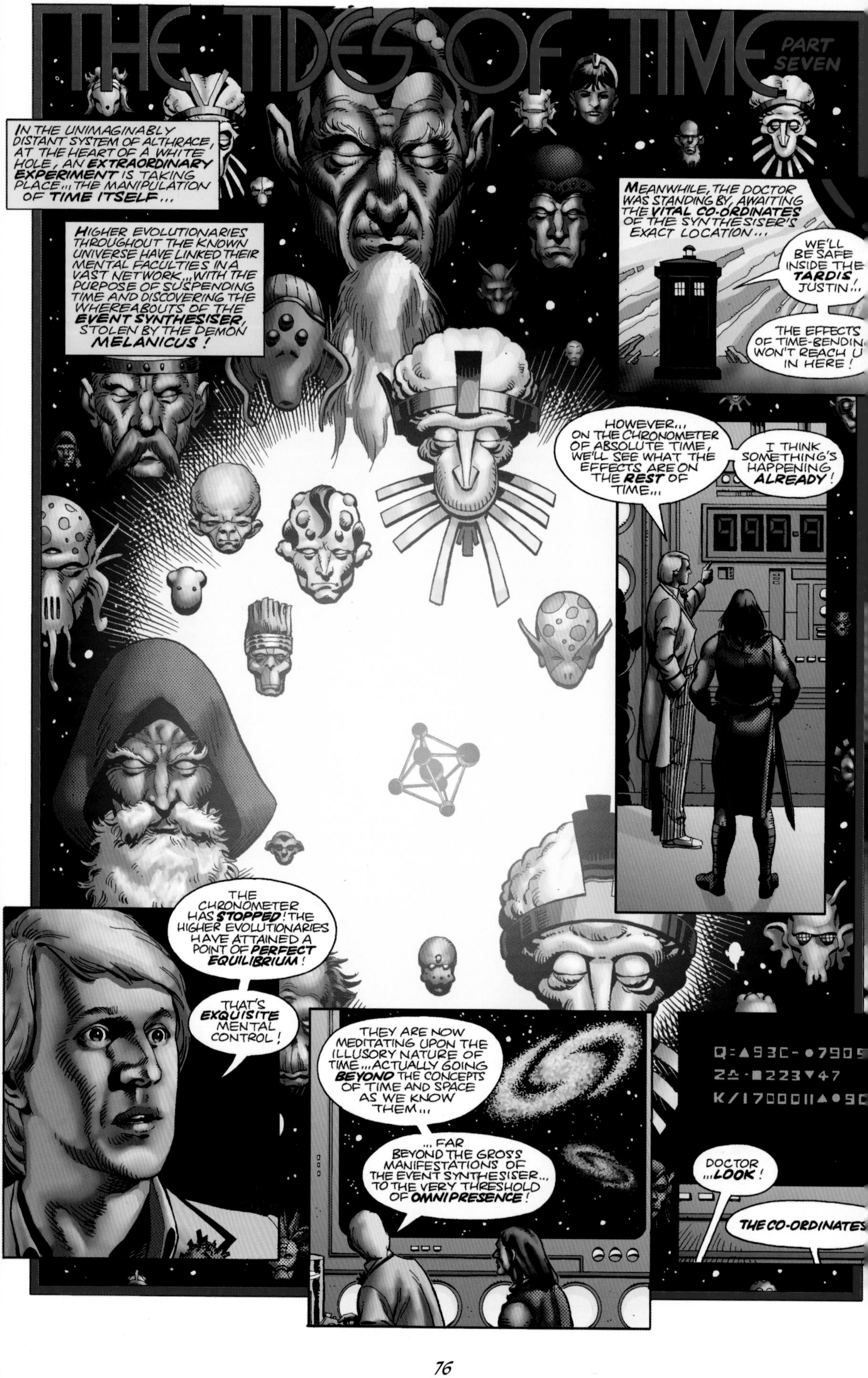
THE TIDES OF TIME
PART SEVEN
IN THE UNIMAGINABLY DISTANT SYSTEM OF ALTHRACE, AT THE HEART OF A WHITE HOLE, AN EXTRAORDINARY EXPERIMENT IS TAKING PLACE... THE MANIPULATION OF TIME ITSELF...
HIGHER EVOLUTIONARIES THROUGHOUT THE KNOWN UNIVERSE HAVE LINKED THEIR MENTAL FACULTIES IN A VAST NETWORK... WITH THE PURPOSE OF SUSPENDING TIME AND DISCOVERING THE WHEREABOUTS OF THE EVENT SYNTHESISER, STOLEN BY THE DEMON MELANICUS!
MEANWHILE, THE DOCTOR WAS STANDING BY, AWAITING THE VITAL CO-ORDINATES OF THE SYNTHESISER'S EXACT LOCATION...
WE'LL BE SAFE INSIDE THE TARDIS, JUSTIN...
THE EFFECTS OF TIME-BENDIN WON'T REACH U IN HERE!
HOWEVER... ON THE CHRONOMETER OF ABSOLUTE TIME, WE'LL SEE WHAT THE EFFECTS ARE ON THE REST OF TIME...
I THINK SOMETHING'S HAPPENING ALREADY!
THE CHRONOMETER HAS STOPPED! THE HIGHER EVOLUTIONARIES HAVE ATTAINED A POINT OF PERFECT EQUILIBRIUM!
THAT'S EXQUISITE MENTAL CONTROL!
THEY ARE NOW MEDITATING UPON THE ILLUSORY NATURE OF TIME... ACTUALLY GOING BEYOND THE CONCEPTS OF TIME AND SPACE AS WE KNOW THEM...
... FAR BEYOND THE GROSS MANIFESTATIONS OF THE EVENT SYNTHESISER... TO THE VERY THRESHOLD OF OMNIPRESENCE!
DOCTOR ...LOOK!
THE CO-ORDINATES

COUNTLESS LIGHT YEARS AWAY... PLANET EARTH LAY IN RUINS. THE **MILLENIUM WARS** HAD BOILED ACROSS HER SURFACE, LEAVING ONLY THE WINDS TO BEMOAN HER FATE...

AND NOW, UPON THAT DESERTED LANDSCAPE, THE TARDIS TOUCHED...

AS IF, IN SOME UN-FATHOMABLE WAY, THE DOCTOR'S DESTINY HAD SWUNG FULL CIRCLE...

VWOOP!

VWHOOP!

JUSTIN, CAN YOU HEAR WHAT I HEAR?

MUSIC FROM AN **ORGAN!**

COMING FROM THE CHURCH!

THIS **IS** EARTH, ISN'T IT, MY FRIEND? I CAN **FEEL** IT!

YES...IT'S EARTH...AT SOME **SUSPENDED** POINT IN TIME! AND YET SOME-ONE, OR SOME**THING** IS STILL ABLE TO FUNCTION...

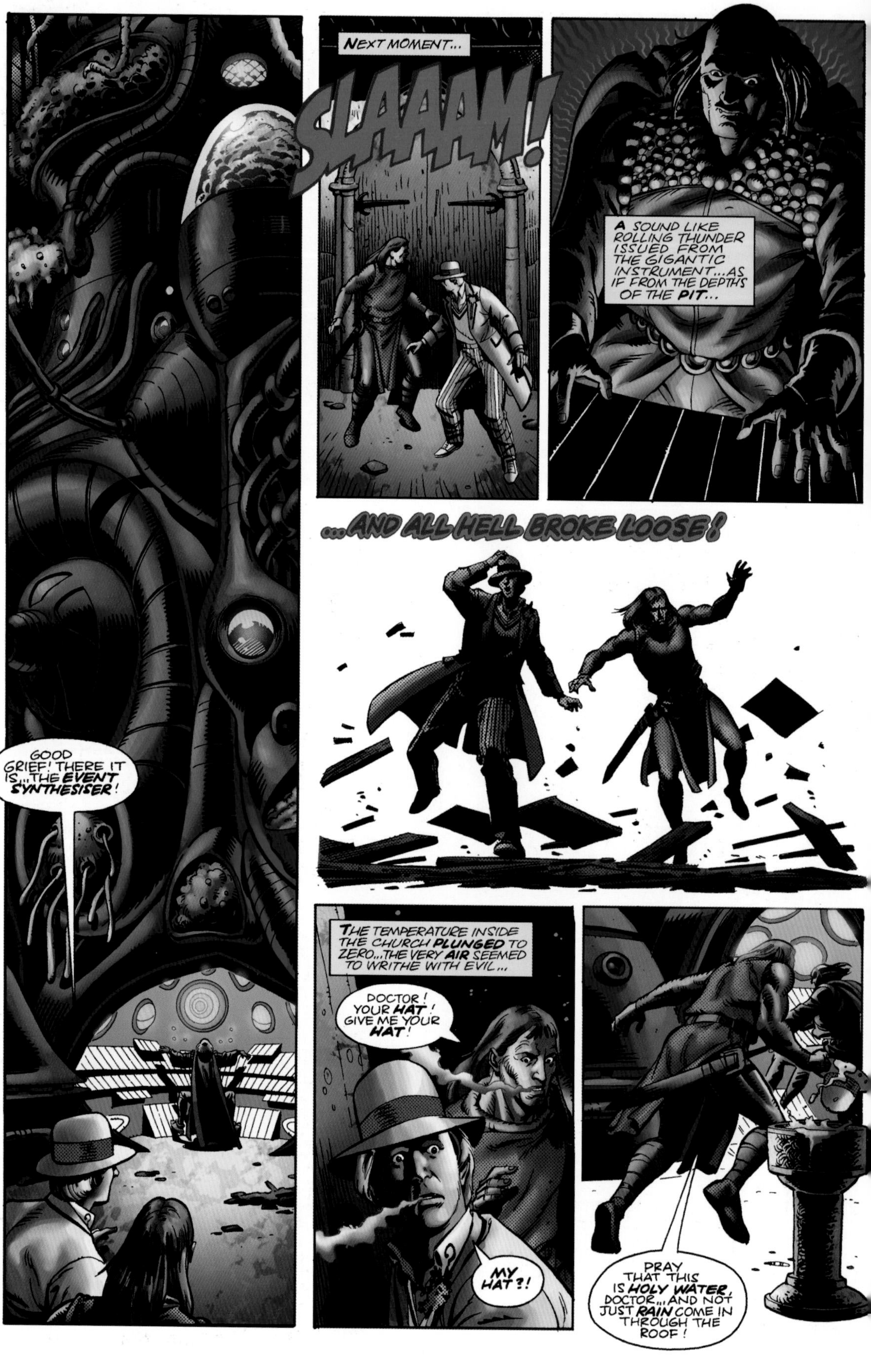
GOOD GRIEF! THERE IT IS... THE EVENT SYNTHESISER!
NEXT MOMENT...
SLAAAM!
A SOUND LIKE ROLLING THUNDER ISSUED FROM THE GIGANTIC INSTRUMENT... AS IF FROM THE DEPTHS OF THE PIT...
...AND ALL HELL BROKE LOOSE!
THE TEMPERATURE INSIDE THE CHURCH PLUNGED TO ZERO... THE VERY AIR SEEMED TO WRITHE WITH EVIL...
DOCTOR! YOUR HAT! GIVE ME YOUR HAT!
MY HAT?!
PRAY THAT THIS IS HOLY WATER, DOCTOR... AND NOT JUST RAIN COME IN THROUGH THE ROOF!

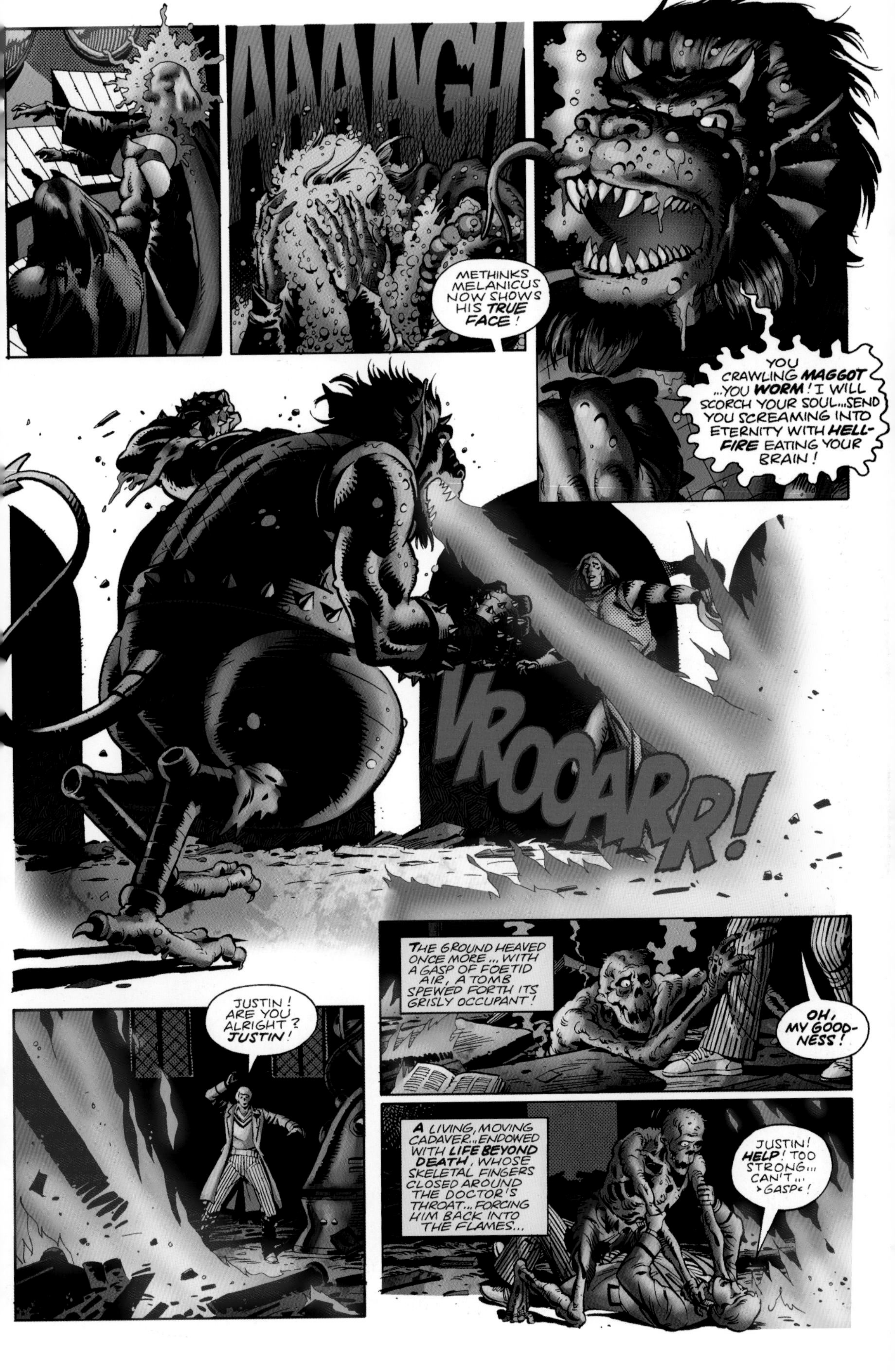
AAAAGH
METHINKS MELANICUS NOW SHOWS HIS TRUE FACE!
YOU CRAWLING MAGGOT ...YOU WORM! I WILL SCORCH YOUR SOUL...SEND YOU SCREAMING INTO ETERNITY WITH HELL-FIRE EATING YOUR BRAIN!
VROOARR!
THE GROUND HEAVED ONCE MORE ... WITH A GASP OF FOETID AIR, A TOMB SPEWED FORTH ITS GRISLY OCCUPANT!
OH, MY GOODNESS!
JUSTIN! ARE YOU ALRIGHT? JUSTIN!
A LIVING, MOVING CADAVER...ENDOWED WITH LIFE BEYOND DEATH, WHOSE SKELETAL FINGERS CLOSED AROUND THE DOCTOR'S THROAT... FORCING HIM BACK INTO THE FLAMES...
JUSTIN! HELP! TOO STRONG... CAN'T... *GASP*!

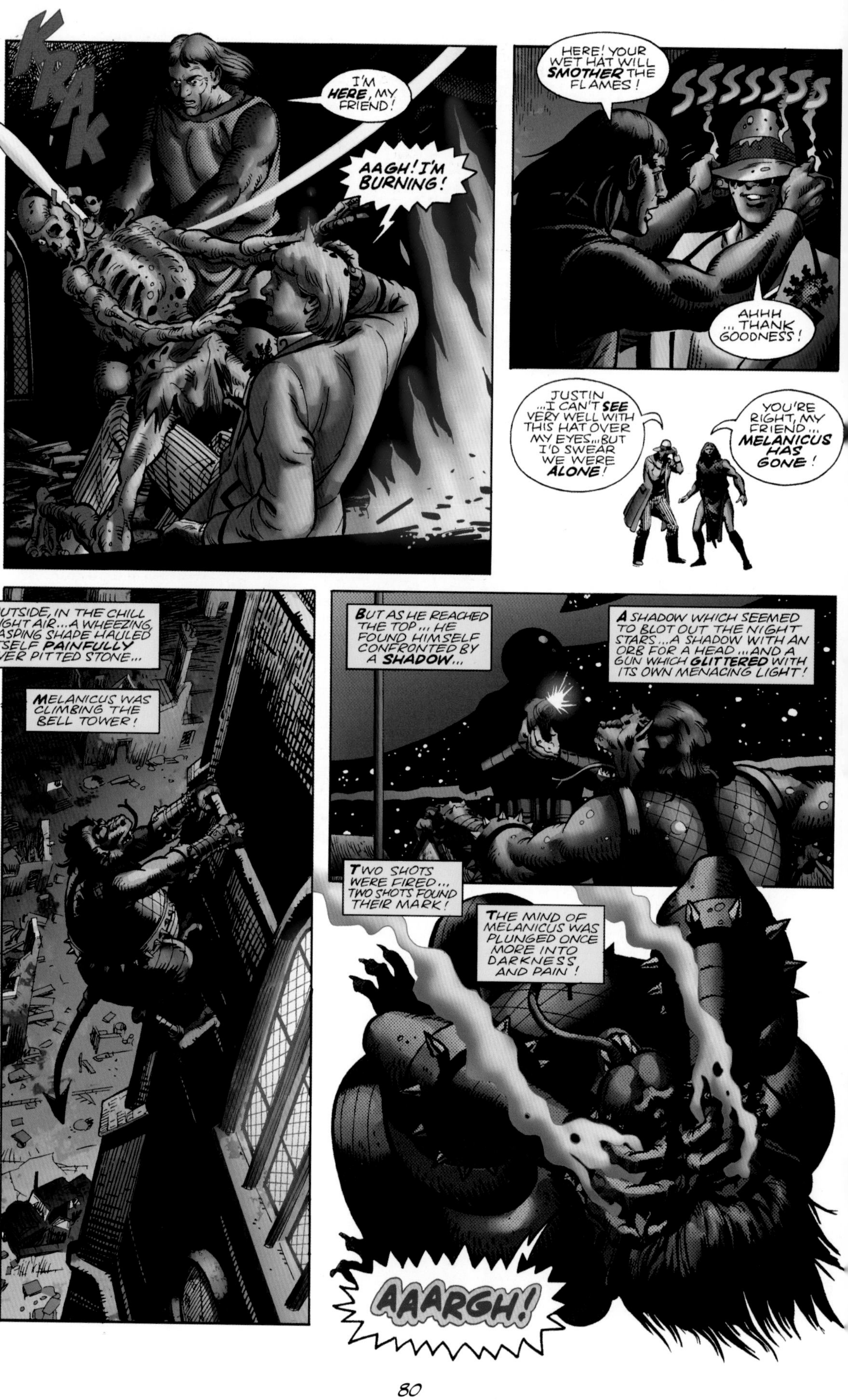
KRAK
I'M HERE, MY FRIEND!
AAGH! I'M BURNING!
HERE! YOUR WET HAT WILL SMOTHER THE FLAMES!
SSSSSSS
AHHH ... THANK GOODNESS!
JUSTIN ...I CAN'T SEE VERY WELL WITH THIS HAT OVER MY EYES...BUT I'D SWEAR WE WERE ALONE!
YOU'RE RIGHT, MY FRIEND... MELANICUS HAS GONE!
OUTSIDE, IN THE CHILL NIGHT AIR... A WHEEZING, GASPING SHAPE HAULED ITSELF PAINFULLY OVER PITTED STONE...
MELANICUS WAS CLIMBING THE BELL TOWER!
BUT AS HE REACHED THE TOP... HE FOUND HIMSELF CONFRONTED BY A SHADOW...
A SHADOW WHICH SEEMED TO BLOT OUT THE NIGHT STARS... A SHADOW WITH AN ORB FOR A HEAD... AND A GUN WHICH GLITTERED WITH ITS OWN MENACING LIGHT!
TWO SHOTS WERE FIRED... TWO SHOTS FOUND THEIR MARK!
THE MIND OF MELANICUS WAS PLUNGED ONCE MORE INTO DARKNESS AND PAIN!
AAARGH!

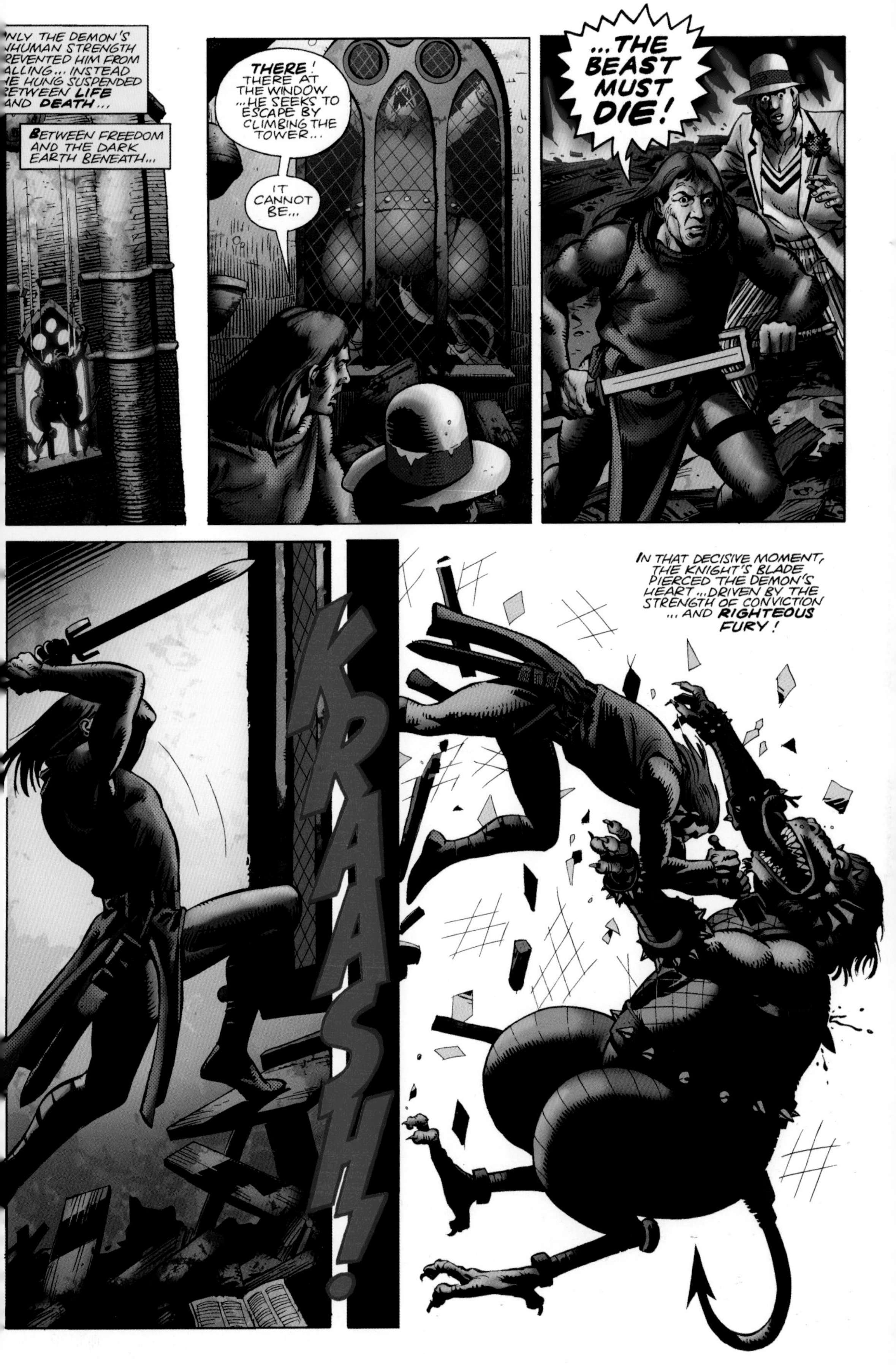
NLY THE DEMON'S NHUMAN STRENGTH REVENTED HIM FROM ALLING... INSTEAD HE HUNG SUSPENDED BETWEEN LIFE AND DEATH...
BETWEEN FREEDOM AND THE DARK EARTH BENEATH...
THERE! THERE AT THE WINDOW ...HE SEEKS TO ESCAPE BY CLIMBING THE TOWER...
IT CANNOT BE...
...THE BEAST MUST DIE!
KRAASH!
IN THAT DECISIVE MOMENT, THE KNIGHT'S BLADE PIERCED THE DEMON'S HEART...DRIVEN BY THE STRENGTH OF CONVICTION ...AND RIGHTEOUS FURY!

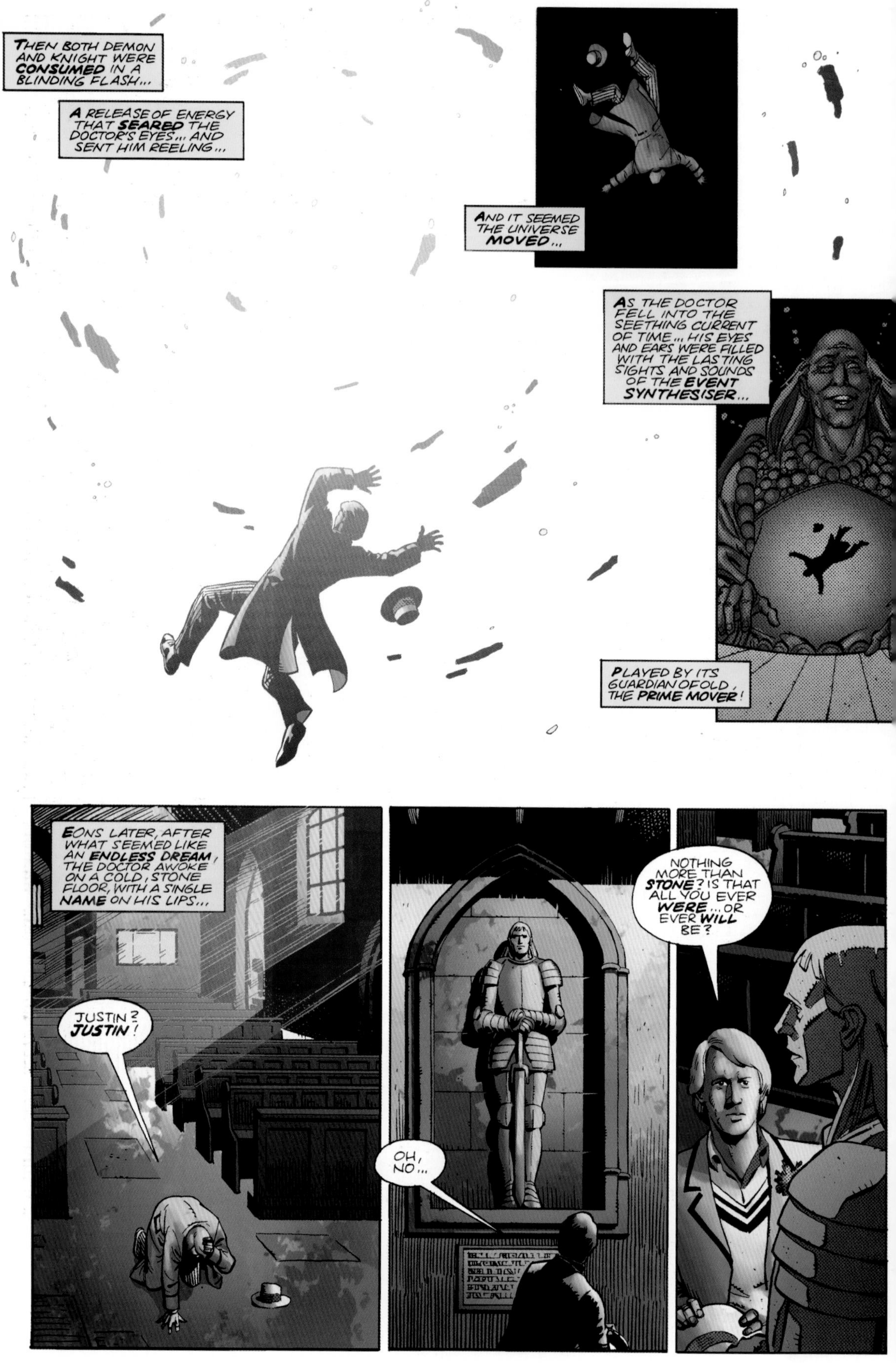
THEN BOTH DEMON AND KNIGHT WERE CONSUMED IN A BLINDING FLASH...
A RELEASE OF ENERGY THAT SEARED THE DOCTOR'S EYES... AND SENT HIM REELING...
AND IT SEEMED THE UNIVERSE MOVED...
AS THE DOCTOR FELL INTO THE SEETHING CURRENT OF TIME... HIS EYES AND EARS WERE FILLED WITH THE LASTING SIGHTS AND SOUNDS OF THE EVENT SYNTHESISER...
PLAYED BY ITS GUARDIAN OF OLD, THE PRIME MOVER!
EONS LATER, AFTER WHAT SEEMED LIKE AN ENDLESS DREAM, THE DOCTOR AWOKE ON A COLD, STONE FLOOR, WITH A SINGLE NAME ON HIS LIPS...
JUSTIN? JUSTIN!
OH, NO...
NOTHING MORE THAN STONE? IS THAT ALL YOU EVER WERE... OR EVER WILL BE?

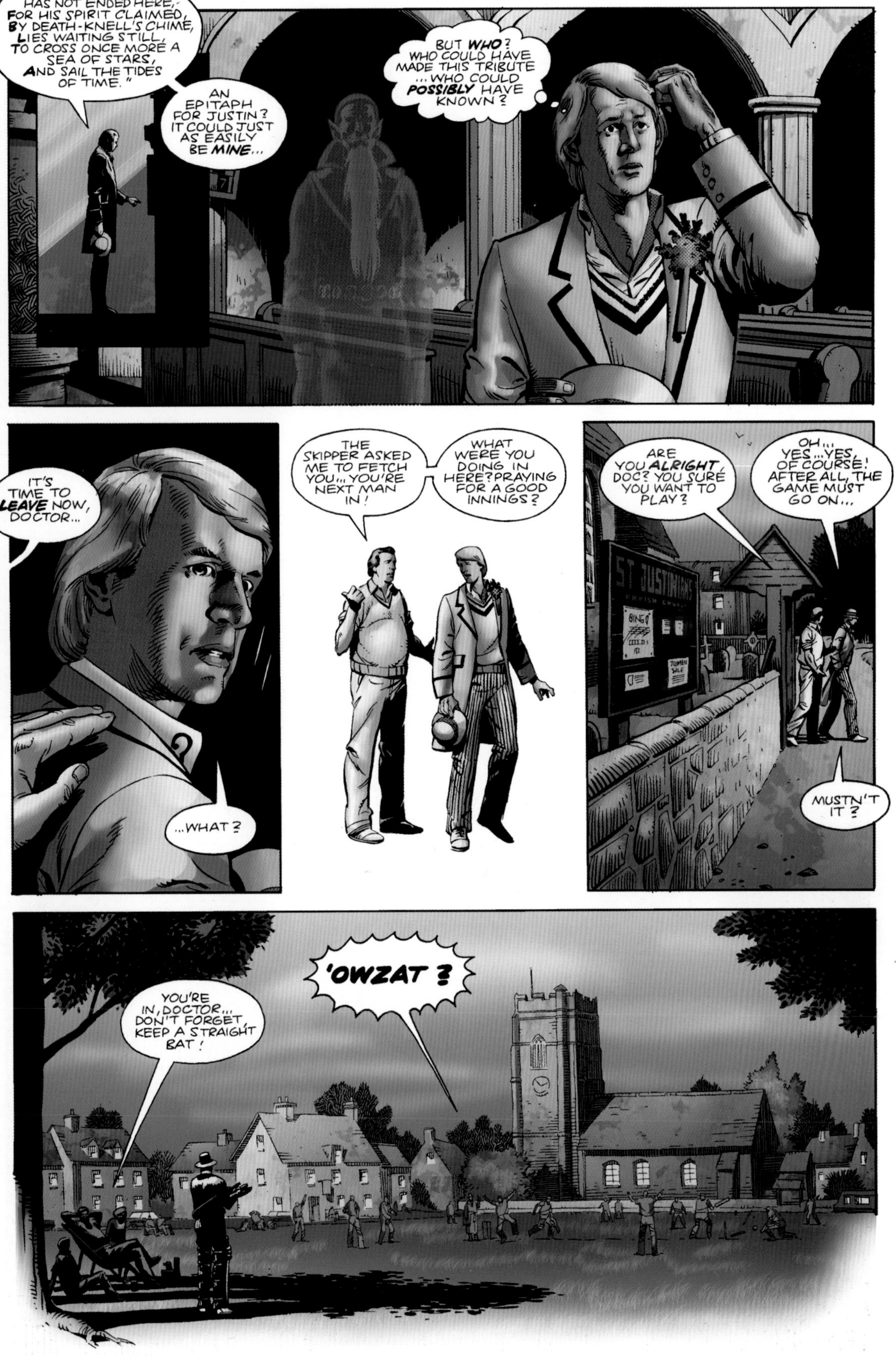

"THE JOURNEY HAS NOT ENDED HERE, FOR HIS SPIRIT CLAIMED, BY DEATH-KNELL'S CHIME, LIES WAITING STILL, TO CROSS ONCE MORE A SEA OF STARS, AND SAIL THE TIDES OF TIME."
AN EPITAPH FOR JUSTIN? IT COULD JUST AS EASILY BE MINE...
BUT WHO? WHO COULD HAVE MADE THIS TRIBUTE ...WHO COULD POSSIBLY HAVE KNOWN?
IT'S TIME TO LEAVE NOW, DOCTOR...
...WHAT?
THE SKIPPER ASKED ME TO FETCH YOU... YOU'RE NEXT MAN IN!
WHAT WERE YOU DOING IN HERE? PRAYING FOR A GOOD INNINGS?
ARE YOU ALRIGHT, DOC? YOU SURE YOU WANT TO PLAY?
OH... YES...YES, OF COURSE! AFTER ALL, THE GAME MUST GO ON...
MUSTN'T IT?
'OWZAT?
YOU'RE IN, DOCTOR... DON'T FORGET, KEEP A STRAIGHT BAT!

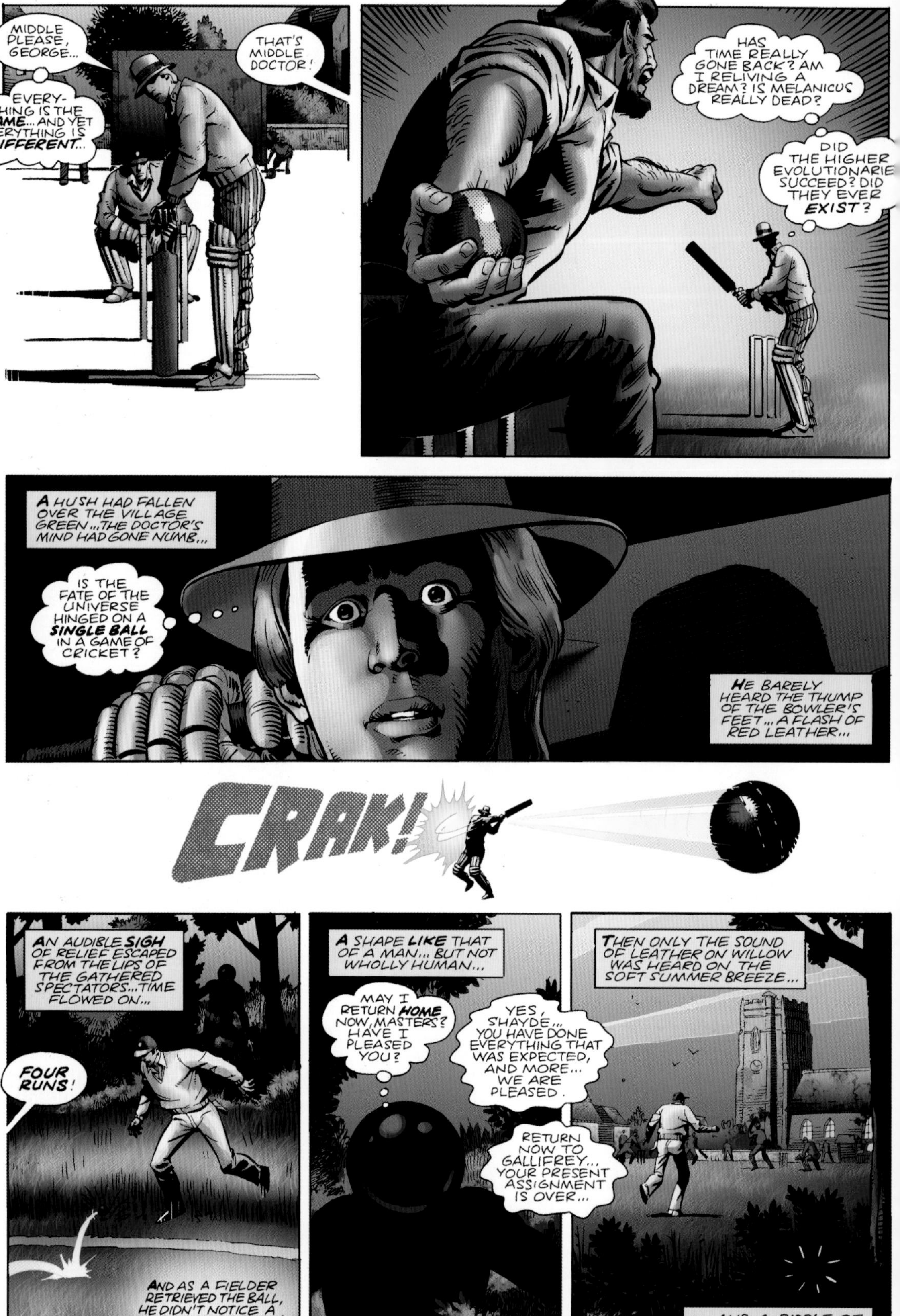
MIDDLE PLEASE, GEORGE...
THAT'S MIDDLE DOCTOR!
EVERY-THING IS THE SAME... AND YET EVERYTHING IS DIFFERENT...
HAS TIME REALLY GONE BACK? AM I RELIVING A DREAM? IS MELANICUS REALLY DEAD?
DID THE HIGHER EVOLUTIONARIE SUCCEED? DID THEY EVER EXIST?
A HUSH HAD FALLEN OVER THE VILLAGE GREEN... THE DOCTOR'S MIND HAD GONE NUMB...
IS THE FATE OF THE UNIVERSE HINGED ON A SINGLE BALL IN A GAME OF CRICKET?
HE BARELY HEARD THE THUMP OF THE BOWLER'S FEET... A FLASH OF RED LEATHER...
CRAK!
AN AUDIBLE SIGH OF RELIEF ESCAPED FROM THE LIPS OF THE GATHERED SPECTATORS... TIME FLOWED ON...
FOUR RUNS!
AND AS A FIELDER RETRIEVED THE BALL, HE DIDN'T NOTICE A DARK SHAPE DETACH ITSELF FROM THE DAPPLED SHADOWS...
A SHAPE LIKE THAT OF A MAN... BUT NOT WHOLLY HUMAN...
MAY I RETURN HOME NOW, MASTERS? HAVE I PLEASED YOU?
YES, SHAYDE... YOU HAVE DONE EVERYTHING THAT WAS EXPECTED, AND MORE... WE ARE PLEASED.
RETURN NOW TO GALLIFREY... YOUR PRESENT ASSIGNMENT IS OVER...
THEN ONLY THE SOUND OF LEATHER ON WILLOW WAS HEARD ON THE SOFT SUMMER BREEZE...
... AND A RIPPLE OF LOW LAUGHTER IN THE AFTERNOON SUN...
THE END.

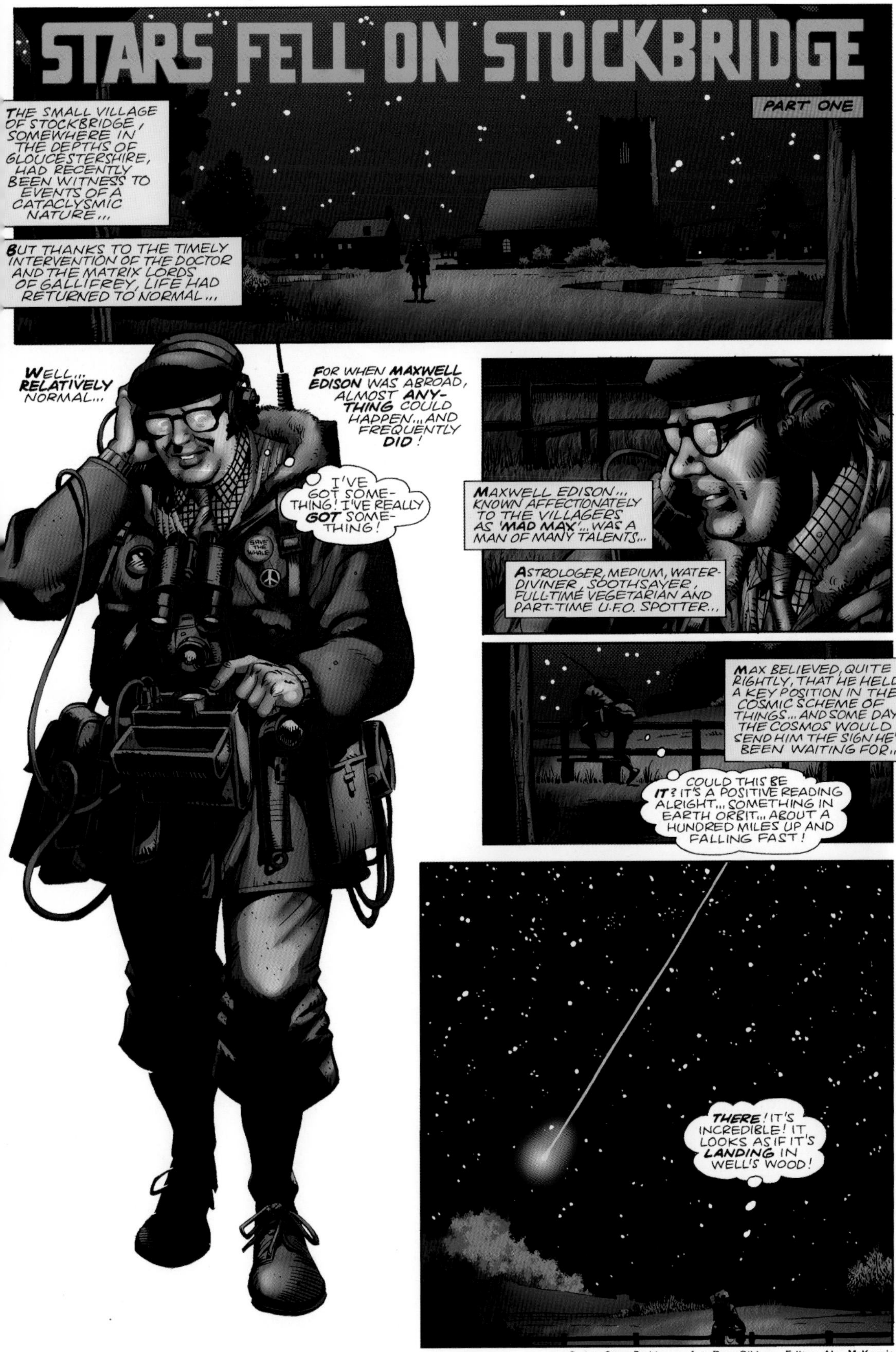

STARS FELL ON STOCKBRIDGE
PART ONE
THE SMALL VILLAGE OF STOCKBRIDGE, SOMEWHERE IN THE DEPTHS OF GLOUCESTERSHIRE, HAD RECENTLY BEEN WITNESS TO EVENTS OF A CATACLYSMIC NATURE...
BUT THANKS TO THE TIMELY INTERVENTION OF THE DOCTOR AND THE MATRIX LORDS OF GALLIFREY, LIFE HAD RETURNED TO NORMAL...
WELL... RELATIVELY NORMAL...
FOR WHEN MAXWELL EDISON WAS ABROAD, ALMOST ANY-THING COULD HAPPEN... AND FREQUENTLY DID!
I'VE GOT SOME-THING! I'VE REALLY GOT SOME-THING!
SAVE THE WHALE
MAXWELL EDISON... KNOWN AFFECTIONATELY TO THE VILLAGERS AS 'MAD MAX'... WAS A MAN OF MANY TALENTS...
ASTROLOGER, MEDIUM, WATER-DIVINER, SOOTHSAYER, FULL-TIME VEGETARIAN AND PART-TIME U.F.O. SPOTTER...
MAX BELIEVED, QUITE RIGHTLY, THAT HE HELD A KEY POSITION IN THE COSMIC SCHEME OF THINGS... AND SOME DAY THE COSMOS WOULD SEND HIM THE SIGN HE'D BEEN WAITING FOR...
COULD THIS BE IT? IT'S A POSITIVE READING ALRIGHT... SOMETHING IN EARTH ORBIT... ABOUT A HUNDRED MILES UP AND FALLING FAST!
THERE! IT'S INCREDIBLE! IT LOOKS AS IF IT'S LANDING IN WELL'S WOOD!

Script: Steve Parkhouse Art: Dave Gibbons Editor: Alan McKenzie

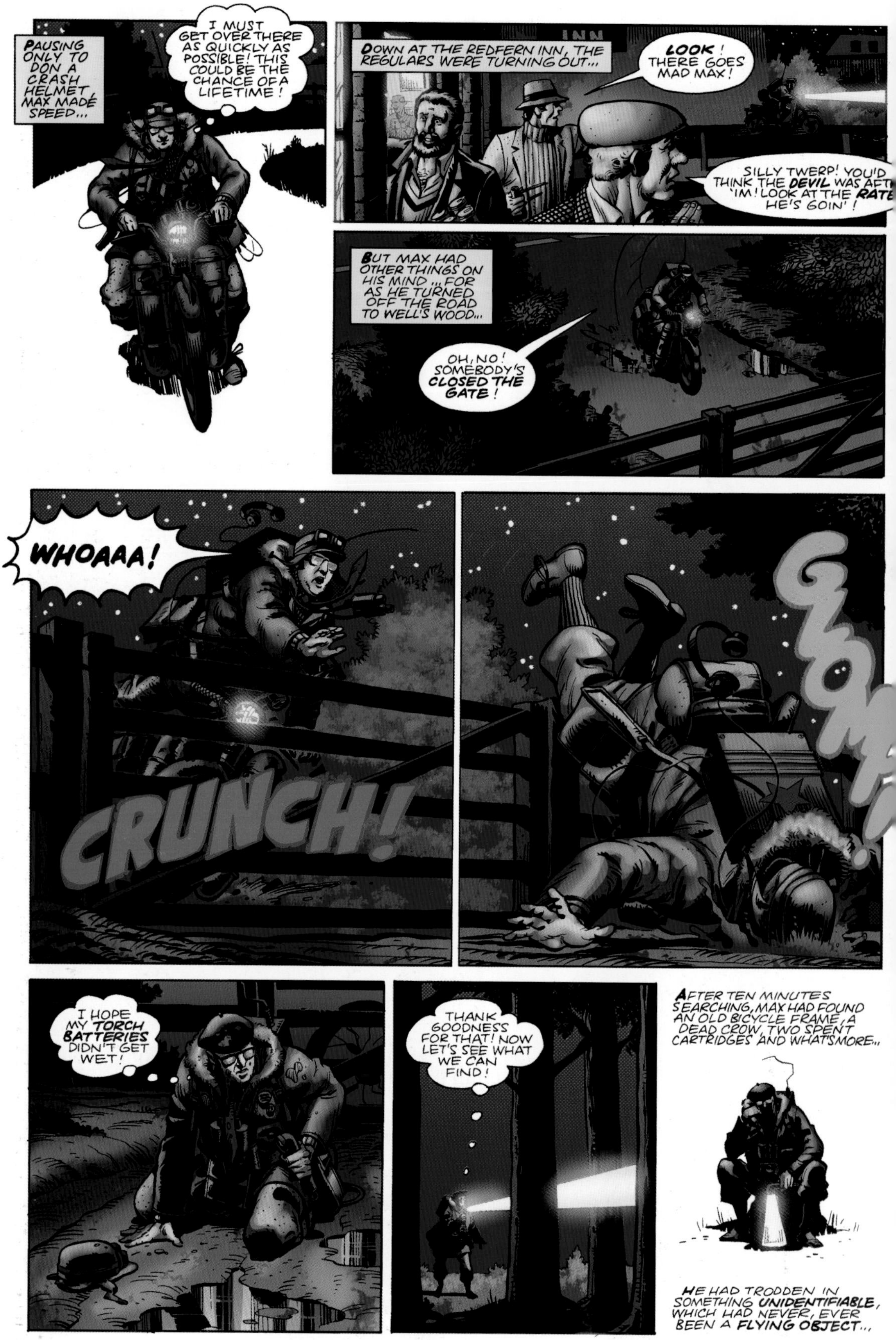
PAUSING ONLY TO DON A CRASH HELMET, MAX MADE SPEED...
I MUST GET OVER THERE AS QUICKLY AS POSSIBLE! THIS COULD BE THE CHANCE OF A LIFETIME!
INN
DOWN AT THE REDFERN INN, THE REGULARS WERE TURNING OUT...
LOOK! THERE GOES MAD MAX!
SILLY TWERP! YOU'D THINK THE DEVIL WAS AFT 'IM! LOOK AT THE RATE HE'S GOIN'!
BUT MAX HAD OTHER THINGS ON HIS MIND... FOR AS HE TURNED OFF THE ROAD TO WELL'S WOOD...
OH, NO! SOMEBODY'S CLOSED THE GATE!
WHOAAA!
CRUNCH!
I HOPE MY TORCH BATTERIES DIDN'T GET WET!
THANK GOODNESS FOR THAT! NOW LET'S SEE WHAT WE CAN FIND!
AFTER TEN MINUTES SEARCHING, MAX HAD FOUND AN OLD BICYCLE FRAME, A DEAD CROW, TWO SPENT CARTRIDGES AND WHAT'S MORE...
HE HAD TRODDEN IN SOMETHING UNIDENTIFIABLE, WHICH HAD NEVER, EVER BEEN A FLYING OBJECT...

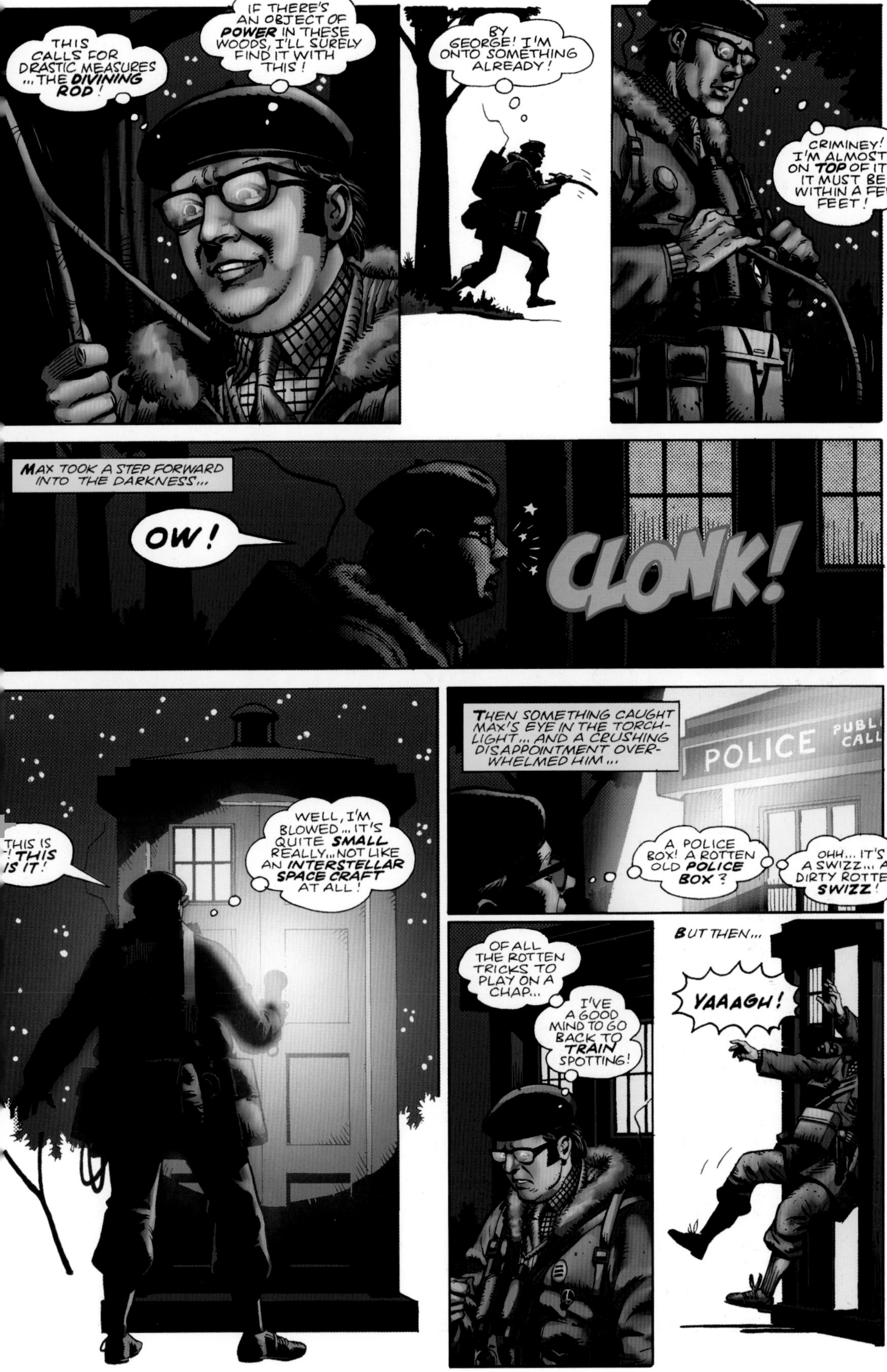
THIS CALLS FOR DRASTIC MEASURES ...THE DIVINING ROD!
IF THERE'S AN OBJECT OF POWER IN THESE WOODS, I'LL SURELY FIND IT WITH THIS!
BY GEORGE! I'M ONTO SOMETHING ALREADY!
CRIMINEY! I'M ALMOST ON TOP OF IT! IT MUST BE WITHIN A FEW FEET!
MAX TOOK A STEP FORWARD INTO THE DARKNESS...
OW!
CLONK!
THIS IS -! THIS IS IT!
WELL, I'M BLOWED... IT'S QUITE SMALL REALLY... NOT LIKE AN INTERSTELLAR SPACE CRAFT AT ALL!
THEN SOMETHING CAUGHT MAX'S EYE IN THE TORCH-LIGHT... AND A CRUSHING DISAPPOINTMENT OVER-WHELMED HIM...
POLICE
PUBLI CALL
A POLICE BOX! A ROTTEN OLD POLICE BOX?
OHH... IT'S A SWIZZ... A DIRTY ROTTEN SWIZZ!
OF ALL THE ROTTEN TRICKS TO PLAY ON A CHAP...
I'VE A GOOD MIND TO GO BACK TO TRAIN SPOTTING!
BUT THEN...
YAAAGH!

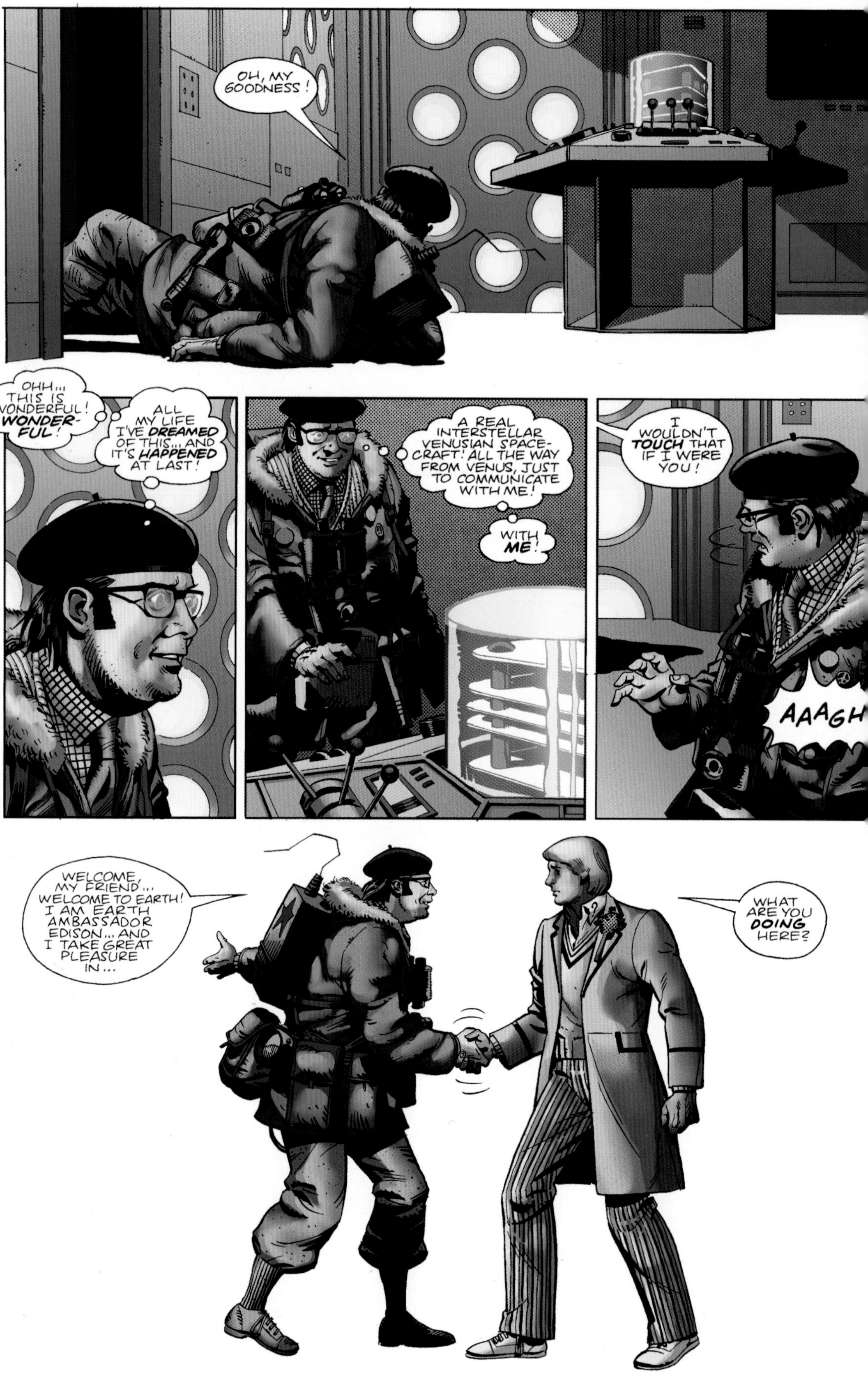
OH, MY GOODNESS!
OHH... THIS IS WONDERFUL! WONDERFUL!
ALL MY LIFE I'VE DREAMED OF THIS... AND IT'S HAPPENED AT LAST!
A REAL INTERSTELLAR VENUSIAN SPACE-CRAFT! ALL THE WAY FROM VENUS, JUST TO COMMUNICATE WITH ME!
WITH ME!
I WOULDN'T TOUCH THAT IF I WERE YOU!
AAAGH
WELCOME, MY FRIEND... WELCOME TO EARTH! I AM EARTH AMBASSADOR EDISON... AND I TAKE GREAT PLEASURE IN...
WHAT ARE YOU DOING HERE?

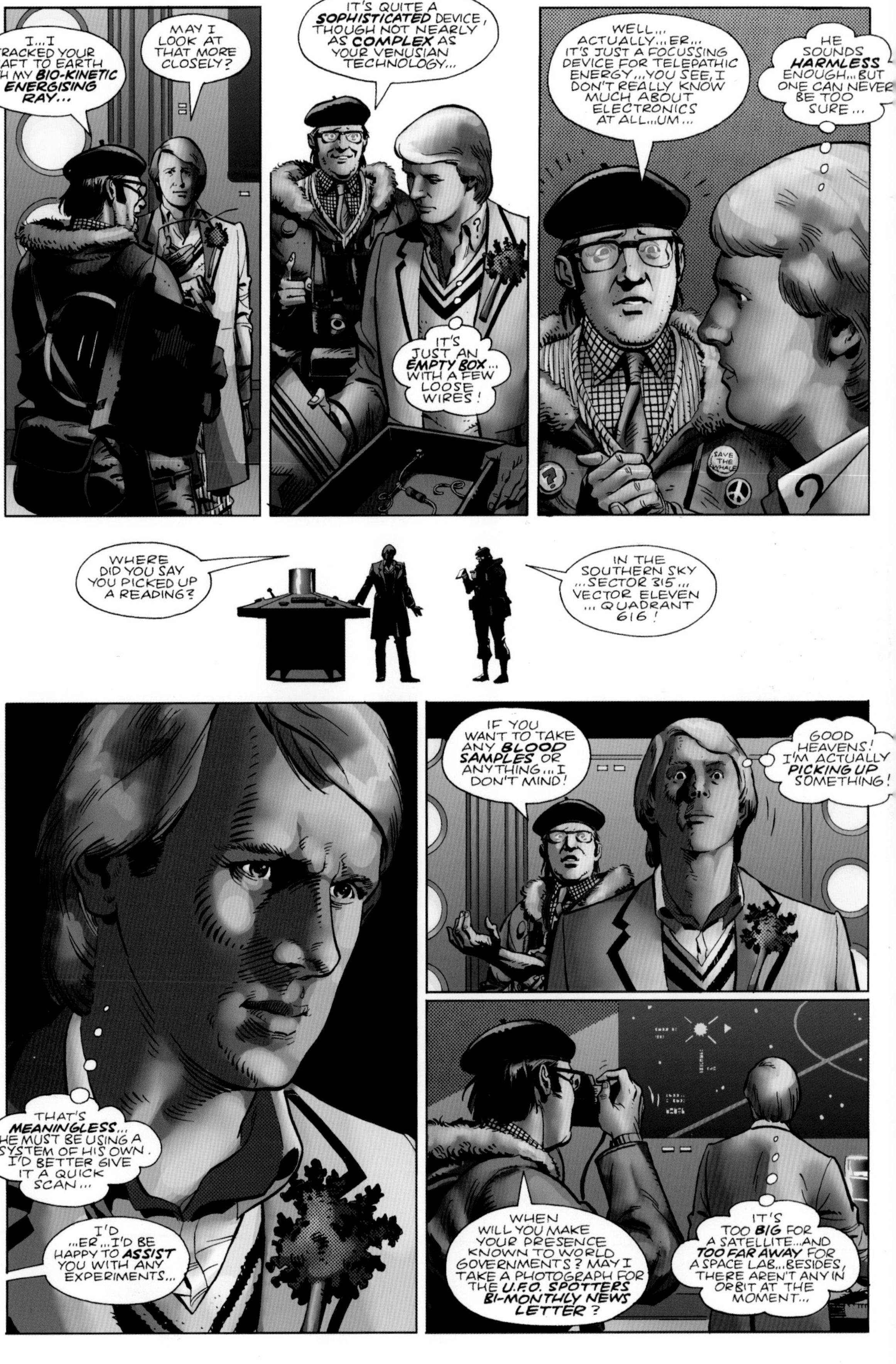

I...I TRACKED YOUR RAFT TO EARTH TH MY BIO-KINETIC ENERGISING RAY...
MAY I LOOK AT THAT MORE CLOSELY?
IT'S QUITE A SOPHISTICATED DEVICE, THOUGH NOT NEARLY AS COMPLEX AS YOUR VENUSIAN TECHNOLOGY...
IT'S JUST AN EMPTY BOX... WITH A FEW LOOSE WIRES!
WELL... ACTUALLY... ER... IT'S JUST A FOCUSSING DEVICE FOR TELEPATHIC ENERGY... YOU SEE, I DON'T REALLY KNOW MUCH ABOUT ELECTRONICS AT ALL... UM...
HE SOUNDS HARMLESS ENOUGH... BUT ONE CAN NEVER BE TOO SURE...
SAVE THE WHALE
WHERE DID YOU SAY YOU PICKED UP A READING?
IN THE SOUTHERN SKY ...SECTOR 315... VECTOR ELEVEN ... QUADRANT 616!
THAT'S MEANINGLESS... HE MUST BE USING A SYSTEM OF HIS OWN. I'D BETTER GIVE IT A QUICK SCAN...
I'D ...ER... I'D BE HAPPY TO ASSIST YOU WITH ANY EXPERIMENTS...
IF YOU WANT TO TAKE ANY BLOOD SAMPLES OR ANYTHING... I DON'T MIND!
GOOD HEAVENS! I'M ACTUALLY PICKING UP SOMETHING!
WHEN WILL YOU MAKE YOUR PRESENCE KNOWN TO WORLD GOVERNMENTS? MAY I TAKE A PHOTOGRAPH FOR THE U.F.O. SPOTTERS BI-MONTHLY NEWS LETTER?
IT'S TOO BIG FOR A SATELLITE... AND TOO FAR AWAY FOR A SPACE LAB... BESIDES, THERE AREN'T ANY IN ORBIT AT THE MOMENT...

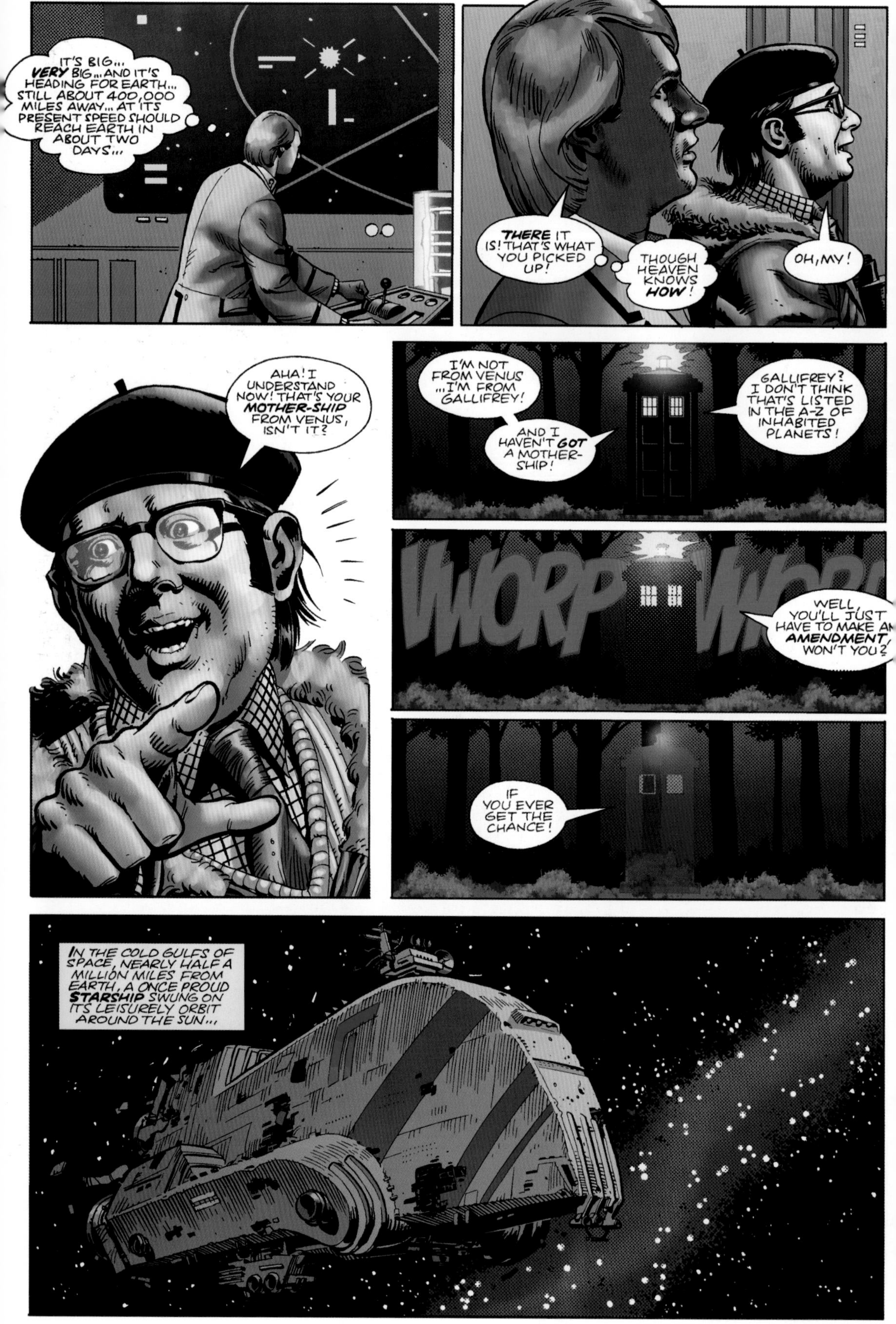
IT'S BIG... VERY BIG... AND IT'S HEADING FOR EARTH... STILL ABOUT 400,000 MILES AWAY... AT ITS PRESENT SPEED SHOULD REACH EARTH IN ABOUT TWO DAYS...
THERE IT IS! THAT'S WHAT YOU PICKED UP!
THOUGH HEAVEN KNOWS HOW!
OH, MY!
AHA! I UNDERSTAND NOW! THAT'S YOUR MOTHER-SHIP FROM VENUS, ISN'T IT?
I'M NOT FROM VENUS ...I'M FROM GALLIFREY!
AND I HAVEN'T GOT A MOTHER-SHIP!
GALLIFREY? I DON'T THINK THAT'S LISTED IN THE A-Z OF INHABITED PLANETS!
VWORP
WELL, YOU'LL JUST HAVE TO MAKE AN AMENDMENT, WON'T YOU?
IF YOU EVER GET THE CHANCE!
IN THE COLD GULFS OF SPACE, NEARLY HALF A MILLION MILES FROM EARTH, A ONCE PROUD STARSHIP SWUNG ON ITS LEISURELY ORBIT AROUND THE SUN...

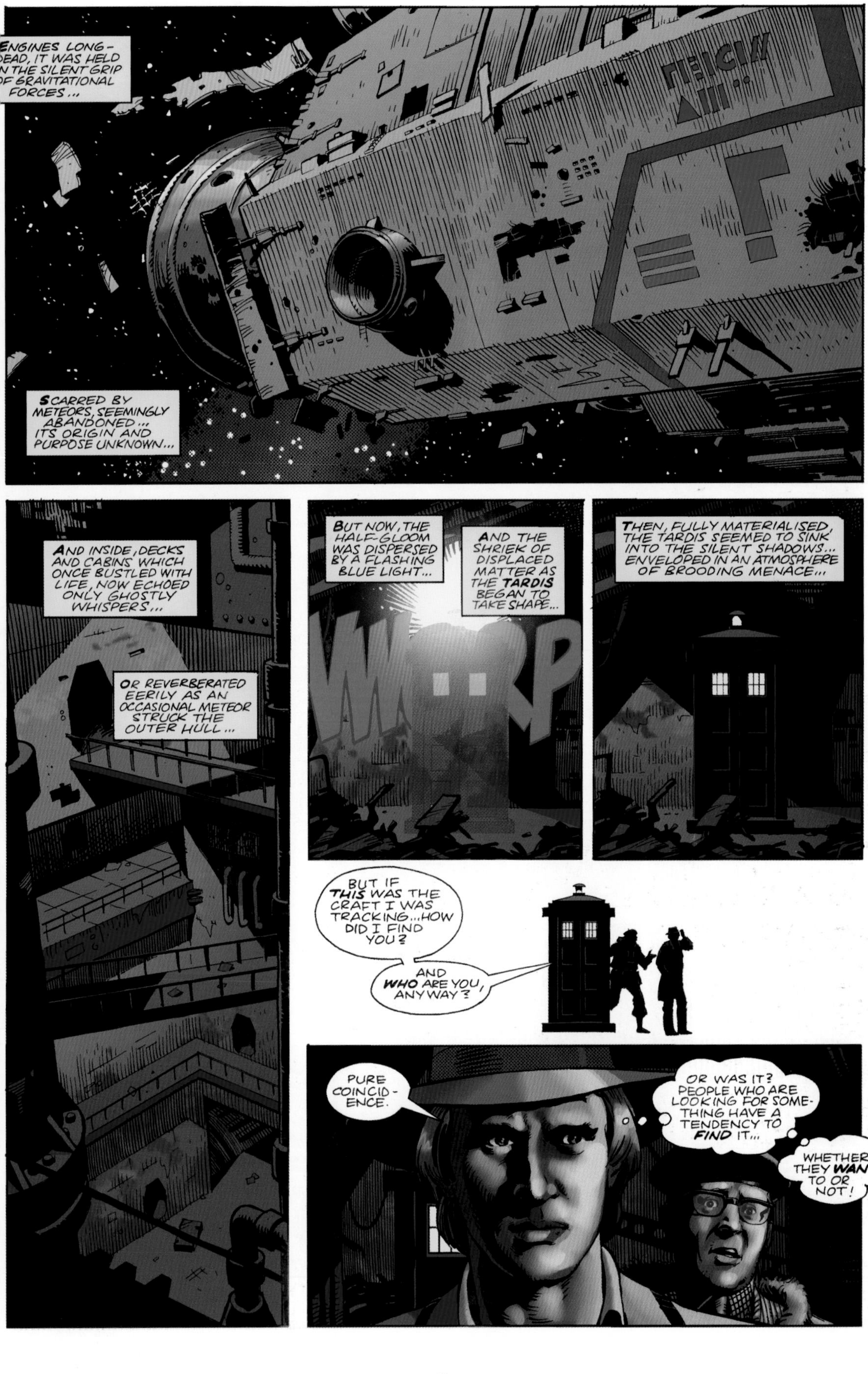
ENGINES LONG-DEAD, IT WAS HELD IN THE SILENT GRIP OF GRAVITATIONAL FORCES...
SCARRED BY METEORS, SEEMINGLY ABANDONED... ITS ORIGIN AND PURPOSE UNKNOWN...
AND INSIDE, DECKS AND CABINS WHICH ONCE BUSTLED WITH LIFE, NOW ECHOED ONLY GHOSTLY WHISPERS...
OR REVERBERATED EERILY AS AN OCCASIONAL METEOR STRUCK THE OUTER HULL...
BUT NOW, THE HALF-GLOOM WAS DISPERSED BY A FLASHING BLUE LIGHT...
AND THE SHRIEK OF DISPLACED MATTER AS THE TARDIS BEGAN TO TAKE SHAPE...
THEN, FULLY MATERIALISED, THE TARDIS SEEMED TO SINK INTO THE SILENT SHADOWS... ENVELOPED IN AN ATMOSPHERE OF BROODING MENACE...
BUT IF THIS WAS THE CRAFT I WAS TRACKING... HOW DID I FIND YOU?
AND WHO ARE YOU, ANYWAY?
PURE COINCIDENCE.
OR WAS IT? PEOPLE WHO ARE LOOKING FOR SOMETHING HAVE A TENDENCY TO FIND IT...
WHETHER THEY WANT TO OR NOT!

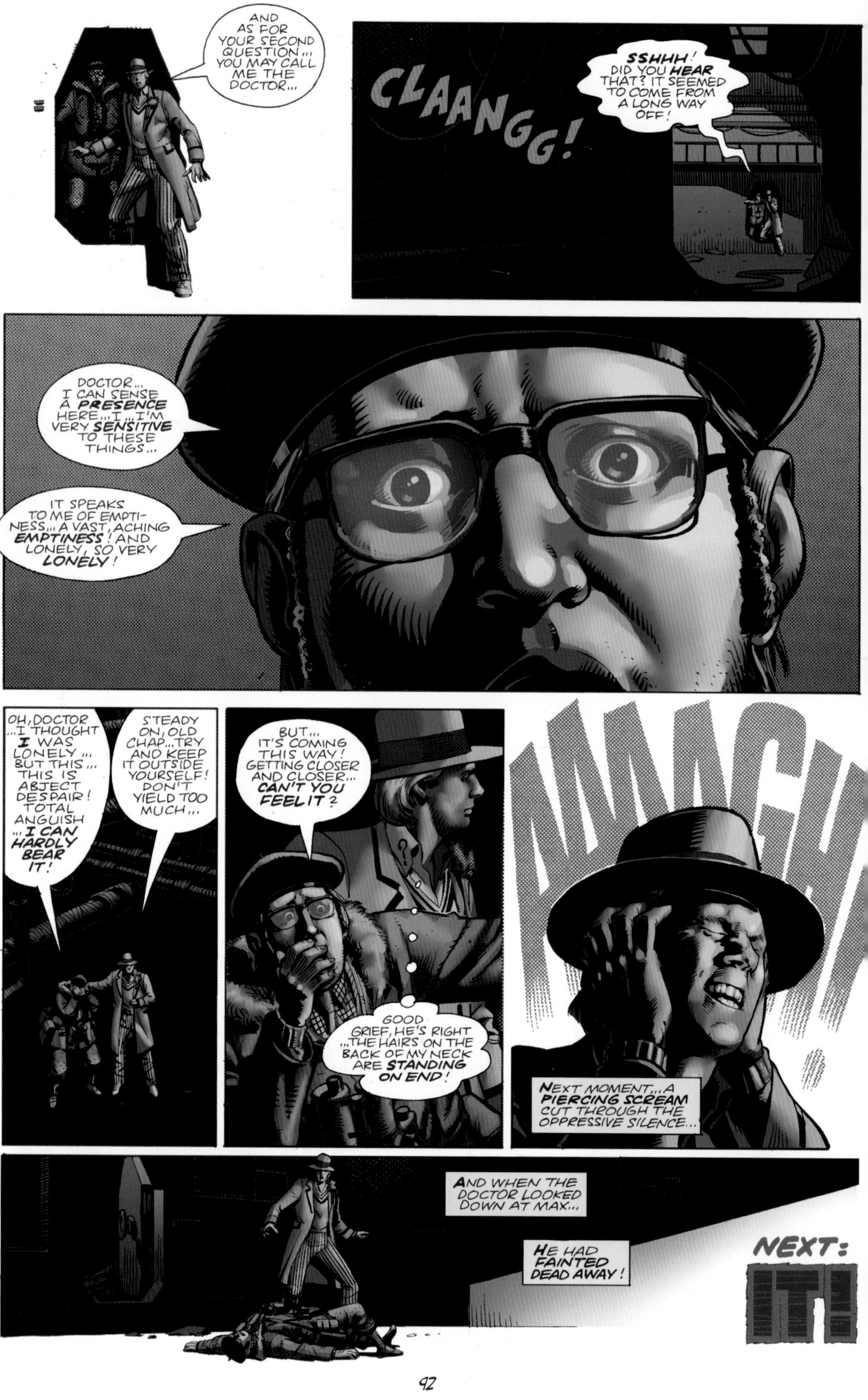
AND AS FOR YOUR SECOND QUESTION... YOU MAY CALL ME THE DOCTOR...
CLAANGG!
SSHHH! DID YOU HEAR THAT? IT SEEMED TO COME FROM A LONG WAY OFF!
DOCTOR... I CAN SENSE A PRESENCE HERE... I... I'M VERY SENSITIVE TO THESE THINGS...
IT SPEAKS TO ME OF EMPTINESS... A VAST, ACHING EMPTINESS! AND LONELY, SO VERY LONELY!
OH, DOCTOR ...I THOUGHT I WAS LONELY... BUT THIS... THIS IS ABJECT DESPAIR! TOTAL ANGUISH ...I CAN HARDLY BEAR IT!
STEADY ON, OLD CHAP... TRY AND KEEP IT OUTSIDE YOURSELF! DON'T YIELD TOO MUCH...
BUT... IT'S COMING THIS WAY! GETTING CLOSER AND CLOSER... CAN'T YOU FEEL IT?
GOOD GRIEF, HE'S RIGHT ...THE HAIRS ON THE BACK OF MY NECK ARE STANDING ON END!
NEXT MOMENT... A PIERCING SCREAM CUT THROUGH THE OPPRESSIVE SILENCE...
AND WHEN THE DOCTOR LOOKED DOWN AT MAX...
HE HAD FAINTED DEAD AWAY!
NEXT: IT!

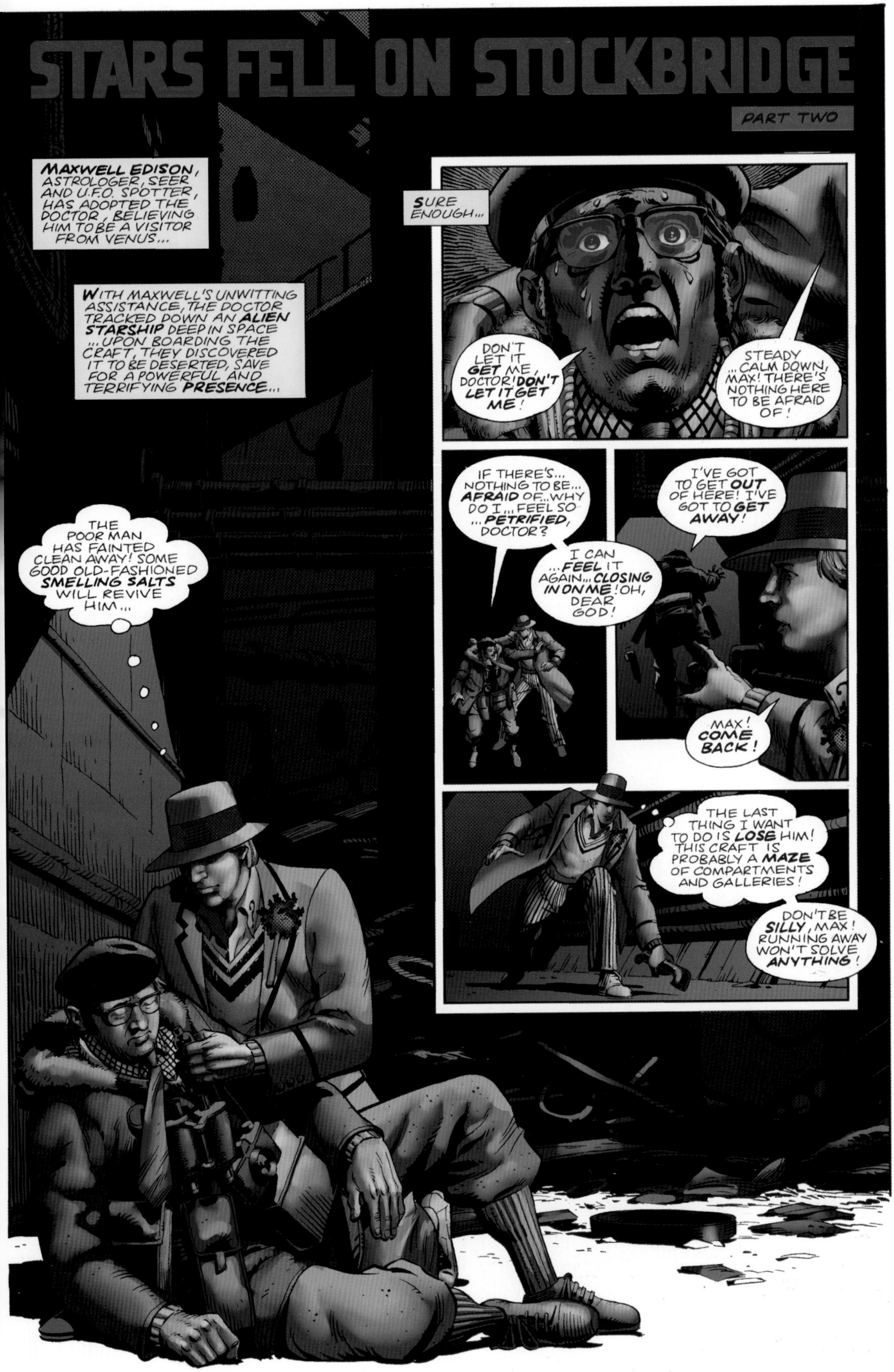

STARS FELL ON STOCKBRIDGE
PART TWO
MAXWELL EDISON, ASTROLOGER, SEER AND U.F.O. SPOTTER, HAS ADOPTED THE DOCTOR, BELIEVING HIM TO BE A VISITOR FROM VENUS...
WITH MAXWELL'S UNWITTING ASSISTANCE, THE DOCTOR TRACKED DOWN AN ALIEN STARSHIP DEEP IN SPACE ...UPON BOARDING THE CRAFT, THEY DISCOVERED IT TO BE DESERTED, SAVE FOR A POWERFUL AND TERRIFYING PRESENCE...
SURE ENOUGH...
DON'T LET IT GET ME, DOCTOR! DON'T LET IT GET ME!
STEADY ...CALM DOWN, MAX! THERE'S NOTHING HERE TO BE AFRAID OF!
IF THERE'S... NOTHING TO BE... AFRAID OF...WHY DO I... FEEL SO ...PETRIFIED, DOCTOR?
I CAN ...FEEL IT AGAIN... CLOSING IN ON ME! OH, DEAR GOD!
I'VE GOT TO GET OUT OF HERE! I'VE GOT TO GET AWAY!
MAX! COME BACK!
THE LAST THING I WANT TO DO IS LOSE HIM! THIS CRAFT IS PROBABLY A MAZE OF COMPARTMENTS AND GALLERIES!
DON'T BE SILLY, MAX! RUNNING AWAY WON'T SOLVE ANYTHING!
THE POOR MAN HAS FAINTED CLEAN AWAY! SOME GOOD OLD-FASHIONED SMELLING SALTS WILL REVIVE HIM...

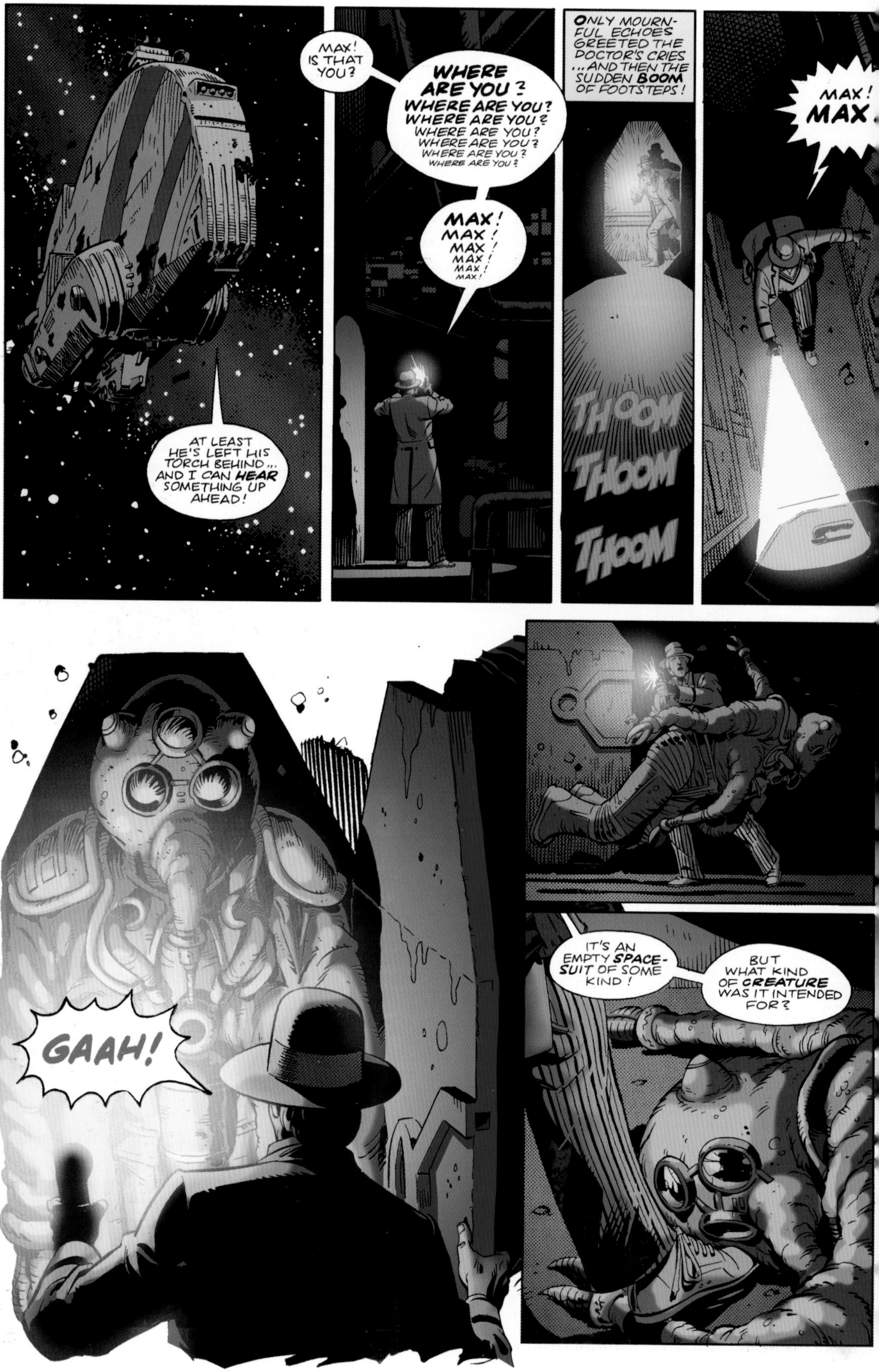

AT LEAST HE'S LEFT HIS TORCH BEHIND... AND I CAN HEAR SOMETHING UP AHEAD!
MAX! IS THAT YOU?
WHERE ARE YOU? WHERE ARE YOU? WHERE ARE YOU? WHERE ARE YOU? WHERE ARE YOU? WHERE ARE YOU? WHERE ARE YOU?
MAX! MAX! MAX! MAX! MAX! MAX!
ONLY MOURNFUL ECHOES GREETED THE DOCTOR'S CRIES ...AND THEN THE SUDDEN BOOM OF FOOTSTEPS!
THOOM THOOM THOOM
MAX! MAX
GAAH!
IT'S AN EMPTY SPACE-SUIT OF SOME KIND!
BUT WHAT KIND OF CREATURE WAS IT INTENDED FOR?

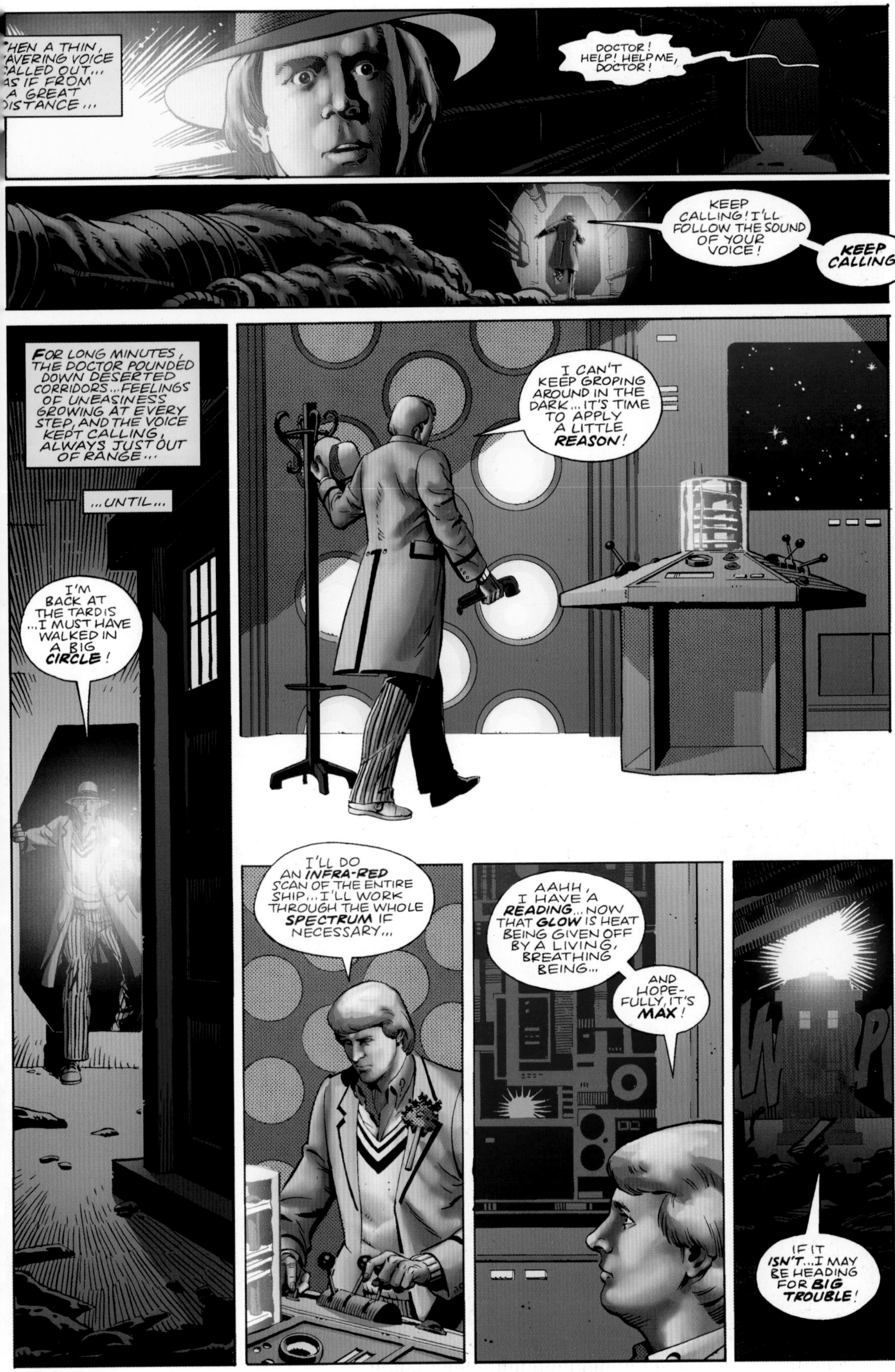
HEN A THIN, AVERING VOICE CALLED OUT... AS IF FROM A GREAT DISTANCE...
DOCTOR! HELP! HELP ME, DOCTOR!
KEEP CALLING! I'LL FOLLOW THE SOUND OF YOUR VOICE!
KEEP CALLING!
FOR LONG MINUTES, THE DOCTOR POUNDED DOWN DESERTED CORRIDORS... FEELINGS OF UNEASINESS GROWING AT EVERY STEP, AND THE VOICE KEPT CALLING, ALWAYS JUST OUT OF RANGE...
...UNTIL...
I'M BACK AT THE TARDIS ...I MUST HAVE WALKED IN A BIG CIRCLE!
I CAN'T KEEP GROPING AROUND IN THE DARK... IT'S TIME TO APPLY A LITTLE REASON!
I'LL DO AN INFRA-RED SCAN OF THE ENTIRE SHIP... I'LL WORK THROUGH THE WHOLE SPECTRUM IF NECESSARY...
AAHH, I HAVE A READING... NOW THAT GLOW IS HEAT BEING GIVEN OFF BY A LIVING, BREATHING BEING...
AND HOPE-FULLY, IT'S MAX!
IF IT ISN'T... I MAY BE HEADING FOR BIG TROUBLE!

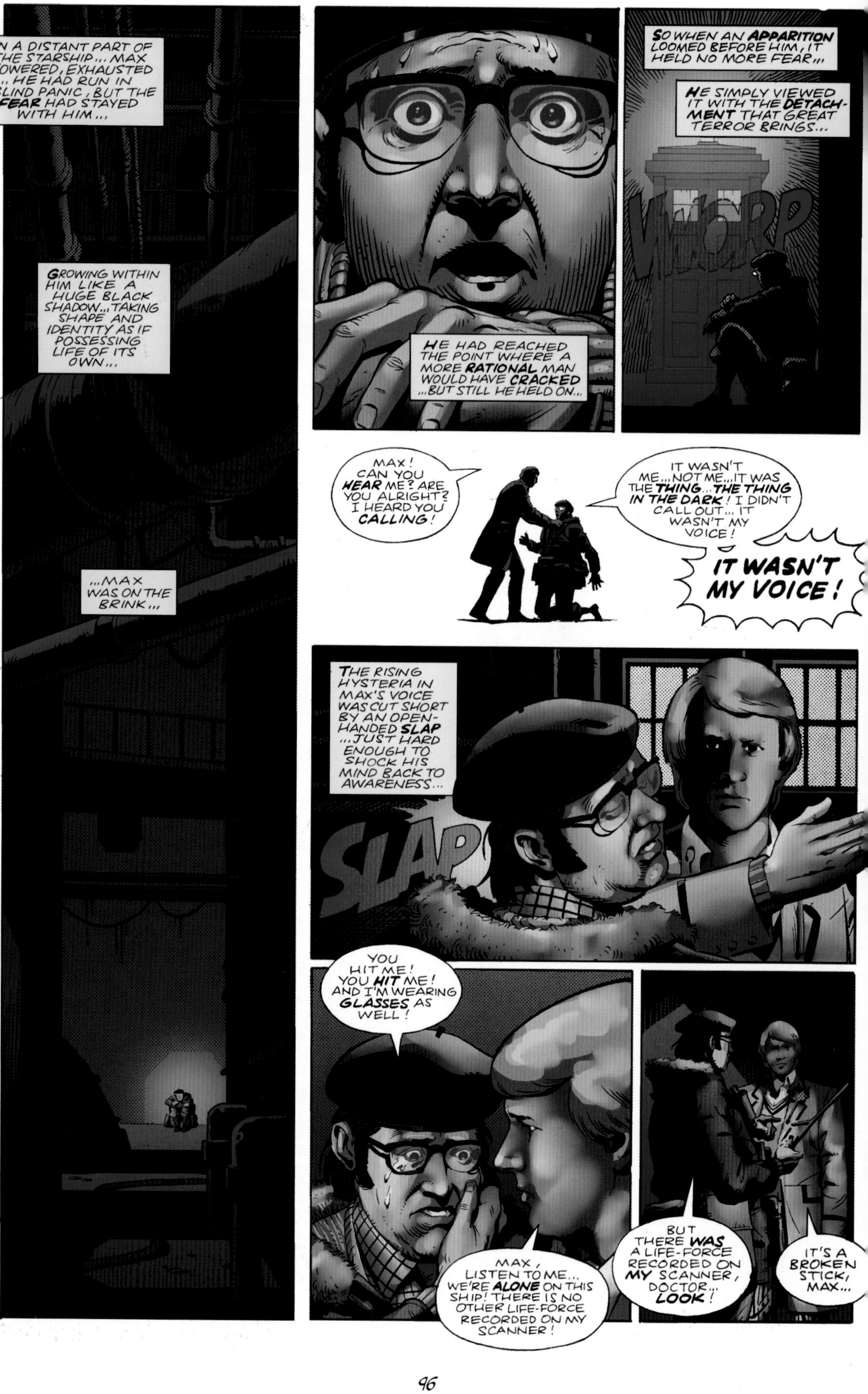
IN A DISTANT PART OF THE STARSHIP... MAX COWERED, EXHAUSTED ... HE HAD RUN IN BLIND PANIC, BUT THE FEAR HAD STAYED WITH HIM...
GROWING WITHIN HIM LIKE A HUGE BLACK SHADOW... TAKING SHAPE AND IDENTITY AS IF POSSESSING LIFE OF ITS OWN...
...MAX WAS ON THE BRINK...
HE HAD REACHED THE POINT WHERE A MORE RATIONAL MAN WOULD HAVE CRACKED ...BUT STILL HE HELD ON...
SO WHEN AN APPARITION LOOMED BEFORE HIM, IT HELD NO MORE FEAR...
HE SIMPLY VIEWED IT WITH THE DETACHMENT THAT GREAT TERROR BRINGS...
MAX! CAN YOU HEAR ME? ARE YOU ALRIGHT? I HEARD YOU CALLING!
IT WASN'T ME... NOT ME... IT WAS THE THING... THE THING IN THE DARK! I DIDN'T CALL OUT... IT WASN'T MY VOICE!
IT WASN'T MY VOICE!
THE RISING HYSTERIA IN MAX'S VOICE WAS CUT SHORT BY AN OPEN-HANDED SLAP ...JUST HARD ENOUGH TO SHOCK HIS MIND BACK TO AWARENESS...
SLAP
YOU HIT ME! YOU HIT ME! AND I'M WEARING GLASSES AS WELL!
MAX, LISTEN TO ME... WE'RE ALONE ON THIS SHIP! THERE IS NO OTHER LIFE-FORCE RECORDED ON MY SCANNER!
BUT THERE WAS A LIFE-FORCE RECORDED ON MY SCANNER, DOCTOR... LOOK!
IT'S A BROKEN STICK, MAX...

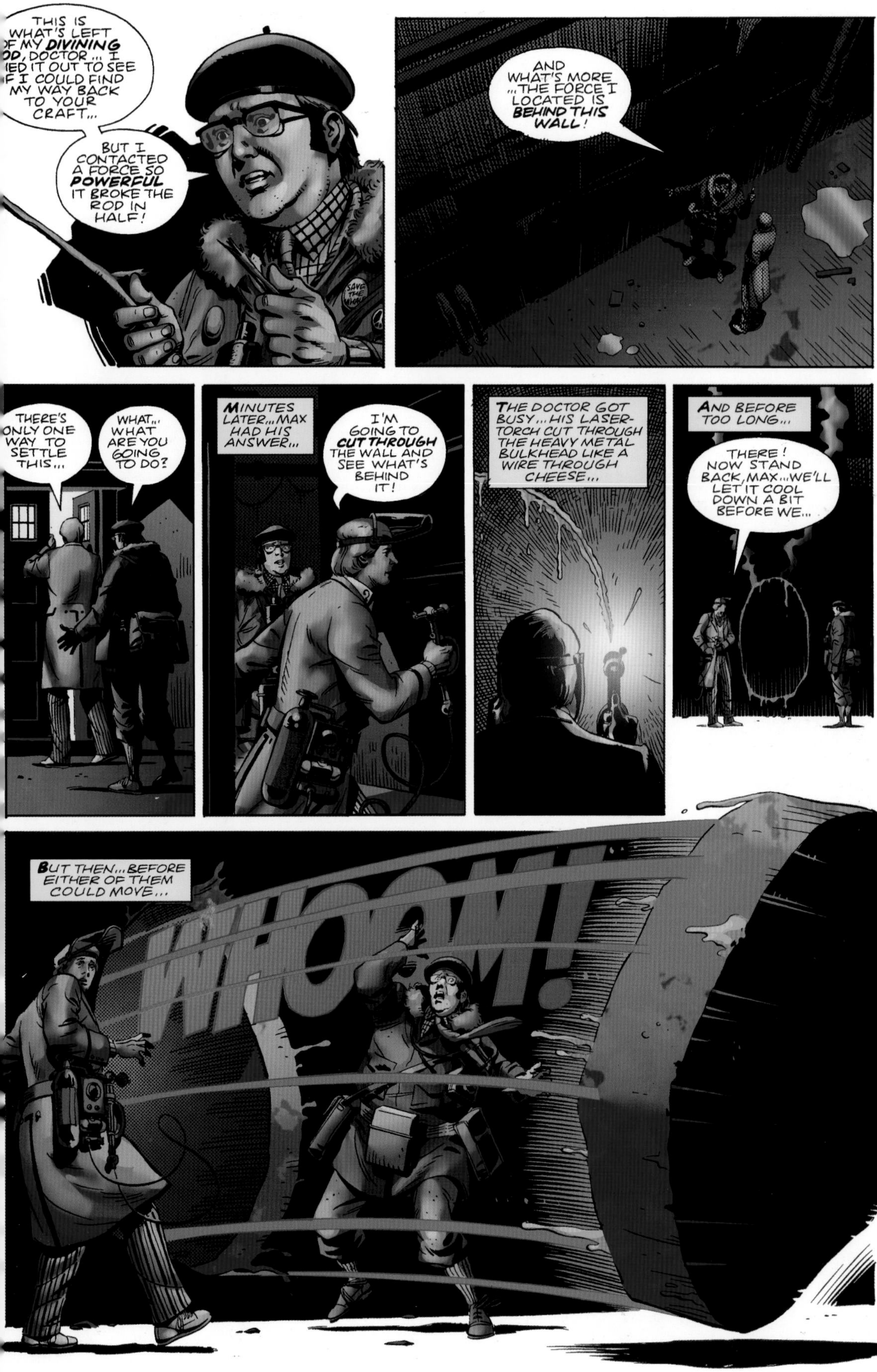

THIS IS WHAT'S LEFT OF MY DIVINING ROD, DOCTOR... I TIED IT OUT TO SEE IF I COULD FIND MY WAY BACK TO YOUR CRAFT...
BUT I CONTACTED A FORCE SO POWERFUL IT BROKE THE ROD IN HALF!
SAVE THE WHALE
AND WHAT'S MORE ...THE FORCE I LOCATED IS BEHIND THIS WALL!
THERE'S ONLY ONE WAY TO SETTLE THIS...
WHAT... WHAT ARE YOU GOING TO DO?
MINUTES LATER... MAX HAD HIS ANSWER...
I'M GOING TO CUT THROUGH THE WALL AND SEE WHAT'S BEHIND IT!
THE DOCTOR GOT BUSY... HIS LASER-TORCH CUT THROUGH THE HEAVY METAL BULKHEAD LIKE A WIRE THROUGH CHEESE...
AND BEFORE TOO LONG...
THERE! NOW STAND BACK, MAX... WE'LL LET IT COOL DOWN A BIT BEFORE WE...
BUT THEN... BEFORE EITHER OF THEM COULD MOVE...
WHOOM!

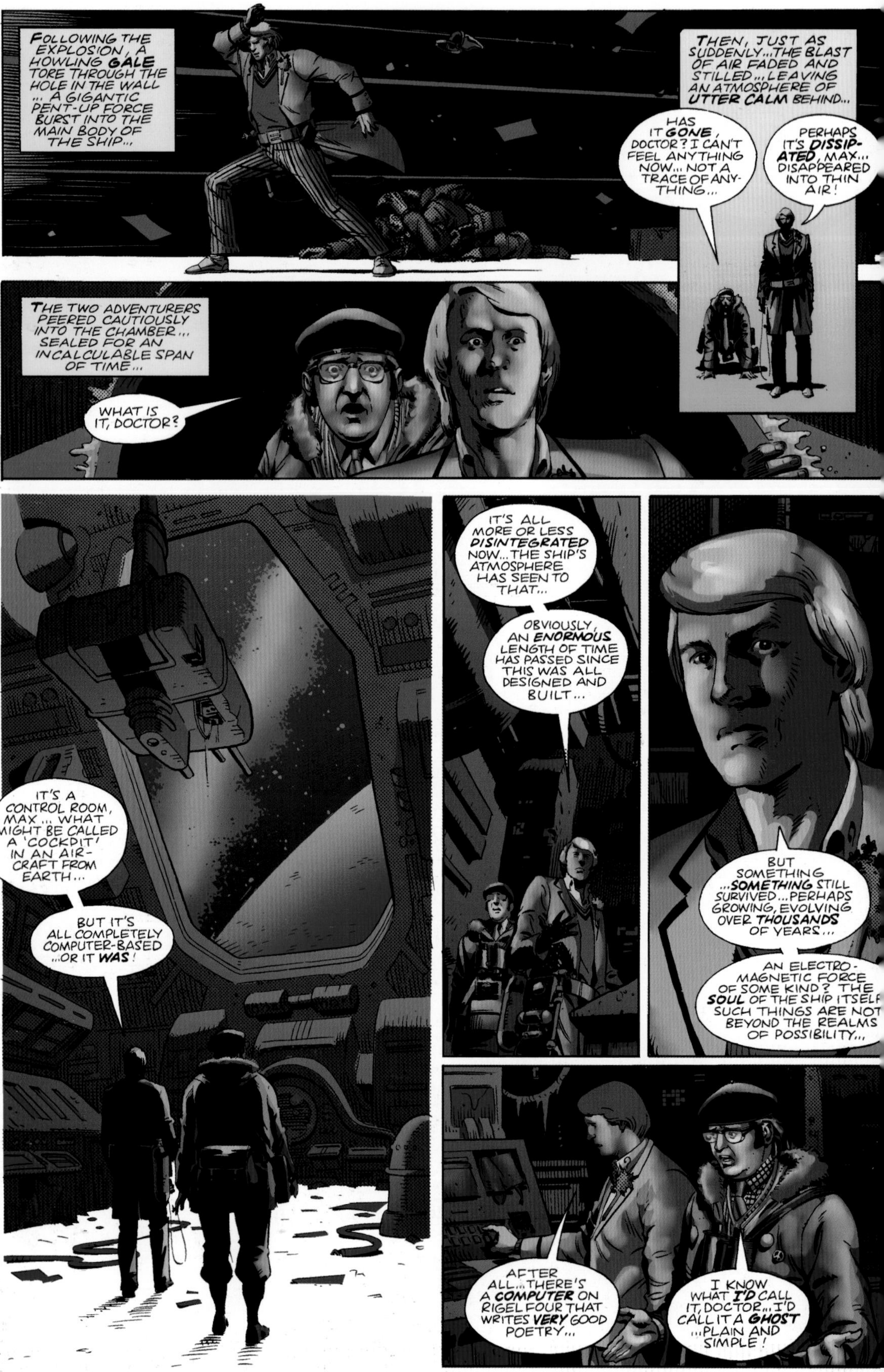
FOLLOWING THE EXPLOSION, A HOWLING GALE TORE THROUGH THE HOLE IN THE WALL ... A GIGANTIC PENT-UP FORCE BURST INTO THE MAIN BODY OF THE SHIP...
THEN, JUST AS SUDDENLY... THE BLAST OF AIR FADED AND STILLED... LEAVING AN ATMOSPHERE OF UTTER CALM BEHIND...
HAS IT GONE, DOCTOR? I CAN'T FEEL ANYTHING NOW... NOT A TRACE OF ANYTHING...
PERHAPS IT'S DISSIPATED, MAX... DISAPPEARED INTO THIN AIR!
THE TWO ADVENTURERS PEERED CAUTIOUSLY INTO THE CHAMBER... SEALED FOR AN INCALCULABLE SPAN OF TIME...
WHAT IS IT, DOCTOR?
IT'S A CONTROL ROOM, MAX ... WHAT MIGHT BE CALLED A 'COCKPIT' IN AN AIRCRAFT FROM EARTH...
BUT IT'S ALL COMPLETELY COMPUTER-BASED ...OR IT WAS!
IT'S ALL MORE OR LESS DISINTEGRATED NOW... THE SHIP'S ATMOSPHERE HAS SEEN TO THAT...
OBVIOUSLY, AN ENORMOUS LENGTH OF TIME HAS PASSED SINCE THIS WAS ALL DESIGNED AND BUILT...
BUT SOMETHING ...SOMETHING STILL SURVIVED... PERHAPS GROWING, EVOLVING OVER THOUSANDS OF YEARS...
AN ELECTRO-MAGNETIC FORCE OF SOME KIND? THE SOUL OF THE SHIP ITSELF SUCH THINGS ARE NOT BEYOND THE REALMS OF POSSIBILITY...
AFTER ALL... THERE'S A COMPUTER ON RIGEL FOUR THAT WRITES VERY GOOD POETRY...
I KNOW WHAT I'D CALL IT, DOCTOR... I'D CALL IT A GHOST ...PLAIN AND SIMPLE!

THAT'S SOMETHING WE MAY *NEVER* *KNOW* FOR SURE, MAX...

ARE WE *LEAVING*?

HAVEN'T YOU NOTICED? THE ATMOSPHERE IS GETTING *WARMER* BY THE MINUTE...

THE SHIP IS *HEATING UP*!

MY GUESS IS IT'S ENCOUNTERING EARTH ATMOSPHERE!

AND WITHOUT HEAT SHIELDS IT WILL *BURN UP* ON ENTRY FAIRLY QUICKLY...

WHORRPP *WORP*

I'D HATE TO BE AROUND WHEN *THAT* HAPPENS!

ON A DARK, MOONLESS NIGHT IN THE WILDS OF GLOUCESTERSHIRE ... THE AREA KNOWN AS *WELLS WOOD* ONCE AGAIN BORE SILENT WITNESS TO THE ARRIVAL OF AN *ALIEN* VISITOR...

IS THIS GOODBYE, DOCTOR?

FOR A WHILE, MAX ... THOUGH I DARESAY WE'LL BUMP INTO EACH OTHER BEFORE LONG ...

ONE LAST QUESTION ... EXACTLY *WHEN* WILL THAT STARSHIP BEGIN TO BREAK UP?

PRECISELY FIFTY SEVEN MINUTES FROM NOW ... THE DEBRIS SHOULD SCATTER FAR AND WIDE ... IT'LL BE QUITE A DISPLAY!

THAT'S ALL I NEEDED TO KNOW...

THANKS, DOCTOR!

DOWN AT THE REDFERN INN, THE REGULARS WERE TURNING OUT AS USUAL AS MAX MADE HIS WAY HOMEWARD...

THERE GOES MAX AGAIN!

HAW, HAW!

WHERE YOU BEEN TONIGHT, MAX...OUT ON YOUR FLYING CARPET?

ACTUALLY, NC... I'VE BEEN TRACKING DOWN LIGHTS IN THE SKY...WITH A *FRIEND*...

LOOK OUT OF YOUR WINDOWS AT ABOUT THREE MINUTES TO MIDNIGHT...YOU MAY SEE SOMETHING *INTERESTING*!

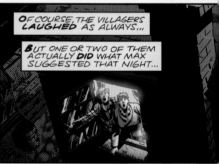

OF COURSE, THE VILLAGERS *LAUGHED* AS ALWAYS...

BUT ONE OR TWO OF THEM ACTUALLY *DID* WHAT MAX SUGGESTED THAT NIGHT...

THE NIGHT THAT MAX GAINED A LITTLE GRUDGING *RESPECT* IN THE VILLAGE...

THE NIGHT THAT STARS FELL ON STOCKBRIDGE...

DAVE GIBBONS

THE END.

Script/pencils: Steve Parkhouse Inks: Paul Neary Editor: Alan McKenzie

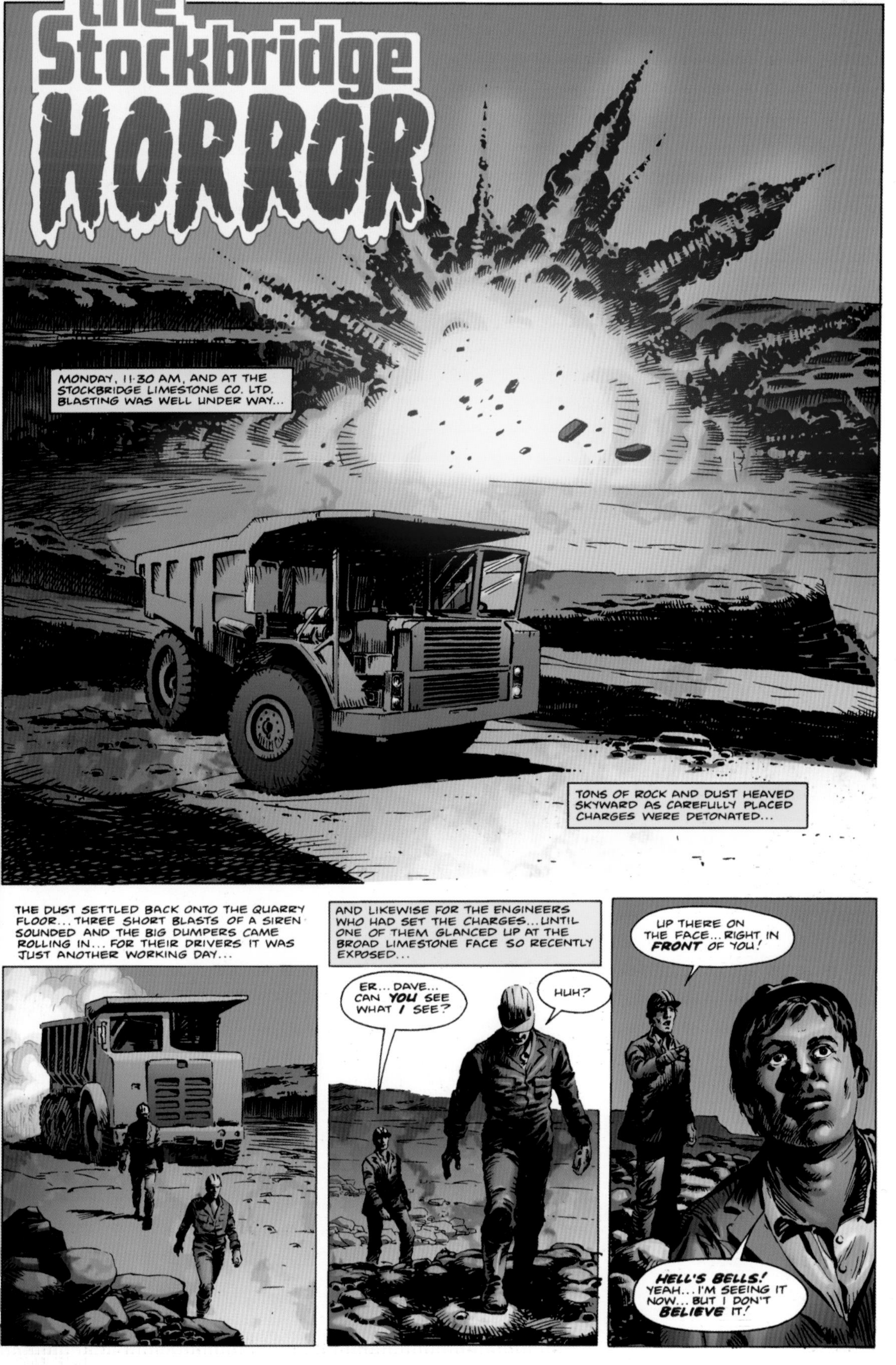
the Stockbridge HORROR
MONDAY, 11:30 AM, AND AT THE STOCKBRIDGE LIMESTONE CO. LTD. BLASTING WAS WELL UNDER WAY...
TONS OF ROCK AND DUST HEAVED SKYWARD AS CAREFULLY PLACED CHARGES WERE DETONATED...
THE DUST SETTLED BACK ONTO THE QUARRY FLOOR... THREE SHORT BLASTS OF A SIREN SOUNDED AND THE BIG DUMPERS CAME ROLLING IN... FOR THEIR DRIVERS IT WAS JUST ANOTHER WORKING DAY...
AND LIKEWISE FOR THE ENGINEERS WHO HAD SET THE CHARGES... UNTIL ONE OF THEM GLANCED UP AT THE BROAD LIMESTONE FACE SO RECENTLY EXPOSED...
ER... DAVE... CAN YOU SEE WHAT I SEE?
HUH?
UP THERE ON THE FACE... RIGHT IN FRONT OF YOU!
HELL'S BELLS! YEAH... I'M SEEING IT NOW... BUT I DON'T BELIEVE IT!

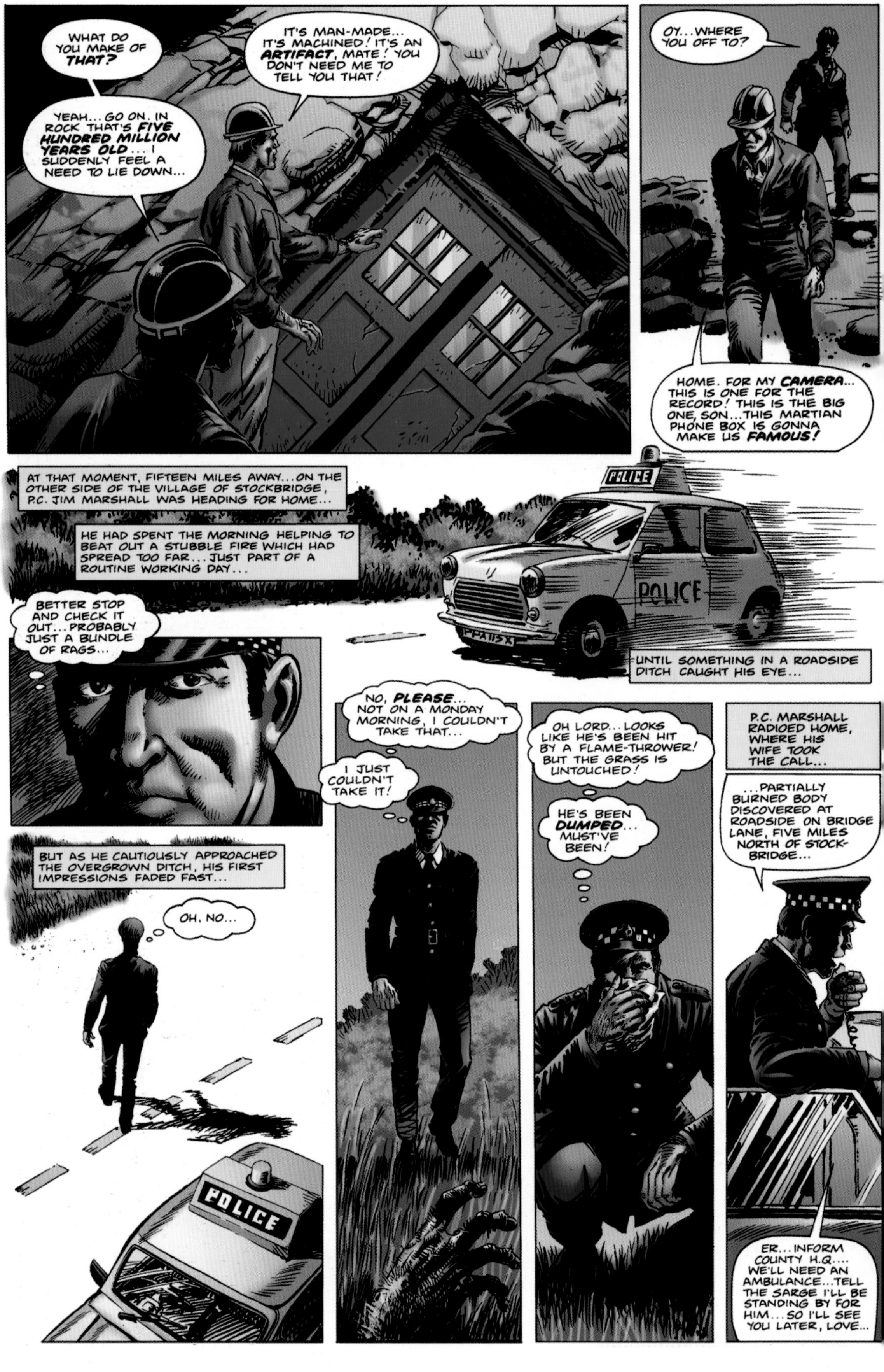

WHAT DO YOU MAKE OF THAT?
IT'S MAN-MADE... IT'S MACHINED! IT'S AN ARTIFACT, MATE! YOU DON'T NEED ME TO TELL YOU THAT!
YEAH... GO ON. IN ROCK THAT'S FIVE HUNDRED MILLION YEARS OLD... I SUDDENLY FEEL A NEED TO LIE DOWN...
OY... WHERE YOU OFF TO?
HOME. FOR MY CAMERA... THIS IS ONE FOR THE RECORD! THIS IS THE BIG ONE, SON... THIS MARTIAN PHONE BOX IS GONNA MAKE US FAMOUS!
AT THAT MOMENT, FIFTEEN MILES AWAY... ON THE OTHER SIDE OF THE VILLAGE OF STOCKBRIDGE, P.C. JIM MARSHALL WAS HEADING FOR HOME...
HE HAD SPENT THE MORNING HELPING TO BEAT OUT A STUBBLE FIRE WHICH HAD SPREAD TOO FAR... JUST PART OF A ROUTINE WORKING DAY...
POLICE
POLICE
UNTIL SOMETHING IN A ROADSIDE DITCH CAUGHT HIS EYE...
BETTER STOP AND CHECK IT OUT... PROBABLY JUST A BUNDLE OF RAGS...
BUT AS HE CAUTIOUSLY APPROACHED THE OVERGROWN DITCH, HIS FIRST IMPRESSIONS FADED FAST...
OH, NO...
POLICE
NO, PLEASE... NOT ON A MONDAY MORNING, I COULDN'T TAKE THAT...
I JUST COULDN'T TAKE IT!
OH LORD... LOOKS LIKE HE'S BEEN HIT BY A FLAME-THROWER! BUT THE GRASS IS UNTOUCHED!
HE'S BEEN DUMPED... MUST'VE BEEN!
P.C. MARSHALL RADIOED HOME, WHERE HIS WIFE TOOK THE CALL...
...PARTIALLY BURNED BODY DISCOVERED AT ROADSIDE ON BRIDGE LANE, FIVE MILES NORTH OF STOCK-BRIDGE...
ER... INFORM COUNTY H.Q.... WE'LL NEED AN AMBULANCE... TELL THE SARGE I'LL BE STANDING BY FOR HIM... SO I'LL SEE YOU LATER, LOVE...

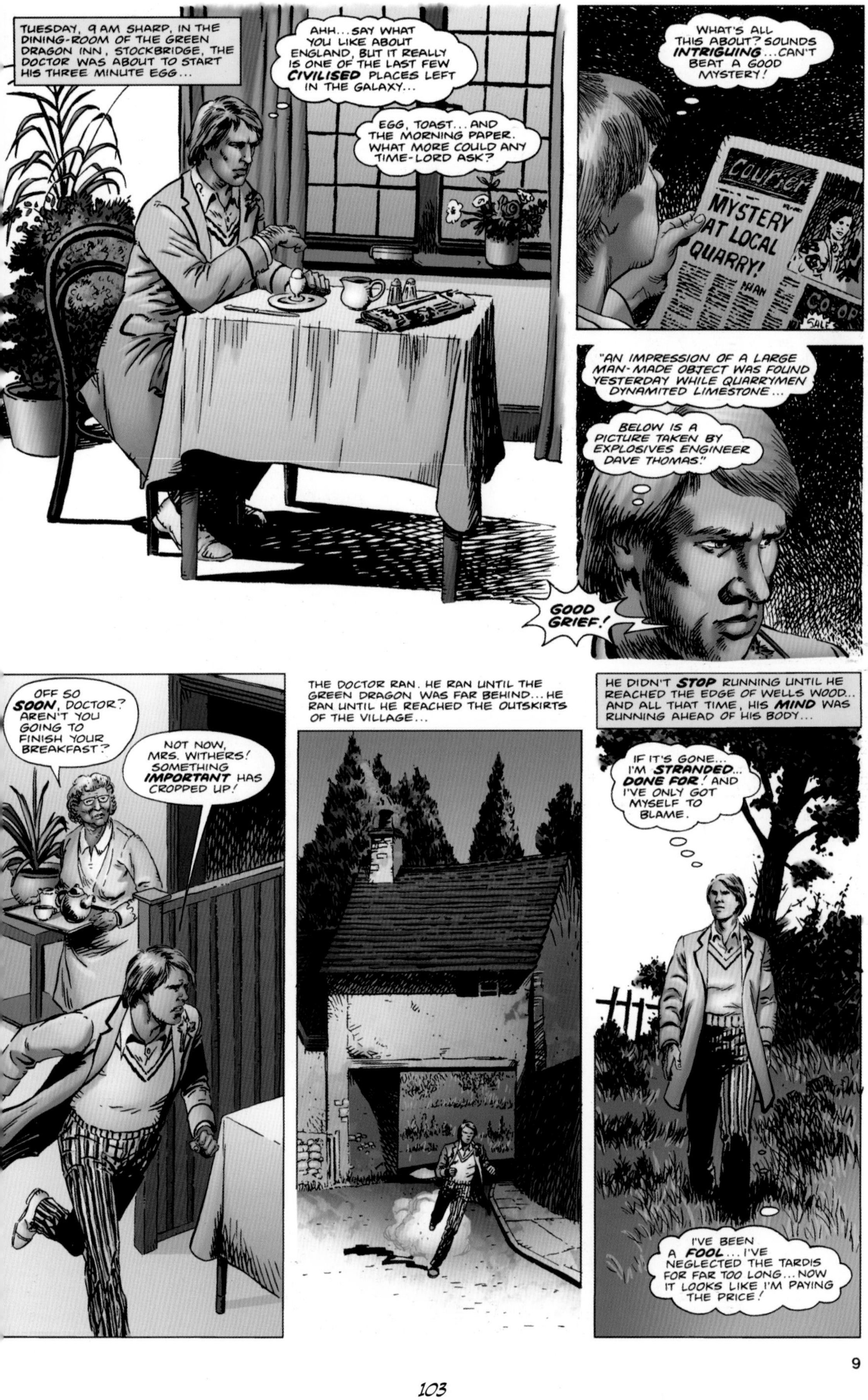
TUESDAY, 9 AM SHARP, IN THE DINING-ROOM OF THE GREEN DRAGON INN, STOCKBRIDGE, THE DOCTOR WAS ABOUT TO START HIS THREE MINUTE EGG...
AHH... SAY WHAT YOU LIKE ABOUT ENGLAND, BUT IT REALLY IS ONE OF THE LAST FEW CIVILISED PLACES LEFT IN THE GALAXY...
EGG, TOAST... AND THE MORNING PAPER. WHAT MORE COULD ANY TIME-LORD ASK?
WHAT'S ALL THIS ABOUT? SOUNDS INTRIGUING...CAN'T BEAT A GOOD MYSTERY!
Courier
MYSTERY AT LOCAL QUARRY!
"AN IMPRESSION OF A LARGE MAN-MADE OBJECT WAS FOUND YESTERDAY WHILE QUARRYMEN DYNAMITED LIMESTONE...
BELOW IS A PICTURE TAKEN BY EXPLOSIVES ENGINEER DAVE THOMAS."
GOOD GRIEF!
OFF SO SOON, DOCTOR? AREN'T YOU GOING TO FINISH YOUR BREAKFAST?
NOT NOW, MRS. WITHERS! SOMETHING IMPORTANT HAS CROPPED UP!
THE DOCTOR RAN. HE RAN UNTIL THE GREEN DRAGON WAS FAR BEHIND... HE RAN UNTIL HE REACHED THE OUTSKIRTS OF THE VILLAGE...
HE DIDN'T STOP RUNNING UNTIL HE REACHED THE EDGE OF WELLS WOOD... AND ALL THAT TIME, HIS MIND WAS RUNNING AHEAD OF HIS BODY...
IF IT'S GONE... I'M STRANDED... DONE FOR! AND I'VE ONLY GOT MYSELF TO BLAME.
I'VE BEEN A FOOL... I'VE NEGLECTED THE TARDIS FOR FAR TOO LONG... NOW IT LOOKS LIKE I'M PAYING THE PRICE!

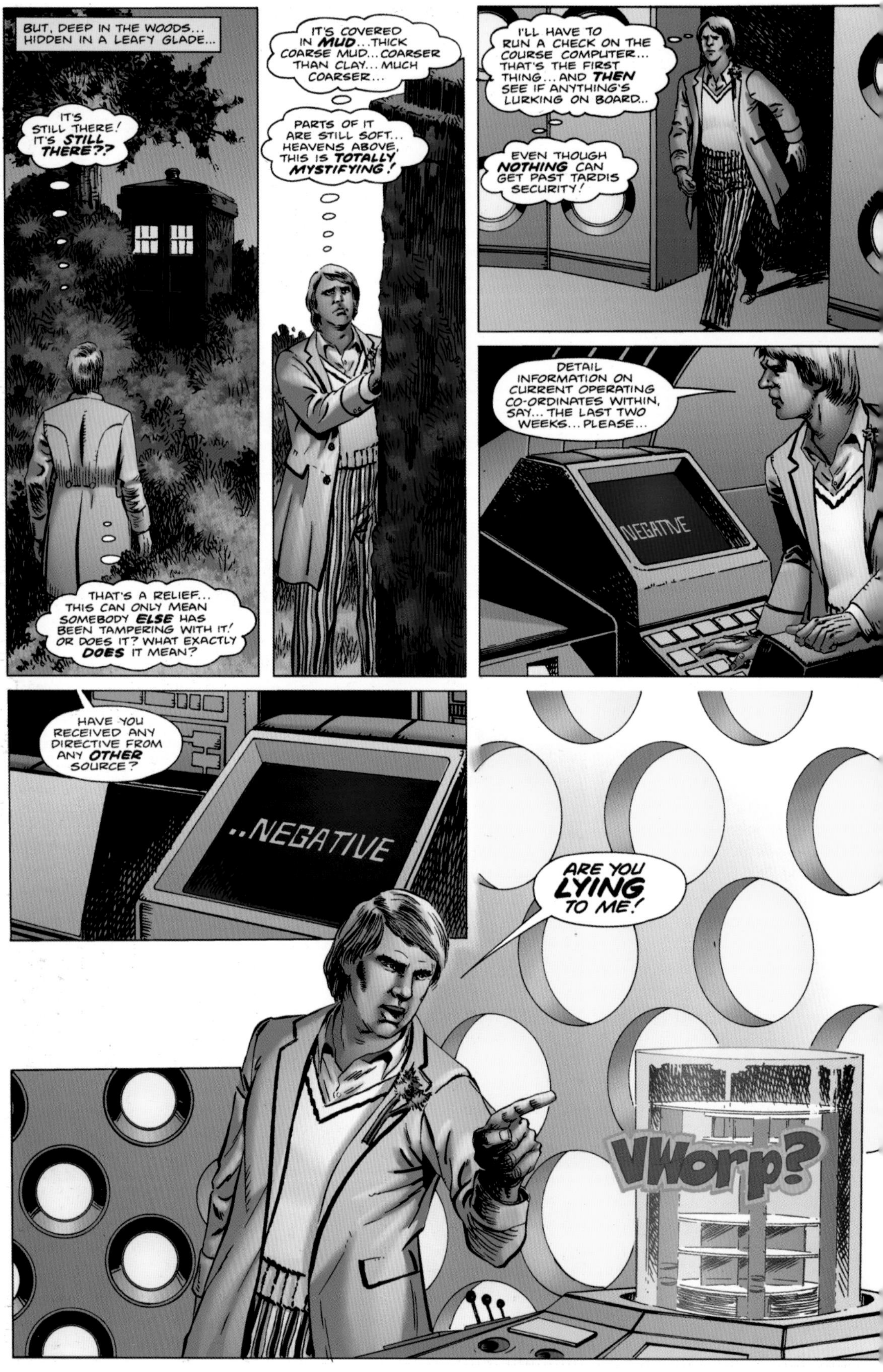
BUT, DEEP IN THE WOODS... HIDDEN IN A LEAFY GLADE...
IT'S STILL THERE! IT'S STILL THERE??
THAT'S A RELIEF... THIS CAN ONLY MEAN SOMEBODY ELSE HAS BEEN TAMPERING WITH IT! OR DOES IT? WHAT EXACTLY DOES IT MEAN?
IT'S COVERED IN MUD... THICK COARSE MUD... COARSER THAN CLAY... MUCH COARSER...
PARTS OF IT ARE STILL SOFT... HEAVENS ABOVE, THIS IS TOTALLY MYSTIFYING!
I'LL HAVE TO RUN A CHECK ON THE COURSE COMPUTER... THAT'S THE FIRST THING... AND THEN SEE IF ANYTHING'S LURKING ON BOARD...
EVEN THOUGH NOTHING CAN GET PAST TARDIS SECURITY!
DETAIL INFORMATION ON CURRENT OPERATING CO-ORDINATES WITHIN, SAY... THE LAST TWO WEEKS... PLEASE...
NEGATIVE
HAVE YOU RECEIVED ANY DIRECTIVE FROM ANY OTHER SOURCE?
..NEGATIVE
ARE YOU LYING TO ME!
VWorp?

THERE'S SOMETHING FISHY GOING ON HERE... I CAN SENSE SOMETHING *RESENTFUL*, ALMOST *REBELLIOUS* ABOUT THE TARDIS...

ALMOST AS IF IT'S BEEN OUT *PLAYING* BY ITSELF WITHOUT MY PERMISSION...

A SAMPLE OF THIS MUD FOR ANALYSIS SHOULD CLARIFY MATTERS...

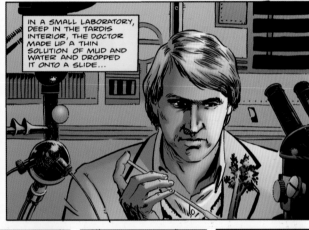

IN A SMALL LABORATORY, DEEP IN THE TARDIS INTERIOR, THE DOCTOR MADE UP A THIN SOLUTION OF MUD AND WATER AND DROPPED IT ONTO A SLIDE...

HMMM...JUST WHAT I EXPECTED REALLY...TINY CORAL-LIKE FOSSILS...THE BASIS OF SEDIMENTARY ROCK...

PROBABLY CARBONIFEROUS... 500,000,000 YEARS OLD OR THEREABOUTS... IN SHORT, *LIMESTONE!*

WHAT APPEARS TO BE A MAN-MADE OBJECT, IN SEDIMENTARY ROCK OF THE CARBONIFEROUS PERIOD, BEFORE LIFE AS TERRESTRIALS KNOW IT HAD EVOLVED!

A DISCOVERY LIKE THIS WILL PRODUCE A *SHOCK-WAVE* OF CONFUSION AND SPECULATION THROUGHOUT THE WORLD COMMUNITY!

AND THE *BLAME* LIES SQUARELY WITH ME!

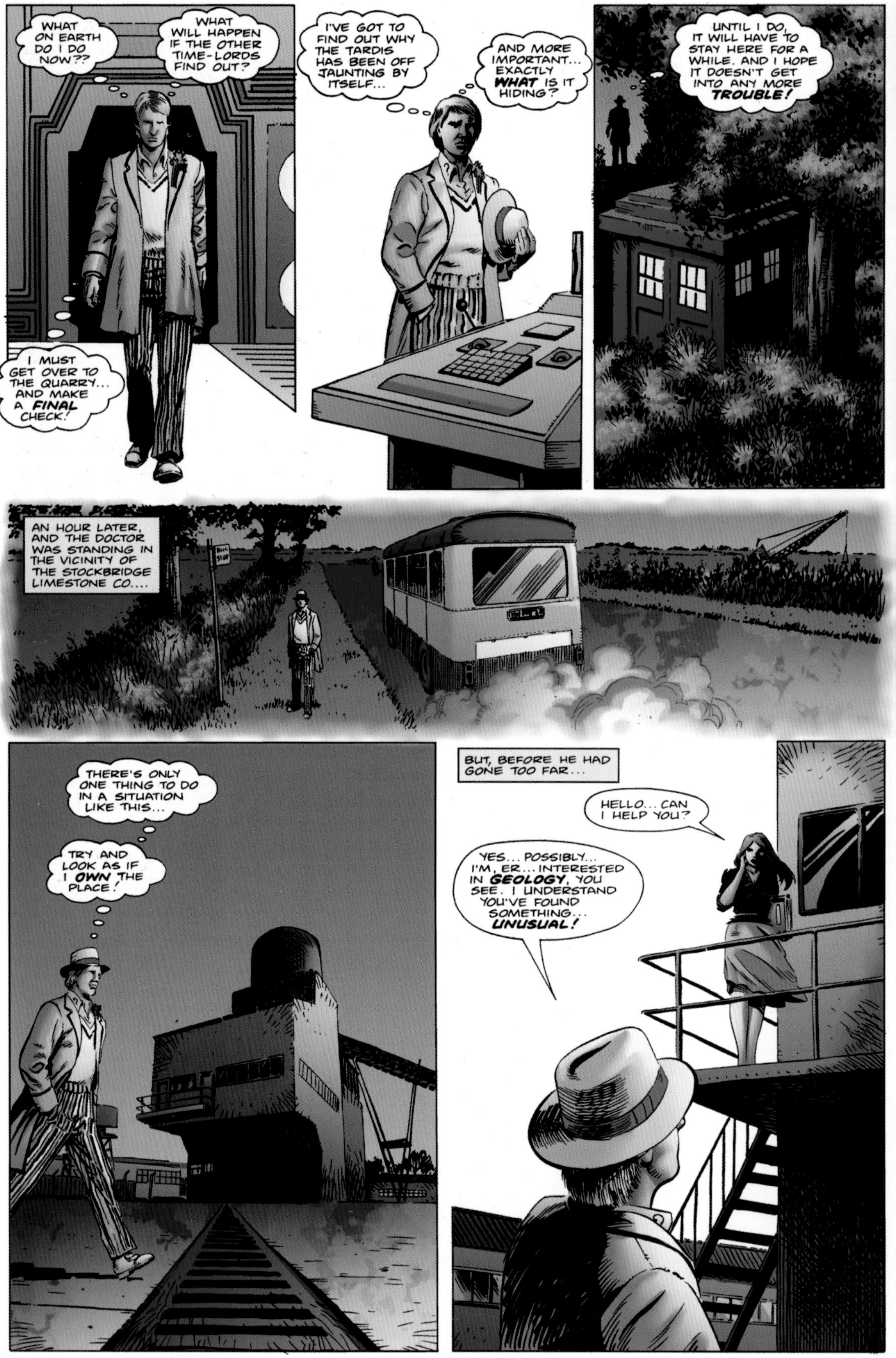
WHAT ON EARTH DO I DO NOW??
WHAT WILL HAPPEN IF THE OTHER TIME-LORDS FIND OUT?
I MUST GET OVER TO THE QUARRY... AND MAKE A FINAL CHECK!
I'VE GOT TO FIND OUT WHY THE TARDIS HAS BEEN OFF JAUNTING BY ITSELF...
AND MORE IMPORTANT... EXACTLY WHAT IS IT HIDING?
UNTIL I DO, IT WILL HAVE TO STAY HERE FOR A WHILE. AND I HOPE IT DOESN'T GET INTO ANY MORE TROUBLE!
AN HOUR LATER, AND THE DOCTOR WAS STANDING IN THE VICINITY OF THE STOCKBRIDGE LIMESTONE CO....
THERE'S ONLY ONE THING TO DO IN A SITUATION LIKE THIS...
TRY AND LOOK AS IF I OWN THE PLACE!
BUT, BEFORE HE HAD GONE TOO FAR...
HELLO... CAN I HELP YOU?
YES... POSSIBLY... I'M, ER... INTERESTED IN GEOLOGY, YOU SEE. I UNDERSTAND YOU'VE FOUND SOMETHING... UNUSUAL!

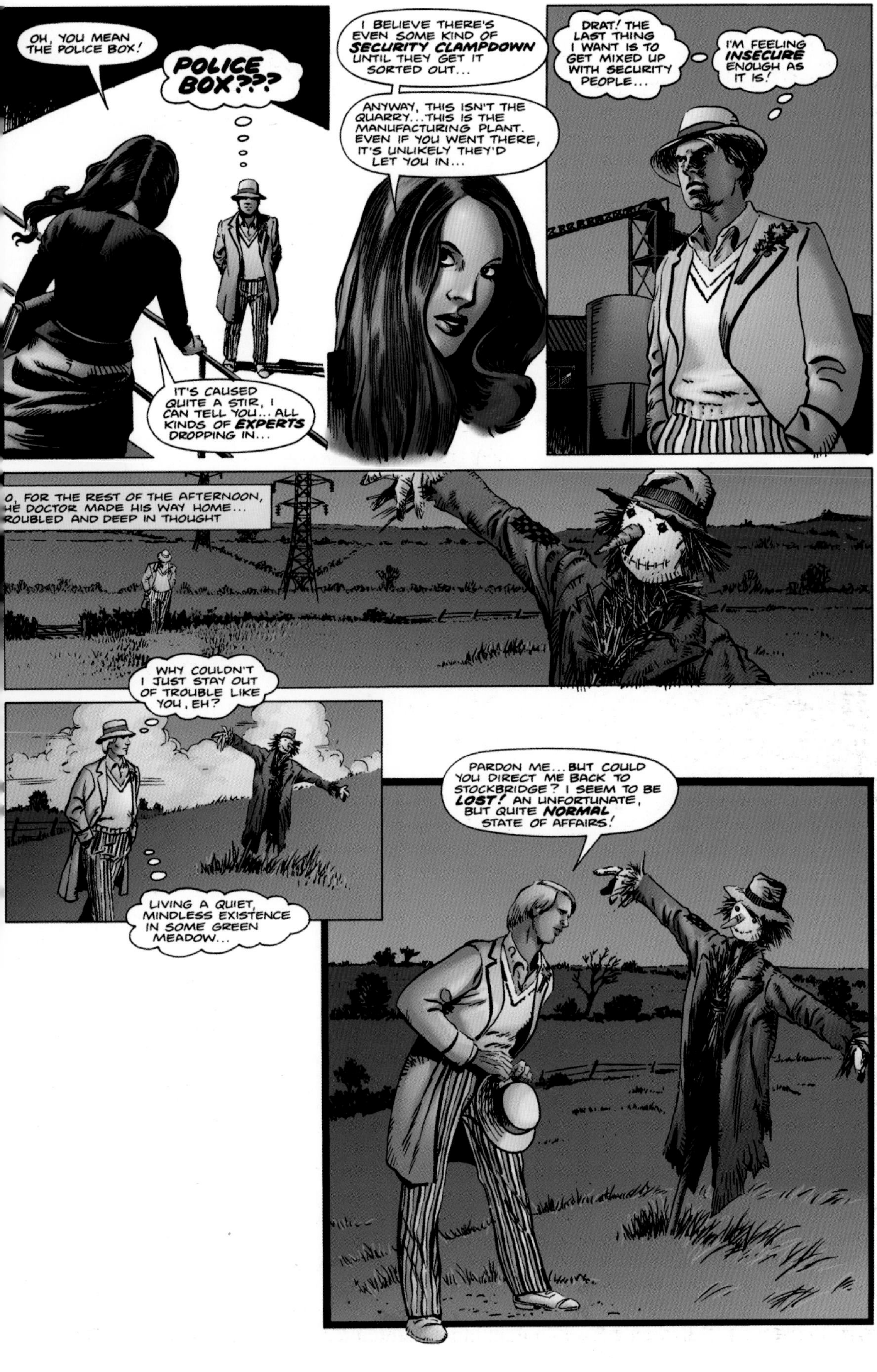
OH, YOU MEAN THE POLICE BOX!
POLICE BOX???
IT'S CAUSED QUITE A STIR, I CAN TELL YOU... ALL KINDS OF EXPERTS DROPPING IN...
I BELIEVE THERE'S EVEN SOME KIND OF SECURITY CLAMPDOWN UNTIL THEY GET IT SORTED OUT...
ANYWAY, THIS ISN'T THE QUARRY... THIS IS THE MANUFACTURING PLANT. EVEN IF YOU WENT THERE, IT'S UNLIKELY THEY'D LET YOU IN...
DRAT! THE LAST THING I WANT IS TO GET MIXED UP WITH SECURITY PEOPLE...
I'M FEELING INSECURE ENOUGH AS IT IS!
O, FOR THE REST OF THE AFTERNOON, HE DOCTOR MADE HIS WAY HOME... ROUBLED AND DEEP IN THOUGHT
WHY COULDN'T I JUST STAY OUT OF TROUBLE LIKE YOU, EH?
LIVING A QUIET, MINDLESS EXISTENCE IN SOME GREEN MEADOW...
PARDON ME... BUT COULD YOU DIRECT ME BACK TO STOCKBRIDGE? I SEEM TO BE LOST! AN UNFORTUNATE, BUT QUITE NORMAL STATE OF AFFAIRS!

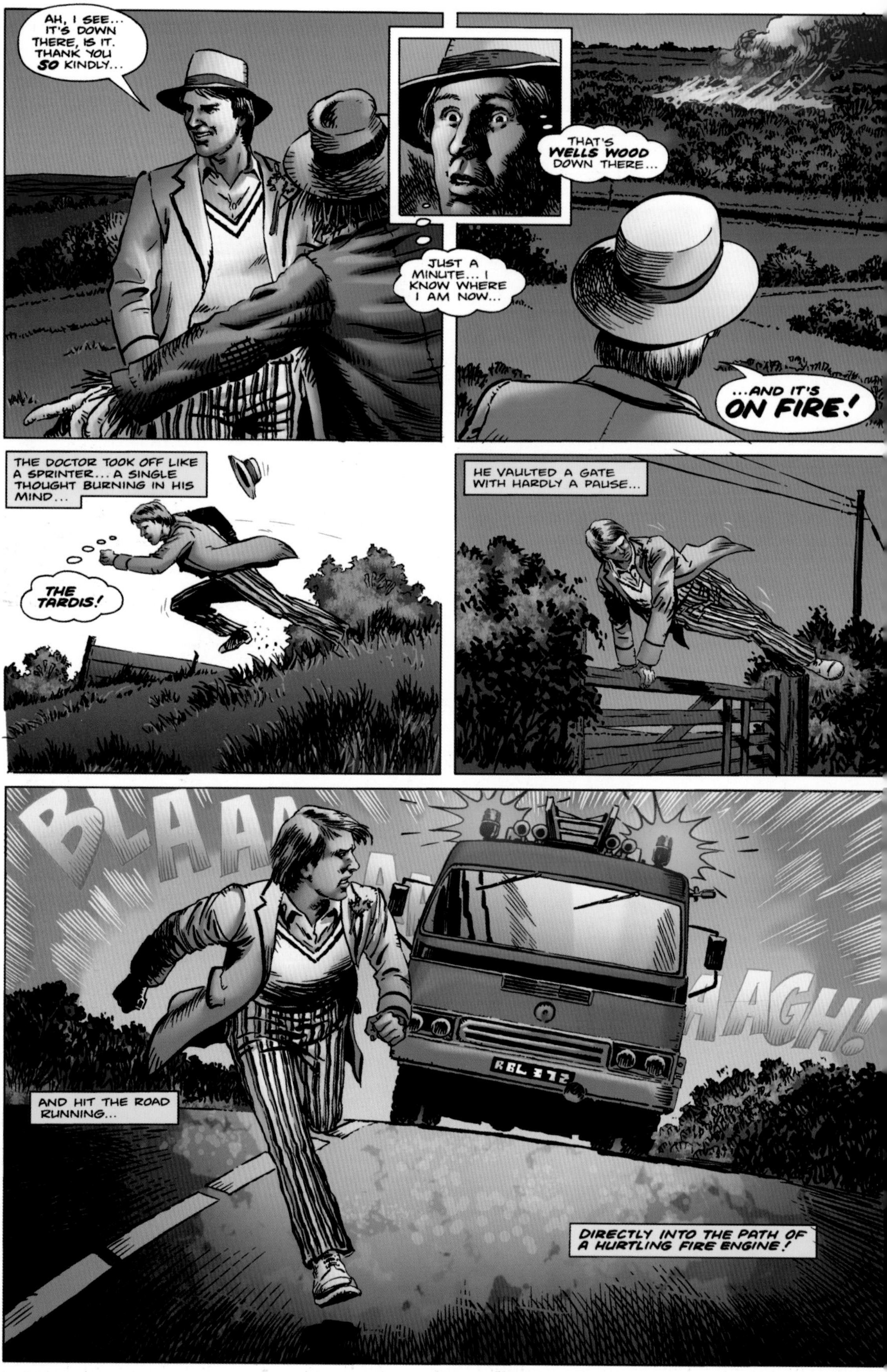

AH, I SEE... IT'S DOWN THERE, IS IT. THANK YOU SO KINDLY...
THAT'S WELLS WOOD DOWN THERE...
JUST A MINUTE... I KNOW WHERE I AM NOW...
...AND IT'S ON FIRE!
THE DOCTOR TOOK OFF LIKE A SPRINTER... A SINGLE THOUGHT BURNING IN HIS MIND...
THE TARDIS!
HE VAULTED A GATE WITH HARDLY A PAUSE...
BLAAAAAAGH!
RBL 372
AND HIT THE ROAD RUNNING...
DIRECTLY INTO THE PATH OF A HURTLING FIRE ENGINE!

Script/pencils: Steve Parkhouse Inks: Paul Neary Editor: Alan McKenzie

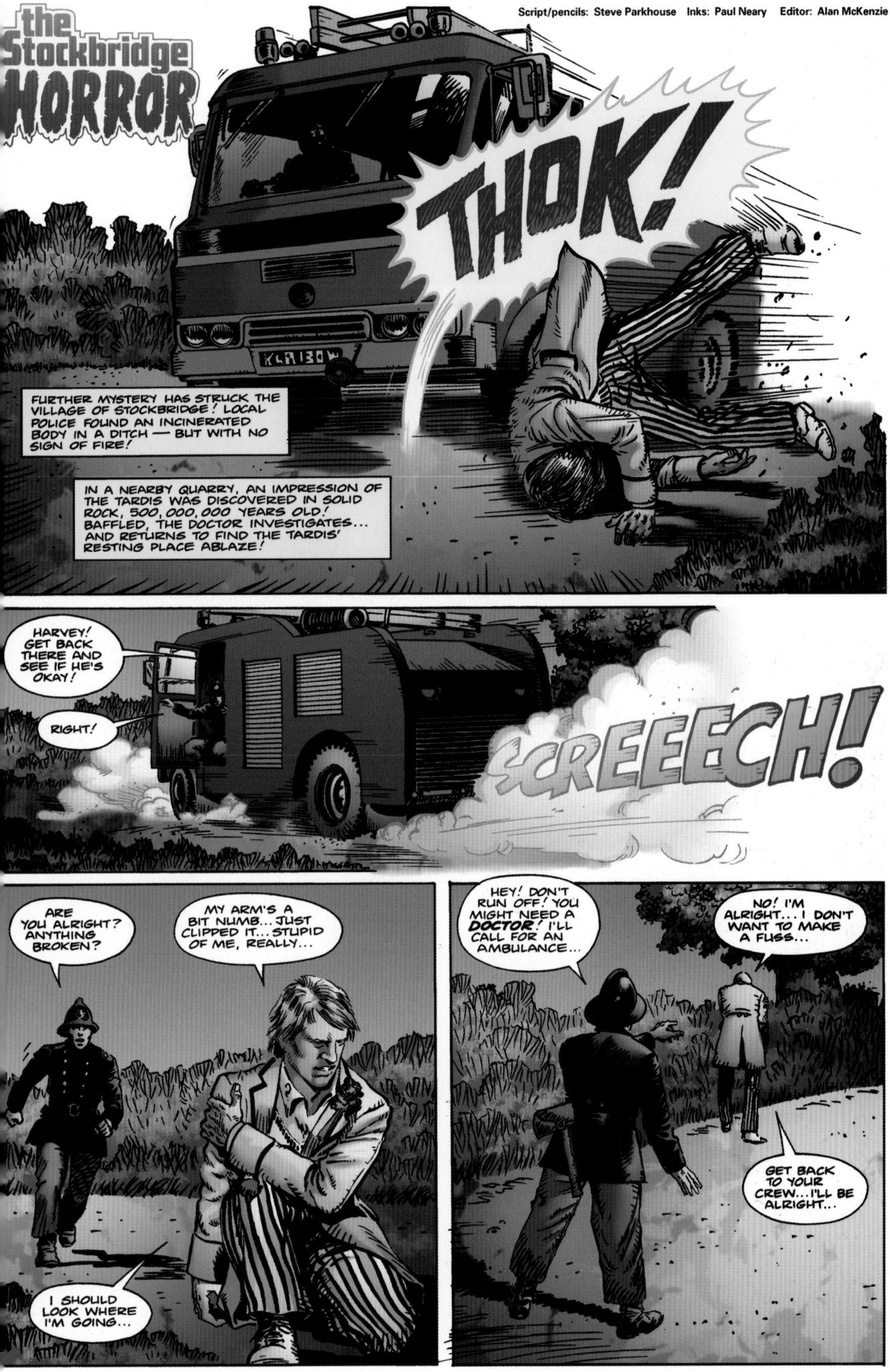
the Stockbridge HORROR
THOK!
KLR 130W
FURTHER MYSTERY HAS STRUCK THE VILLAGE OF STOCKBRIDGE! LOCAL POLICE FOUND AN INCINERATED BODY IN A DITCH — BUT WITH NO SIGN OF FIRE!
IN A NEARBY QUARRY, AN IMPRESSION OF THE TARDIS WAS DISCOVERED IN SOLID ROCK, 500,000,000 YEARS OLD! BAFFLED, THE DOCTOR INVESTIGATES... AND RETURNS TO FIND THE TARDIS' RESTING PLACE ABLAZE!
HARVEY! GET BACK THERE AND SEE IF HE'S OKAY!
RIGHT!
SCREEECH!
ARE YOU ALRIGHT? ANYTHING BROKEN?
MY ARM'S A BIT NUMB... JUST CLIPPED IT... STUPID OF ME, REALLY...
I SHOULD LOOK WHERE I'M GOING...
HEY! DON'T RUN OFF! YOU MIGHT NEED A DOCTOR! I'LL CALL FOR AN AMBULANCE...
NO! I'M ALRIGHT... I DON'T WANT TO MAKE A FUSS...
GET BACK TO YOUR CREW... I'LL BE ALRIGHT...

OH, NO! NOW THE ENGINE'S GONE OFF AND *LEFT* ME!

AND THAT POOR BLIGHTER'S MADE IT OFF INTO THE WOODS...

I'D BETTER KEEP AN *EYE* ON HIM, OR THE CHIEF'LL HAVE MY GUTS FOR GARTERS...

THE DOCTOR STUMBLED THROUGH THE EDGE OF THE WOODS, MUSTERING ALL HIS PHYSICAL AND MENTAL RESOURCES TO OVERCOME THE *PAIN* IN HIS BATTERED BODY...

AND ALREADY HE COULD FEEL THE *HEAT* ON HIS FACE...AND THE SHARP SMELL OF WOODSMOKE FILLED HIS NOSTRILS...

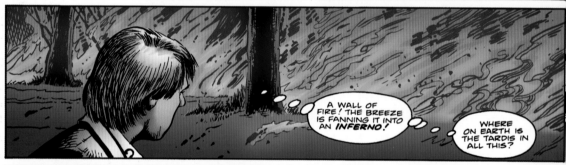

A WALL OF FIRE! THE BREEZE IS FANNING IT INTO AN *INFERNO!*

WHERE ON EARTH IS THE TARDIS IN ALL THIS?

THERE! THE FLAMES HAVEN'T REACHED IT YET!

I'VE GOT TO GET IT *OUT* OF HERE...THE PLACE WILL BE SWARMING WITH FIREMEN...

THERE'S NO WAY I CAN GET THROUGH THESE FLAMES...

I'LL HAVE TO SKIRT *ROUND* THEM...

THEN THE *FEAR* HIT HIM... A PALPABLE, TANGIBLE *FORCE* DEEP IN HIS STOMACH...

A LIVING HAND *GRASPED* HIS INNARDS, A WRENCHING, TWISTING *TERROR* THAT DOUBLED HIM UP...

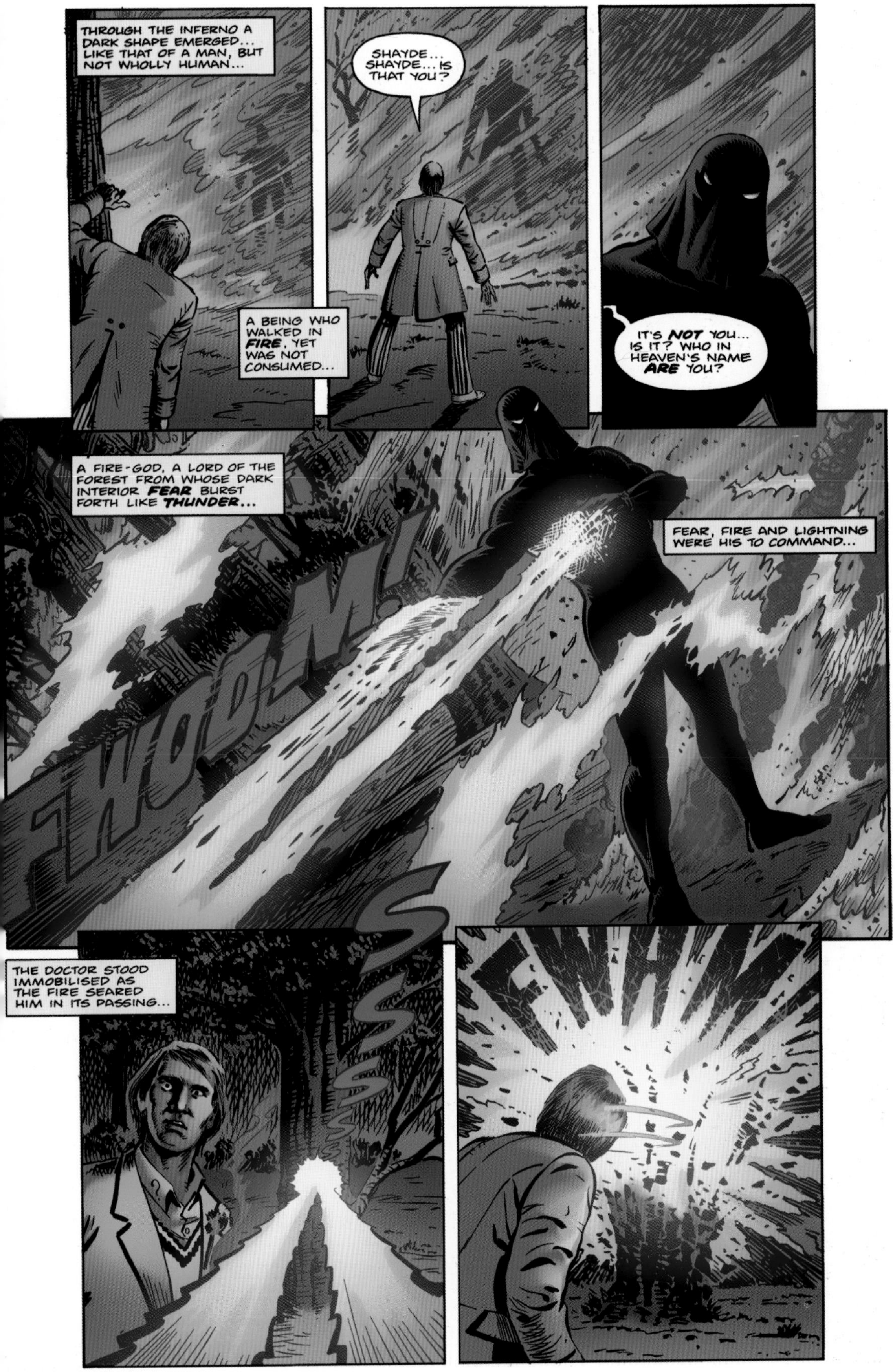
THROUGH THE INFERNO A DARK SHAPE EMERGED... LIKE THAT OF A MAN, BUT NOT WHOLLY HUMAN...
SHAYDE... SHAYDE... IS THAT YOU?
A BEING WHO WALKED IN FIRE, YET WAS NOT CONSUMED...
IT'S NOT YOU... IS IT? WHO IN HEAVEN'S NAME ARE YOU?
A FIRE-GOD, A LORD OF THE FOREST FROM WHOSE DARK INTERIOR FEAR BURST FORTH LIKE THUNDER...
FEAR, FIRE AND LIGHTNING WERE HIS TO COMMAND...
FWOOM!
THE DOCTOR STOOD IMMOBILISED AS THE FIRE SEARED HIM IN ITS PASSING...
SSSSS

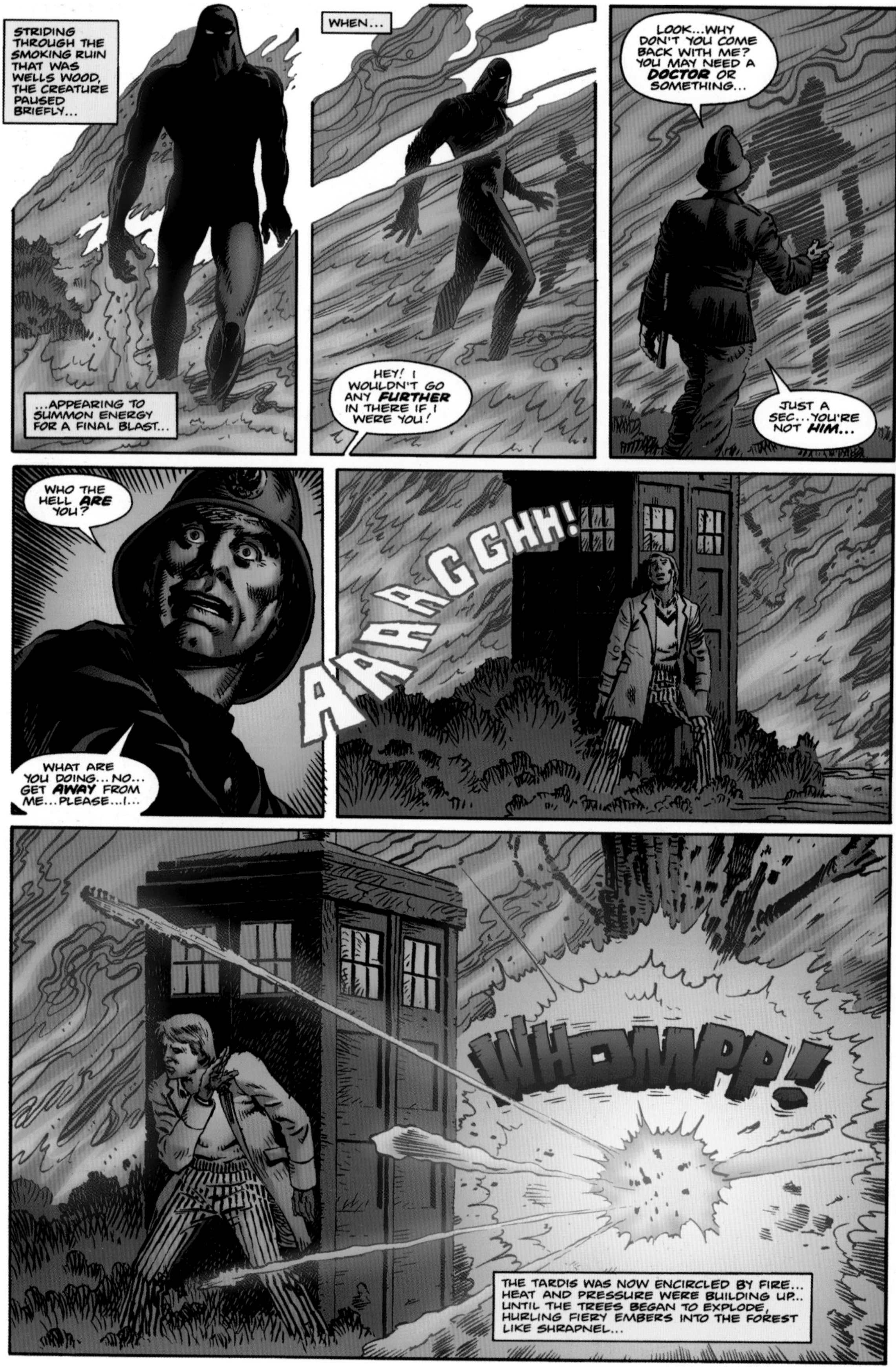

STRIDING THROUGH THE SMOKING RUIN THAT WAS WELLS WOOD, THE CREATURE PAUSED BRIEFLY...
...APPEARING TO SUMMON ENERGY FOR A FINAL BLAST...
WHEN...
HEY! I WOULDN'T GO ANY FURTHER IN THERE IF I WERE YOU!
LOOK...WHY DON'T YOU COME BACK WITH ME? YOU MAY NEED A DOCTOR OR SOMETHING...
JUST A SEC...YOU'RE NOT HIM...
WHO THE HELL ARE YOU?
WHAT ARE YOU DOING...NO... GET AWAY FROM ME...PLEASE...I...
AAAAGGHH!
WHOMPP!
THE TARDIS WAS NOW ENCIRCLED BY FIRE... HEAT AND PRESSURE WERE BUILDING UP... UNTIL THE TREES BEGAN TO EXPLODE, HURLING FIERY EMBERS INTO THE FOREST LIKE SHRAPNEL...

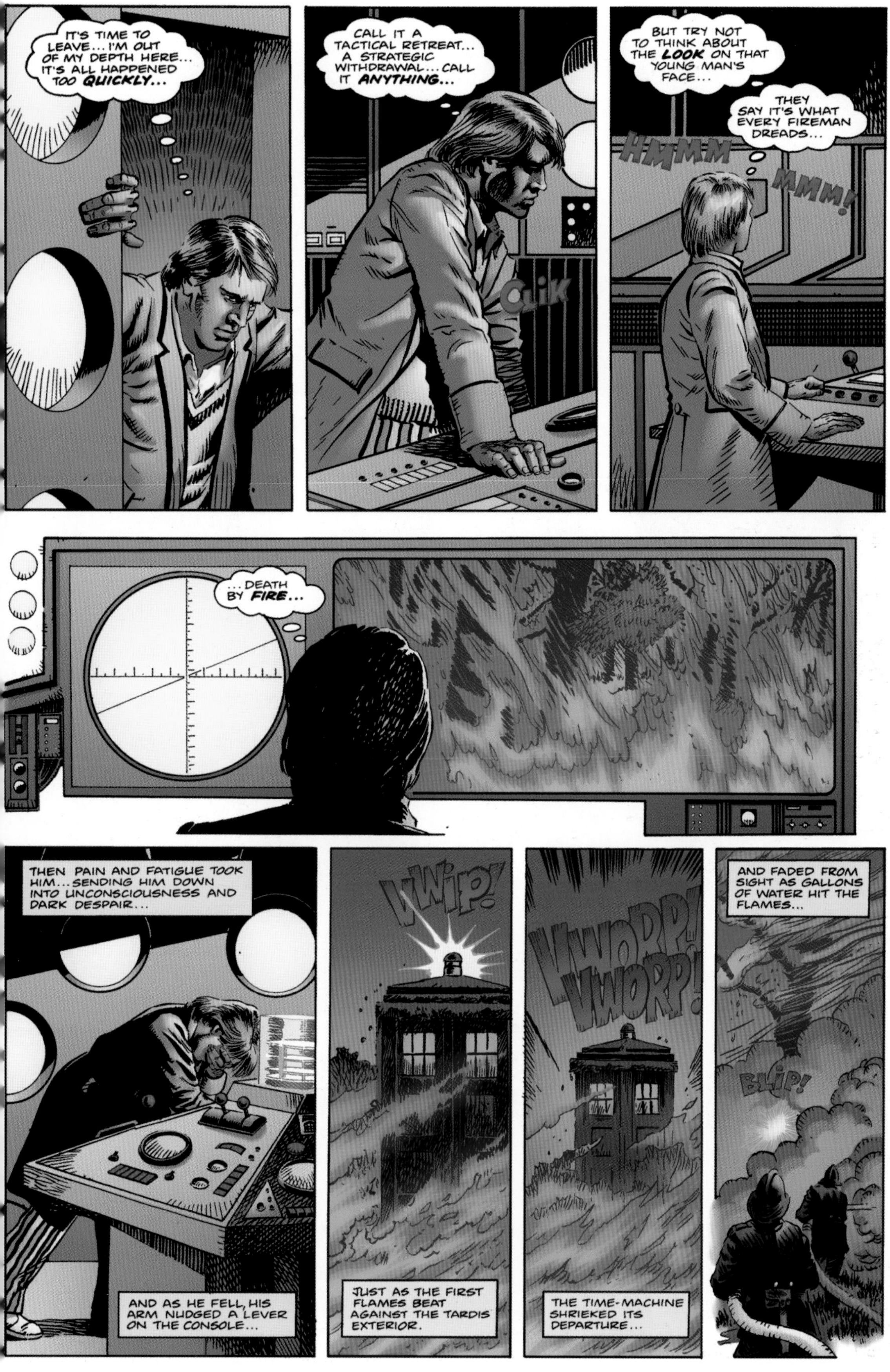
IT'S TIME TO LEAVE... I'M OUT OF MY DEPTH HERE... IT'S ALL HAPPENED TOO **QUICKLY...**
CALL IT A TACTICAL RETREAT... A STRATEGIC WITHDRAWAL... CALL IT **ANYTHING...**
CLIK
BUT TRY NOT TO THINK ABOUT THE **LOOK** ON THAT YOUNG MAN'S FACE...
THEY SAY IT'S WHAT EVERY FIREMAN DREADS...
HMMM MMM!
... DEATH BY **FIRE...**
THEN PAIN AND FATIGUE TOOK HIM... SENDING HIM DOWN INTO UNCONSCIOUSNESS AND DARK DESPAIR...
AND AS HE FELL, HIS ARM NUDGED A LEVER ON THE CONSOLE...
VWIP!
JUST AS THE FIRST FLAMES BEAT AGAINST THE TARDIS EXTERIOR.
VWORP! VWORP!
THE TIME-MACHINE SHRIEKED ITS DEPARTURE...
AND FADED FROM SIGHT AS GALLONS OF WATER HIT THE FLAMES...
BLIP!

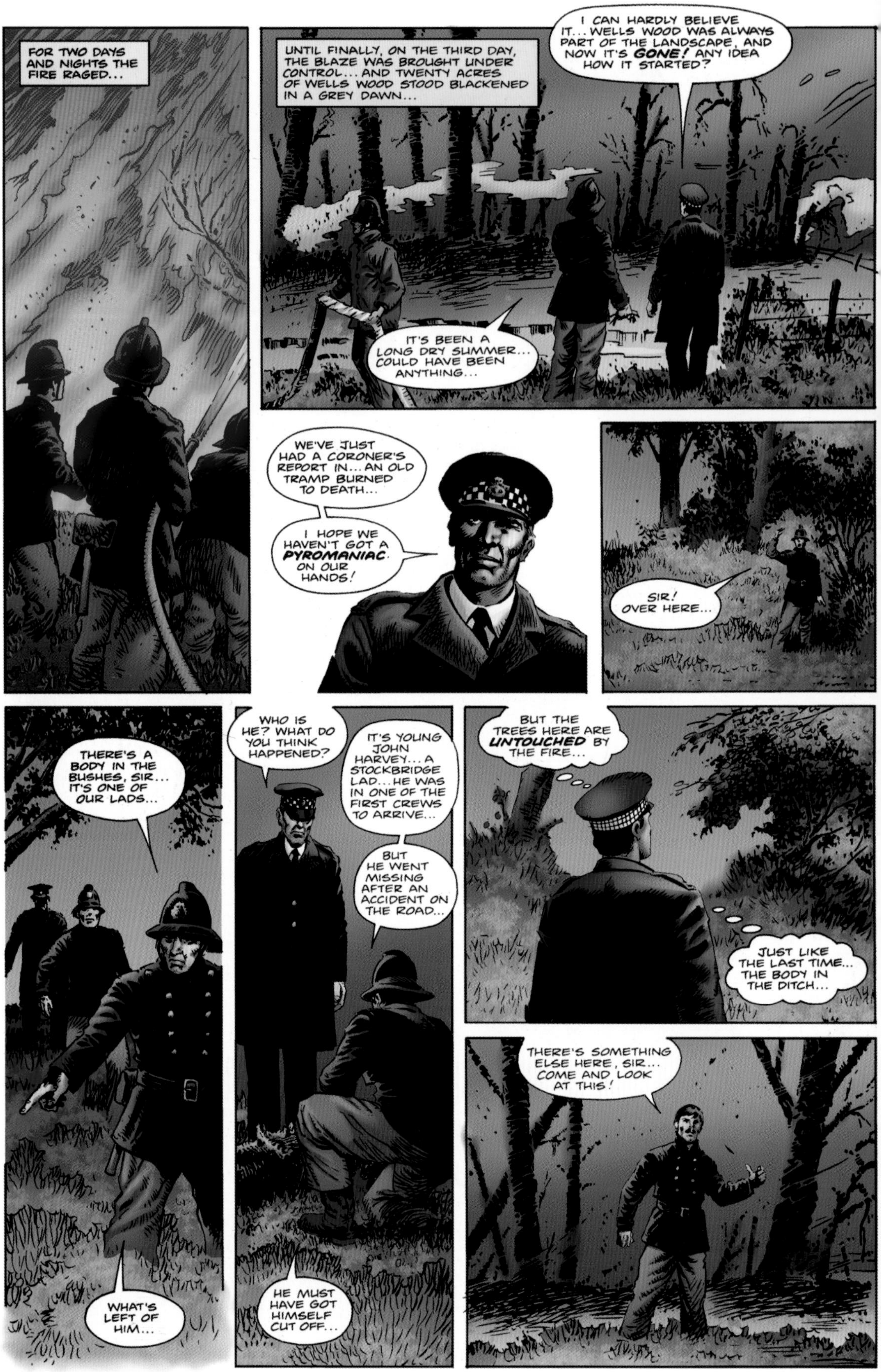
FOR TWO DAYS AND NIGHTS THE FIRE RAGED...
UNTIL FINALLY, ON THE THIRD DAY, THE BLAZE WAS BROUGHT UNDER CONTROL... AND TWENTY ACRES OF WELLS WOOD STOOD BLACKENED IN A GREY DAWN...
I CAN HARDLY BELIEVE IT... WELLS WOOD WAS ALWAYS PART OF THE LANDSCAPE, AND NOW IT'S GONE! ANY IDEA HOW IT STARTED?
IT'S BEEN A LONG DRY SUMMER... COULD HAVE BEEN ANYTHING...
WE'VE JUST HAD A CORONER'S REPORT IN... AN OLD TRAMP BURNED TO DEATH...
I HOPE WE HAVEN'T GOT A PYROMANIAC ON OUR HANDS!
SIR! OVER HERE...
THERE'S A BODY IN THE BUSHES, SIR... IT'S ONE OF OUR LADS...
WHAT'S LEFT OF HIM...
WHO IS HE? WHAT DO YOU THINK HAPPENED?
IT'S YOUNG JOHN HARVEY... A STOCKBRIDGE LAD... HE WAS IN ONE OF THE FIRST CREWS TO ARRIVE...
BUT HE WENT MISSING AFTER AN ACCIDENT ON THE ROAD...
HE MUST HAVE GOT HIMSELF CUT OFF...
BUT THE TREES HERE ARE UNTOUCHED BY THE FIRE...
JUST LIKE THE LAST TIME... THE BODY IN THE DITCH...
THERE'S SOMETHING ELSE HERE, SIR... COME AND LOOK AT THIS!

LOOK AT THIS PATCH OF GRASS...COMPLETELY UNBURNT, YET THE GRASS AROUND IT IS SCORCHED BLACK!

IT'S A PERFECT SQUARE, AND *YELLOW*... AS IF SOMETHING HAD BEEN *STANDING* THERE!

THE PLOT THICKENS, EH?

THIS LOOKS LIKE ONE FOR YOU BLOKES...WE'VE DONE OUR BIT...

GET OUT YOUR *MAGNIFYING GLASS* AND GET STARTED ON THIS LOT...

WEARILY, P.C. MARSHALL WALKED BACK TO HIS CAR...FRAMING HIS REPORT IN HIS MIND...

TWO BADLY BURNED BODIES IN THE SPACE OF A FEW DAYS WAS *MORE* THAN COINCIDENCE...IT WAS ALMOST AN *EPIDEMIC*...

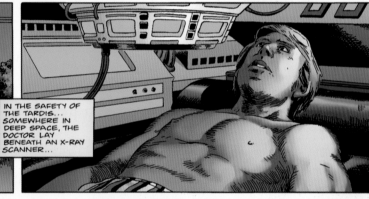

IN THE SAFETY OF THE TARDIS... SOMEWHERE IN DEEP SPACE, THE DOCTOR LAY BENEATH AN X-RAY SCANNER...

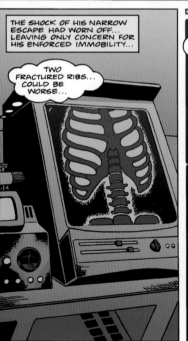

THE SHOCK OF HIS NARROW ESCAPE HAD WORN OFF... LEAVING ONLY CONCERN FOR HIS ENFORCED IMMOBILITY...

TWO FRACTURED RIBS... COULD BE WORSE...

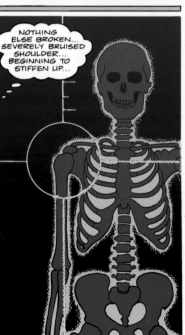

NOTHING ELSE BROKEN... SEVERELY BRUISED SHOULDER... BEGINNING TO STIFFEN UP...

I NEED REST... BUT MY MIND WON'T LET GO OF THAT... THAT *THING* I SAW IN THE WOODS...

LIKE SOME KIND OF *MONSTER!*

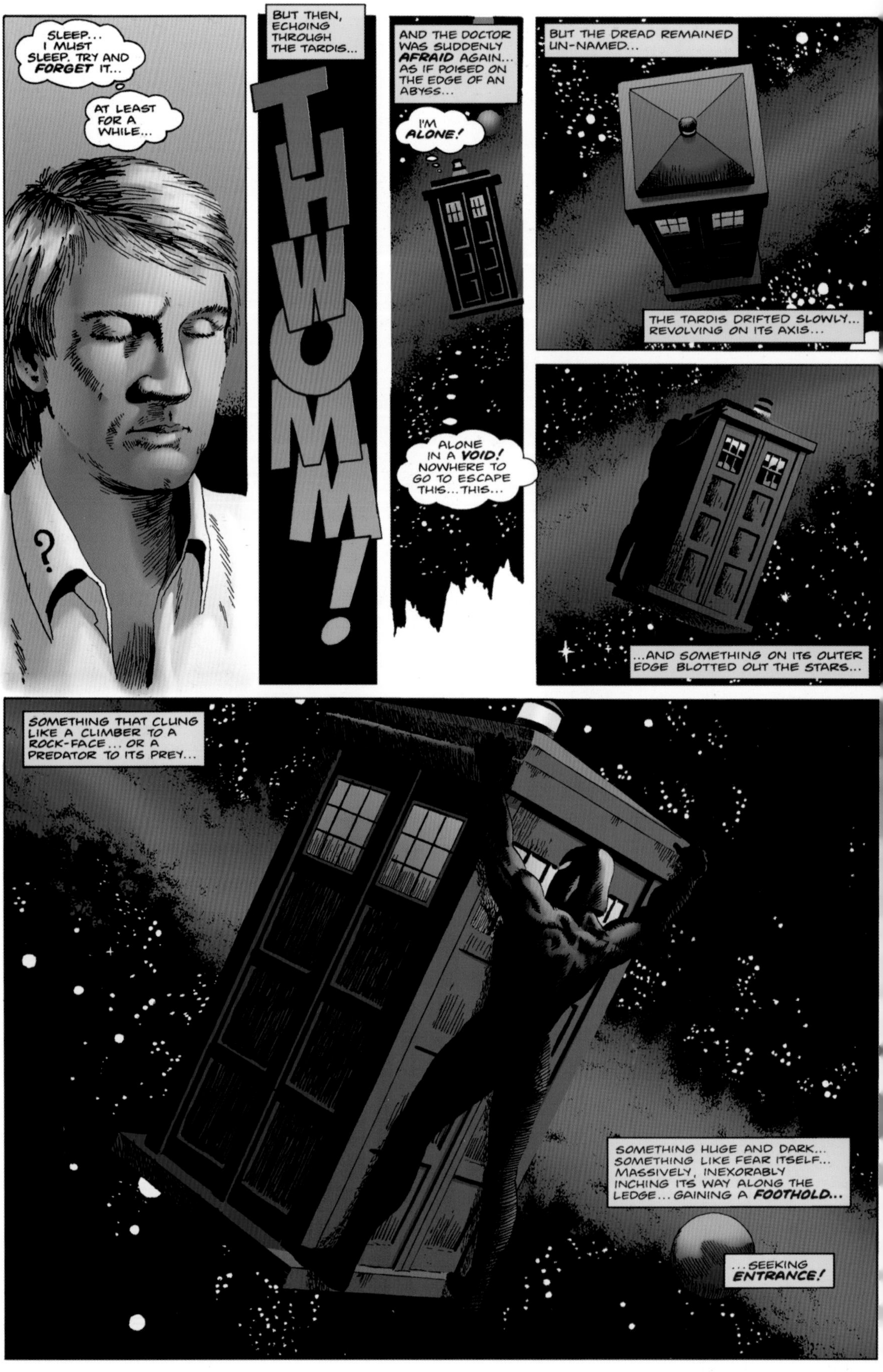

SLEEP... I MUST SLEEP. TRY AND FORGET IT...
AT LEAST FOR A WHILE...
BUT THEN, ECHOING THROUGH THE TARDIS...
THWOMM!
AND THE DOCTOR WAS SUDDENLY AFRAID AGAIN... AS IF POISED ON THE EDGE OF AN ABYSS...
I'M ALONE!
ALONE IN A VOID! NOWHERE TO GO TO ESCAPE THIS... THIS...
BUT THE DREAD REMAINED UN-NAMED...
THE TARDIS DRIFTED SLOWLY... REVOLVING ON ITS AXIS...
...AND SOMETHING ON ITS OUTER EDGE BLOTTED OUT THE STARS...
SOMETHING THAT CLUNG LIKE A CLIMBER TO A ROCK-FACE... OR A PREDATOR TO ITS PREY...
SOMETHING HUGE AND DARK... SOMETHING LIKE FEAR ITSELF... MASSIVELY, INEXORABLY INCHING ITS WAY ALONG THE LEDGE... GAINING A FOOTHOLD...
...SEEKING ENTRANCE!

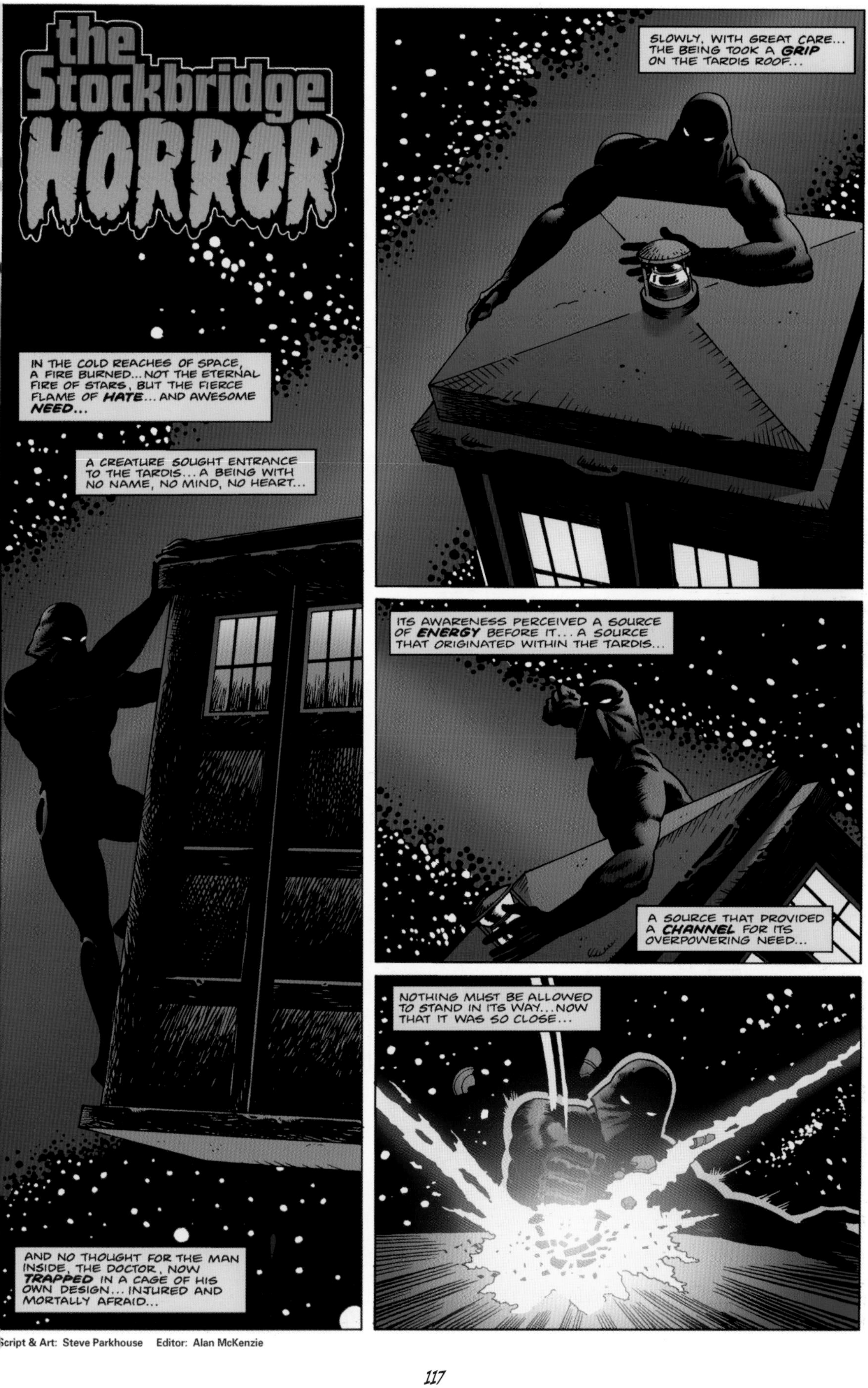
the Stockbridge HORROR
IN THE COLD REACHES OF SPACE, A FIRE BURNED... NOT THE ETERNAL FIRE OF STARS, BUT THE FIERCE FLAME OF HATE... AND AWESOME NEED...
A CREATURE SOUGHT ENTRANCE TO THE TARDIS... A BEING WITH NO NAME, NO MIND, NO HEART...
AND NO THOUGHT FOR THE MAN INSIDE, THE DOCTOR, NOW TRAPPED IN A CAGE OF HIS OWN DESIGN... INJURED AND MORTALLY AFRAID...
SLOWLY, WITH GREAT CARE... THE BEING TOOK A GRIP ON THE TARDIS ROOF...
ITS AWARENESS PERCEIVED A SOURCE OF ENERGY BEFORE IT... A SOURCE THAT ORIGINATED WITHIN THE TARDIS...
A SOURCE THAT PROVIDED A CHANNEL FOR ITS OVERPOWERING NEED...
NOTHING MUST BE ALLOWED TO STAND IN ITS WAY... NOW THAT IT WAS SO CLOSE...

Script & Art: Steve Parkhouse Editor: Alan McKenzie

GRASPING THE TERMINALS WITH BOTH HANDS, THE CREATURE ALLOWED ITS OWN ENERGY TO FLOW IN A GREAT SURGE...WITH ALL THE PENT-UP **POWER** OF AN ELECTRICAL STORM...

THE LIFE-FORCE **SEARED** INTO THE TARDIS' POWER SYSTEM...

UNTIL, OVERLOADED, THE SYSTEM GAVE OUT... **SUNDERING** THE CONSOLE IN A VIOLENT EXPLOSION!

FZAT!

GOOD GRIEF!

AN OVERLOAD... A MASSIVE **FAULT**... IT MUST HAVE BEEN...

...UNLESS...

I'LL SWITCH OVER TO SUPPLEMENTARY POWER...

GET A REPORT ON THE DAMAGE TO THE MAIN SYSTEM...

REQUESTING REPORT ON EXTENT OF DAMAGE TO MAIN POWER UNITS...AND CONSOLE SYSTEMS...IMPERATIVE...

REPEAT IMPERATIVE...

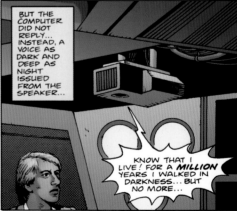

BUT THE COMPUTER DID NOT REPLY...INSTEAD, A VOICE AS DARK AND DEEP AS NIGHT ISSUED FROM THE SPEAKER...

KNOW THAT I LIVE! FOR A **MILLION** YEARS I WALKED IN DARKNESS...BUT NO MORE...

118

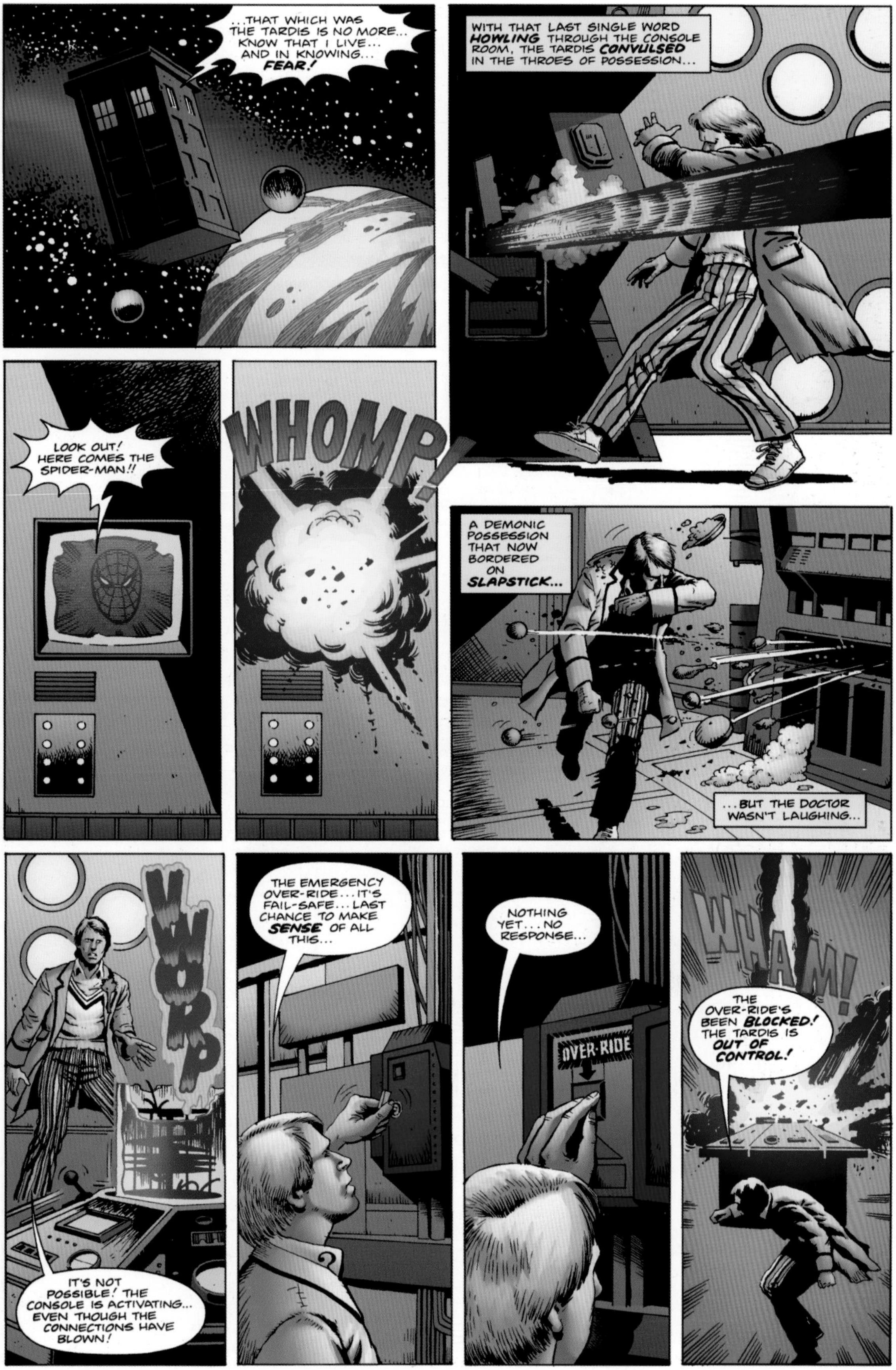

...THAT WHICH WAS THE TARDIS IS NO MORE... KNOW THAT I LIVE... AND IN KNOWING... FEAR!
WITH THAT LAST SINGLE WORD HOWLING THROUGH THE CONSOLE ROOM, THE TARDIS CONVULSED IN THE THROES OF POSSESSION...
LOOK OUT! HERE COMES THE SPIDER-MAN!!
WHOMP!
A DEMONIC POSSESSION THAT NOW BORDERED ON SLAPSTICK...
...BUT THE DOCTOR WASN'T LAUGHING...
VWORP
IT'S NOT POSSIBLE! THE CONSOLE IS ACTIVATING... EVEN THOUGH THE CONNECTIONS HAVE BLOWN!
THE EMERGENCY OVER-RIDE... IT'S FAIL-SAFE... LAST CHANCE TO MAKE SENSE OF ALL THIS...
NOTHING YET... NO RESPONSE...
OVER-RIDE
WHAM!
THE OVER-RIDE'S BEEN BLOCKED! THE TARDIS IS OUT OF CONTROL!

I'VE GOT TO TAKE IT OUT... **SHUT THE WHOLE THING DOWN!**

UNKNOWN TO THE DOCTOR, THE EMERGENCY OVER-RIDE SWITCH HAD ACTIVATED A **SIGNAL**... A SIGNAL THAT EVEN NOW WAS BEING BEAMED TO A CONTROL ROOM ON **GALLIFREY**...

AT SOMETHING APPROACHING THE SPEED OF **LIGHT**...

EMERGENCY CODE THREE ZERO ONE FOUR ONE BEING TRANSFERRED TO MATRIX CENTRAL...

CLEAR ALL CHANNELS FOR EMERGENCY CODE THREE ZERO ONE FOUR ONE...

DEEP IN THE MATRIX DATA BANK, THE EMERGENCY CODE TRIPPED A PRE-PROGRAMMED SEQUENCE OF EVENTS...

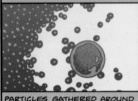

PARTICLES GATHERED AROUND A SINGLE **NUCLEUS**

WHICH THEN MULTIPLIED ITSELF AT AN ALARMING RATE ...FORMING A PRE-DETERMINED **PATTERN**...

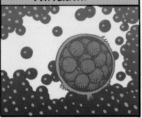

UNTIL A **SHAPE** BEGAN TO COALESCE BENEATH A TERMINAL...

A SHAPE **LIKE** THAT OF A MAN...YET NOT WHOLLY HUMAN...

SHAYDE, SECONDARY AGENT OF THE MATRIX-LORDS OF GALLIFREY, REACHED AROUND FOR A **DIRECTIVE**...

BUT FOUND NONE...

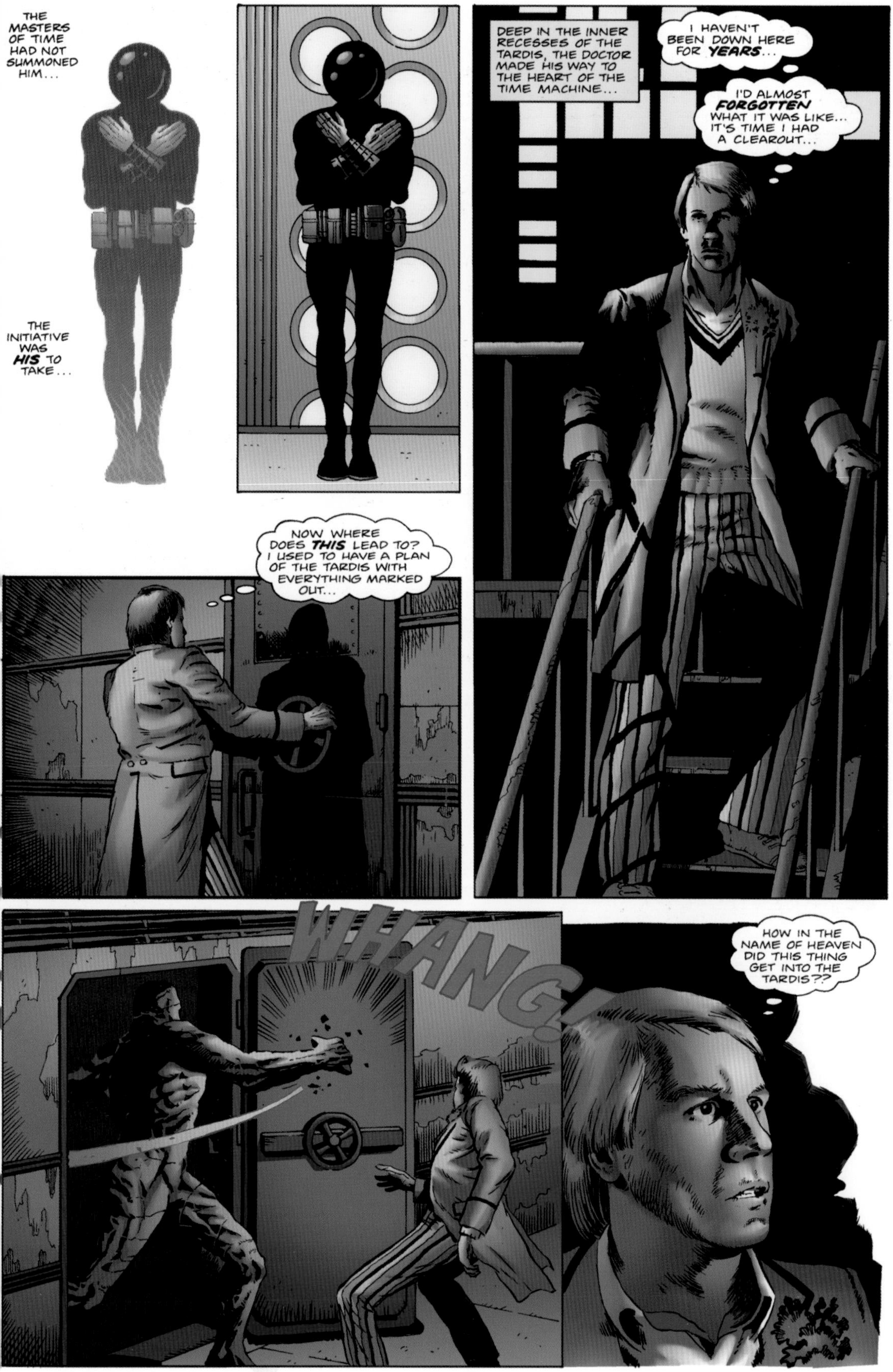
THE MASTERS OF TIME HAD NOT SUMMONED HIM...
THE INITIATIVE WAS HIS TO TAKE...
DEEP IN THE INNER RECESSES OF THE TARDIS, THE DOCTOR MADE HIS WAY TO THE HEART OF THE TIME MACHINE...
I HAVEN'T BEEN DOWN HERE FOR YEARS...
I'D ALMOST FORGOTTEN WHAT IT WAS LIKE... IT'S TIME I HAD A CLEAROUT...
NOW WHERE DOES THIS LEAD TO? I USED TO HAVE A PLAN OF THE TARDIS WITH EVERYTHING MARKED OUT...
WHANG!
HOW IN THE NAME OF HEAVEN DID THIS THING GET INTO THE TARDIS??

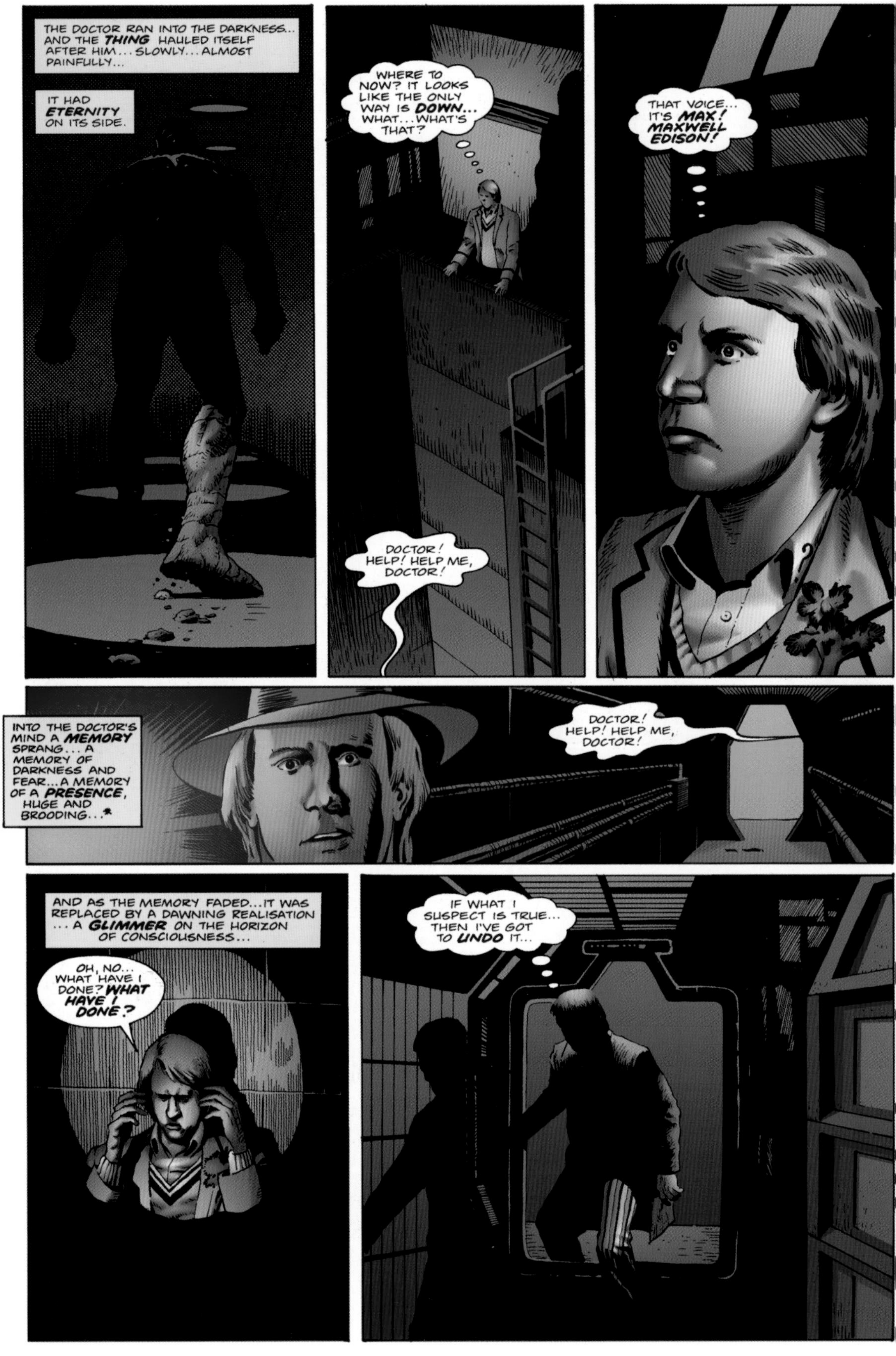
THE DOCTOR RAN INTO THE DARKNESS... AND THE THING HAULED ITSELF AFTER HIM... SLOWLY... ALMOST PAINFULLY...
IT HAD ETERNITY ON ITS SIDE.
WHERE TO NOW? IT LOOKS LIKE THE ONLY WAY IS DOWN... WHAT... WHAT'S THAT?
DOCTOR! HELP! HELP ME, DOCTOR!
THAT VOICE... IT'S MAX! MAXWELL EDISON!
INTO THE DOCTOR'S MIND A MEMORY SPRANG... A MEMORY OF DARKNESS AND FEAR... A MEMORY OF A PRESENCE, HUGE AND BROODING...*
DOCTOR! HELP! HELP ME, DOCTOR!
AND AS THE MEMORY FADED... IT WAS REPLACED BY A DAWNING REALISATION ... A GLIMMER ON THE HORIZON OF CONSCIOUSNESS...
OH, NO... WHAT HAVE I DONE? WHAT HAVE I DONE?
IF WHAT I SUSPECT IS TRUE... THEN I'VE GOT TO UNDO IT...

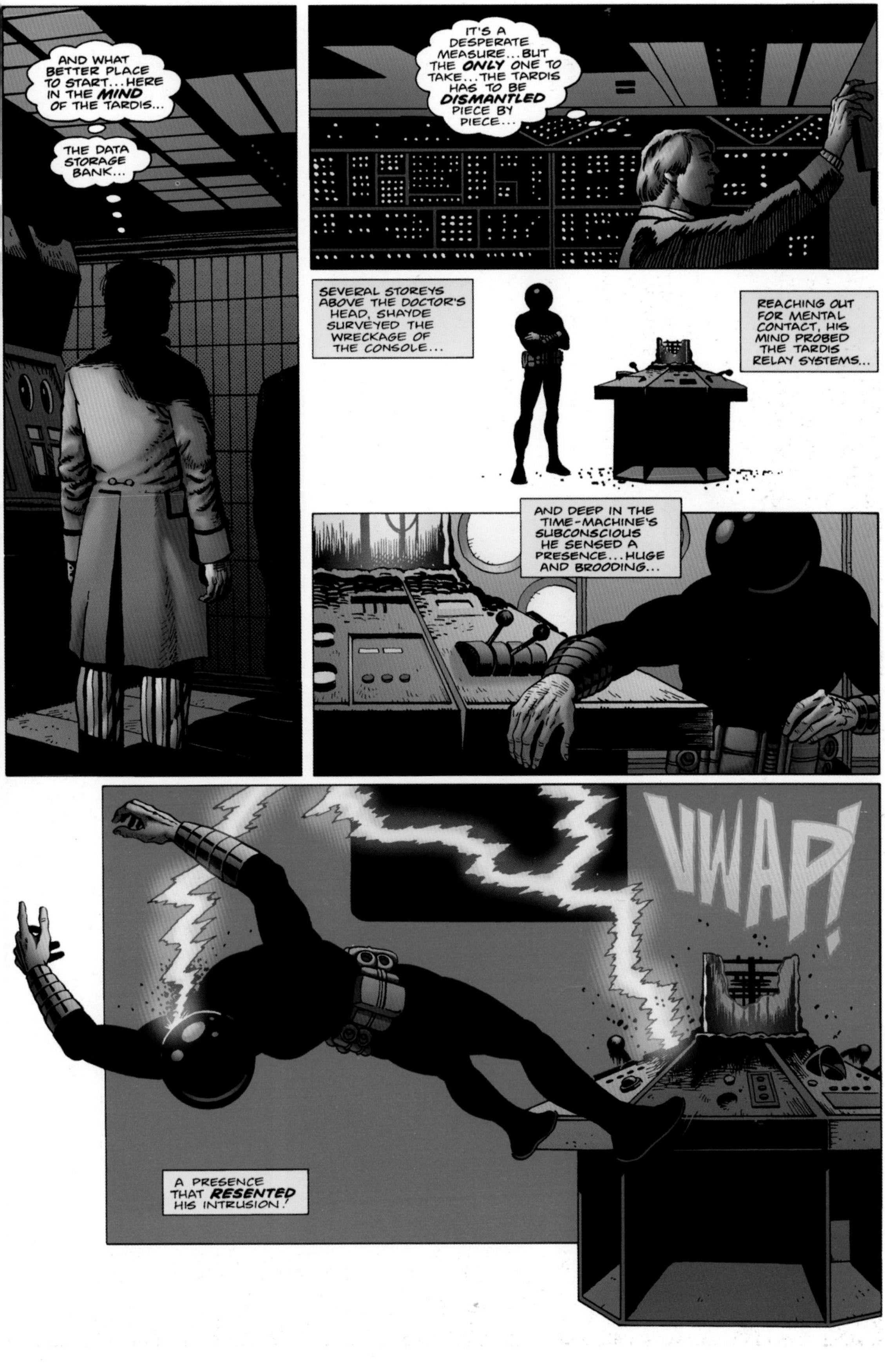
AND WHAT BETTER PLACE TO START... HERE IN THE MIND OF THE TARDIS...
THE DATA STORAGE BANK...
IT'S A DESPERATE MEASURE... BUT THE ONLY ONE TO TAKE... THE TARDIS HAS TO BE DISMANTLED PIECE BY PIECE...
SEVERAL STOREYS ABOVE THE DOCTOR'S HEAD, SHAYDE SURVEYED THE WRECKAGE OF THE CONSOLE...
REACHING OUT FOR MENTAL CONTACT, HIS MIND PROBED THE TARDIS RELAY SYSTEMS...
AND DEEP IN THE TIME-MACHINE'S SUBCONSCIOUS HE SENSED A PRESENCE... HUGE AND BROODING...
VWAP!
A PRESENCE THAT RESENTED HIS INTRUSION!

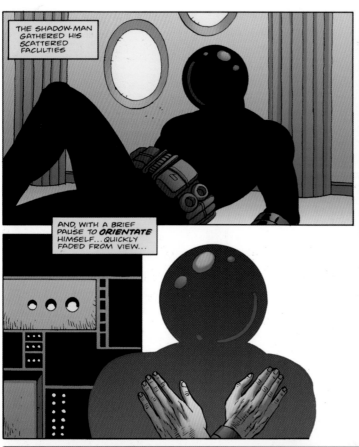

THE SHADOW-MAN GATHERED HIS SCATTERED FACULTIES

AND, WITH A BRIEF PAUSE TO *ORIENTATE* HIMSELF...QUICKLY FADED FROM VIEW...

IN A WELL OF DARKNESS, A THING OF EARTH AND STONE WAS DRAWING NEAR TO ITS INTENDED PREY...

ONCE IT HAD BEEN A GOD OF FIRE, A LORD OF LIGHTNING, CLAIMING VICTIMS IN THE HEART OF A STORM...

BUT NOW IT NEEDED *MASS*... AND SO IT HAD CHANGED...

BUT THE FIRE STILL RAGED WITHIN... FIRE AND THE NEED TO DESTROY...

TO DESTROY THE BEING WHO HAD *SET IT FREE!*

Script: Steve Parkhouse Pencil art. Mick Austin Inks: Paul Neary Editor: Alan McKenzie

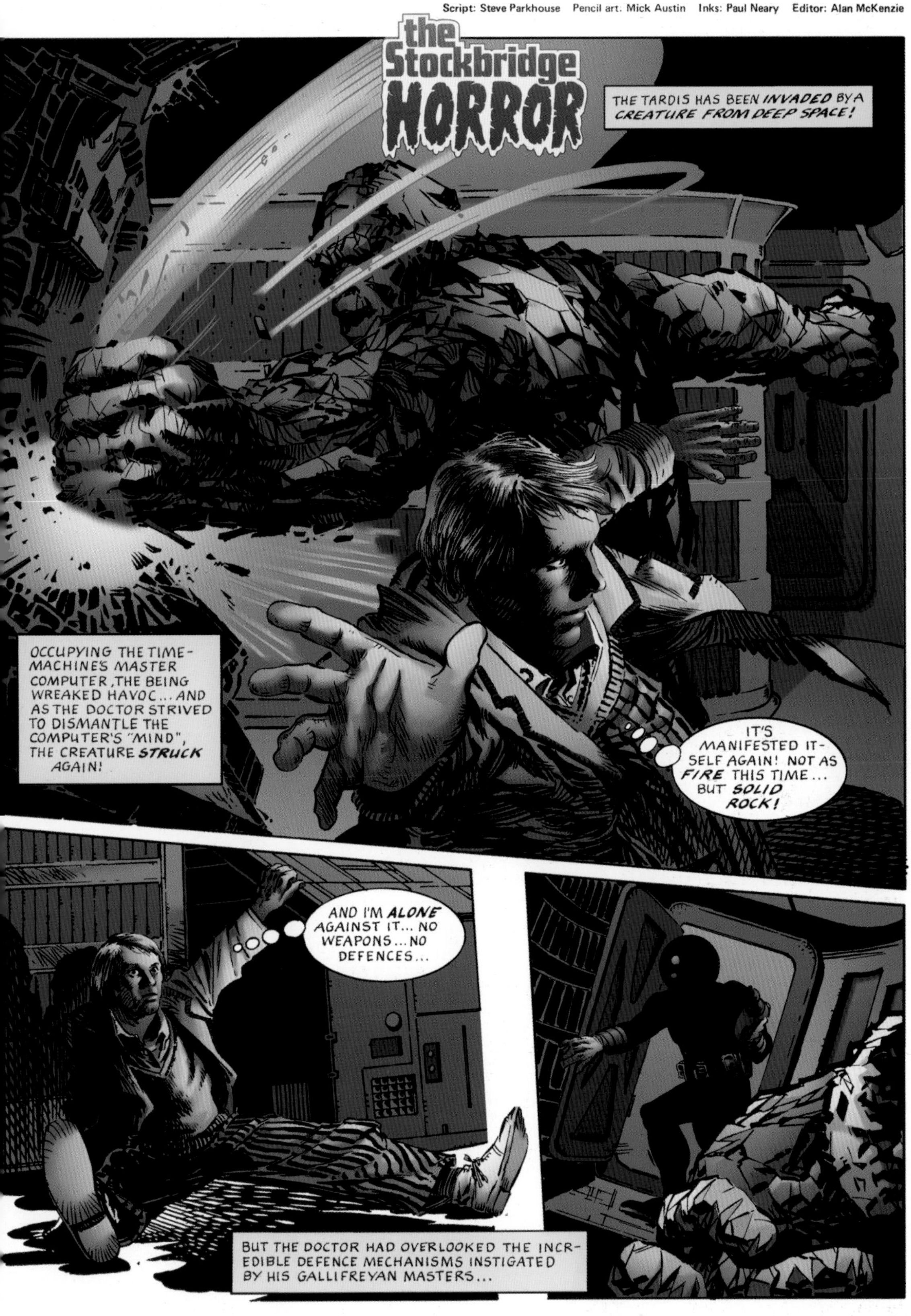
the Stockbridge HORROR
THE TARDIS HAS BEEN INVADED BY A CREATURE FROM DEEP SPACE!
OCCUPYING THE TIME-MACHINE'S MASTER COMPUTER, THE BEING WREAKED HAVOC... AND AS THE DOCTOR STRIVED TO DISMANTLE THE COMPUTER'S "MIND", THE CREATURE STRUCK AGAIN!
IT'S MANIFESTED IT-SELF AGAIN! NOT AS FIRE THIS TIME... BUT SOLID ROCK!
AND I'M ALONE AGAINST IT... NO WEAPONS... NO DEFENCES...
BUT THE DOCTOR HAD OVERLOOKED THE INCREDIBLE DEFENCE MECHANISMS INSTIGATED BY HIS GALLIFREYAN MASTERS...

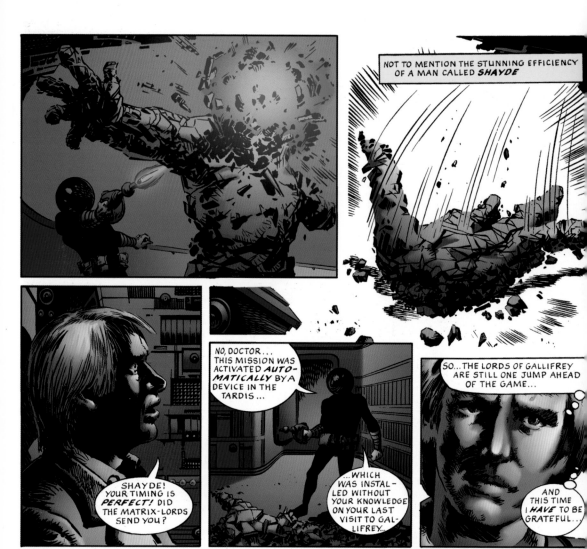

NOT TO MENTION THE STUNNING EFFICIENCY OF A MAN CALLED *SHAYDE*

SHAYDE! YOUR TIMING IS *PERFECT!* DID THE MATRIX-LORDS SEND YOU?

NO, DOCTOR... THIS MISSION WAS ACTIVATED *AUTO-MATICALLY* BY A DEVICE IN THE TARDIS...

...WHICH WAS INSTAL-LED WITHOUT YOUR KNOWLEDGE ON YOUR LAST VISIT TO GAL-LIFREY...

SO...THE LORDS OF GALLIFREY ARE STILL ONE JUMP AHEAD OF THE GAME...

AND THIS TIME I *HAVE* TO BE GRATEFUL...

DOCTOR... YOUR TIME MACHINE HAS BEEN COMMANDEERED BY AN *UN-IDENTIFIABLE FORCE...*

THE TARDIS IS *POSESSED!*

YES...I KNOW... I SUSPEC-TED IT ALL ALONG. I JUST DIDN'T WANT TO *ADMIT* IT TO MYSELF...

YOU SEE... THERE'S A GREAT DEAL I DON'T UNDER-STAND. BUT THERE ALWAYS *IS* WHEN *YOU'RE* INVOLVED... ISN'T THERE?

YOU MAY HAVE TO *ABANDON* THE TARDIS! LIKE A DISEASED MIND, THE TARDIS IS INFECTED BY SOME KIND OF PARASITE... THERE MAY BE *NO* CURE!

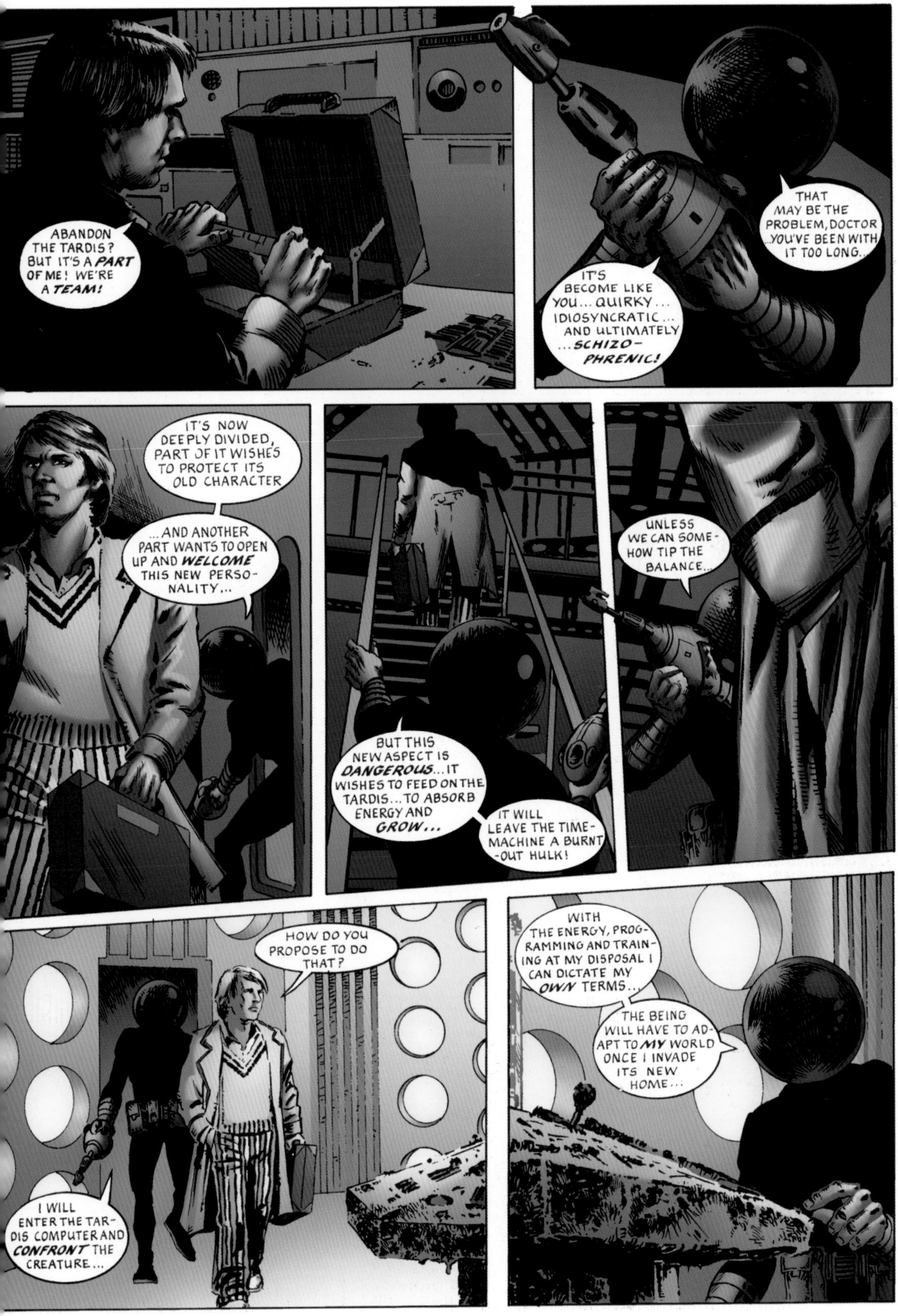
ABANDON THE TARDIS? BUT IT'S A PART OF ME! WE'RE A TEAM!
THAT MAY BE THE PROBLEM, DOCTOR ...YOU'VE BEEN WITH IT TOO LONG...
IT'S BECOME LIKE YOU... QUIRKY... IDIOSYNCRATIC... AND ULTIMATELY ...SCHIZO-PHRENIC!
IT'S NOW DEEPLY DIVIDED, PART OF IT WISHES TO PROTECT ITS OLD CHARACTER
...AND ANOTHER PART WANTS TO OPEN UP AND WELCOME THIS NEW PERSO-NALITY...
BUT THIS NEW ASPECT IS DANGEROUS...IT WISHES TO FEED ON THE TARDIS...TO ABSORB ENERGY AND GROW...
IT WILL LEAVE THE TIME-MACHINE A BURNT-OUT HULK!
UNLESS WE CAN SOME-HOW TIP THE BALANCE...
HOW DO YOU PROPOSE TO DO THAT?
I WILL ENTER THE TAR-DIS COMPUTER AND CONFRONT THE CREATURE...
WITH THE ENERGY, PROG-RAMMING AND TRAIN-ING AT MY DISPOSAL I CAN DICTATE MY OWN TERMS...
THE BEING WILL HAVE TO AD-APT TO MY WORLD ONCE I INVADE ITS NEW HOME...

AND IF YOU *FAIL?*

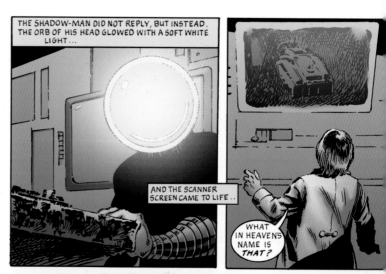

THE SHADOW-MAN DID NOT REPLY, BUT INSTEAD, THE ORB OF HIS HEAD GLOWED WITH A SOFT WHITE LIGHT...

AND THE SCANNER SCREEN CAME TO LIFE...

WHAT IN HEAVEN'S NAME IS *THAT?*

YOU'VE BEEN AWAY TOO LONG, DOCTOR... YOU'VE *LOST TOUCH* WITH DEVELOPMENTS ON GALLIFREY...

YOU KNOW THAT THE MILITARY HAVE BEEN DEVELOP-ING A TARDIS FOR THEIR OWN PURPOSES...

WHAT YOU'RE LOOKING AT IS THEIR LATEST MODEL ....IF WE FAIL...THEY WILL QUITE SIMPLY *BLOW YOUR SHIP TO ATOMS!*

ON WHOSE *AUTHORITY* HAVE YOU DONE THIS? WHO IS IN COMMAND OF THAT THING?

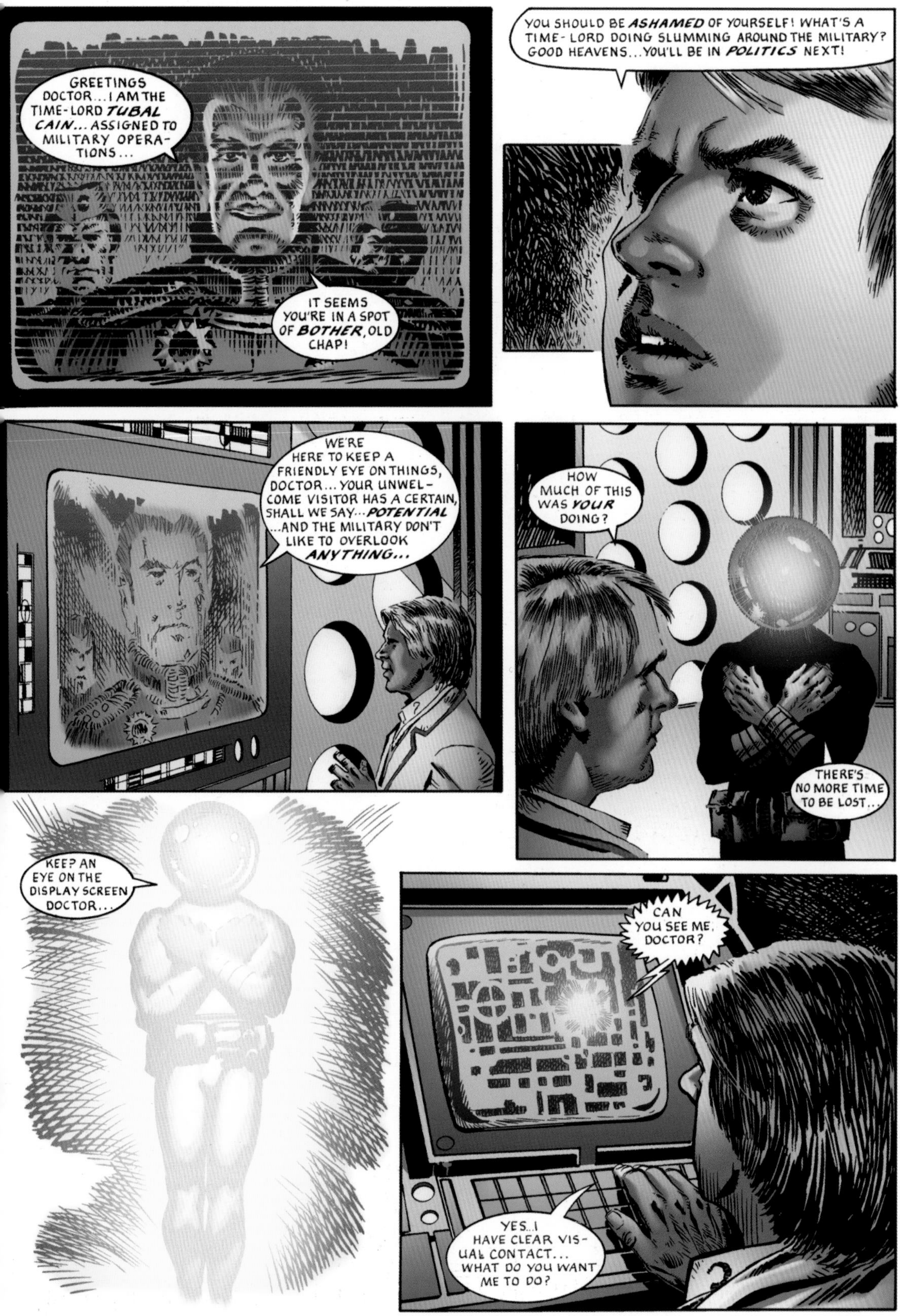
GREETINGS DOCTOR... I AM THE TIME-LORD TUBAL CAIN... ASSIGNED TO MILITARY OPERATIONS...
IT SEEMS YOU'RE IN A SPOT OF BOTHER, OLD CHAP!
YOU SHOULD BE ASHAMED OF YOURSELF! WHAT'S A TIME-LORD DOING SLUMMING AROUND THE MILITARY? GOOD HEAVENS... YOU'LL BE IN POLITICS NEXT!
WE'RE HERE TO KEEP A FRIENDLY EYE ON THINGS, DOCTOR... YOUR UNWELCOME VISITOR HAS A CERTAIN, SHALL WE SAY... POTENTIAL ...AND THE MILITARY DON'T LIKE TO OVERLOOK ANYTHING...
HOW MUCH OF THIS WAS YOUR DOING?
THERE'S NO MORE TIME TO BE LOST...
KEEP AN EYE ON THE DISPLAY SCREEN DOCTOR...
CAN YOU SEE ME, DOCTOR?
YES... I HAVE CLEAR VISUAL CONTACT... WHAT DO YOU WANT ME TO DO?

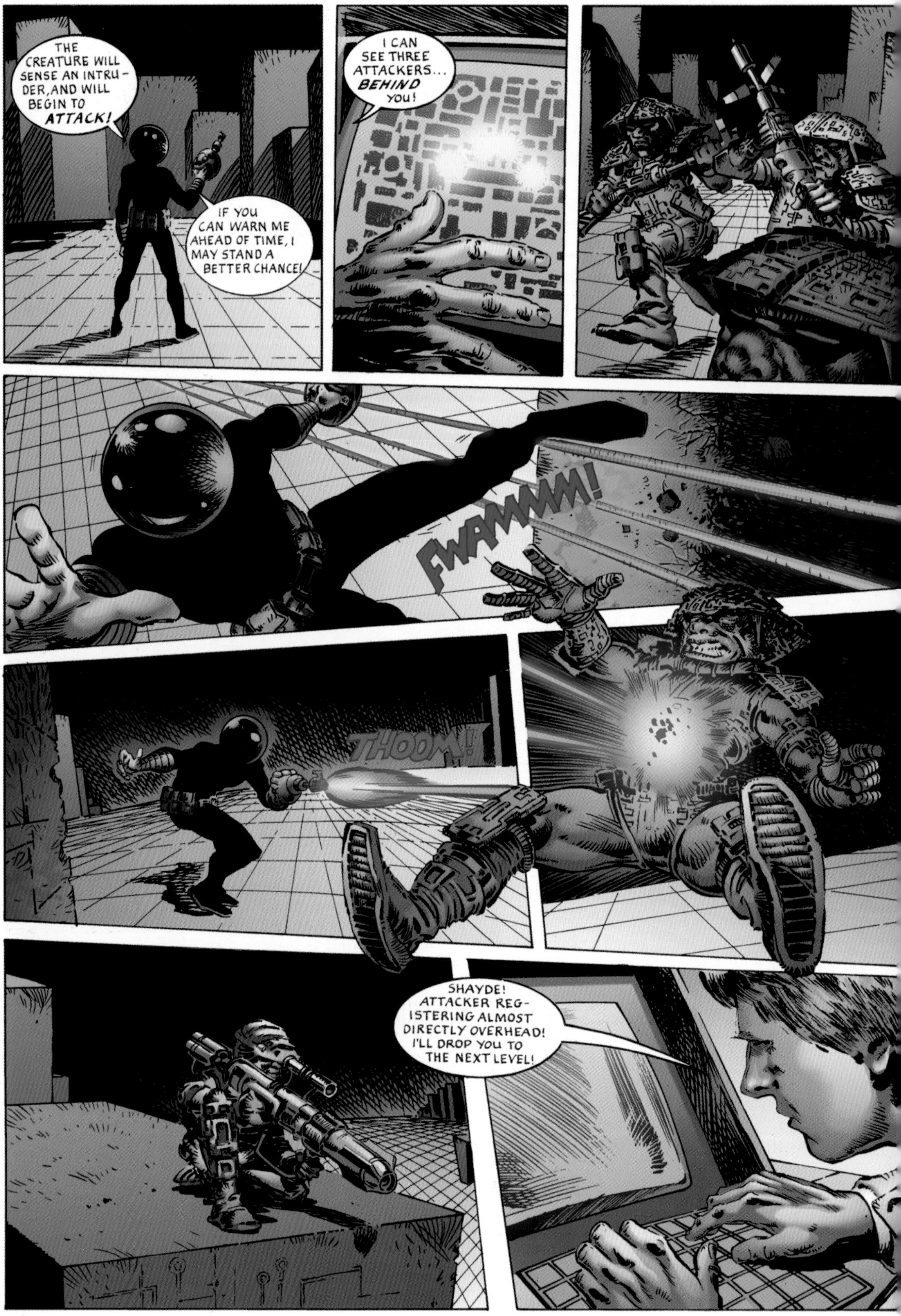
THE CREATURE WILL SENSE AN INTRUDER, AND WILL BEGIN TO ATTACK!
IF YOU CAN WARN ME AHEAD OF TIME, I MAY STAND A BETTER CHANCE!
I CAN SEE THREE ATTACKERS... BEHIND YOU!
FWAMMM!
THOOM!
SHAYDE! ATTACKER REGISTERING ALMOST DIRECTLY OVERHEAD! I'LL DROP YOU TO THE NEXT LEVEL!

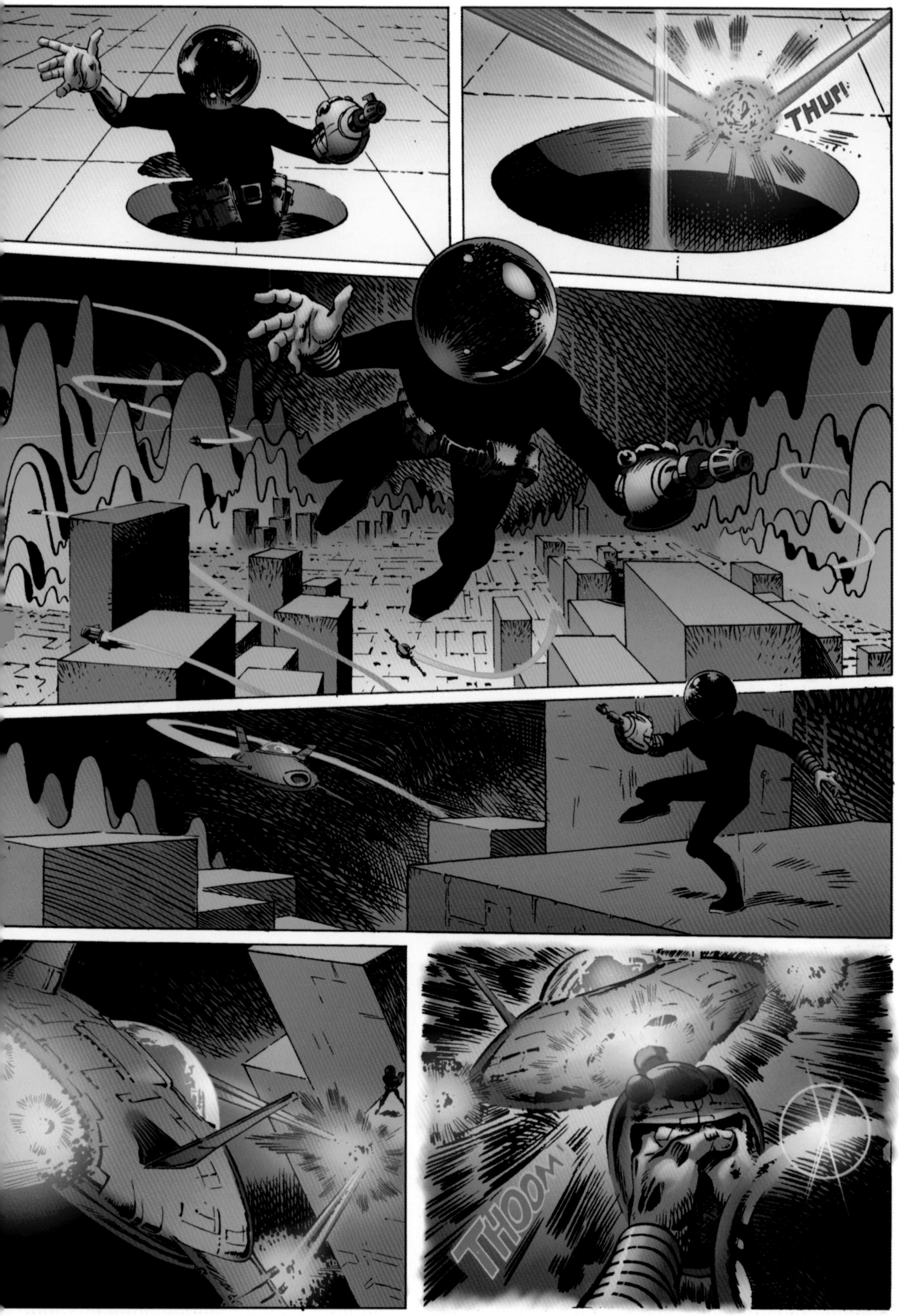
THUP!
THOOM!

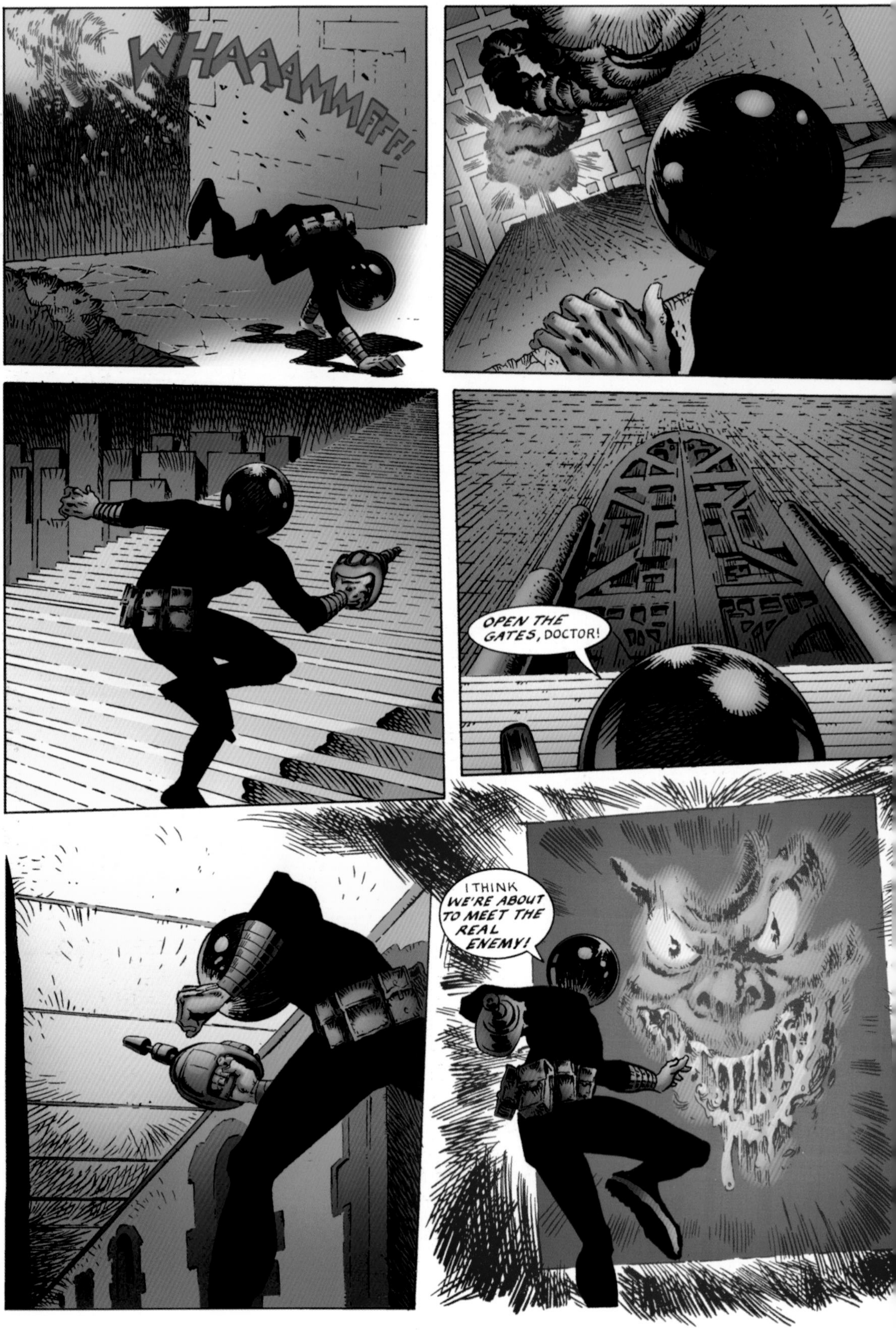
WHAAAMMFFF!
OPEN THE GATES, DOCTOR!
I THINK WE'RE ABOUT TO MEET THE REAL ENEMY!

Script: Steve Parkhouse Art: Mick Austin & Paul Neary Editor: Alan McKenzie

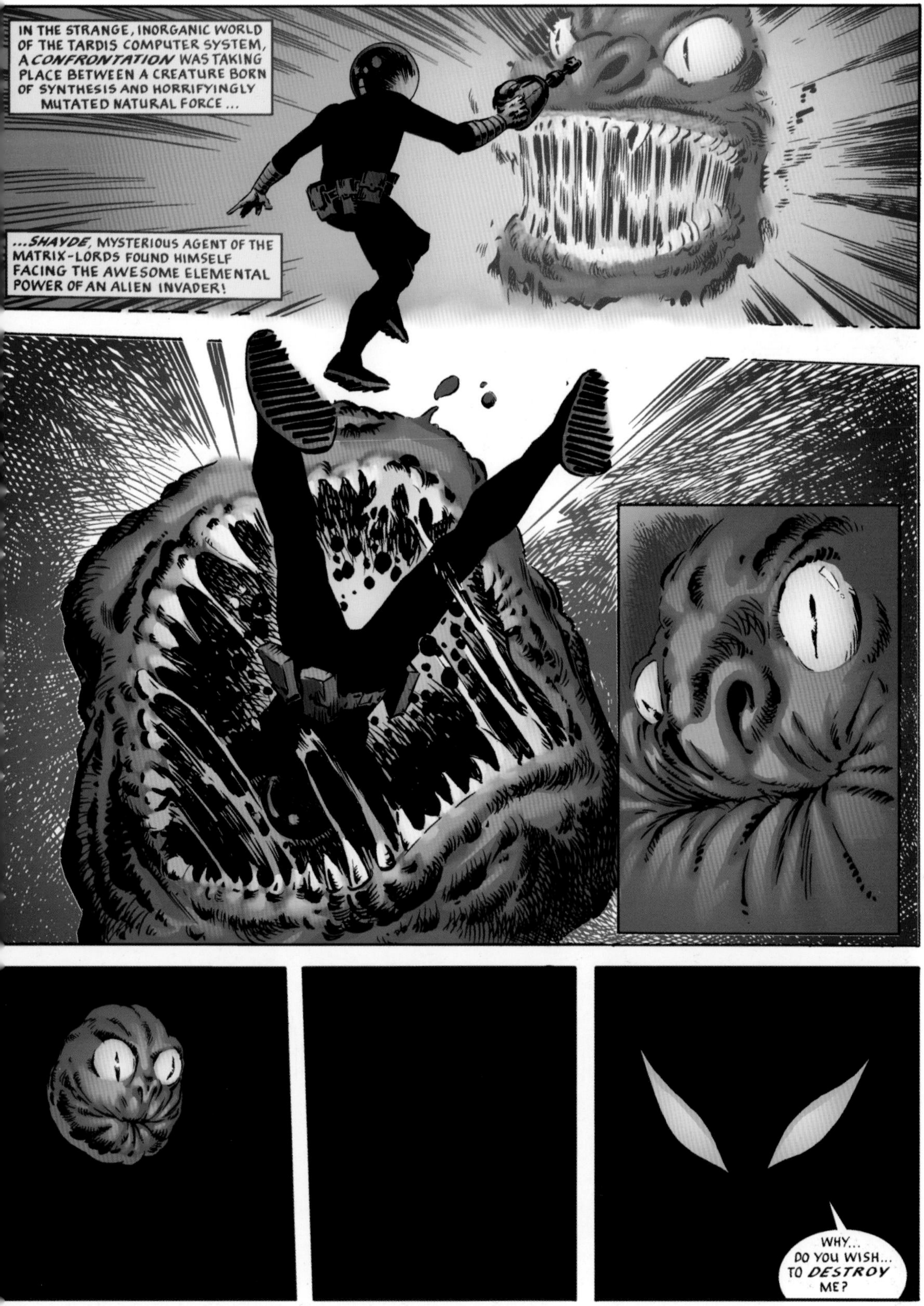

IN THE STRANGE, INORGANIC WORLD OF THE TARDIS COMPUTER SYSTEM, A CONFRONTATION WAS TAKING PLACE BETWEEN A CREATURE BORN OF SYNTHESIS AND HORRIFYINGLY MUTATED NATURAL FORCE...
...SHAYDE, MYSTERIOUS AGENT OF THE MATRIX-LORDS FOUND HIMSELF FACING THE AWESOME ELEMENTAL POWER OF AN ALIEN INVADER!
WHY... DO YOU WISH... TO DESTROY ME?

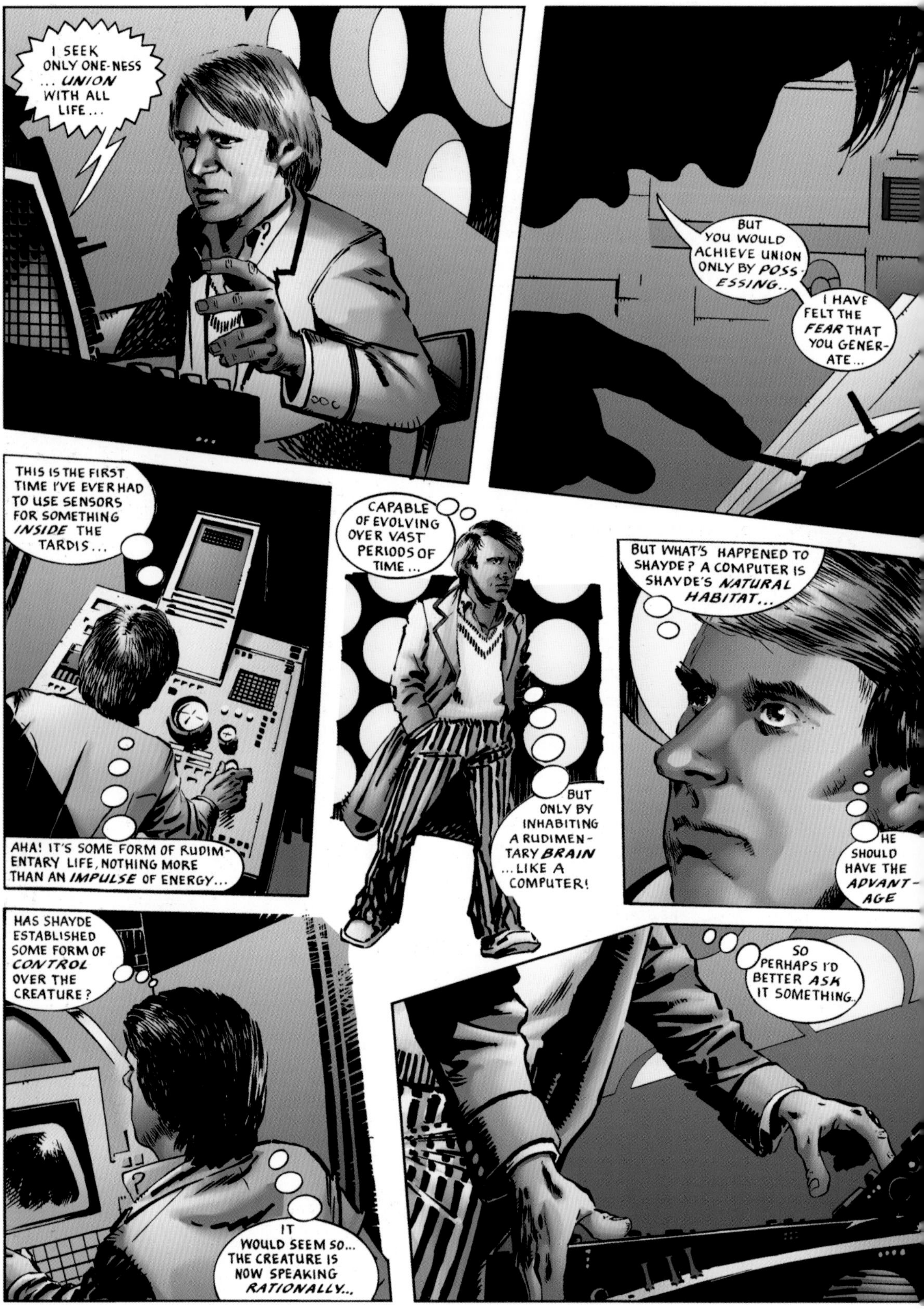

I SEEK ONLY ONE-NESS ... UNION WITH ALL LIFE...
BUT YOU WOULD ACHIEVE UNION ONLY BY POSSESSING..
I HAVE FELT THE FEAR THAT YOU GENERATE...
THIS IS THE FIRST TIME I'VE EVER HAD TO USE SENSORS FOR SOMETHING INSIDE THE TARDIS...
AHA! IT'S SOME FORM OF RUDIMENTARY LIFE, NOTHING MORE THAN AN IMPULSE OF ENERGY...
CAPABLE OF EVOLVING OVER VAST PERIODS OF TIME...
BUT ONLY BY INHABITING A RUDIMENTARY BRAIN ...LIKE A COMPUTER!
BUT WHAT'S HAPPENED TO SHAYDE? A COMPUTER IS SHAYDE'S NATURAL HABITAT...
HE SHOULD HAVE THE ADVANTAGE
HAS SHAYDE ESTABLISHED SOME FORM OF CONTROL OVER THE CREATURE?
IT WOULD SEEM SO... THE CREATURE IS NOW SPEAKING RATIONALLY...
SO PERHAPS I'D BETTER ASK IT SOMETHING..

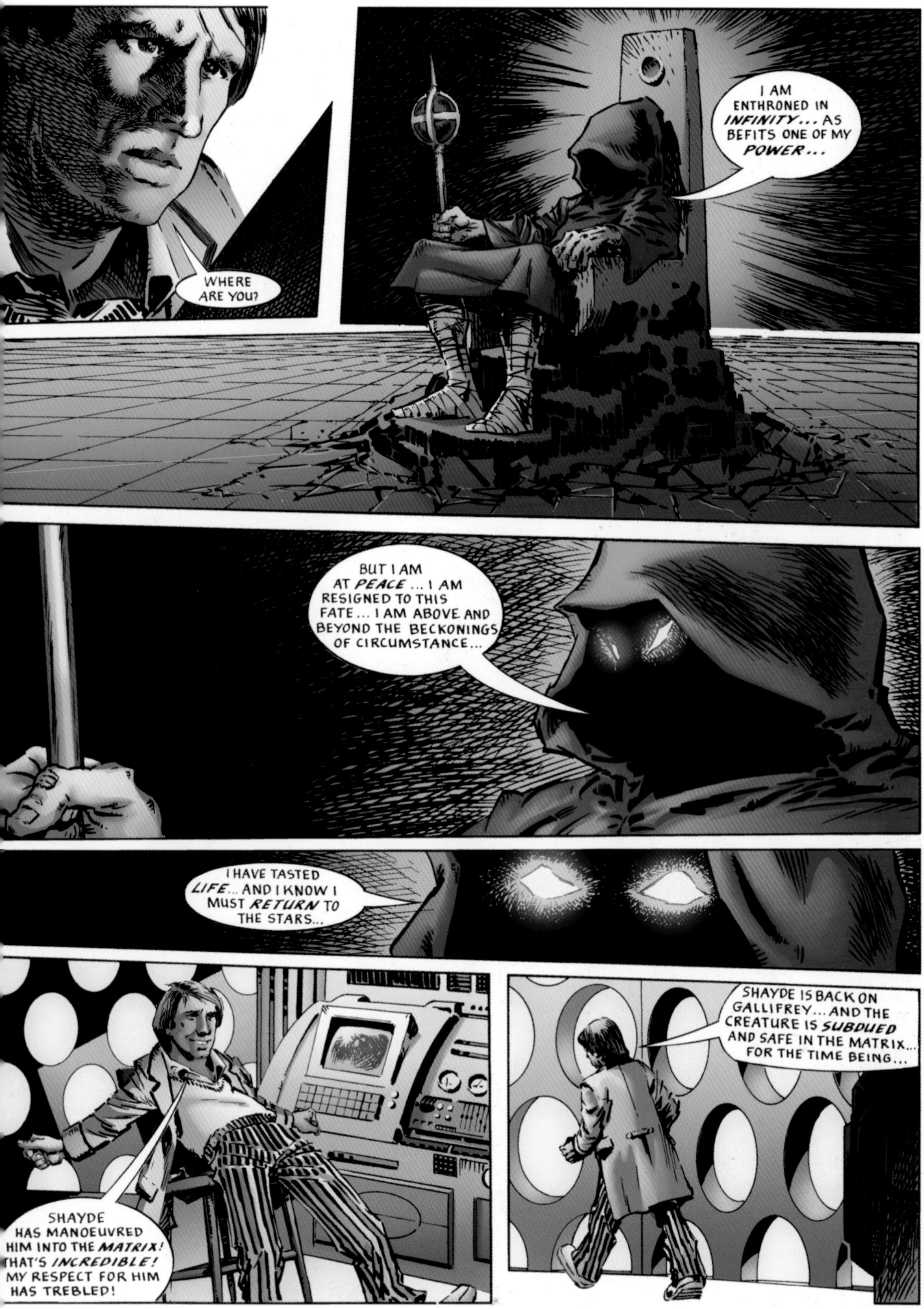

WHERE ARE YOU?
I AM ENTHRONED IN INFINITY... AS BEFITS ONE OF MY POWER...
BUT I AM AT PEACE ... I AM RESIGNED TO THIS FATE... I AM ABOVE AND BEYOND THE BECKONINGS OF CIRCUMSTANCE...
I HAVE TASTED LIFE... AND I KNOW I MUST RETURN TO THE STARS...
SHAYDE HAS MANOEUVRED HIM INTO THE MATRIX! THAT'S INCREDIBLE! MY RESPECT FOR HIM HAS TREBLED!
SHAYDE IS BACK ON GALLIFREY... AND THE CREATURE IS SUBDUED AND SAFE IN THE MATRIX... FOR THE TIME BEING...

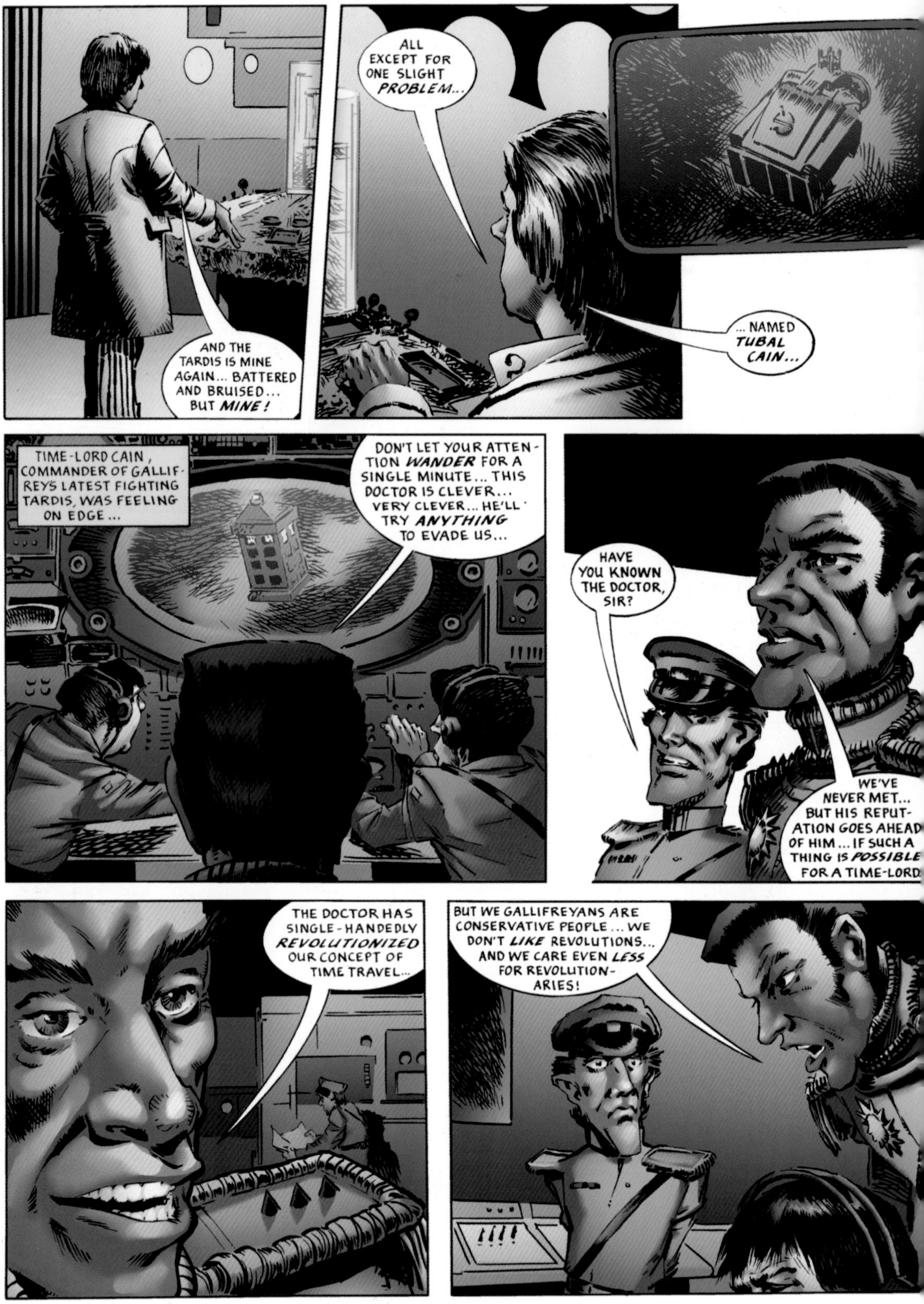
AND THE TARDIS IS MINE AGAIN... BATTERED AND BRUISED... BUT MINE!
ALL EXCEPT FOR ONE SLIGHT PROBLEM...
...NAMED TUBAL CAIN...
TIME-LORD CAIN, COMMANDER OF GALLIFREY'S LATEST FIGHTING TARDIS, WAS FEELING ON EDGE...
DON'T LET YOUR ATTENTION WANDER FOR A SINGLE MINUTE... THIS DOCTOR IS CLEVER... VERY CLEVER... HE'LL TRY ANYTHING TO EVADE US...
HAVE YOU KNOWN THE DOCTOR, SIR?
WE'VE NEVER MET... BUT HIS REPUTATION GOES AHEAD OF HIM... IF SUCH A THING IS POSSIBLE FOR A TIME-LORD
THE DOCTOR HAS SINGLE-HANDEDLY REVOLUTIONIZED OUR CONCEPT OF TIME TRAVEL...
BUT WE GALLIFREYANS ARE CONSERVATIVE PEOPLE... WE DON'T LIKE REVOLUTIONS... AND WE CARE EVEN LESS FOR REVOLUTIONARIES!

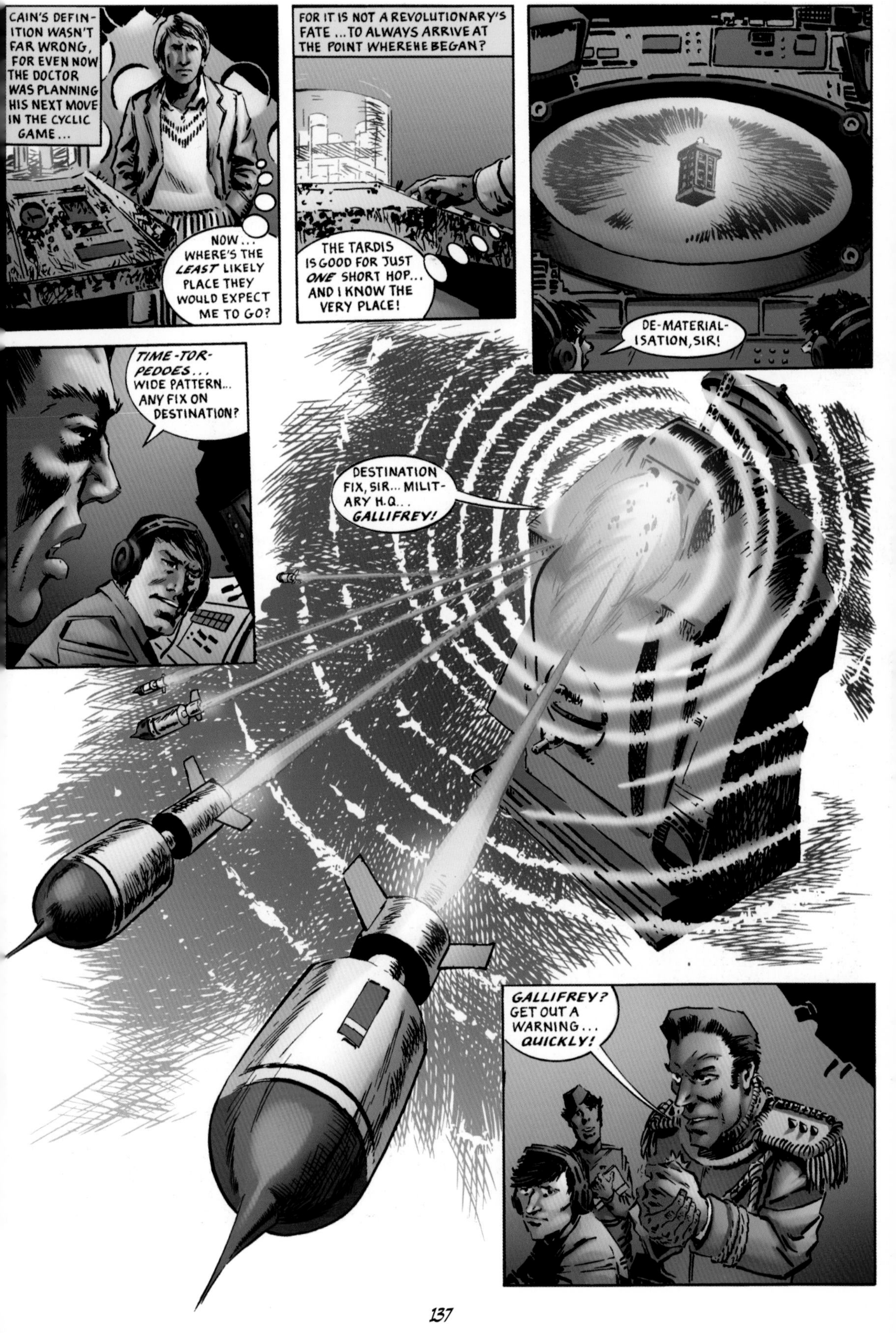
CAIN'S DEFINITION WASN'T FAR WRONG, FOR EVEN NOW THE DOCTOR WAS PLANNING HIS NEXT MOVE IN THE CYCLIC GAME...
NOW... WHERE'S THE LEAST LIKELY PLACE THEY WOULD EXPECT ME TO GO?
FOR IT IS NOT A REVOLUTIONARY'S FATE ...TO ALWAYS ARRIVE AT THE POINT WHEREHE BEGAN?
THE TARDIS IS GOOD FOR JUST ONE SHORT HOP... AND I KNOW THE VERY PLACE!
DE-MATERIALISATION, SIR!
TIME-TORPEDOES... WIDE PATTERN... ANY FIX ON DESTINATION?
DESTINATION FIX, SIR... MILITARY H.Q... GALLIFREY!
GALLIFREY? GET OUT A WARNING... QUICKLY!

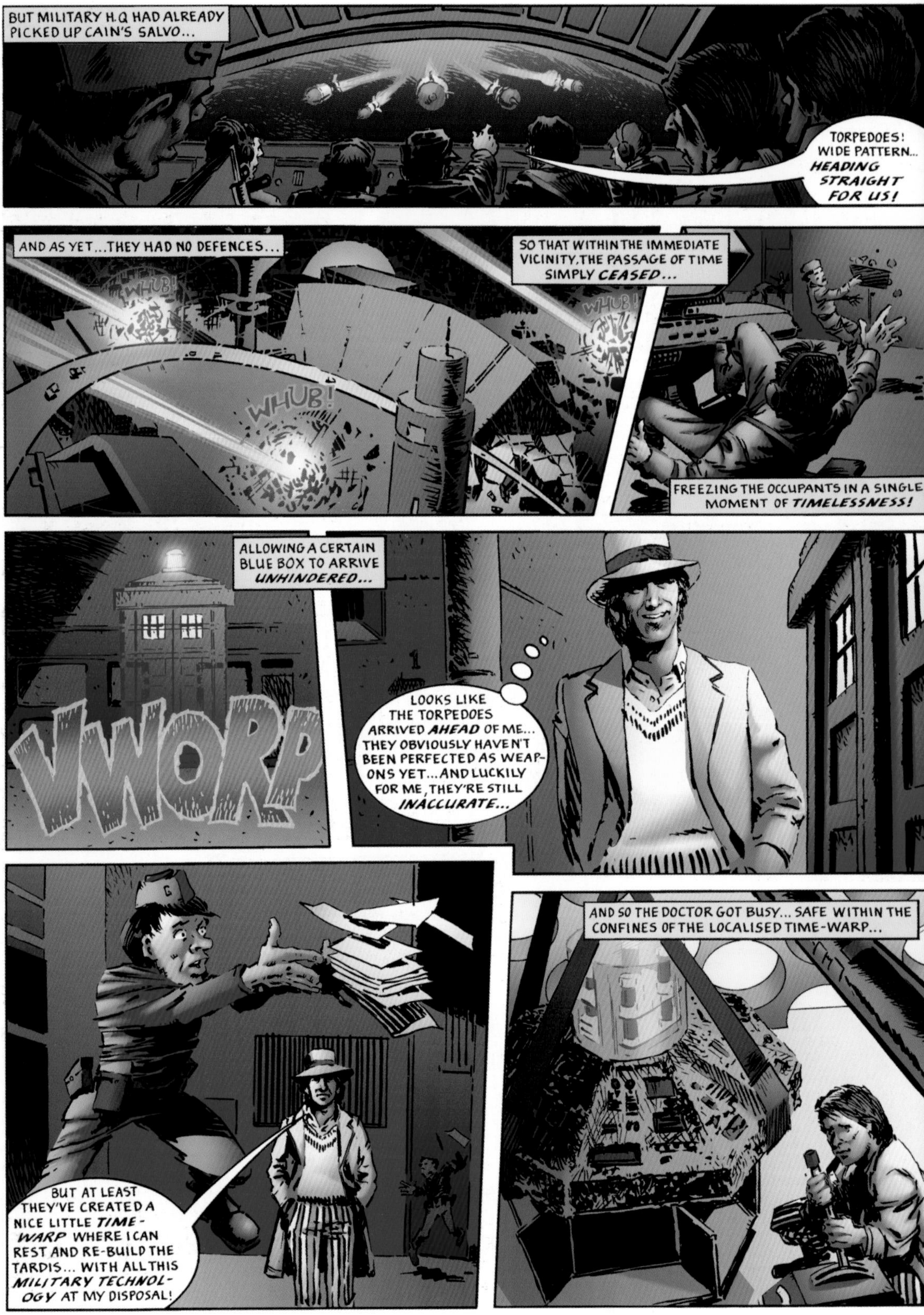
BUT MILITARY H.Q HAD ALREADY PICKED UP CAIN'S SALVO...
TORPEDOES! WIDE PATTERN... HEADING STRAIGHT FOR US!
AND AS YET...THEY HAD NO DEFENCES...
WHUB!
WHUB!
WHUB!
SO THAT WITHIN THE IMMEDIATE VICINITY, THE PASSAGE OF TIME SIMPLY CEASED...
FREEZING THE OCCUPANTS IN A SINGLE MOMENT OF TIMELESSNESS!
ALLOWING A CERTAIN BLUE BOX TO ARRIVE UNHINDERED...
VWORP
LOOKS LIKE THE TORPEDOES ARRIVED AHEAD OF ME... THEY OBVIOUSLY HAVEN'T BEEN PERFECTED AS WEAPONS YET... AND LUCKILY FOR ME, THEY'RE STILL INACCURATE...
BUT AT LEAST THEY'VE CREATED A NICE LITTLE TIME-WARP WHERE I CAN REST AND RE-BUILD THE TARDIS... WITH ALL THIS MILITARY TECHNOLOGY AT MY DISPOSAL!
AND SO THE DOCTOR GOT BUSY... SAFE WITHIN THE CONFINES OF THE LOCALISED TIME-WARP...

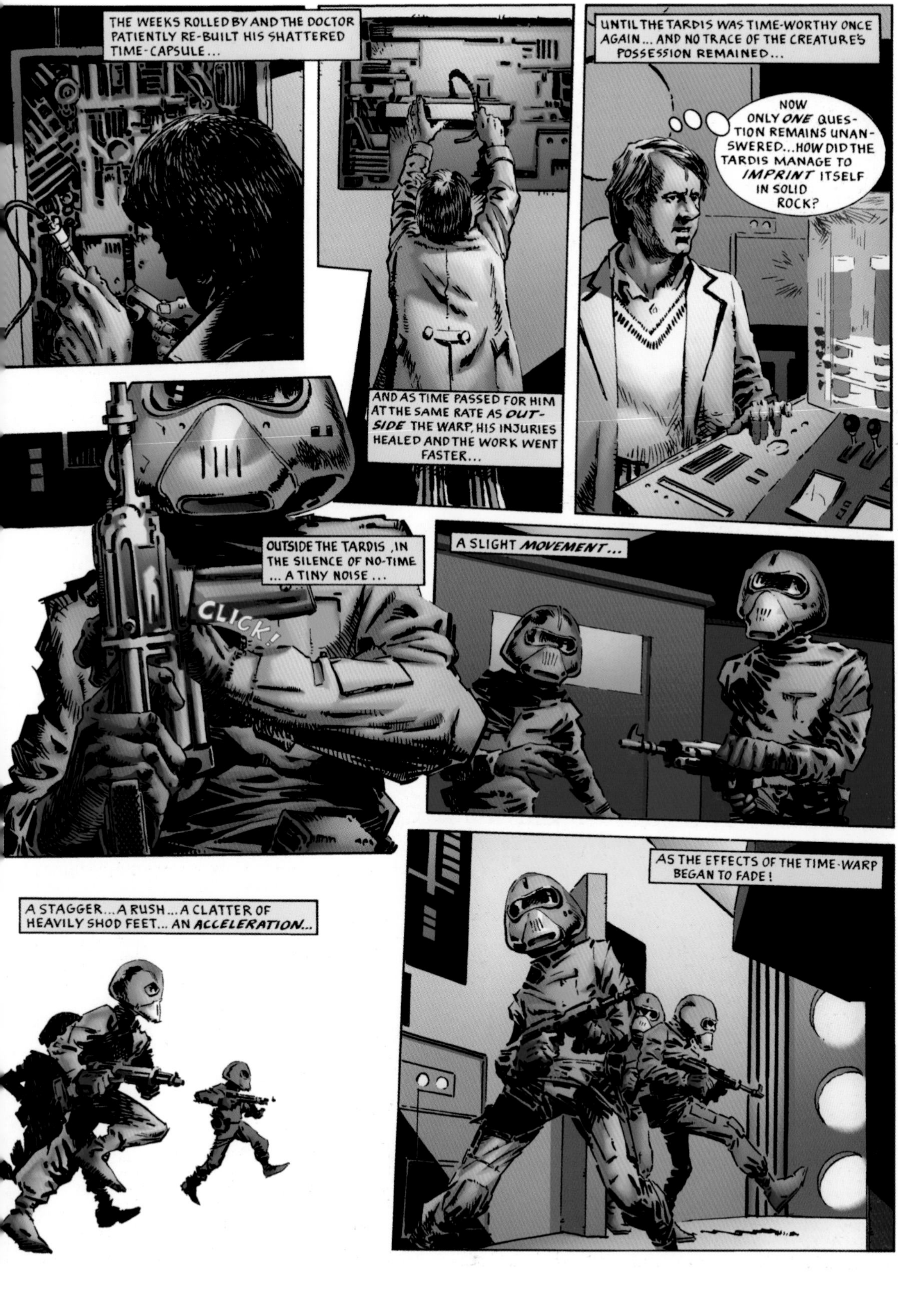
THE WEEKS ROLLED BY AND THE DOCTOR PATIENTLY RE-BUILT HIS SHATTERED TIME-CAPSULE...
AND AS TIME PASSED FOR HIM AT THE SAME RATE AS OUT-SIDE THE WARP, HIS INJURIES HEALED AND THE WORK WENT FASTER...
UNTIL THE TARDIS WAS TIME-WORTHY ONCE AGAIN... AND NO TRACE OF THE CREATURE'S POSSESSION REMAINED...
NOW ONLY ONE QUESTION REMAINS UNANSWERED...HOW DID THE TARDIS MANAGE TO IMPRINT ITSELF IN SOLID ROCK?
OUTSIDE THE TARDIS, IN THE SILENCE OF NO-TIME ...A TINY NOISE...
CLICK!
A SLIGHT MOVEMENT...
A STAGGER...A RUSH...A CLATTER OF HEAVILY SHOD FEET... AN ACCELERATION...
AS THE EFFECTS OF THE TIME-WARP BEGAN TO FADE!

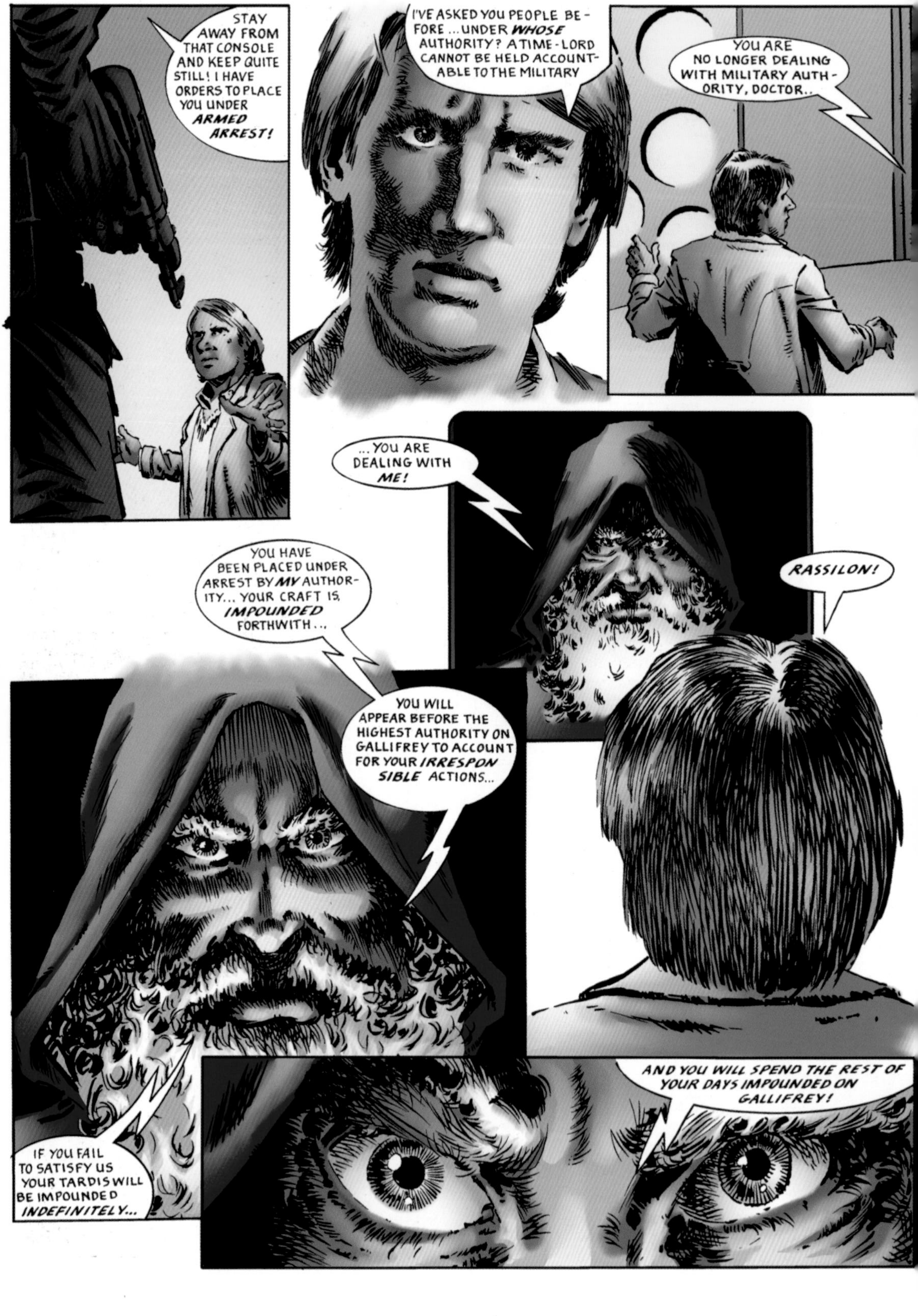

STAY AWAY FROM THAT CONSOLE AND KEEP QUITE STILL! I HAVE ORDERS TO PLACE YOU UNDER ARMED ARREST!
I'VE ASKED YOU PEOPLE BE-FORE ... UNDER WHOSE AUTHORITY? A TIME-LORD CANNOT BE HELD ACCOUNT-ABLE TO THE MILITARY
YOU ARE NO LONGER DEALING WITH MILITARY AUTH-ORITY, DOCTOR..
...YOU ARE DEALING WITH ME!
RASSILON!
YOU HAVE BEEN PLACED UNDER ARREST BY MY AUTHOR-ITY... YOUR CRAFT IS IMPOUNDED FORTHWITH...
YOU WILL APPEAR BEFORE THE HIGHEST AUTHORITY ON GALLIFREY TO ACCOUNT FOR YOUR IRRESPON SIBLE ACTIONS...
IF YOU FAIL TO SATISFY US YOUR TARDIS WILL BE IMPOUNDED INDEFINITELY...
AND YOU WILL SPEND THE REST OF YOUR DAYS IMPOUNDED ON GALLIFREY!

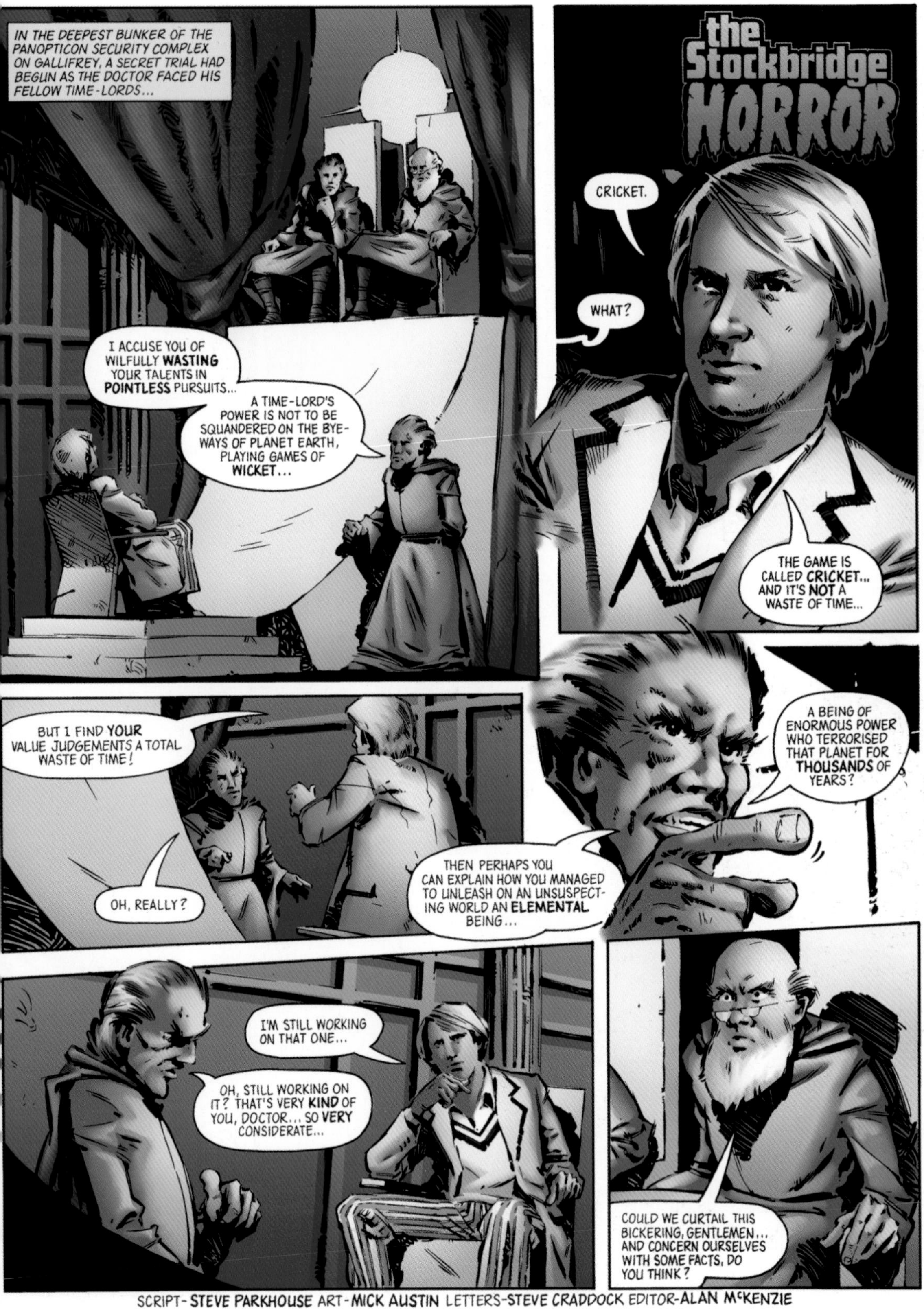

IN THE DEEPEST BUNKER OF THE PANOPTICON SECURITY COMPLEX ON GALLIFREY, A SECRET TRIAL HAD BEGUN AS THE DOCTOR FACED HIS FELLOW TIME-LORDS...
I ACCUSE YOU OF WILFULLY WASTING YOUR TALENTS IN POINTLESS PURSUITS...
A TIME-LORD'S POWER IS NOT TO BE SQUANDERED ON THE BYE-WAYS OF PLANET EARTH, PLAYING GAMES OF WICKET...
the Stockbridge HORROR
CRICKET.
WHAT?
THE GAME IS CALLED CRICKET... AND IT'S NOT A WASTE OF TIME...
BUT I FIND YOUR VALUE JUDGEMENTS A TOTAL WASTE OF TIME!
OH, REALLY?
THEN PERHAPS YOU CAN EXPLAIN HOW YOU MANAGED TO UNLEASH ON AN UNSUSPECTING WORLD AN ELEMENTAL BEING...
A BEING OF ENORMOUS POWER WHO TERRORISED THAT PLANET FOR THOUSANDS OF YEARS?
I'M STILL WORKING ON THAT ONE...
OH, STILL WORKING ON IT? THAT'S VERY KIND OF YOU, DOCTOR... SO VERY CONSIDERATE...
COULD WE CURTAIL THIS BICKERING, GENTLEMEN... AND CONCERN OURSELVES WITH SOME FACTS, DO YOU THINK?

SCRIPT-STEVE PARKHOUSE ART-MICK AUSTIN LETTERS-STEVE CRADDOCK EDITOR-ALAN McKENZIE

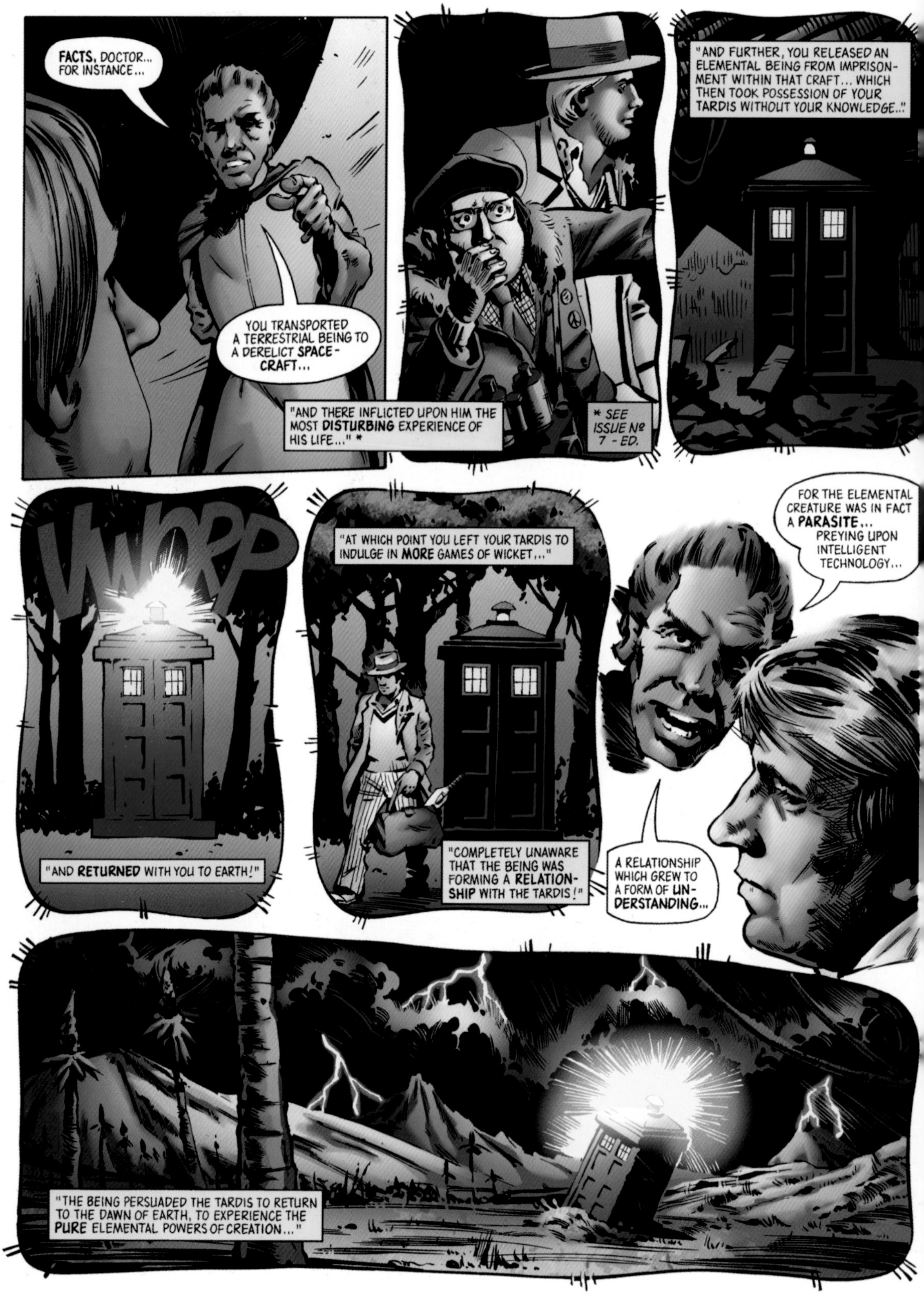

FACTS, DOCTOR... FOR INSTANCE...
YOU TRANSPORTED A TERRESTRIAL BEING TO A DERELICT SPACE-CRAFT...
"AND THERE INFLICTED UPON HIM THE MOST DISTURBING EXPERIENCE OF HIS LIFE..." *
* SEE ISSUE Nº 7 - ED.
"AND FURTHER, YOU RELEASED AN ELEMENTAL BEING FROM IMPRISON-MENT WITHIN THAT CRAFT... WHICH THEN TOOK POSSESSION OF YOUR TARDIS WITHOUT YOUR KNOWLEDGE..."
VWORP
"AND RETURNED WITH YOU TO EARTH!"
"AT WHICH POINT YOU LEFT YOUR TARDIS TO INDULGE IN MORE GAMES OF WICKET..."
"COMPLETELY UNAWARE THAT THE BEING WAS FORMING A RELATION-SHIP WITH THE TARDIS!"
FOR THE ELEMENTAL CREATURE WAS IN FACT A PARASITE... PREYING UPON INTELLIGENT TECHNOLOGY...
A RELATIONSHIP WHICH GREW TO A FORM OF UN-DERSTANDING...
"THE BEING PERSUADED THE TARDIS TO RETURN TO THE DAWN OF EARTH, TO EXPERIENCE THE PURE ELEMENTAL POWERS OF CREATION..."

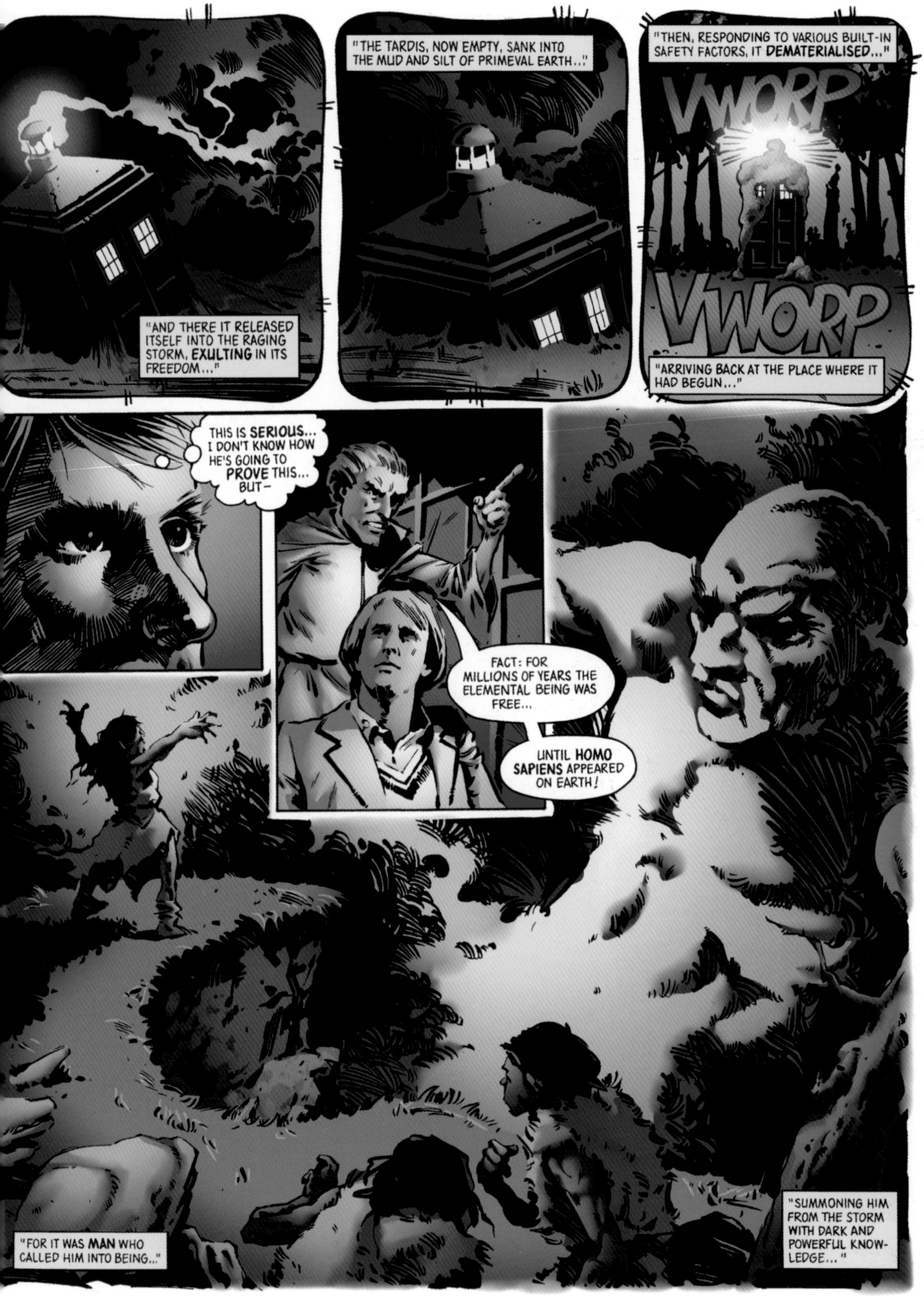
"AND THERE IT RELEASED ITSELF INTO THE RAGING STORM, **EXULTING** IN ITS FREEDOM..."
"THE TARDIS, NOW EMPTY, SANK INTO THE MUD AND SILT OF PRIMEVAL EARTH..."
"THEN, RESPONDING TO VARIOUS BUILT-IN SAFETY FACTORS, IT **DEMATERIALISED...**"
VWORP
VWORP
"ARRIVING BACK AT THE PLACE WHERE IT HAD BEGUN..."
THIS IS **SERIOUS...** I DON'T KNOW HOW HE'S GOING TO **PROVE** THIS... BUT–
FACT: FOR MILLIONS OF YEARS THE ELEMENTAL BEING WAS FREE...
UNTIL **HOMO SAPIENS** APPEARED ON EARTH!
"FOR IT WAS **MAN** WHO CALLED HIM INTO BEING..."
"SUMMONING HIM FROM THE STORM WITH DARK AND POWERFUL KNOW-LEDGE..."

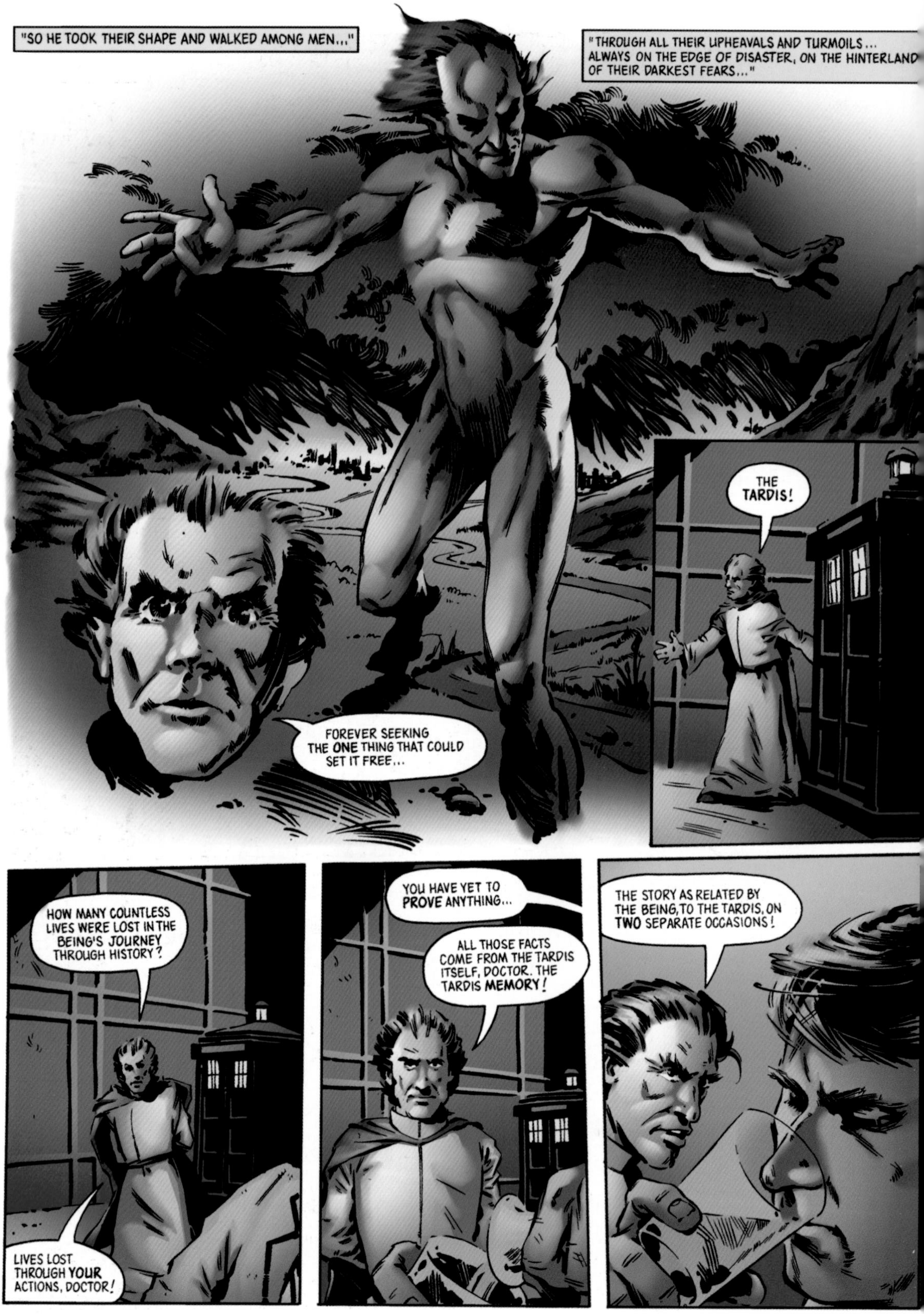
"SO HE TOOK THEIR SHAPE AND WALKED AMONG MEN..."
"THROUGH ALL THEIR UPHEAVALS AND TURMOILS... ALWAYS ON THE EDGE OF DISASTER, ON THE HINTERLAND OF THEIR DARKEST FEARS..."
FOREVER SEEKING THE ONE THING THAT COULD SET IT FREE...
THE TARDIS!
HOW MANY COUNTLESS LIVES WERE LOST IN THE BEING'S JOURNEY THROUGH HISTORY?
LIVES LOST THROUGH YOUR ACTIONS, DOCTOR!
YOU HAVE YET TO PROVE ANYTHING...
ALL THOSE FACTS COME FROM THE TARDIS ITSELF, DOCTOR. THE TARDIS MEMORY!
THE STORY AS RELATED BY THE BEING, TO THE TARDIS, ON TWO SEPARATE OCCASIONS!

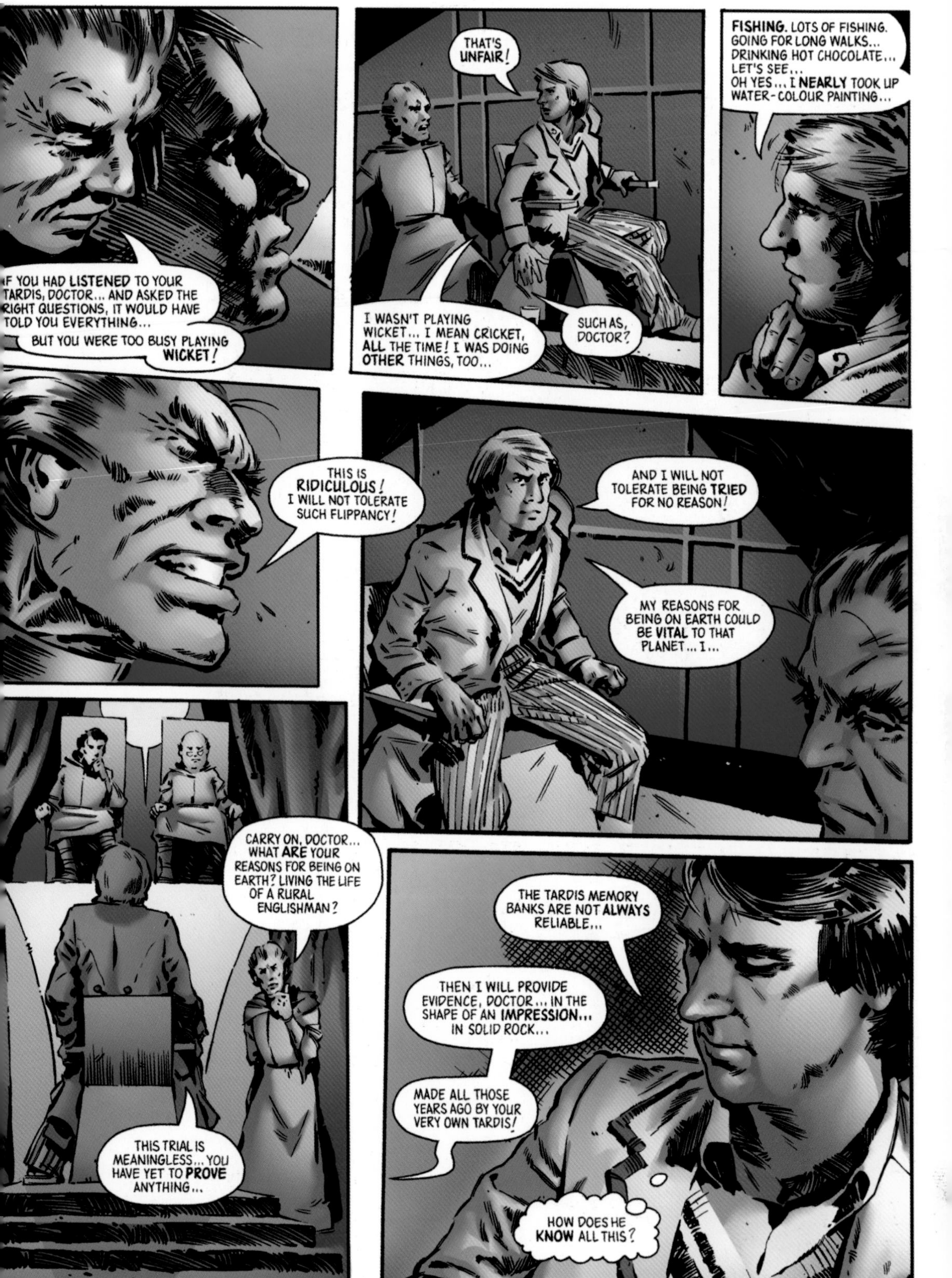
IF YOU HAD LISTENED TO YOUR TARDIS, DOCTOR... AND ASKED THE RIGHT QUESTIONS, IT WOULD HAVE TOLD YOU EVERYTHING...
BUT YOU WERE TOO BUSY PLAYING WICKET!
THAT'S UNFAIR!
I WASN'T PLAYING WICKET... I MEAN CRICKET, ALL THE TIME! I WAS DOING OTHER THINGS, TOO...
SUCH AS, DOCTOR?
FISHING. LOTS OF FISHING. GOING FOR LONG WALKS... DRINKING HOT CHOCOLATE... LET'S SEE... OH YES... I NEARLY TOOK UP WATER-COLOUR PAINTING...
THIS IS RIDICULOUS! I WILL NOT TOLERATE SUCH FLIPPANCY!
AND I WILL NOT TOLERATE BEING TRIED FOR NO REASON!
MY REASONS FOR BEING ON EARTH COULD BE VITAL TO THAT PLANET... I...
CARRY ON, DOCTOR... WHAT ARE YOUR REASONS FOR BEING ON EARTH? LIVING THE LIFE OF A RURAL ENGLISHMAN?
THIS TRIAL IS MEANINGLESS... YOU HAVE YET TO PROVE ANYTHING...
THE TARDIS MEMORY BANKS ARE NOT ALWAYS RELIABLE...
THEN I WILL PROVIDE EVIDENCE, DOCTOR... IN THE SHAPE OF AN IMPRESSION... IN SOLID ROCK...
MADE ALL THOSE YEARS AGO BY YOUR VERY OWN TARDIS!
HOW DOES HE KNOW ALL THIS?

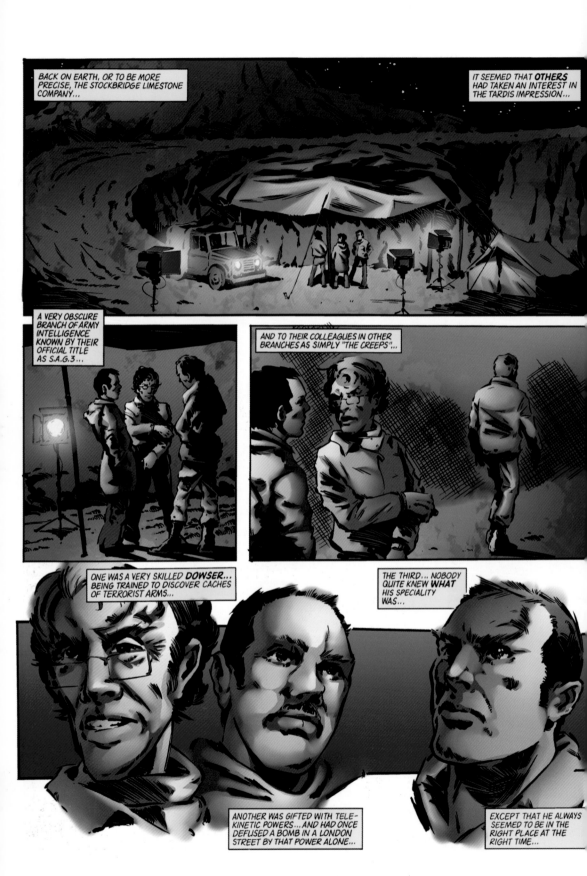

BACK ON EARTH, OR TO BE MORE PRECISE, THE STOCKBRIDGE LIMESTONE COMPANY...

IT SEEMED THAT **OTHERS** HAD TAKEN AN INTEREST IN THE TARDIS IMPRESSION...

A VERY OBSCURE BRANCH OF ARMY INTELLIGENCE KNOWN BY THEIR OFFICIAL TITLE AS S.A.G.3...

AND TO THEIR COLLEAGUES IN OTHER BRANCHES AS SIMPLY "THE CREEPS"...

ONE WAS A VERY SKILLED **DOWSER**... BEING TRAINED TO DISCOVER CACHES OF TERRORIST ARMS...

THE THIRD... NOBODY QUITE KNEW **WHAT** HIS SPECIALITY WAS...

ANOTHER WAS GIFTED WITH TELE-KINETIC POWERS...AND HAD ONCE DEFUSED A BOMB IN A LONDON STREET BY THAT POWER ALONE...

EXCEPT THAT HE ALWAYS SEEMED TO BE IN THE RIGHT PLACE AT THE RIGHT TIME...

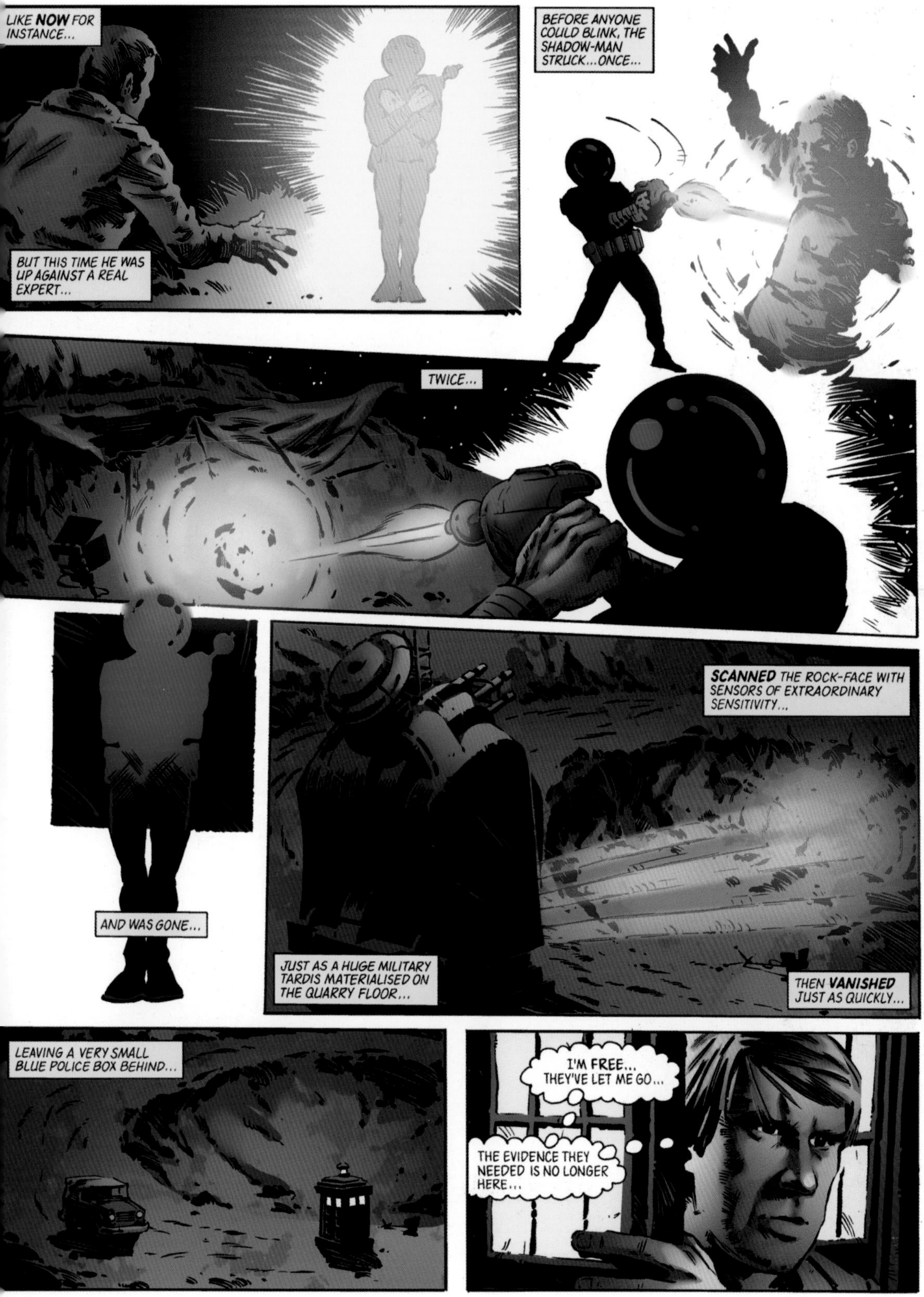
LIKE NOW FOR INSTANCE...
BUT THIS TIME HE WAS UP AGAINST A REAL EXPERT...
BEFORE ANYONE COULD BLINK, THE SHADOW-MAN STRUCK...ONCE...
TWICE...
AND WAS GONE...
JUST AS A HUGE MILITARY TARDIS MATERIALISED ON THE QUARRY FLOOR...
SCANNED THE ROCK-FACE WITH SENSORS OF EXTRAORDINARY SENSITIVITY...
THEN VANISHED JUST AS QUICKLY...
LEAVING A VERY SMALL BLUE POLICE BOX BEHIND...
I'M FREE... THEY'VE LET ME GO...
THE EVIDENCE THEY NEEDED IS NO LONGER HERE...

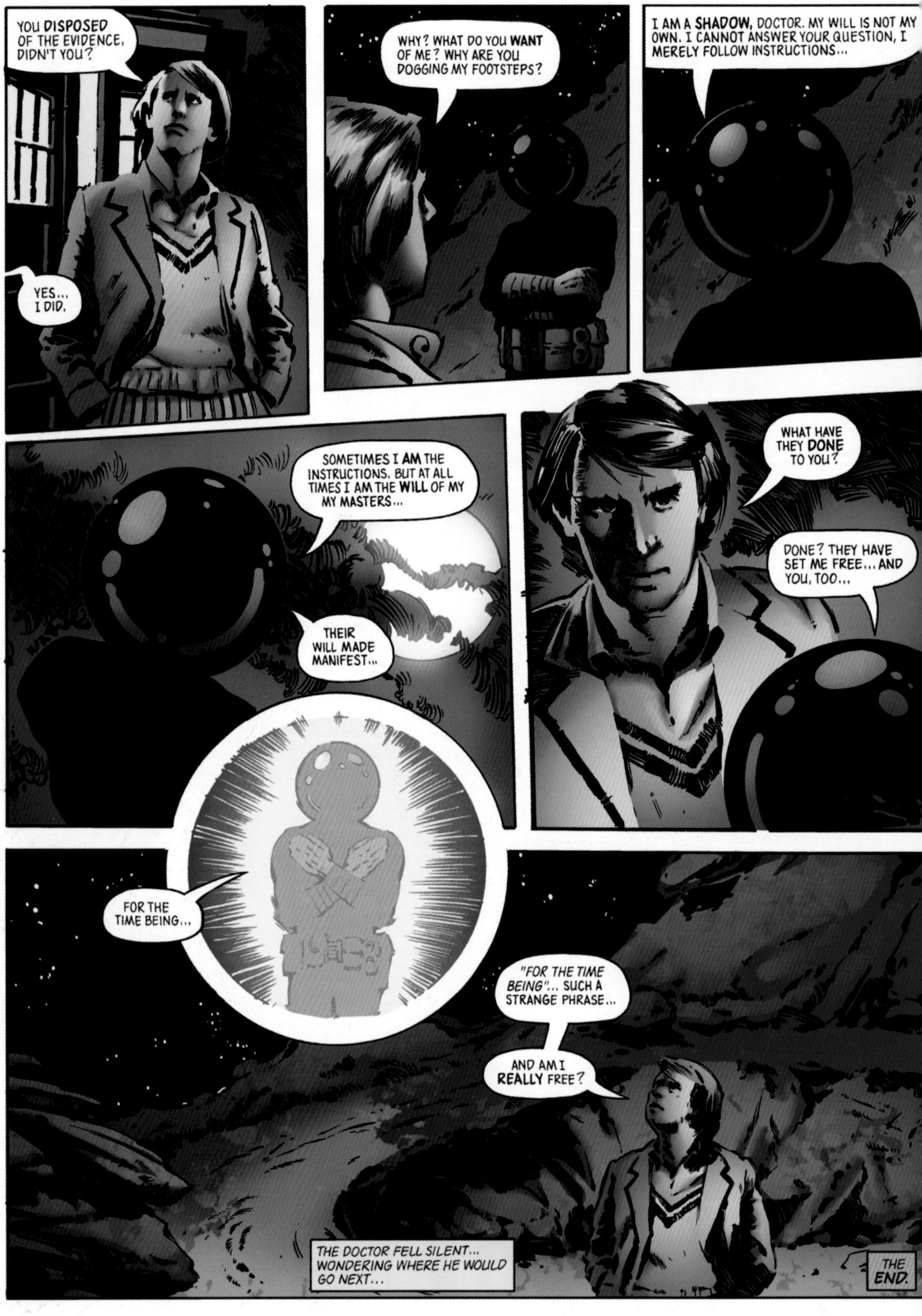
YOU DISPOSED OF THE EVIDENCE, DIDN'T YOU?
YES... I DID.
WHY? WHAT DO YOU WANT OF ME? WHY ARE YOU DOGGING MY FOOTSTEPS?
I AM A SHADOW, DOCTOR. MY WILL IS NOT MY OWN. I CANNOT ANSWER YOUR QUESTION, I MERELY FOLLOW INSTRUCTIONS...
SOMETIMES I AM THE INSTRUCTIONS, BUT AT ALL TIMES I AM THE WILL OF MY MY MASTERS...
THEIR WILL MADE MANIFEST...
WHAT HAVE THEY DONE TO YOU?
DONE? THEY HAVE SET ME FREE... AND YOU, TOO...
FOR THE TIME BEING...
"FOR THE TIME BEING"... SUCH A STRANGE PHRASE...
AND AM I REALLY FREE?
THE DOCTOR FELL SILENT... WONDERING WHERE HE WOULD GO NEXT...
THE END.

ART GALLERY

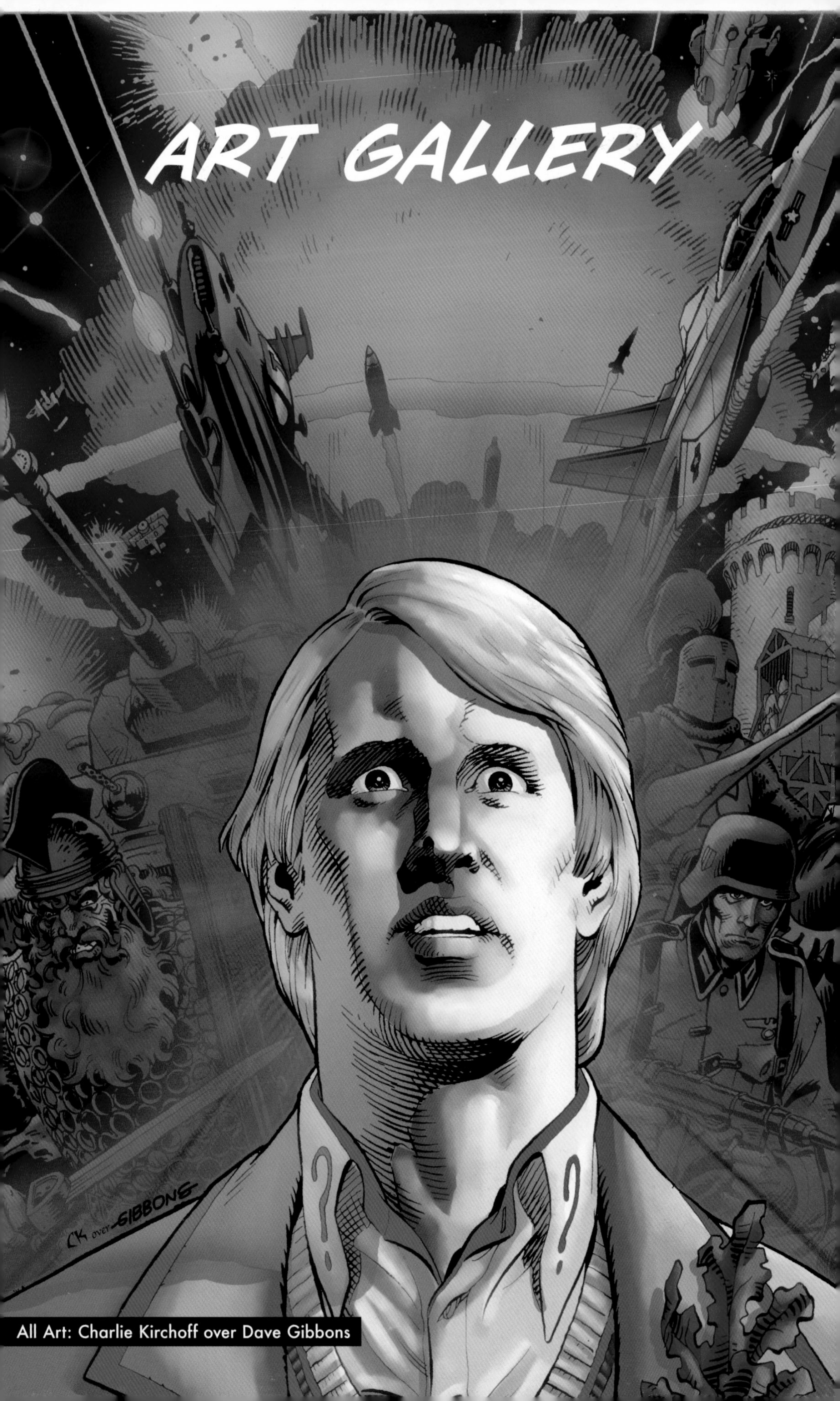
CK over GIBBONS

All Art: Charlie Kirchoff over Dave Gibbons

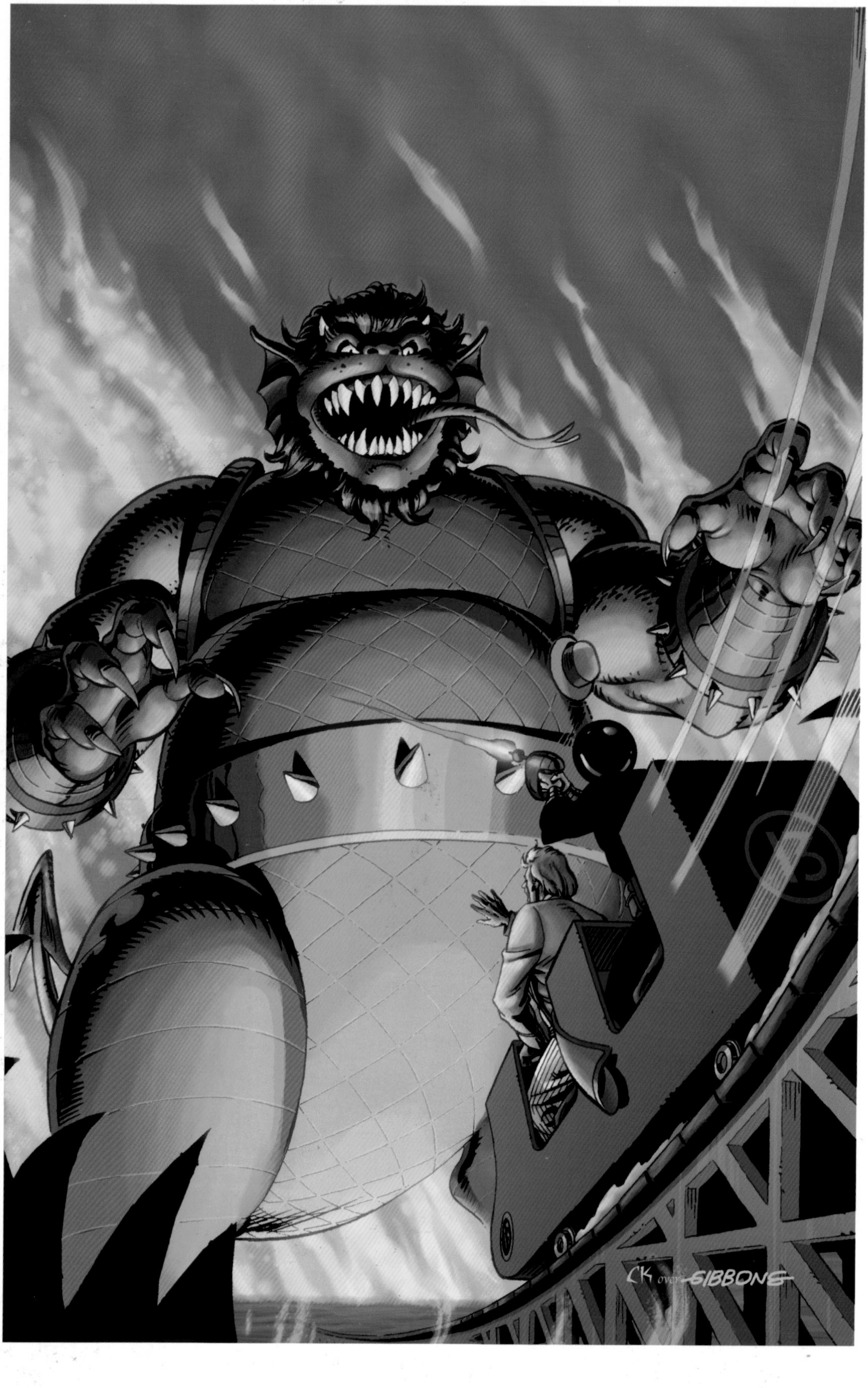
CK over GIBBONS

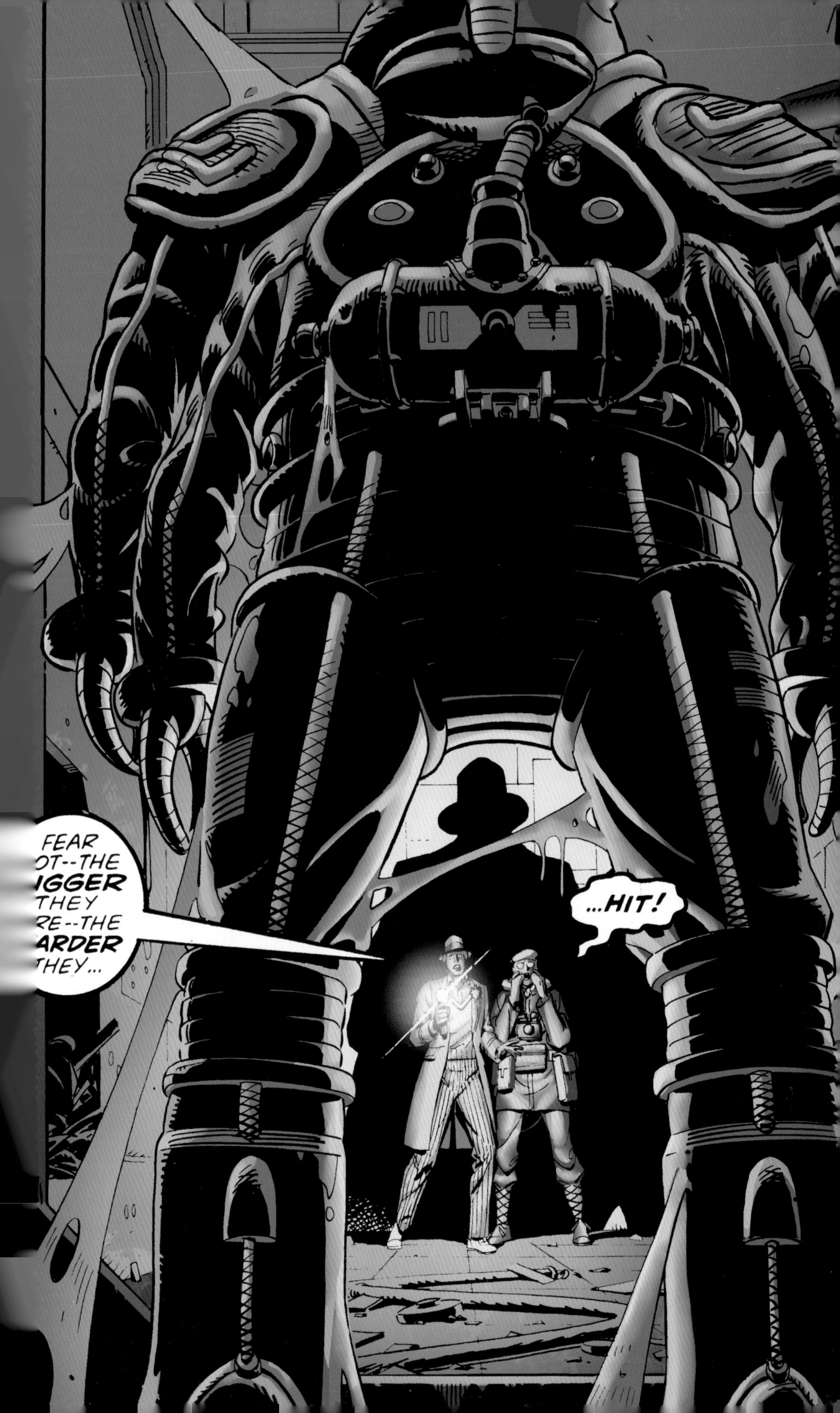
FEAR
OT--THE
IGGER
THEY
RE--THE
ARDER
THEY...
...HIT!

DOCTOR WHO CLASSICS

VOLUME 4